P9-DHA-373

THE CELEBRATION CHRONICLES

Also by Andrew Ross

Real Love

The Chicago Gangster Theory of Life

Strange Weather

No Respect

The Failure of Modernism

No Sweat (editor)

Science Wars (editor)

Microphone Fiends (editor, with T. Rose)

Technoculture (coeditor, with C. Penley)

Universal Abandon? (editor)

THE CELEBRATION CHRONICLES

LIFE, LIBERTY, AND THE PURSUIT OF PROPERTY VALUE IN DISNEY'S NEW TOWN

ANDREW ROSS

BALLANTINE BOOKS • NEW YORK

A Ballantine Book
Published by The Ballantine Publishing Group

Published in the United States by The Ballantine Publishing Group, a division of
Random House, Inc., New York, and simultaneously in Canada by
Random House of Canada Limited, Toronto.

www.randomhouse.com/BB/

Library of Congress Cataloging-in-Publication Data
Ross, Andrew, 1956–
The celebration chronicles : life, liberty, and the pursuit of
property value in Disney's new town / Andrew Ross.
p. cm.
ISBN 0-345-41751-8 (hard : alk. paper)
1. Celebration (Fla.) 2. New towns—Florida Case studies.
3. City and town life—Florida—Celebration. 4. City planning—
Florida—Celebration. 5. Walt Disney Enterprises. I. Title. II. Title:
Life, liberty, and the pursuit of property value in Disney's new town.
HT169.57.U62C457 1999
307.76'09759'25—dc21 99-26403
CIP

Text design by Ann Gold

Manufactured in the United States of America

First Edition: August 1999

10 9 8 7 6 5 4 3 2 1

CONTENTS

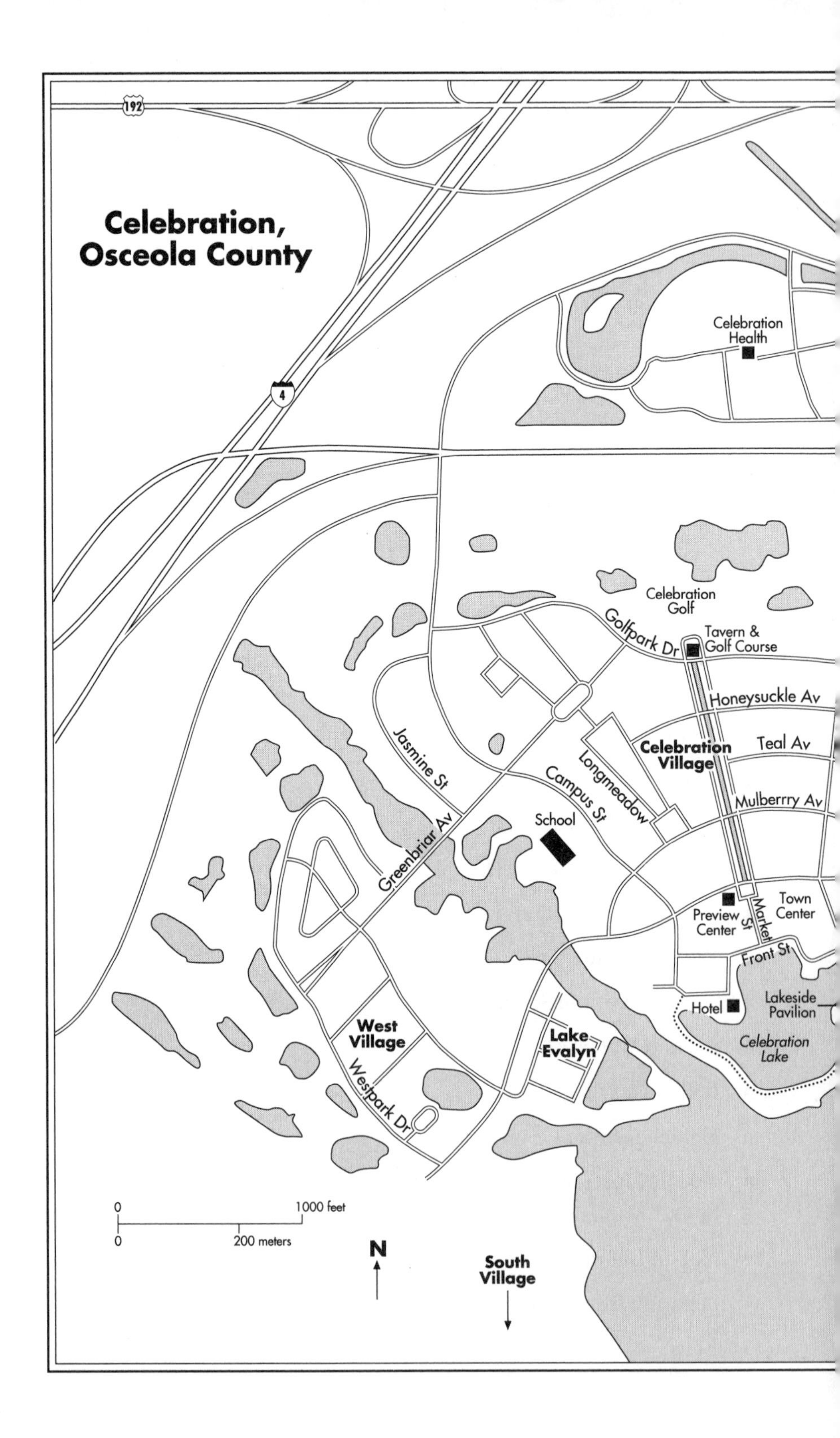

Celebration, Osceola County
192
4
Celebration Health
Celebration Golf
Golfpark Dr
Tavern & Golf Course
Honeysuckle Av
Teal Av
Celebration Village
Jasmine St
Longmeadow
Campus St
Mulberrry Av
School
Greenbriar Av
Market St
Town Center
Preview Center
Front St
Hotel
Lakeside Pavilion
Celebration Lake
West Village
Lake Evalyn
Westpark Dr
0
1000 feet
0
200 meters
N
South Village

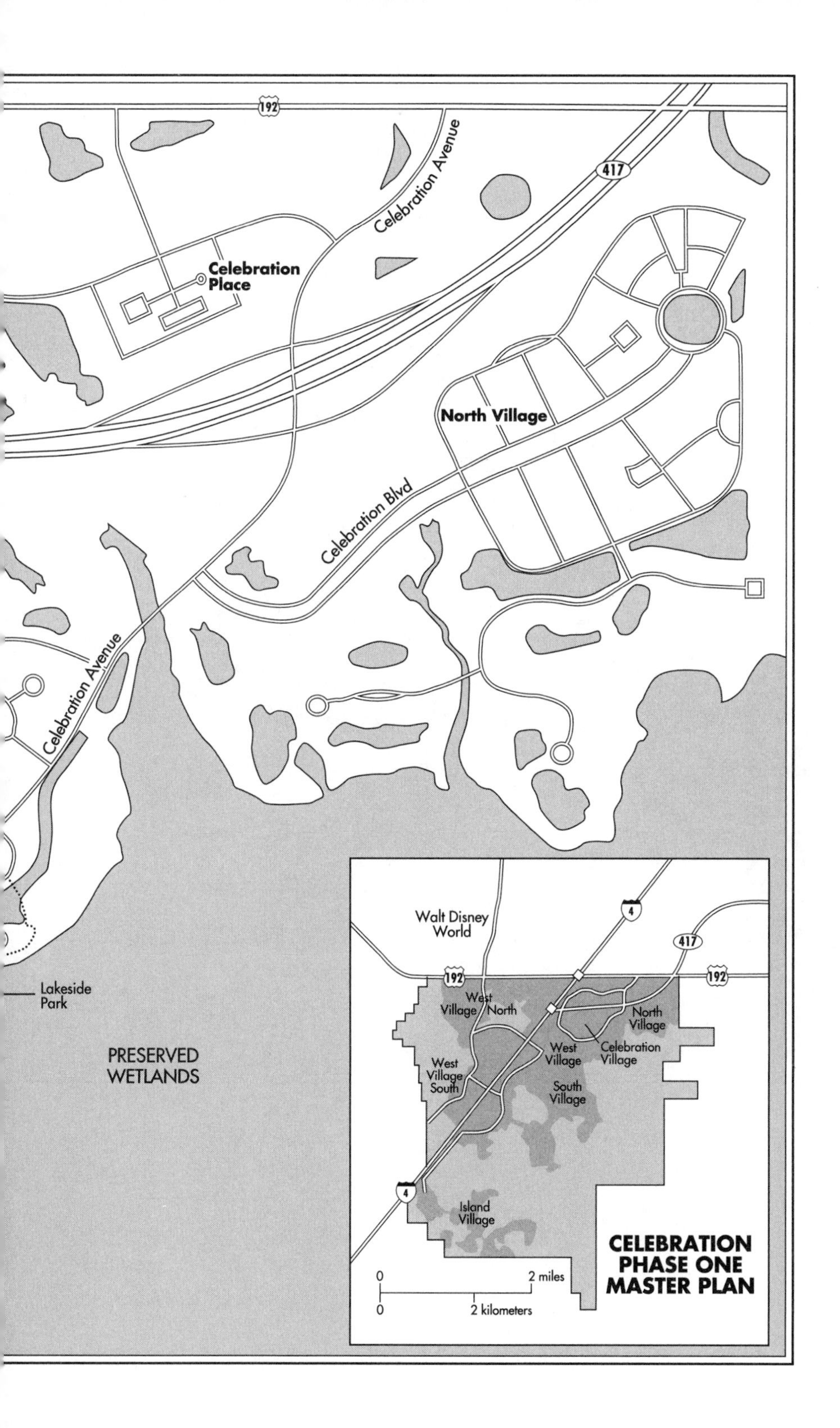
192
417
Celebration Avenue
Celebration Place
North Village
Celebration Blvd
Celebration Avenue
Lakeside Park
PRESERVED WETLANDS
Walt Disney World
4
417
192
192
West Village North
North Village
West Village
Celebration Village
West Village South
South Village
4
Island Village
0
2 miles
0
2 kilometers
CELEBRATION PHASE ONE MASTER PLAN

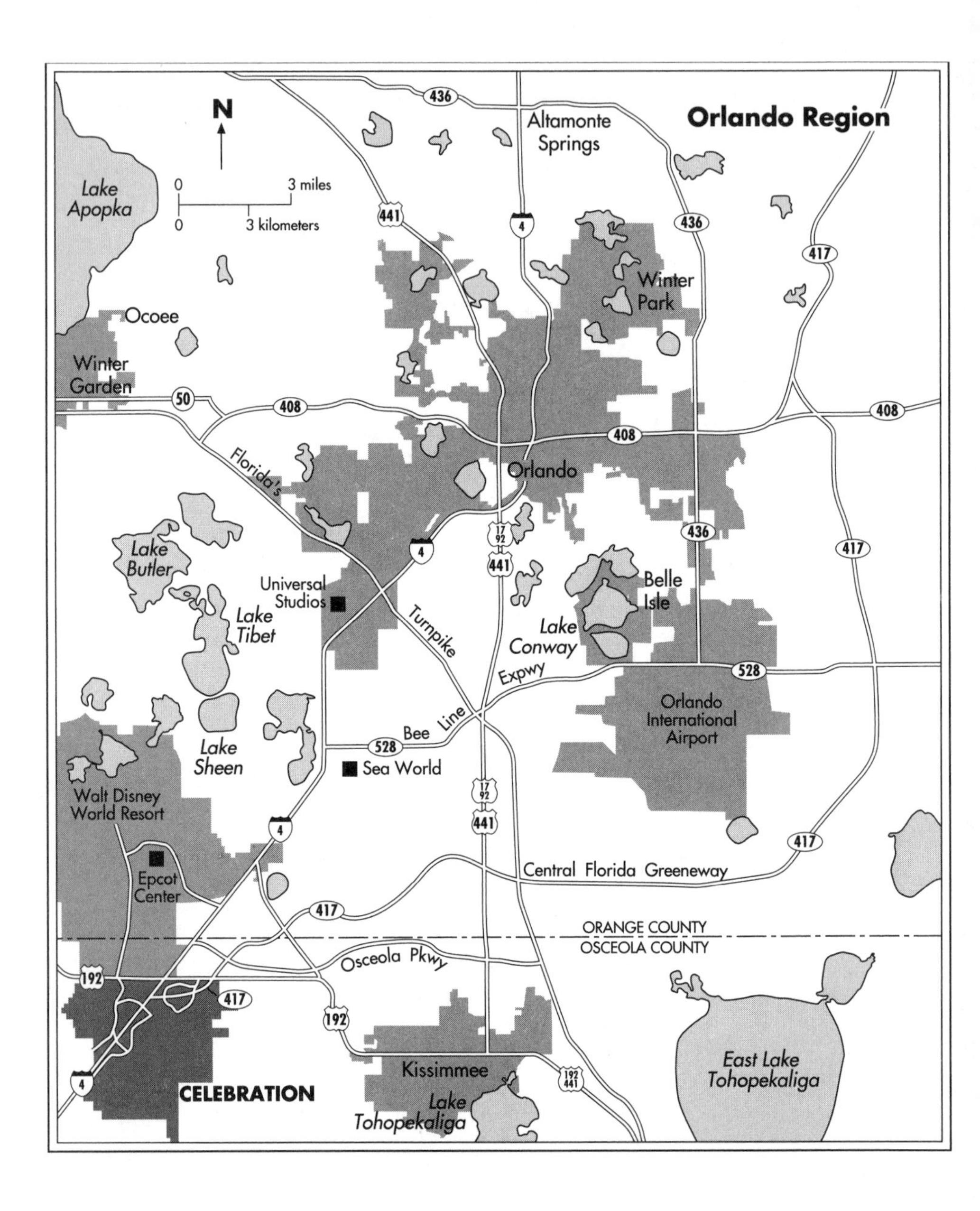
Orlando Region
N
0
3 miles
0
3 kilometers
Lake Apopka
Altamonte Springs
436
441
4
436
417
Winter Park
Ocoee
Winter Garden
50
408
408
408
Florida's
Orlando
Lake Butler
17 92
441
436
417
4
Universal Studios
Belle Isle
Lake Tibet
Lake Conway
Turnpike
Expwy
528
Orlando International Airport
Bee Line
528
Lake Sheen
Sea World
Walt Disney World Resort
17 92
441
4
417
Epcot Center
Central Florida Greeneway
417
ORANGE COUNTY
OSCEOLA COUNTY
Osceola Pkwy
192
417
192
Kissimmee
192 441
4
CELEBRATION
Lake Tohopekaliga
East Lake Tohopekaliga

ACKNOWLEDGMENTS

This book chronicles a year I spent in residence in Celebration from September 1997 to August 1998, in addition to several visits before and after that period. During that time, I participated fully in the community life of Celebration, and conducted six or seven hundred hours of interviews, primarily with town residents, company employees, and area inhabitants. Unless otherwise cited, quotations in the book are from these interviews, or from comments made in public meetings and in semi-public settings. *The Celebration Chronicles* is primarily based on the stories of the people I talked to. Some of the names of residents have been altered to protect their privacy.

I had no association with the Walt Disney Company, but Ann-Marie Matthews, Ralph Kline, and Marilyn Waters, each of whom served as communications officers of The Celebration Company, responded promptly to my requests for information and for interviews with Disney employees.

My special gratitude goes to Dave Eaton, Brian Haas, and Diane Polsen-Haas, who showed particular kindness and generosity during my residence.

There were many others in Celebration whose help and hospitality I enjoyed. Among them were:

Christine Herzog, Larry Rosen, Brent Herrington, Dawn Thomas,

Ron Dickson, Jackson and Sarah Mumey, Lenny Savino, Scott Biehler, Sarai Cowin, Donald and Joan Jones, Carolyn Hopp, Melissa Rodriguez, Donna Leinsing, Charmaine Gabel, Jackie Flanigan, Bob Shinn, Jim Whelan, Marty Treu, Margo Schwartz, Charlie Rogers, Leonard Timm, Robin Delaney, Pam and Bob Morris, Debbie Lehman, Charles Adams, Perry Reeder, Tom Dunn, Karen and Tom Zirbes, Beulah Farquarson, Larry Haber, Jeff La Mendola, Debbie Delevan, Joseph Palacios, Peter Rummell, Paul and Iris Kraft, Alex Morton, Tom Vitale, Heather Krawsczyk, Ron Clifton, Ray and Debbie Chiaramonte, Andy Carson, Dot Davis, Rachel Binns, Sarah Fields, Kennedy Donofrio, Peg and Rod Owens, John Arcuri, Joe Barnes, Todd Mansfield, Dee Stevens, Kathy Johnson, Gregory Ross, Jim and Shirley Bailey, Melie Ablang, Don Killoren, David Pace, Lise and Ron Juneman, Wanda Wade, David and Jo Ann Tennant, Al and Judy Ziffer, Bob Stern, Andres Duany, Betty and Roger Popp, Patrick Wrisley, Rodney and Debbie Jones, Mike and Lorraine Turner, Tom Lewis, Lance and Karin Boyer, Raffaello, Lisa, Max and Caitlin Sessoms, and Fred and Darlene Rapanotti.

All the best to the Honeysuckle Potluckers and the Montessori Initiative!

Thanks to John Hayt, who was kind enough to take some photographs for me.

A big shout-out to my cronies in Orlando, especially to Lisa Stokes and Michael Hoover, whose fulsome comradeship knew no bounds. All hail to the deathless ninja soul of Tyler Stokes! To Wendy Brandon, I owe many thanks for the culinary wisdom, and the vibe from that white Porsche. And to Kevin Meehan—let us salute the rockin' memory of the Shirtless Wonder.

Jeff Truesdell, editor of the *Orlando Weekly*, and Rick Bernhardt, at the City of Orlando Planning Department, were both helpful and gracious.

Constance Penley first introduced me to the people and landscapes of Central Florida through family visits.

Many thanks to my colleagues at NYU—George Yudice, Lisa Duggan, Nikhil Pal Singh, and Philip Brian Harper—who all filled in for me during my year's sabbatical, and my students, who either respected my leave, or, better still, who came to visit, like Mabel Wilson, Alondra Nelson, Kitty Krupat, and Nichole Rustin.

Lisa Maya Knauer, Robyn Dutra, and Alison Reddick all provided essential research assistance, early and late.

Faye Ginsburg read a manuscript draft and offered valuable suggestions, and Emily Grayson, at Ballantine, provided crucial help.

A deep debt lies with Katherine Silberger, who never lived there, but who lived with Celebration each day of the year that I did.

Peter Borland, my unflappable editor at Ballantine, and Elyse Cheney, my unstoppable agent at Sanford Greenburger, cooked up this assignment for me over a portentous lunch. Peter kept me on track, while Elyse was an energy source of ideas and inspirations. I am very grateful for all of their attention, support, and hard work.

1

HOMEWARD BOUND

"Home is where the mortgage is." —American proverb

I live in a country that never runs out of promises. There is always a fresh start, a new frontier, a shiny next step, opportunity, or bargain for which enough people will put down some cash, or pick up all their things, and go for broke. Even in the rosiest of times, the prospect of satisfaction is not much better than the chances of coming out on top after a casino visit. Running on such odds, the long-distance stamina of the American Dream is pretty impressive. But much more startling is the widespread tolerance for lesser outcomes when that wobbly old dream, in whatever shape, goes unrealized, as it must for the majority. Most people accept that there exists a cruel gulf between the soapy promises of the hucksters and boosters and the school of hard knocks that is their daily lot. Tacit acknowledgment of this gap has become a staple of American life. As a result, the landscape out there is not a junkyard of dreams, though there are many shabby memorials and woebegone ruins. It is the messy result of what people have to settle for when their aspirations fall short of the mark.

This book has a lot to do with dreams, because it is about people who regularly used that term when they spoke to me and to each other about their recent lives. Whatever their dreams had been in the past, they had become lately entangled with the designs of a company that controls a lion's share of the dream business, and had opted to offer, in the realm of real estate, some of the wish fulfillment it had long traded in the realm of make-believe. Selling dream homes is not unlike selling dream vacations, but for the live-in consumer, it's quite a different story. My book draws upon a year in the life and times of a new town built by the Walt Disney Company amid the cypress swamp, open pineland, and palmetto groves of Central Florida. Named in the hopeful American tradition of towns like Harmony, Eden, Experiment, and Amity, Celebration is not just a constellation of dream homes, lavishly packaged by a canny developer. It is also the product of a company that merchandizes the semi-real with an attitude that the architectural historian Vincent Scully once described as "unacceptably optimistic."[1] Many of the pioneers who flocked to the new settlement were plainly charmed by the prospect of living, and dying, on Disney land. Yet they would spend a good part of their fledgling years here trying to prove to themselves and to the outside world that this was a real place, "with real problems," and not a theme park village cooked up by the Imagineers. In the process, they would be under pressure to perform above par while everyone else was watching.

WHEN YOU BANK UPON A STAR

What sets such people in motion? Treasure seekers, colonists, settlers, runaways, frontier homesteaders, and immigrants of every stripe can testify abundantly to the original motive for their movements. America has always been a harvest of advertising. From mythic word of mouth to Renaissance travelers' tales about the Blessed Isles and the Fountain of Youth, and from emigrant societies' breathless pamphlets to realtors' lustrous brochures, the odysseys across prairie, mountain, ocean, and Jim Crow state line have been spurred on by consistently good advertising copy. The same pledges and guarantees crop up over and over again, like so many versions of a single promissory note. Florida has cornered the market on many of them. The state's reputation as a haven for migrants has been actively promoted for over three centuries in successive policies offering religious sanctuary, free land, low taxes, and Medicare. At times, its climate of warm expectations has been oversold by bogus

Nonstandard real estate advertising, on Route 192. (Photo: the author)

assurances, earning it the title of "the most lied-about state," most notably during the notorious land boom of the 1920s, when unbridled speculation caused land to change hands several times a day, sometimes tripling in price. At the height of the boom, national anti-Florida sentiment about realty fraud forced the governor and a group of businessmen to invite the national press to a promotional "Truth About Florida" meeting at the Waldorf-Astoria Hotel in New York City.

It's best, then, to start with the ads. By the time I moved into Celebration, advertising for the new town was featuring a bold pun—"Isn't this reason enough for Celebration?" On the billboards outside of town, this slogan ran below an image of two girls savoring their go on a playground swingset. Their fresh gusto was bathed in radiant sunlight as they rose up into a blue-sky future. Their self-assurance was barely tempered by the giddy liberty felt at the summit of the swing's arc. Almost at once, you could see that this picture of carefree play was meant to contrast with the risky thrills and spills of the tourist attractions that vie for the attention of visitors to this part of the world. The homey technology of the traditional playground swing evokes a world of values quite at odds with the over-mechanized apparatus of terror that fills the theme parks and their spin-offs lining the tourist strips of the Orlando region. In that other realm of vicious vertigo machines and virtual bungee-jumps, there is a clear contempt for balance, let alone gravity. Adjacent to Celebration itself is a tourist site that features "the tallest swing in the world," a freaky contraption that plunges riders into a cardiac-challenging arc from its 200-foot-high tower.

So the real message of this and other Celebration ads was not visible on the billboards themselves; it lay in the contrast with their surroundings. Located on arteries that steer motorists past concrete and neon thickets of fast-food shacks and discount malls, acres of asphalt parking lots, and subdivisions of dull duplicate housing, the ads could afford to be subtle. The reason for Celebration lay all around, though to call too direct attention to this fact would be unneighborly. Playing to people's loathing for the strip-mall landscape, its gaudy commercialism and plug-in housing tracts, was the best tactic for selling this new town. Over time, the ads began to approximate the typical Florida developer's pitch—"Buy a New House and Get a New Town! From 160s to 750+"—but even then you could still feel the subtle twist of the knife.

Like most new blueprints for the pursuit of happiness, the reason for Celebration was rooted in repulsion for the existing order of things. In the early 1950s, Walt Disney's disgust for the postwar urban sprawl of Los Angeles (and his distaste for the lack of hygiene in other popular entertainment facilities) fueled his idea to build a theme park in Anaheim. Disneyland sprang up as a quarantine zone, artificially purged of the urban ills, design tragedies, and traffic atrocities that plagued its California area surroundings. Almost overnight, however, the park spawned a commercial tourist sprawl directly outside its gates.

A land grab of 28,000 acres in Central Florida in 1966 promised enough space for the company to deliver a second, more self-contained solution—Disney World, with its own resorts and full menu of visitor facilities. Walt's designs even included plans for a utopian residential city, the EPCOT that was never realized. In turn, of course, the collateral impact of Disney World, soon to become the planet's number one tourist destination, transformed the entire landscape of Central Florida's sleepy lakeside towns and cow pastures into a purgatory of fast growth and fast food. The Orlando region became a three-alarm signal for runaway strip mall development everywhere.

Solution number three—a showcase town for 20,000 residents, designed as a corrective to sprawl—broke ground in Osceola County to the south of the theme parks in 1994. First and foremost, this master-planned community was a bid to maximize the value of 10,000 acres of company land, de-annexed from the virtually autonomous Reedy Creek Improvement District that governs Disney World. With half the site preserved for a wetland greenbelt, Osceola Multi-Use Development, as it was called in early planning stages, promised to earn the company a much-needed reputation as a Good Neighbor, since Disney was operating for the first time in the public domain and under the klieg-light scrutiny of the media. In addition, the town was to be a stepchild of New Urbanism, a zealous new movement in town planning that had declared war on auto-driven development and vowed to reintroduce suburban Americans to the civic virtues of active community involvement. Flush with utopian assurances handed down from centuries of American pioneer settlement, Celebration would be yet another fresh start in a world gone wrong.

So what was I doing here? Unlike most of the new residents streaming into town in the late summer of 1997, neither attraction nor repulsion had drawn me to Celebration. I was on a year's sabbatical from New York City. The dense turbulence, multicultural throngs, and ultra-liberal lifestyles of downtown Manhattan, where I live and work, seem to repel more Americans than they attract. For people like myself, it is a step closer to utopia than just about anywhere else (and about as far from a master-planned community as you could imagine). But Manhattanites are chronically insular and loath to recognize other signs of terrestrial life, especially the quality and purpose of suburban Middle America. If we are ever to be good neighbors in the larger landscape, there is much to learn about places and people that do not feature on Saul Steinberg's famous cartoon map of the "New Yorker's View of the

World." It was partly in this spirit that I accepted my publisher's assignment to live and work in Celebration. Friends, colleagues, and familiars of my past writings were dubious of my motive. Disney-bashing is a favored sport in New York City, and has taken on a fresh vigor with the company's new presence on 42nd Street. I left behind a town frothing with offense at the Disneyfication of Times Square. But if Disney-bashing had been my chief goal, I could have written this book from a safe distance, in common with most armchair practitioners of that ballooning genre. Conversely, once in Celebration, it would take some energy on my part to dispel the suspicion, inside and outside of town, that I was somehow in cahoots with the Walt Disney Company.

With two marriages under my belt and no offspring to rear, my resident's profile would be matched by very few. This was a family town, and with many more outsize families (three or four children) than you would expect from its highly educated late boomer parents. Like most of my new neighbors, however, I had been highly mobile in my history of residence. Americans normally move every five years or so, and I was batting above average in the seventeen years I had lived in the United States, with spells in California, the Midwest, and various Northeast locations, but never in full-blown suburbia or the South. In common with many Celebration residents, I had grown up in a small town. Mine was in a patchwork part of Scotland where notches of the lowland industrial belt sit alongside farmland and upland grazing country. For a town that was not in the least wealthy, the housing mix was as varied as could be. About half of it was public housing, including some of the most notorious slums in the country. Among the private, single-family houses were one or two new subdivisions and a sprinkling of mansions and estates kept by the local aristocracy and well-to-do. Through a relic of the feudal system, my family still paid a small sum (a "feu") to the former owner of the land on which our house was built. The settlement was several hundred years old, and its communal memory bore the legacies of many waves of economic and religious change. In the 1970s, the town's social fabric had been rent apart by de-industrialization, and most of its residents had been in survival mode ever since. It was a very unpretentious place, and impossible to idealize or endow with sentimental qualities, even in the rosy mood of retrospection.

By contrast, the small-town idealism of my new residence in Osceola County was easy to grasp. Even if you were not the kind to swallow the sugary brew of sentiment attached to the traditional small American town, a quick jaunt around Florida's highways, condo canyons, and honky-tonk strips would be enough to prep you for the girls on the swing or the hard sell of Celebration Realty. The whole state was in pretty bad shape. At some point in mid-century, after Florida stopped building communities around people and started building them around automobiles, its population growth pattern locked into a woozy spiral. "Keep the World Coming to Florida" has ever been the state's calling card. Recent estimates of growth project an increase of between 6 and 13 million new residents by 2020, when Celebration's own buildout is complete. Each year, assuming the lower, more conservative estimate of 6 million new residents, the state will need 120,000 new dwelling units, 40 million more gallons of fresh water, 800 miles of new roads, and, as a result, will lose 164, 250 acres of forest and 149, 650 acres of farmland.[2] It will be catastrophic to accommodate this growth on open space in the current fashion: cranking out new exurban subdivisions of three-bedroom, two-bath ranch homes on half-acre lots at five-mile distances from the mall clusters of Wal-Mart, Home Depot, and Burger King. The toll on water, energy and land will simply be unsustainable. The damage wrought by thirty years of this kind of market-driven development, propelled by short-term profit and asleep-at-the-wheel planning, is painfully evident on all sides. The second and third rings of suburban development around city cores now host semi-abandoned strip malls and miles of decaying housing stock. Some of these places are becoming virtually obsolete within a single generation. The cost of maintaining the infrastructure of the low-density suburban housing formula has begun to outstrip the budgets of middle-class residents and tax-starved local governments. Those who can afford it seek refuge in prestigious, gated communities on the outer, pastoral necklace and enjoy forms of private government that capture their tax assessments for internal use. In the meantime, Florida's rich wetland and lake ecosystems have deteriorated to the point where the hatching rate of its alligators—prehistoric creatures with a time-proven capacity to survive—has begun to plummet.

Celebration joined the small but growing rank of towns and neighborhoods that were creating alternatives in the name of sustainable development. Seaside, ground zero of the New Urbanist movement, and Windsor, its most tony offspring; city neighborhoods like Boca Raton's Mizner Park, Tampa's Hyde Park, and Orlando's South-East Corridor; retrofitted centers like Haile Village, near Gainesville, and West Palm Beach; new developments like the Tampa-area cluster of Longleaf, Silver Oaks, Rivendell, Westchase, and Connerton; and large municipalities, like Jacksonville and Orlando—all have forged and adopted planning principles that stress mixed land use, compact residential and commercial density, pedestrian or mass-transit orientation, and, where it still exists, greenfield preservation. Growth management legislation, passed in 1985, has catapulted Florida from being almost derelict on the regulation of developers to one of the more stringent of the Sunbelt states. The regulations still lack the teeth to make regional planning effective, but they have forced developers to acknowledge, and enter into dialogue with, environmentalists. In time, every city and county in the state might come to weigh anti-sprawl planning ordinances. If the sales figures shift enough, key players in the housing industry and investment banking might be persuaded to amend their formulaic habits of "blow and go" subdivision production. The pursuit of a Dream Home, lately endangered as housing costs have outstripped median incomes, might be redeemed as a result of savings on transportation and unit density. And, who knows?, the restoration of civic spirit in tightly knit new traditional neighborhoods might help to breathe new life into a moribund democracy at large. These, at least, were some of the hopes borne along by New Urbanism's winds of change.

However unique in its market offerings, then, Celebration was not exactly a one-shot wonder. Disney's decision to develop was a shrewd bet on a horse with everything going for it: timing, turf, and a critical mass of influential advocates. For seekers of property value, it also seemed like a sure thing, since it was backed by a company with one of the most profitable land development performances in history. Devised by the original developer of Never-Never Land, Celebration simply could not avoid its baptism as an instant utopia, nor could it ever live this identity down. In mock-heroic moments, I would picture myself in the footsteps of the classical narrators of utopian travelogues. Writers like Thomas More, Francis Bacon, Jonathan Swift, William Morris, Edward Bellamy, H. G. Wells, and Ursula Le Guin had sent themselves or fictional travelers to new places, whether real or imagined, to report on the existence of better worlds, wondrous alternatives to the corrupt and decadent societies they had left behind. But I had promised myself to be true to residents' experience of daily life in Celebration, and I soon found that they had brought along as much nonutopian residue from their former lives as I had.

FIRST DAY

On my first day in Celebration, I am still battling a light New York flu that often pulses through the city's population around Labor Day, as if to remind us that no season holds a copyright on mortality. My movers have not arrived. They call to report that they have broken down twice already, once in Virginia and then in North Carolina. Like many of the employees in the moving business in New York City, they are young Israeli men, fresh from their army training and, I assume, accustomed to hardship and uncompromising orders. They are quick to point out that native-born Americans would not deign to do their job. Unsure about this assertion, I spare them my phlegm on the phone and brace myself for a rough-and-ready weekend. I am about to share a common experience of new Celebration residents—an uncertain wait to move properly into my home.

Kennedy Donofrio, Celebration's rental property manager, is eager to help out. It is a relief to see a real personality emerge from the phone voice through which I have gotten to know her. The Disney hospitality voice is a formidable thing; the unstoppable friendliness of its tenor, pitch, and intonation is designed to disarm the skepticism of everyone it encounters. Finely calibrated at Disney University, where all new employees (or "cast members") are trained, this voice is the official greeter of consumer capitalist America, as distinctively authoritative a form of English speech as the pukka curtness of a British colonial administrator might have been for an earlier time. Things are not always what they seem in Celebration, however, and it turns out that Kennedy and her assistant Dawn Thomas, whose Trinidadian lilt has been flattened but not vanquished, are not Disney employees at all. Their management company, ZOM, is one of the many subcontractors in town, delicately buffering relations between residents and the world-famous underwriter of this new community.

Kennedy had found me a downtown apartment at the foot of Market Street, with a balcony view of the central lake. If nearby Kissimmee had not snagged the name over a century ago (Osceola County forbids the repetition of street names), I would be living on Main Street, as Walt once did in his Disneyland apartment, ostensibly to take delight in the first reactions of visitors to the idealized town square setting. Everyone who visits or takes a stroll in downtown Celebration will pass beneath my perch along the petite, palm-lined promenade. In no time, I would become familiar with the traffic in and out of the stores across the street: Max's Café, the bakery Bread Alone, M Fashion's fragrant boutique, the more casual Soft as a Grape, Dunn's antique furniture, and Goodings' grocery store. I would soon get used to street conversation drifting up from the sidewalk bench outside Village Mercantile, mecca for youth gear, and would even learn to endure the Muzak piped into the street from speakers buried in the bases of the palm trees. As I make a debut appearance on my balcony, the first of many pictures is snapped by tourists below, as eager to document a native resident of this town as they would be to snap an Amazon rain-forest dweller, a kilted Highlander, or a Bedouin on a camel.

Downtown is made up of diverse two- or three-story apartment buildings, with restaurants and stores at street level. Because the town is supposed to have grown up organically over time, master planners Robert Stern and Jaquelin Robertson wanted some to look as if they were apartment buildings all along, and others to look like grand houses that were later converted to use as apartments. This habit of posterior dating has a pedigree in Florida. The most renowned example is northern industrialist James Deering's winter villa, Vizcaya, in Biscayne—an elegant Renaissance estate built in 1916 in a highly weathered style to suggest occupation and languid restoration by several generations of a titled Italian family. In Celebration, however, everything, even if it is "slightly aged" in this manner, looks freshly minted. The preference for porches and gingerbread detail made of polymerized materials instead of wood (highly rottable in this climate) means that the real aging process will have a struggle on its hands. My duplex apartment, in a sturdy, coral-colored, stucco building with a clock tower, is atop a dinky shopping arcade that provides shade from the punishing midday sun. Right now, the late summer air is a river of scalding breath, ferrying pairs of fat lovebugs that stick to my skin and burst apart like overripe Champagne grapes if I slap them. Patch-eyed birds glide in on the breeze from the lake, and use Market Street for a landing strip. But there are scant pickings for them on the ground. From my earlier, flying visits to Celebration, advertised at that time as an "honest to goodness town," I already know these street surfaces are vacuum-cleaned every morning by early-bird company employees. At this time of year, late-afternoon gully washers drench the whole place. Even so, the power washers on the dawn patrol are never too far way.

I do the Celebration thing and introduce myself to a neighbor, Raffaello Sessoms, who is surveying the parking lot from the common walkway at the back of our apartment block. Every bit the casual and courteous Carolinian, he welcomes me cordially and fills the air with lively praise of downtown apartment life. When asked, I tell him up front, as I'll do with everyone in town, that I am here to write a book about the community. Biting down on the quid of tobacco in his mouth, his blithe mood shifts, his voice lowers, and he coyly advises me that I'll soon learn "the pixie dust wears off quickly here." This is too much like the beginning of a southern gothic screenplay for me, so I nod knowingly and change the subject. After all, I want to inhale some of that pixie dust before it wears off. Six months down from Charleston, Raffaello works evenings at the Macaroni Grill out on the Kissimmee strip and minds his irresistible kids, Caitlin and Max, during the day, while his wife Lisa teaches at a middle school. "That's the secret of keeping a marriage afloat," he jokes. I grit my teeth as I smile, wondering how I will keep my own Manhattan-stranded romance afloat in the year ahead.

Unruffled and vigilant, Raffaello has the proficient air of a town-watcher, and I can see one of the reasons why. Directly below us, children are playing in the gardens, bordered by a busy parking lot that services not only the residences but also the backs of stores and restaurants. I suspect that the pedestrian traffic across this interior lot could tell me a good deal about the doings of this town, much more so than

The Sessoms family and apartments on Market Street. (Photo: Jonathan Hayt)

on Market Street, the main thoroughfare on the other side of our apartments. The town hall and the post office occupy one corner, the bank sits in another, the cinema and half the town's restaurants and stores back on to the square, and directly opposite from us is the Seminole Building, housing the offices of the Celebration Company (TCC), the Disney subsidiary that is developing the town. Everyone's paths cross here at some point or another. My neighbor seems to know many of the people in motion below, and in time so will I. Eyes on the street in Celebration are for more than safety. Residents like Raffaello are surveying and assessing how well this new town actually works. Are there unforeseen traffic problems? Do the restaurant kitchens have enough back space to function? Where do people cluster and what do they talk about? In other words, residents are already doing what urbanologists do—what I have been sent to do. Flush with the grand romance of being Celebration pioneers, they are monitoring the town's every step, from behind the scenes, on the backlot, even as the world's media survey the life of its front porches, parks, and avenues.

Despite the extensive spraying, everyone, Raffaello tells me, is panicking about the encephalitis-bearing mosquitoes that have recently moved into the area and have started to take human lives. Town Hall has issued advisories about venturing out after sunset. The much-vaunted porch life of the residents is on hold, and community activity is subdued. Sectors of Disney World have been shut down. In the absence of a hurricane season, courtesy of El Niño, lesser natural threats are taking on a fresh prominence. A fourteen-foot gator, an alleged mankiller on several occasions, has just been captured in an adjoining county—the biggest specimen in recorded state history, although the claim is being hotly disputed. Since I was last here in the spring, several alligators had taken up residence in Celebration Lake and been benignly evicted. I later learn that waivers in homeowners' contracts exempt the developer from liability for residents' harmful encounters with alligators. An article about alligator habits is even included in the contracts. Why this special attention? Apparently, the swampland on which Celebration is being built was used as a dumping ground for gators cleared out of the Lake Buena Vista area when the foundations of Disney World were being excavated. Celebrationites were sharing their new habitat with this scaly army of Disney refugees. Of course, the gators are not anxious for human contact, but on occasion, five-footers show up in residents' swimming pools.

Notable birds, like sandhill cranes, have begun to adopt Celebration's lavish parks as a port of call, keeping company with other fauna in and around the wetland areas: the cottonmouth moccasin snakes and eastern diamondbacks, great blue herons, snowy and great egrets, gopher frogs, stinkpot musk turtles, cooters, bald eagles, parakeets, wild turkeys, and, most wondrous to me at least, the anhingas, drying off their clumsy wings by the lake before taking flight, like latter-day pterodactyls. For a northern urbanite, there is more than a touch of the Lost World about Central Florida, a region that played host to a Noah's ark of animals fleeing the southward advance of the Pleistocene ice sheets eons before it welcomed the hordes of human "snowbirds" fleeing modern northern winters.

Later in the season, Nala, a clawless 450-pound lion, will escape from nearby Jungle Land, precipitating a massive three-day hunt along route 192 outside of Celebration. Lt. Dennis Parker of the state game commission will tell residents that if they are attacked, they should "present an arm or something that isn't vital." Nala, rescued in a terrified condition from an adjacent thicket, turns out to be the least of the powerful natural threats, most of them meteorological, that will visit destruction and hardship on Central Florida in the months to come. Flood, fire, and winds from hell will lend an end-days backdrop to my year in Osceola County.

Just across from my balcony, three solid wooden rocking chairs are set out on the lakeside promenade. Unoccupied, they still look like three elderly citizens holding a leisurely conversation. The rockers are placed there for public use and they command the best downtown vantage point. From there, the view up Market Street is unimpeded, and you can see the entire sweep of Front Street and Bloom Street as they hug the northern portion of the lake. Their facades all glowing brightly in the sun, the downtown buildings draw on regional styles and borrow liberally from much-admired southern townscapes. There are balconies from New Orleans on Market Street, and Charleston sideyard porches on Front Street. According to the Architectural Walking Tour pamphlet, which you can pick up from the sales Preview Center, the garden apartment buildings on Campus Street, to the west, with their green clapboard upper stories, steep gabled roofs, and shallow eaves are "inspired by the traditional houses of St. Augustine." On Bloom Street, the model is the Low Country houses found in the coastal areas of the Carolinas. Many of the background buildings on Market and Front draw on Anglo-Caribbean "cross-bred" styles that mix colonial and classical architecture.

By the lakefront on Front Street stands a large plantation house, with the posture of Deep South comfort. Its solid, round columns rise above a ground floor that houses Café D'Antonio. The upper-floor apartments in the building opposite, hosting Max's Café, are shaded by outsize Bermuda shutters. Columbia, a branch of a famous family restaurant from the old Cuban cigar-making community of Ybor City, near Tampa, is nearing completion farther along Front. According to the pamphlet, it displays "the transfer of architectural ideas from Spain to Florida via Cuba" in the sweeping pediment marking its entryway and in its latticed lakefront porch. Next door, Cesar Pelli's deco cinema, with its two slender towers aimed skyward like impatient launch rockets, is a flamboyant tribute to the showy era of picture palaces. Few small towns these days boast a working downtown theater, and even fewer advertise their presence from a great distance as this one does. Also rare on the nation's Main Streets are the chunky, old-fashioned commercial signs, like this cinema's wheel-shaped marquees, or the boxy icons of Chambers' the jewelers and Max's, projecting out from their buildings and into the streets. Under pressure from preservationists, the signage on Main Streets' commercial buildings nationwide has been denuded or compressed in order to focus attention on the facades.[3] Here in Celebration, the variety of the signage, and what Jaquelin Robertson calls the "urban jewelry" of the town, is sumptuous enough, but still bears the mark of a single author, in this case the New York design firm of Pentagram.

Farther back, at the top of Market Street, is the town's tallest structure, currently in use as the Preview Center for realty sales. The last building to be designed by the quixotic Charles Moore, it is topped off by a stair-wrapped tower that harkens back to earlier years of Florida settlement, when such towers beckoned newcomers to town and served as a vantage point for homesteaders to pick out a lot. In Celebration, however, this tower, like the watertower at the entrance off route 192, is purely for show—you can't climb above the second floor. Across the square sits Michael Graves's faintly nautical, open-air post office. Next to it rises Philip Johnson's Town Hall, its grove of spindly columns mocking the solemnity of civic architecture. Just beyond the eighteen-acre downtown, an Old Glory big enough to grace a medium-size car dealership flaps above Founder's Park. At the back of the park are the stubby towers and muscle-bound facade of the newly completed school. In view of the bloody trials it will shortly undergo, this building appropriately resembles a military fortification built to withstand a siege. Farther out but still within easy walking distance, the streets of the main residential lots—with names like Mulberry Avenue, Longmeadow, Elderberry Court, Sycamore Street, Honeysuckle Avenue, Arbor Circle, Wisteria Court, Veranda Place, and Jasmine Street—are filling rapidly with porched houses of different sizes and styles. From

Stores and apartments on Market Street (Robert Stern, architect). (Photo: the author)

the lakefront rockers to the golf clubhouse at the end of the formal Beaux Arts canal corridor on Water Street, the Celebration logo—a dog tagging behind a ponytailed girl riding a bicycle past a picket fence and a spreading oak tree—dots the streetscape, appealing shamelessly to the iconography of innocence.

The lake itself is manmade, but has been skillfully sculpted by Disney's water engineers, preeminent in a state renowned for its dubious dredging feats. The creek that runs off to the east by Lakeside Park is pumped, but already boasts a surface carpet of algae. In almost any other master-planned development, the lake would be encircled by fancy houses, commanding a high premium for their waterfront location (and in some earlier plans for the site these houses do appear). Instead, Celebration's lake is ringed by a greenbelt of preserved wetlands and walking trails. In like fashion, the expensive estate homes that sit on the outer belt of Celebration Village are separated from the public golf course by a curving road and sidewalk, preserving the green expanse for walks and views. These exorbitant mansions, with builders' names that are 100 percent *nouveau riche* Anglo (Bromley Hall, Belle Manor, Creighton Hall, and Downing Hall), share narrow back alleyways with middle-income homes, and some of them are a spit away from multi-family apartments. There are many such departures from the conventional suburban landscape. By suburban standards, houses here have modest lots (the very largest are only 90 feet wide by 130 feet deep), scanty setbacks from the street where broad porches address passersby, and garages, with granny flats on top, tucked in at the back.

But the biggest violation of convention is the downtown area. No one in modern building history has opened a full-fledged town center on day one before 98 percent of the residences have even broken ground. It flies in the face of the cardinal rule of development that all commercial realty must be demand driven. Only a developer with very deep pockets, and the PR resources to pull in tourists, could underwrite this risk simply to beget an instantly vibrant town center. With barely five hundred residents, downtown already boasts fifteen stores, three restaurants, a coffeehouse, a cinema, a sprinkling of services, and about a dozen offices. Clearly chosen for the upscale tourist market (many of them are boutique retailers from bijou Winter Park, north of Orlando), the merchants I talk to are having a tough time making sales. The visitors ambling their way down Market Street are easily identifiable as denizens of Middle America. High socks cling tightly to the bare upper calves of the men, floral tote bags hang from the forearms of the women. None of them look as if they will be shelling out top dollar for a bar of Provençal soap at L'Occitane, the parfumerie, or a sylphic size 4 cocktail dress from M Fashion, or a twee English curio from Thomas Dunn, the antique furniture store. Time, repute, and retail Darwinism, I have been told, will take care of this problem. But things in Celebration, as I will soon learn, tend to happen prematurely.

THE BIG DRAW

Less than two years before, on Founders Day (November 18, 1995), almost five thousand people thronged around the marquees on an open field between route 192 and Celebration Place, the town's 100-acre business park (opened six months earlier). Three hundred and fifty home sites were up for lottery, and prospective buyers waited, checkbooks in hand, to lay down a deposit if they drew a respectable number. A good deal more orderly than the Oklahoma land rush, it was still a scene from the storyboards—a heady stir of Disney fever, America fever, and property fever. A brass band played, and the county-fair ambience included balloons, hot dogs, and puppet shows. The assembled were from far and wide, but mostly from Florida, the eastern seaboard, and the Midwest. Few of the people standing in line had seen anything like a detailed rendering of a house, let alone a floor plan. They had been drawn there by gilded rumor and a boffo advertising campaign that often read like scenes from a Ray Bradbury story stripped of all the stuff that makes your scalp stiffen:

> There once was a place where neighbors greeted neighbors in the quiet of summer twilight. Where children chased fireflies. And porch swings provided easy refuge from the care of the day. The movie house showed cartoons on Saturday. The grocery store delivered. And there was one teacher who always knew you who had that "special something." Remember that place? Perhaps from your childhood. Or maybe just from stories. It held a magic all its own. The special magic of an American home town. Now, the people at Disney—itself an American family tradition—are creating a place that celebrates this legacy. A place that recalls the timeless traditions and boundless spirit that are the best parts of who we are.
>
> Or
>
> There is a place that takes you back to that time of innocence. A place where the biggest decision is whether to play Kick the Can or King of the Hill. A place of caramel apples and cotton candy, secret forts, and hopscotch on the streets. That place is here again, in a new town called Celebration. . . . A new American town of block parties and Fourth of July parades. Of spaghetti dinners and school bake sales, lollipops, and fireflies in a jar. And while we can't return to these times we can arrive at a place that embraces all of these things. Someday, 20,000 people will live in Celebration, and for each and every one of them, it will be home.

The brochures also promised them a state-of-the-art package of progressive education, high technology, unequaled health facilities, and quality homes, but the fantasy glue that sealed the package was a story about going home again. Traditionally, this country's luckier migrants have always been promised something new, somewhere different, some place in the future they had never been before—whether in a little house on the prairie, a brownstone apartment in the city, a bungalow in a canyon, or a Cape Cod in the suburbs. This was a different kind of promise. It seemed to be channeling the sharp rush of baby-boomer hunger to be homeward bound to a place that lies well off the century's main drag—behind the fast curve of modernity, where their grandparents had once lived. At prices ranging from $150,000 for a townhouse all the way to a cool million for a mansion, it would not be a cheap detour.

Farther along route 192, Disney was drawing a different kind of migrant to Osceola County. Workers from Central America and the Caribbean were arriving to fill minimum-wage jobs at the theme parks. The same day that families from the suburbs of Detroit and Miami were banking on Disney's gilt-edged name in the Celebration drawing, families from San Juan and Guadalajara with the promise of a thin Disney pay slip in hand were combing the apartment complexes just off the Kissimmee strip for affordable shelter. The company had at least two hands at work on this land, ushering people hither and thither, and the left one did not always care to know what the right one was up to.

In the meantime, back on my first day in residence, in a place where I had imagined I would feel a little like a Hell's Angel, I have already been upstaged. Real bikers have come to town! The leathery visitors—the men sporting a few too many whiskers and the women way too much mascara—are clustered in Sweet's ice cream bar on Front Street, digesting the wares and absorbing the lakeside vibes. It's a long way from Hollister, California, where the ton-up mavericks made their most infamous appearance almost exactly fifty years before (providing the storyline for the *The Wild One*), and yet Sweet's, modeled to evoke that era, is a suggestive backdrop. These might well be the baddest boys and girls I am likely to see here, and yet they could have been hired hands, absorbed into the scenery. It will take a little while for this illusion of stagecraft to wear off. Celebration is a picture-book town with a

Kodak moment on every corner, and it reminds all first-time visitors of a film set.

My biker urges dissipate overnight, and the next day I trade them for a different American fantasy—a Cadillac of a certain age. Scouring the classified pages, I seek out a vehicle distinct from the freshly polished new cars in Celebration's streets and parking lots, but respectable enough not to violate the town's aesthetic standards ("unsightly vehicles" are prohibited, according to my rental agreement). After an adventurous foray around the metro region, I lay down cash for an '85 Coupe de Ville, champagne colored and handsomely maintained. According to the ad, it is "fully loaded," which appeals to the long-dormant road warrior in me, though I have little idea what the phrase means and will often wonder as the car gradually turns into a money pit, losing its life gracelessly in the last weeks of my Florida residence. As we cruise across the North Orlando mallscapes to an insurance shack to complete the sale, the owner, soft-spoken and bashful, casually reveals that he is an ex–bounty hunter. He even has an unpublished book manuscript detailing his exploits. Without much further prompting, he delivers a few gamey stories about the pursuit of outlaws with a price on their heads. He still sleeps with a shotgun under his bed. I resolve to change the tags as soon as I can.

Back in Celebration, and en route to the DMV office in Kissimmee, I pick up a British tabloid newspaper, readily available for visiting tourists in the Goodings grocery store. It carries the story of Becky Howell, an Orlando waitress who has won a Porsche in an endurance contest. Her winning performance involves kissing the car continuously for 33 hours and 17 minutes, a feat that required medical attention to her cramped legs, swollen neck, and two loose teeth. Life without automobiles—the far-fetched dream of places like Celebration—would surely be dull for some, but people like Becky might soon learn to apply their affection in ways less hazardous to their health.

2

THE PRICE OF TRADITION

"The dampers for some bathroom fans have been painted shut and therefore the fans cannot remove air. To test for this condition, pull off 4 sheets of toilet tissue. Moisten one end and stick the tissue on the end of a broom handle. Turn on the fan and hold the handle near the fan's grill. The fan should pull the tissue up vigorously across the entire grill, not just part of the grill. Otherwise the damper is not free to open." —extract from the renegade Celebration Homeowners Association's "Town House Bulletin"

By the time Celebration's lake was being scooped out of the soggy soil, Osceola had become one of the most schizophrenic, and fastest-growing, counties in the United States. But you didn't have to go very far to run into Old Florida. The county's pine and palmetto prairie that ran south from the nineteenth-century cowboy towns of Kissimmee and St. Cloud to Yeehaw Junction was still under the sway of the Cattlemen's Association and the old ranching families. Over 80 percent farmland and water, Osceola boasted a huge chunk of the largest ranch east of the Mississippi: the Mormon Church–owned Deseret Ranch, at 316,000 acres all told, with its thousands of head of Brahma cattle (the only breed with sweat glands). Cowboys, crackers, good old boys, and the Klu Klux Klan were no longer all-powerful, but they had not quite relaxed their grip on the county's legislature. To the north and west, on the tourist strip between Walt Disney World and Kissimmee, the scrubland was now ruled by brand names: CK, Ray-Ban, Seiko, Reebok, Timberland. Haunted Gothic mansions, Pizza Huts, Denim Kingdoms, electronics flea markets, trailer parks, and time-share apartment blocks had sprouted overnight in fields still freshly splashed with cattle dung. Over half of Osceola's jobs were now in tourism, residential land use had doubled between 1990 and 1997, and, at peak times, its seasonal visitors added another 70,000 to its standing population.[1]

Celebration, at the far western end, is the new kid on this block. It is the indirect legacy of the short-lived local residency of Elias Disney, Walt's father, who married Flora McCall, a vacationing Ohio schoolteacher, in Kissimmee, and then tried his luck, and failed, as a citrus grower in the late 1880s. But if you drive out west along the strip and make the turn left into town, expecting to see the future of the county, you will be met by rows of sumptuous, porch-saddled houses that have not been built in Florida for well over sixty years. You may be excused for asking, in the words of urban theorist Kevin Lynch, "What time is this place?"[2] This is a version of the future, but it doesn't look futuristic, not like the one you passed en route—Xanadu, the House of the Future (a space-agey tourist attraction that was outdated even when it was built well over a decade ago). Back in the earliest planning stages, there had been some talk about "dating" this town by providing it, Disney style, with a themed backstory. In one rendering, the town was built by survivors of a shipwrecked Spanish galleon, and the residents had an elaborate monument in the town square by which to remember their heroic ancestors.[3] In another, Celebration had been built anew out of the rubble left by General Sherman's ruinous march through the South.[4] Thankfully, for the sake of the current residents, this planning approach, which bore the jaunty trademark of the Imagineers, was shelved. Instead, Celebration came into being as a neotraditional town, the product, among other things, of market research that showed how much prospective homebuyers would be prepared to pay for re-creating the past while preserving their modernity.

CONSUMER SCIENCE

Not long after I moved into my Celebration apartment, I took a house call from representatives of a company called European Lifestyle. This was a local start-up on route 192, outside of town, that offers interior design consulting, along with a range of other domestic services, including uniformed maids and car valeting. A lush brochure left at my door had guaranteed "bespoke, upscale" results that drew upon "centuries of traditional service," and promised that I would be the envy of my neighbors. Clients in pursuit of the elegance and sophistication of Europe could choose from the "simple, functional and practical styles of Scandinavia" or the "reserved, classic originality" of Britain, the "flamboyant and laissez-faire liberalism" of France, the "formality" of Teutonic styles, or the "creativity" of Italy. From the evidence of their advertising, the company had probably assumed that recently moved-in Celebrationites would be ideal customers. So I made an appointment, hoping to learn something about how outsiders saw us.

In deference to the crisp authority of the brochure, I had prepared myself for some fierce autocrat of style, a Cruella De Vil who would issue design edicts as she swanned around my apartment. I did not bargain for an hour of strenuous people pleasing from my visitors. The owner, Gail, had a relaxed and homespun manner, and a distinctly northern English accent with no superclass overtones. She had set up near Orlando because the embassy was willing to grant her a visa to work in a region with the highest rates of home building in the nation, and where there would be a crying need for her services. Sure enough, she had estimated that Celebration residents would be a steady source of income.

Gail had just returned from a design show in London, and was full of news about what's in at Harrods. Alice, her senior designer, was more tightly wound-up. A fast-talking, tanned blonde from Alabama, she warned me that she was itching to be let loose to redesign my "little space." Protocol demanded that she consult my tastes, however, and she promised that when the time came we would go shopping together to the showrooms. Passing on each of the national traditions on offer, I expressed my preference for Mediterranean colors and local decorative elements. This was a frank provocation, because it did not cater directly to the expertise of my guests. Tourists and part-time residents of Florida are expected to favor this indigenous style, which is basically a knock-off of the Hispanic fantasies woven by Addison Mizner in the first Palm Beach resort after the First World War. Tom Wolfe would call it something like Time Share Mediterranean. Gail and Alice were supposed to be offering something else, for residents with cosmopolitan taste, who don't necessarily want to be reminded that they live in or near Orlando. But they were undeterred by my lack of imagination. What colors interested me? Turquoise and jasmine. Both were "in" at the moment. Everything I mentioned happened to be "in." We agreed on leopard-skin prints, a choice my Cruella might have approved. Gail assured me they were "very masculine" and, of course, they were still "in at Harrods," and would lend some dash to the stark black leather furniture I had brought down from New York. Gail suggested some "window treatments," which I took to mean curtains, and a "faux finish to the back walls," which I simply let pass with approving silence.

So far, they had done a good job of flattering this sadly uninformed consumer. Having established I was not her ideal client, Alice asked, a little curtly, if I would be favoring nontraditional furniture, too. Gail intervened to soften the tension. In England, she assured me, people are not obliged to choose between traditional and modern. They mix and match at will, and are comfortable with all sorts of combinations of taste. Happy eclecticism of this sort may not sit well with upscale American suburban living, but if the English condone it, then I should be able to rest easy with my choice. With that clarified, and with the uncertain promise that they would return at some later date to do business, they took their leave.

I never saw them again and heard that they had packed up and left within the year, having overestimated the local demand for their services. Above all, it seems, they had misjudged the Celebration market. A month after Gail and Alice's visit, a domestic cleaner called me, claiming that he often worked for them, but could offer me much lower rates if I employed him directly. A recent immigrant from the English Midlands, he was caught, like so many others, in the low-wage trap of a tourist economy, where jobs abound but a livable income is hard to come by. I would meet many such souls in the dollar-poor purgatory of Central Florida, including a teacher, freshly fired from an elementary school, who was now working as Winnie-the-Pooh in the Magic Kingdom for just under $6 an hour. Apparently, the coveted task of animating the famous bear for an hour is worth less than the price of a ticket for a Disney film of the same length.

For professionals like Gail and Alice, the Great Divide between modern and traditional is their bread and butter, even as they seemed willing to stretch the definitions for an ornery client like myself. In the everbooming building economy of Orlando Metro—next to Las Vegas, the fastest growing city in the United States—this divide is clearly visible all across the busy landscape, flush with stucco-sheathed subdivisions, criss-crossed by the adobe walls of gated developments, and swelled by the clusters of vacation homes that ring the Big Three attractions: Disney World, Universal Studios, and Sea World. In step with the ethos of the preservation and environmental movements, much of the middle- to high-end housing built in the last two decades defers, in some outward show of respect, to a traditional, or at least a prewar look. There are few developers who do not pay lip service to the heritage formula of selling the trappings of tradition along with the conveniences of modernity. Celebration had taken this formula to another level, offering a traditional townscape along with an advanced technical infrastructure from the age of yahoo.com. As one sales brochure put it, "Except for all the newfangled, modern stuff, it's just like the town your grandparents grew up in."

Celebration's facades attract all the attention, and so initially I was more curious about the interiors. During my first weeks in town, before I had started visiting resident's houses, I spent a portion of each day inside the town's model homes to see what an ideal interior was supposed to look like. Entering these houses was like boarding a suburban version of the ghost ship, the *Maria Celeste*—stocked and decorated as if a real family were living there and had evacuated in a great hurry. Framed family portraits sat on furniture tops, snapshots were magnet-hung on the fridge doors, books lay open on beds, Web sites were frozen on computer screens, a mud-stained baseball outfit was tossed on one bedroom chair, a majorette's hat on another. In the larger model homes, marks of wealth and taste were flaunted—vast facsimiles of Gobelin tapestries stretched along the hallway, classical architectural drawings and hunting-dog portraits lined the walls; fine wines, cigars, old maps, oak panels, and legal tomes filled the study; and elaborate themes were evoked in the childrens' bedrooms—*Star Trek,* Rainforest Botanist, Ballerina Russe, Noah's Ark. In contrast to the tightly packed *Reader's Digest* volumes and *National Geographic* issues found in the smaller houses, the shelves here were lined with upper-middle-brow reading material: John Steinbeck, Barbara Taylor Bradford, George Orwell, Louisa May Alcott, James Michener, Russell Baker, and the five-foot shelf of Harvard Classics. Elaborate flower arrangements and herbal bouquets set off a display of gourmet foods, lying in wait for the chef of the house, while luxurious oils and salts lined the bathtubs, anticipating the weary body. The Celebration rumor mill reported that these model homes had to be continually restocked, since visitors persisted in walking off with the pricey accessories. Minor acts of vandalism were also reported.

These were not simply what builders call "twenty-minute houses," designed to register an immediate visual impression for first-time visitors. They were intact living environments, with preselected taste and decor choices, and they lacked nothing except the presence of warm bodies. Market-researched and brand-approved, with advanced infrastructure and appliances from the likes of Honeywell, General Electric, and Kohler, these interiors were products of an industry that had defined personal taste through the precision science of focus groups and opinion polling. The same consumer science had selected the six housing styles adopted for the developer's traditionalist offerings: Classical, "inspired by the gracious houses of the Old South," and derived primarily from nineteenth-century Greek Revival architecture; Victorian, "whimsical and cheerful," "asymmetrical and picturesque," and drawing heavily on the pattern books of the nineteenth century; Colonial Revival, an "optimistic" commemoration of the popular 1920s–1940s style, and especially typical of traditional neighborhoods in Orlando and Tampa; Coastal, "stately and relaxed," and based on Acadian and Low Country traditions of the southern Atlantic states; Mediterranean, the honeybrown twentieth-century Florida style with stucco and tile roofs; and French, based on the "simple and elegant" farmhouse architecture made popular by veterans on their return from the Great War in Europe.

Consumer market research also lay at the origins of "neotraditionalism," the preferred ethos and style of New Urbanism, the planning movement of which Celebration is largely a spinoff. When I queried Andres Duany, the charismatic, Miami-based figurehead of the movement, about this concept, he cited a slide presentation of a consumer study he attended in a Disney office building in the late 1980s: "It changed my life," he declared with vigorous clarity. "My mind-set, my method of operation was born there." The report, summarizing the results of eighteen years of annual research by the firm Yankelovich Clancy Shulman, was a fast and loose assessment of how boomer consumer attitudes had changed since their "outright rejection" of the "traditional values system" twenty years before.

> We are now developing an entirely new social climate in this country. . . . This new approach to life, which we call Neotraditionalism, is *not* a rejection of what came before, as the "Me Generation" values were. Rather, it is a synthesis of the best parts of the two previous value systems, combining the security and responsibility of the 50s with the individual freedoms and personal choice of the "Me Generation." Consumers seem to be seeking a state of equilibrium, a balance between these extremes.[5]

Duany recalled how the report was presented:

> They showed a photograph of a Victorian mantelpiece with a Braun alarm clock sitting on it. The neotraditionalists, they argued, might choose an old-fashioned room, but they wouldn't buy a Victorian clock that has to be wound and might not be accurate. They would choose an up-to-date German clock. Moreover, the neotraditionalists would have modern plumbing and kitchens in their old houses. Now, a traditionalist would restore a Victorian bathroom, clawfoot tub and all, while a modernist would think it improper to live in a Victorian house.[6]

Tom Lewis, vice president of Walt Disney Imagineering and one of the original members of the Celebration planning team, could not recall this report but acknowledged that a real estate study had been commissioned from the Robert Charles Lesser group (the country's premier real estate valuation firm) when the team was looking at target markets for residential developments in the region. They also talked to a group of futurists about "consumer preferences in the nineties and into the next century," and conducted market research with visitors to Innoventions at EPCOT and through postal surveys sent to stockholders about the kinds of communities, lifestyles, and products they would want in a new town. The results clearly fed into the final conception of the town as a place with "old houses and new toys."

It's not clear that this formula differs so radically from that espoused by the upwardly mobile in previous decades of the century. Didn't all such homeowners want the outward marks of antique prestige while enjoying mod cons inside their homes? On the other hand, if this really was an accurate boomer profile, there was a visible history behind it. The epic 1960s' revolts of boomer teens against a formulaic planet of canned laughter, plastic packaging, and cookie-cutter housing had spawned an ambivalent attitude toward mass-produced modernity. A good deal of the energy of these revolts was channeled into restorative causes like housing preservation and environmentalism, both valuing an undefiled past. But the legacy of the 1960s counterculture also gave birth to the idea that high technology could be utilized as a medium of personal freedom. This was the germ of the personal computer revolution in the West Coast subcultures that formed around Apple and fed, ultimately, into the brave new world of self-publishing on the World Wide Web. Here, then, was the Janus face of the neotraditionalist boomer: ever responsive to promises of self-liberation through high technology, and yet still ravenous for authentic, original stuff, untainted by mass commercialism. Celebration was designed as a happy hunting ground for people who fit this consumer profile.

MAKING ENDS MEET

In this town, where Victorian dormer windows vie with Windows 98, every building and landscape detail—facades, loggias, pediments, cornices, eaves, setbacks, fence heights, and shrubbery—is governed by the style prescriptions, or "recommendations," laid out in the town's Pattern Book. Very little is left to chance, or, more precisely, to the mood of the capricious resident or the impatient builder. Everything that con-

Village homes on Celebration Avenue. (Photo: the author)

tributes visually to the public realm is regulated by codes aimed at refining the "conversation" between buildings and the streetscape. But the Pattern Book does not apply behind the Victorian and Colonial Revival facades, and so the insides and outsides of houses are as different as chalk from cheese.

As far as I could see, the interiors followed conventional suburban floor-plan standards and bore little historical correlation to the deep wraparound porches, hipped roofs, and classical columns of the facades. This was just as well, since modern American families do not use space in the same way as did families of an earlier era. The homes that I had begun to visit boasted cathedral ceilings, open plan floors, with kitchen parlors bleeding into reception and dining spaces, and, in the larger ones, monster master bedrooms off to the side with bathrooms the size of Manhattan studios. In some of the custom-built estate homes, I was more likely to come across attempts at period styling—antique furniture and factory versions of original hand-carved moldings, medallions, casings, and wood paneling. In pursuit of design details for their Classical estate home on Water Street, Rodney and Debbie Jones visited Savannah, Charleston, Asheville, and Raleigh, following portions of the "Disney trail" blazed by the Celebration development team during their own research on traditional southern towns. The framing on the Joneses' doors and interior windows, moldings on their skirtboards, and paneling on the pillars and window grills had all been copied from houses they visited. Customized with similar touches of period detail, the walls featured one very contemporary item: a series of Rodney's abstract paintings, culled from his studio in the garage apartment. An insurance agent with State Farm and a leader of the community's Catholic group, Rodney served tirelessly on almost every community committee in town, yet still had time to work in the "fluidist" style he conceived back in his Penascola high school days. His paintings, executed in oil, acrylic, plaster, and gel, were virtually the only nonfigurative artworks I ever saw in Celebration.

At least one other likely venue for a Jones painting was Dave Eaton's epicene home on Longmeadow. From the outside, it looked like a courteous Coastal, with wicker chairs spreading out all over the endless porch, but when the front doors opened, I found myself in a Mediterranean villa, cunningly laid out around a central courtyard pool and fountain. "Things are seldom what they seem," mused Eaton. As befits the home of the founder of the Celebration Players, the two wings were decorated with high theatrical flair, each hosting a succession of rooms that could have been stage sets for entirely different plays: a Victorian sitting room over here, a deco bedroom over there, and, in front, like some Cole Porter–inspired hotel vestibule, an airy, yellow-hued room with a piano.

In all my early visits to homes, the most surprising finding was the frequency of relatively empty interiors. It was as if the contents of entire rooms had been sucked away by a careful tornado. Boomers often favor uncluttered space, in contrast with the dense, tchotchke-crammed rooms of their parents' homes. But it did not look as if these interiors were a bow to minimalism; their sparseness had more to do with cash flow. A sizable number of residents were chronically short of disposable income after stretching to buy homes priced almost 35 percent above the equivalent in nearby developments with similar amenities. Most homes in New Urbanist developments command a significant premium, since anything novel or unconventional in the housing industry tends to cost more to get built, but 35 percent was uncommonly high.[7] David Weekley, one of the production (non-estate) builders in Celebration, claimed that the design "purity" demanded by the developer's architectural Pattern Book drove their cost up by 30 percent, but most residents, especially those with experience in real estate, took this assertion with a grain of salt.[8] With the range of options on offer, and an additional premium for a desirable lot, sticker shock was a common experience around town. David Tennant, a Scottish resident who had grown up in a cramped Glasgow tenement and was now the owner of a Charleston siderow on a Cottage lot across from the school, offered a typically wry description: "You start out thinking you're going to buy a VW, and end up with a BMW." Ron Dickson, a townhouse resident on the Academy Row section of Campus Street, with a background in the housing industry, put a different spin on his experience: "We thought we were buying a BMW and ended up with a VW." He was referring to the cheap outfitting of much of the production housing in the Townhouse, Garden, Village, and Cottage ranges. Indeed, as residents like Dickson were dismayed to find, these homes came with bottom-of-the-line kitchen appliances, bathroom fixtures, doors, windows, and HVAC installations that you could find on the low-end shelves of any Home Depot store.

Having begged and borrowed to pony up the town's "expensive entrance fee," as some folks describe the cost of setting up in Celebration, furniture and interior decoration are generally not a top priority. Gail and Alice would indeed have had a tough time here finding clients for their deluxe services. Gregory Schroeder, a pianist for the Community Presbyterian Church who works as an interior designer, confirmed that the town had not provided anything like the level of custom he had hoped for. Thomas Dunn, owner of the town's traditional furniture store, gets very little business from Celebration residents. His English imports are passed over in favor of the "authentic reproductions" that residents order by catalog from Karen and Tom Zirbes, who own the adventurous bric-a-brac store on the other side of the street. Even the Zirbes, among the more popular of the town's merchants, estimate that only 2 percent of their sales are from residents. The industry norm for expenditure on home decor, they say, is 25 percent of the price of the home. Celebration, it appeared, was coming in well under the median.

I had been in town for only a few days when I first heard the Celebration mantra that mostly everyone here was "house-rich and cash-poor." There were variations on this theme, such as "We used to have money, before we came to Celebration." Aside from its plausible truth value, I took this comment to be a functional element of community folklore. Such a belief helped to soften the clear inequalities between people living in close proximity in mixed-income neighborhoods. Accustomed to being graded into pods or clusters that correspond to their incomes, this was a highly unusual situation for suburban Americans to find themselves in. In addition, the Celebration ethos of communitarianism demands that everyone is understood to be in the same boat, with no special advantages. While the housing equity and incomes of residents on neighboring blocks may differ substantially (each block consists of the same lot sizes, though no two houses are permitted to be identical), all are assumed to be spending every available dollar on their mortgages. Inside the town's property line, the boomer sensibilities of most Celebrationites insist that they think of themselves as "average people." Airs and graces are discouraged. Outside of town, they are viewed as befits the highest income residents in the region. Many residents professed bemusement at the opinion of county locals that Celebrationites were wealthy and snooty, although several confided their guilty pleasure to me: "I like the idea that other people might think I'm rich." Jonathan Ferenczi, a forty-something townhouse resident with independent wealth and bohemian gusto, gleefully observed that he had moved to a place "where the poor masquerade as rich, and the rich pretend they are poor."

There is some truth on both sides. With the average price of a production home in Phase One running at about $220,000—almost twice the median for a single family home in the Orlando region—there is a manifest concentration of equity wealth in the community. If you included estate homes, the first nine months of 1997 showed an average house sale of $330,000, and in the first half of 1998 this figure rose to $377,300, almost $150,000 more than the average for any other top-selling development in Central Florida.[9] While it was not kosher to flaunt your fortune, Celebration had a good slice of wealthy, and professionally successful, residents.[10] On the other hand, there were many families in town who were living beyond their means, who certainly could not afford the private school fees customary in upscale developments in Florida, and who had to budget hard for family meals and outings. In the frenzy to buy into the Phase One lottery, too little attention was paid to the fine print. Some who had moved from different kinds of housing were dismayed to learn they would be hit for hefty assessments and other maintenance fees in addition to their mortgages.[11] Closing costs were high, and many out-of-state pioneers misjudged the difference between Florida property taxes based on the value of their land, in the first year, and those based on their house value that kicked in a year later.[12] Some claimed they were unaware they would be paying additional premiums for desirable lots (up to $50,000 for production homes and up to $200,000 for estates). In retrospect, they felt that the hard financial information provided by Celebration salespeople was played down in the rush of sales hype. Such discrepancies are commonplace in the world of real estate, but they came as a shock to residents sold on the credo of "In Disney We Trust."

The thin myth of financial egalitarianism aside, there was talk aplenty about the "millionaires on Golfpark Drive" (the road that boasts the most expensive estate houses in the central village), but even they were commonly described as "regular people." I was often informed that some millionaires had chosen to live among the downtown renters, but their modest lifestyles meant that they escaped detection by me. The rumor of their existence was important, however, for it helped erase the ingrained bias against downtown—the habitation of the nonenfranchised and potentially transient renters, with no need to respect the cardinal rule of maintaining property value. Knowing my own location, homeowners frequently commented on how nice it would be to live in a downtown apartment, although those who had done so (while waiting for their house to be built) were usually not among their number. For all the good faith about ignoring income differences, every so often, class assumptions about renters were confirmed. One evening, Linda Frayn, a homeowner who works part-time as a server at Chef Mickey's in the Contemporary Resort (and who earns more in three days than she could in a week locally in her profession as a teacher), waited on two customers who were proud to declare that they had just moved onto Golfpark Drive in Celebration. The couple asked her where she lived. "I'm from Celebration, too." "Really?" they replied, momentarily off guard, but quickly recovering, "Do you live in an apartment?"

To be sure, the financial pinch was felt most among renters. Twenty-four percent of my fellow renters had household incomes of less than $30,000 (21 percent had incomes above $100,000). They included tenants like Miriam Blake, a single mother with three children, who told me she could barely afford to shop in the Goodings grocery store, the one merchant that everyone in town frequented. The apartments hosted several tenants, like Blake, who had come to realize they could not afford a house, but had decided to stay for the school and for the friendliness of the community. Other pioneers, like John Crawford, a retiree prominently featured in the sales center's promotional video, had been faced with a similar dilemma, sharpened by what he saw as excessive annual rent increases, and had opted reluctantly to move into an adult community in Lake County to the north. Like many of the renters, both Blake and Crawford had found part-time jobs in the theme parks.

Celebration has its working class, young and elderly. In local parlance they are referred to as "people on a budget." So, too, the high cost of making ends meet was hitting middle-income dwellers. The school's volunteer pool, overflowing in its first year of operation, suffered noticeably as many homemakers sought employment to meet mortgage payments and hiked property tax assessments.

For many strapped homeowners, the starkest pill to swallow was a much smaller house and lot than they could get elsewhere for the same price. However hard to stomach at first, most could see that the sacrifice of lot size was connected to the "sense of community" they had bought into. The volume of their public life, gauged in social interaction with neighbors and passersby on the street, was supposed to be directly and inversely related to their lot size. This is a basic assumption of New Urbanist planning, extended to the town as a whole. Could it also help explain the underdecorated state of the interiors? One resident who thought so was Ramond Chiaramonte, a savvy town planner with the Hillsborough County Commission in Tampa. Ray and his family had moved to town for a trial run, and they had become New Urbanist converts within a matter of months. He was one of the few residents who responded vigorously, in the press, to presumptuous attacks on Celebration, giving hell to journalists and architects jaundiced against the town.[13] In response to my question, he speculated that the rich public life of Celebration may well translate into a certain indifference to the domestic environment, as residents spend less and less time in the home. "People are not working less," he added, "but they are spending more time together, primarily because you don't lose time driving everywhere."

All the same, Chiaramonte, among many others, drives substantial distances to work outside of Celebration, and a serious shopping trip entails driving well outside the orbit of what the town's own stores can offer. In a place designed for walkability, it is also surprising how often residents still use their cars to drive downtown and elsewhere. Virtually every private party I attended was easy to locate by the small throng of cars parked outside the house. Geographically marooned in a tourist sector, Celebration is probably not the best gauge of the New Urbanist promise of reduced car use, and, as I would later discover, the Disney regional plan, of which Celebration is a cornerstone, was actually based around upgrading auto access to the theme parks. As for the superfluous traffic within the town's property line, that seemed to me to have more to do with the complex and persistent habits of daily auto dependence, a psychology that street planning alone would not alter easily. Adopting the profile of a resolute pedestrian, I regularly turned down offers of rides from one part of town to another. I found it was easy to provoke auto guilt, and harder to detect auto-free pride, among my fellow residents. But the design of Celebration did offer a choice between walking and driving, and choice, dethroning necessity, is the first step toward peacable coexistence with the automobile.[14] Largely because of its location, I found few families for whom the town's walkability had allowed them to give up one of their cars (according to Andres Duany, the average car in suburbia costs its owner $6,400 a year, which translates into $60,000 of housing purchase).[15]

What do residents feel they get for the 35 percent premium paid on their houses or apartments? For a very few, the Disney name is sufficient, even though this is a high price to pay for a town where Disney is nowhere to be seen. Celebration is the only place for miles around where you cannot buy a Mickey Mouse T-shirt. For others, the promise of high resale value justifies their outlay. Property appreciated about 15 percent annually in the first few years, and as much as 30 percent in some cases. In addition, the public school is a payoff for parents, representing a huge savings on private school bills. Many such parents tend to treat the educational offerings accordingly—as an investment on which they expect to see a quarterly return in the form of improving test scores. A substantial minority see the premium as the price to pay for the town's common amenities, and the chance to enjoy the fellowship of the people who have been drawn to the town. It is a generous subsidy for the public affluence of Celebration's streetscapes, parks, trails and promenades, fountains, squares, lakeside access, and downtown ambience, accessible not just to residents but to all who choose to motor into town.

This public realm is real enough, despite the lingering effect of a stage set. But what about the infrastructure behind the brightly painted verandas, expansive porches, gleaming picket fences, and gingerbread eaves? There lies one of the town's most calamitous stories. Unlike the controversy surrounding the school, the jerry-rigging of Celebration never made it into any press headlines.

BUTCHER BUILDERS

Once I started doing my rounds of house visits, I discovered there were few buyers of production houses who did not have atrocity stories to tell about the shoddiness of the construction work on their homes. Some were almost apoplectic when the subject was broached, and found it difficult to recount calmly everything that had gone wrong: porches and roofs that had to be torn down and rebuilt, tilted beams and uneven rafters, plumbing leaks, fissures, and holes, drainage nightmares, doors that won't close, cracks in the foundations, collapsing floors and driveways, interior walls and fireplaces where they should not be, chronic delamination, loose braces, and improper nailing, vapor barriers installed on the wrong side of walls, chimneys out of plumb, and so on. Complaints about builders are legion in any new development, but it was difficult to imagine that so many things could have gone wrong on so many occasions. The way that some of the aggrieved talked, it sounded like one big lawsuit waiting to happen.

Over two hundred production builders had applied for the prestigious Celebration contract, and after extensive reviewing Disney had chosen two: Chicago's number one home builder, Town and Country, which earned the lowest points from Celebration residents; and David Weekley, from Houston, which performed better but did not escape unscathed. Ironically, David Pace, director of residential real estate development for the Celebration Company (TCC), noted early on that "our biggest risk at Celebration wasn't financial," it was selecting builders who wouldn't tarnish Disney's name.[16] With so little competition among builders (six more were chosen to offer estate homes) and with seemingly minimal oversight from TCC, the price of construction appeared to soar as the wage floor sank. It was easy to suspect price gouging on Disney land. Indeed, when the estimated construction cost for the school came in at $134 per square foot, as compared to an average of $80 elsewhere in the county, school board members were more than curious to know why subcontractors felt they could charge such inflated prices to work in Disney's town.

The big builders both came with national prize-winning reputations, but all construction, like politics, is local. Accustomed to a union labor force in the Midwest, Town and Country made it known that they were having difficulty locating skilled workers in the boom construction economy of Orlando, where unemployment in the building industry is minimal, and where Weekley, already building homes in the region, had cornered the labor market in the vicinity of Celebration. Several residents familiar with the industry suggested that Town and Country had been unwilling to pay the bonuses necessary to attract craftsmen from well-known area contractors, nor did they offer to help defray their commuting expenses. Others felt that, as newcomers to the area, the builder simply got "slamdunked by subcontractors." Understaffed and overworked, county building inspectors had a tough time keeping up with the construction boom. As a result, many of those who began to build Celebration were undocumented Mexican agricultural workers, unskilled in construction and underpaid for the semi-skilled work for which they were hastily recruited. Workers proficient in planting crops were learning how to do stucco jobs overnight. Jorge Comesanas, formerly in the building trade, who was one of the first residents to move into town, warned me early in the fall: "If the INS came in here and rounded up the illegals, Celebration wouldn't exist." Sure enough, in February, U.S. Border Patrol agents raided one of the town's construction sites and arrested sixteen undocumented workers. A whistle blower claimed that as many as ninety of the site's one hundred workers were undocumented. The employer, Gables Residential, builder of the site's luxury multifamily apartments, blamed the Orlando labor shortage. The workers were deported south of the border. In common with INS practice—too many cases, not enough manpower to file charges—the company escaped being cited by the agents.[17]

Not a few of Celebration's homebuyers were so relieved to move in after waits, in some cases, of almost two years from the promised completion date, that they overlooked, or decided to forget, many of the flaws in their homes. Others gave up long before the closing date and allowed the builders to sell their houses at an inflated price. One Cottage homeowner on Jasmine Street confessed that he lost sleep every so often mulling over potential structural defects, and imagining that his house might simply fall apart some day, or be felled by a Florida storm. The quality of construction was a running joke around town. Several of my fellow apartment dwellers decided to stay put after watching the carnage on some of the construction sites. When I asked when they would be buying a house, the answer was always something like "Right after you do," or "When a good builder comes to town." Given TCC's one year anti-speculator rule (requiring sellers to relinquish any capital gains within that time to the nonprofit Celebration Foundation), many buyers said they felt trapped, and there was a general expectation of residential flight once the probationary period was over. A good few residents I knew seized their first chance to move, after the year was up, but no mass exodus occurred, as had been widely feared.

Unable to believe that such mishaps could occur on Disney's watch, it took a while for residents to react publicly. One exception was Town and Country homeowner, and ex–building contractor, Ron Dickson, who was active in the community from an early point. In the summer of 1997, he began to circulate an extensive "Checklist for Inspecting a House," designed to help residents look for construction flaws on their own. A straight-talking Carolinian, with a sideline as a merry prankster, Dickson was an old hand in this area of community service. While working as a facility manager for Unysis in Charlotte, he had devoted his after-hours office time to writing (on the company's "$6 million personal word processor") two book-length documents, *Buy a Home Without Losing Your Assets* and *The Management of Homebuilding*, for the benefit of employees and area residents likely to be fleeced by rapscallion builders and realtors. In these manuals, Dickson offers his services as a Sherlock Holmes interpreting the clues of "crimes of construction" for the "potential fools who rush in where agents fear to tread." Both books are a gold mine of tips for the unsuspecting. His other publications include *The Joy of Checks*—on how to balance your bankbook—and *The Great American Moon Pie Handbook*—dedicated to the virtues of "the noble snack" of the marshmallow sandwich, for which he was a ceaseless advocate around town as self-styled president of the elusive Moon Pie Cultural Club.

Dickson was a fix-it kind of person, and his literary ventures had an equally practical flavor. He expected no less of me, and often lectured me about how my book should set things straight in this town and others like it. A master of deadpan, his "checklist" of flaws bore a faintly whimsical tone. In a slight twist on Celebration's family-oriented ethos, he invites homebuyers to go through his list with the help of the whole household: "Make it a fun thing for the family. Let kids spray water on the windows and doors. Use a round brass nozzle, not the pistol grip style, to get a long stream of water. Look for the 'Flying Turkey' test and the 'Old Faithful Geyser' test." What follows is an exhaustive inventory of common defects he had found in neighbors' houses in the areas of plumbing, HVAC, appliances, carpentry, electrical, irrigation, and exterior construction: "If the stove is free standing (sits on the floor), open the oven door all the way and push down hard on it to see if the stove will tip over. If the stove tips, it could send a large turkey flying across the room. An 'anti-tipping' device is supposed to be installed behind the stove to stabilize it." "Flush all toilets and drain all tubs and showers as simultaneously as possible. Station an observer at a toilet on the first floor (powder room). See if water backs up into the bowl of this toilet or leaks at the floor under the toilet. Be prepared to cut off all water quickly if sewer backs up. . . . You do not want your toilet to resemble Old Faithful."

By the fall of 1997, Town and Country's (by now nicknamed "Town and Homeless") record of construction, completion, and warranty repair was so hapless that Dickson ("If the ground slopes down towards the house, walk away") teamed up with a neighbor, Donald Jones, a retired Bible studies teacher and evangelist pastor ("I am under orders from my Commander-in-Chief to promote the life of Jesus wherever I go") to organize homeowners into a pressure group, with legal backing if necessary. Several residents had already contacted personal injury lawyers on their own, and there was talk about class action lawsuits. Dickson collected and typed up thirty pages of common complaints from a questionnaire survey, and established a pattern of sizable discrepancies between what homebuyers felt they had been promised by the developer and what had been delivered by the builders. The leading edge of their grievance was that Disney and/or TCC had "misrepresented" the housing quality in their sales process, and had failed to adequately supervise the course of building. Most residents, after all, had acted on their trust in the Disney name, and not that of the builder, in deciding to buy. Dickson made several suggestions for improving the situation: more company supervision of builders' performance; adoption of a set of standard building practices; provision of detailed plans and specifications to buyers before contracts are signed; a specified completion date; and a "mediation board" to "evaluate complaints from home buyers" and "resolve disputes before they reached the levels of formal arbitration and law suits." He also assembled a media kit, with extensive photo documentation of the construction disasters, and threatened to go to the press. At Town Hall, Dickson reported that he was told "to quit behaving like Moses coming down from the mountain with stone tablets and telling Disney what to do."

This was not the only occasion for a dogged Dickson visit to Town Hall. Postal couriers had balked at delivering mail in the front of his Campus Street house, where parked cars obscured access to the mailbox, and at the back, where the long narrow alley posed some traffic problems. One rainy day in January, Ron attached a long plastic pipe to his mailbox, looped it over the cars into the street, and attached a makeshift delivery box. He distributed some flyers advertising the virtues of the contraption. His mail was delivered, but Town Hall was alerted. By the time an amused local sheriff arrived, the pipe had been swung back into his garden, thus evading a summons for traffic obstruction. Dickson, however, was summoned to Town Hall to explain

Townhouses on Campus Street. (Photo: the author)

his prank. A few days later, he got results. An agreement was reached with the post office in Kissimmee to deliver in the rear alleyway.

Citizen action like this could often take on a surreal air. Later in the year, a lawyer resident pursued a more public form of protest against her builder David Weekley. She plastered stickers, depicting lemons and with slogans about how Weekley had ruined her life, all over her car and her house on West Park Drive. The car was parked downtown on weekends for all to see. While many sympathized with the plight of the Lemon Lady, as she came to be known, her public self-indulgence was widely perceived as a thoughtless menace to her neighbors' property values. Nonetheless, other disgruntled Weekley buyers would adopt the stickers, over time.

At Town and Country, foremen and field superintendents were coming and going on a revolving-door basis, and things seemed to be getting worse. By the end of 1997, despairing complaints about the situation prompted community manager Brent Herrington, the clement czar of Town Hall, to commission an independent engineer's survey on the townhouses—gruesome epicenter of the despair—on Campus Street, Savannah Square, and Mulberry Street. The report, completed in March, was a sweeping indictment of the substandard workmanship and deficiencies in construction of the townhouse buildings. Copies of the report were leaked, and they circulated informally among residents along with the warning, "Don't read it before bedtime." Apocalyptic forecasts about the shoddy construction flourished. The region's subcontractors, it was rumored, were refusing to work at Celebration because of the pay, working conditions, and lack of quality control. Local realtors were also telling clients not to buy here because of the poor construction. With the prospect of Town and Country pulling out altogether, townhouse residents, fed up with their treatment so far, were worried sick about the short-term future of their investment. Several had stopped paying their maintenance fees, in protest. After a year plus of living with chronic leaks, sloping floors, fixture malfunctions, and drainage ordeals, and with most attempts at repair generating new problems, they now learned from the engineer's report that the substandard work "could jeopardize the structural integrity of each building."

With this quality of smoke on the horizon, Herrington, himself a Town and Country homeowner, called a residents' meeting in June to speak with the builder's new division manager, Tim Kelly. A blunt Chicago negotiator, neither unctuous nor easily belligerent, he looked as if he would rather be nursing a martini than facing a room full of Celebration's angriest. "I can't be on the same emotional plane as you people," he acknowledged with terse candor, but promised a new start. By meeting's end, he had vowed to replace all the roofs, unit by unit, and correct all the deficiencies in flashing, bracing, framing, sheathing, and shingle and stucco work. An arsenal of video cameras, cassette recorders, and legal representatives were on hand to document the promises, and the high emotions of the aggrieved were on display. "We paid a lot of money, we got a lot of crap," declared one irate homeowner. There was a flood of talk about quality control, insurer's responsibilities, and responsiveness to punchlists, but nothing about the town's dirty secret—the low wages paid to construction workers by the builder and subcontractors. So I asked Kelly, from the floor, about these conditions. He smiled wanly, and acknowledged there were some local circumstances beyond his company's control. He was referring to the notorious Orlando "labor shortage," which had recently prompted Disney and other area companies to recruit south of the border, rather than raise their rock-bottom wages. The father of one resident, with experience in contracting, illustrated this response by describing a scenario typical of the building industry in Florida: "Droves of people come up here from anywhere, and they get off the back of a truck, and are asked, 'What do you want to be? Painters or carpenters?' "

Robin Stone, an inspector from the county's building department whom I interviewed much later, concurred: "They were pretty much hiring anyone. On most sites there is a majority of guys who know what they're doing, and maybe one helper." On the early Celebration sites, what was more common was "one skilled professional trying to keep track of three unskilled workers." Stone had written violation after violation, as many as eight on some houses, and warned early on that the poor supervision on the developer's part would result in mayhem down the line. "It was too much, too fast," she recalled, and the result was "every kind of repair you could imagine, from foundational to cosmetic." A seasoned inspector, she said she had seen "many strange things" in Celebration. Above all, she expressed sympathy for the residents. "They weren't allowed to see the drawings beforehand," and "the sales agents told them they could have what they wanted" in blithe disregard for what the building codes legally allowed.

By July, TCC had decided to cease serving as a sales broker for the builders, and was allowing prospective homebuyers to meet with the builders' own sales agents in the Preview Center. The official reason was that the builders' agents were more "hungry," but the change in policy was widely seen as a move to stave off future legal action, resulting from the gulf between residents' expectations of the Disney name and what the builders delivered. It fueled suspicions that the company was backing off from the town to protect against any tarnishing of its name. Six years before, in Dade County, a related turn of events had occurred. Country Walk, a planned community built by Arvida, a Disney subsidiary at the time, was flattened by Hurricane Andrew, sustaining much greater damage than neighboring housing developments. The aftermath of the hurricane damage, in Carl Hiassen's account in *Team Rodent*, exposed a trail of sloppy construction: "Engineers discovered rows and rows of nails that were purely decorative, having cleanly missed the trusses they were supposed to secure."[18] Lawsuits followed, in which homeowners tried to claim that Disney's magical name had been invoked by sales agents to secure their purchase. Disney succeeded, through extensive legal pressure, in keeping its name out of the courts.

With or without a hurricane, for a while it looked as if Celebration might be headed down the same path. Dickson and Jones had formed an entity called the Celebration Homeowners' Association, "not affiliated in any way with the Celebration Company," or with the official association. Partly a pressure group, and partly an information resource, the association was a clear alternative to Town Hall's official channels for dealing with the builders. With its motto, "Working Together to Fulfill the Dream of Celebration," it would serve as a ready-made legal convenience if things got much uglier than they already were. It would take the combined effort, finally, of Disney pressure, the county inspectors' issuance of code violations, and threats of resident insurrections to force Town and Country to make good on some of the repairs. In the fall of 1998, workers set about tearing off the rooftops, filling the quiet air below with a shower of shingle. Within weeks, some of the new roofs would be sprouting leaks. Grateful for any attention to the repair of their homes, several residents nevertheless seized the moment to sell and move out. They included Ron Dickson himself, who returned to the Charlotte area to live "on the biggest lake in North Carolina." As a result of his departure, the alternative Homeowners' Association lost much of its steam and fell apart. But Ron had not withdrawn from the fray. "Once I take up a cause, I don't give up easily," he declared when I caught up with him seven months after he moved north. He was still busy penning letters to the new town managers and consulting with lawyers about the builders and the school. "A lot of people are afraid to speak out down there," he explained, "so they ask me to do it." No longer a resident, he was getting even less satisfaction in his petitioning.

With or without Dickson, the ever-elusive class action lawsuit against Disney was not likely to materialize, but the memory of at least one brush with the law was firmly deposited in the town's stash of legends. In a certain townhouse on a bad day, one resident's difference of opinion with a Town and Country employee had escalated into a physical brawl. The employee moved to charge the resident with attempted second-degree murder. After many twists and turns, the suit was eventually dropped. Violence had come to town, notably, in a struggle over property.

3
THE NEW GEEWHIZZERY

"How does the future appear?" —Karl Marx

"Believe me, that was a happy age, before the days of architects, before the days of builders." —Seneca

The Disney name has long been a catchphrase for false-front architecture and optical illusions, and so the last thing the company needed was to be accused of "Mickey Mouse construction." Yet the expected headlines never appeared in print. On the face of it, this was surprising. Journalists were popping in and out of town all the time, and the strength of feeling among residents about their housing hardships could not easily be stifled. Sooner or later, some scandal-seeking reporter would surely have come across this story. I had been in residence myself for only a few weeks when I learned, without inquiring, all about the butcher builders. A resident hailed me—a stranger to him—as I passed by his home. He was bemoaning the waterlogged state of his lawn, and clearly wanted to share his drainage predicament, even with someone he did not know. Inviting me inside, he pointed to the lopsided floor, a door hanging askew, water stains all over the ceiling and walls, and other visible legacies of the poor workmanship.

Public openness proved more rare than I had been led to assume from this encounter. From week to week, I expected to see the story break in the media. But clearly there was a much stronger countervailing force at work. Residents' common interest in protecting the town's property values prevailed. This was one story that no one in town wanted to see in the newspapers, and so, despite the ever-present threat on the part of wronged residents to go to the press, none broke ranks to do so.

Of course, the Mickey Mouse construction in town had nothing directly to do with Disney's own know-how in assembling buildings, let alone two-dimensional stage sets. But the homeowners who had been shortchanged felt that their plight said something about how the company interpreted its responsibilities in creating a model public environment. Saddled with a dubious reputation for building only phoney places, there was nothing company managers would like more than to earn credit for fashioning a real bricks-and-mortar habitat that would help awaken public life from its suburban slumber. What stood in the way? In addition to the housing glitch, it turned out that there were some obvious anachronisms involved in creating the kind of town that hasn't been built for many decades.

For one thing, ideas about what constitutes the public interest change over time. The technical master plan for the town had not always accounted for the way in which public needs have been redefined in the course of a century. For example, I learned early on that the building of the Phase One infrastructure made little provision for disabled access, and was in violation of federal requirements. Under pressure from residents who used wheelchairs, TCC had to spend a small fortune remodeling bridges, sidewalks, parks, and waterfront access paths in order to meet ADA standards that were not a legal requirement in the earliest part of the century when towns like this were built. I came across few residents who knew about this, and indeed, if they had, they may have wondered whether their homeowners' assessments were footing the bill for the company's costly oversight. Even with the rectifications, residents in wheelchairs would have a tough time with the three, four, or five steps that lead onto the porches of Celebration's homes. Unlike most houses in Florida, they are built on raised slabs well above the grade of the land, ostensibly to give residents a sense of

Cottage homes in Celebration Village. (Photo: the author)

security. To make these houses wheelchair accessible would require up to twenty-four feet of ramping, and would surely disrupt the aesthetic unity of the facades so well protected by the Pattern Book.

Similarly, the task of re-creating traditional housing designs in an industry that had forgotten how to build them was fraught with obvious pitfalls, especially in a town being thrown up so quickly. The outward period styling of these homes suggested painstaking craft and long durability, while much of the infrastructure was inexpensive, inferior, and likely to be obsolete after a few decades. Die-hard traditionalists maintain that if a Victorian home is not built with the methods, materials, and careful craft of that age, it will deteriorate rapidly. The more pragmatic neotraditionalists insist that the latest technical improvements, if properly installed, will do the job. Many Celebrationites told me they could not be sure of how long their houses would last. Mostly everyone knew there was a disparity between the "body" and the "dress" of the housing.

In Disney World, I learned, they use especially hardy "theme park–quality paint" to weather the daily contact with millions of visitors. Building a public realm involves much more than pleasing the mass of people with aesthetics. How the builder of a public environment budgets and guarantees its infrastructure is no less significant than the designs or the architectural styles that are chosen to express civic ideals. Look at the great public building feats of this century. The public works of the New Deal—the TVA, the rebuilt infrastructure of many cities, the Greenbelt towns, the great rural parkways and dams—became objects of immense popular pride, especially for those who had worked on these projects. FDR's Works Progress Administration, Public Works Administration, and Resettlement Administration not only put people back to work but also produced buildings, roads, and environments that were clearly intended to symbolize the achievements of public will and public commitment. These were projects with common benefits, aimed at the social well-being of vast sectors of the population. Naturally, once the federal pipeline was open, public money flowed in the direction of votes and vested interests. Postwar suburbanization was massively funded by the public purse, whether to build roads and infrastructure, guarantee rock-bottom mortgage rates, or absorb homeowner tax deductions. Public money, in this period, directly financed a privatized, suburban landscape, almost exclusively for white families, while it was building cheap Corbusian knockoffs in city projects for predominantly minority residents. Both were products of public policy, and they were inextricably linked. Neither has survived terribly well. Whether unaffordable or unlivable, large portions of both landscapes are falling to pieces.

While few of its residents would regard Celebration as a direct result of public policy, the building of the town had been fully shaped and approved by public government agencies, though not without a struggle. Bob Stern assured me that he and the other planners had to "beat back the system" all the way. The outcome was a town with much more public space than is usually permitted by these same regulatory agencies, accustomed to zoning around the automobile. In fact, one of the reasons I had taken up residence there was that I believed there might be some lessons to be learned from Celebration about the direction of public life at the end of the century. The last two decades of suburban tax revolts, government's forced retreat from public spending, and the epidemic of privatization have meant that we can no longer take for granted our society's will to build and maintain the basic framework of public life. Here, in the Osceola scrub, a giant beneficiary of the private marketplace entered the business of sponsoring the public realm and of infusing suburbia—the bastion of social and economic privacy—with a revived public spirit. But what kind of business is this, and what is its future? Isn't the public everyone's business? And how accountable can a private company be to the public interest if its ultimate priority is to protect its name and self-interest? Will it always back off when the heat is on? Celebration would not provide full answers to these questions, but living there convinced me it is a good place to ask them. Every time a new set of tensions developed within the town, I watched as the company's commitment "to act in the sunshine" (as Florida's public officials are directed to do by the state's Sunshine Laws) was put to the test.

THE PUBLIC IS NOT FREE?

The company's declared interest in restoring public space dates from Walt's distaste for what Southern California had become by the mid-1950s, and his intent to market Disneyland as a remedy. In 1965, Robert Stern, then editor of the Yale journal *Perspecta*, published an essay by Charles Moore, the renowned postmodernist architect, whose last design, before his death, turned out to be the sales Preview Center in Celebration. Entitled "You Have to Pay for the Public Life," the essay was the first significant mark of recognition for Disneyland from within the elite quarters of the architectural profession. Searching for public monumental architecture in Southern California, where public space had become an endangered species, Moore could only find what he was looking for in Disneyland. In that auto-free environment, people could commonly mingle in ways that were impossible in their daily suburban environments. He concluded that the future creation of public space may well lie with entities like Disney, if only they were prepared to "submerge their own Mickey Mouse visions in a broader prospect of greater public interest." Indeed, he declared, with a brash nonchalance available only to a professionally secure avant-gardist seeking to shock his peers,

> Disneyland must be regarded as the most important single piece of construction in the West in the past several decades. . . . Single-handedly, it is engaged in replacing and extending many of those elements of the public realm that have vanished in the featureless, private, floating world of Southern California, whose only edge is the ocean, and whose center is undiscoverable. Curiously, for a public place, Disneyland is not free. You buy your tickets at the gate. But then Versailles cost someone a great deal of money. Now, as then, you have to pay for the public life.[1]

Moore got no points for his flip analogy with Versailles, which was such an obscene example of personal opulence at public expense that it helped to foment a popular revolution. But his comments about Disneyland, however provocative in intent, proved to have a long and sprightly life among architects and planners for whom the theme park's urbanism was held in a perilous balance; much admired by fans for its bustling ambience and spotless efficiency, much reviled by critics for its near-totalitarian forms of crowd control.

For one thing, the success of Disneyland was a chilling premonition of the day when shopping malls, controlled by private developers, would come to function as just about the only version of public space available to a sizable chunk of the North American middle class. These biblically proportioned zones, which swelled in scale from 50,000 square feet in the early 1950s to over ten times as large in the 1990s, became mandatory destinations for all and sundry, from the makeshift youth subcultures of mall rats to the elderly legions who use their retail corridors and stairways as exercise opportunities. In George Romero's prescient film *Dawn of the Dead*, the mall was a gathering point for zombies whose return from the dead led them, by force of glutted habit, to congregate in the only place where they remembered each other collectively to be alive. Increasingly, malls have threatened to displace parks, schools, libraries, post offices, town halls, and community centers as civic meeting places and points of assembly. Architecturally, they include evocations of the traditional marketplace, plaza, or village green, and many have walkways that simulate the public bustle of urban streets. Soon, whole suburbs began to name themselves after malls, and vast private developments sprang up in the form of city malls, often run by corporate boards with no trace of civic accountability.

The creators of Celebration were well aware of Moore's prophecy about Disney's future role as a promoter of public space. Proud of the subsequent attention devoted to the theme parks by architects and planners, Michael Eisner told me he has always thought of the theme parks as "public places in private communities." Celebration could comfortably fit under this description. Since there is no visible evidence, for the unwitting visitor, of the Disney connection, this town could indeed claim to be the literal outcome of Disney "submerging its Mickey Mouse visions in the broader prospect of greater public interest." Locating Disney iconography in downtown Celebration is like looking for graven images in a mosque. When Joseph Judge, a bicycle retailer, set up shop in the fall of 1997, he raised a Mickey Mouse banner above his storefront for two heroic weeks before he was obliged to remove it, as indeed he had predicted to me. If you look hard enough you can find discreet Disney jewelry and vintage Disneyana collectibles in one or two stores, but keeping Mickey out of sight is consistent with canons of good taste dictated in the downtown area. The mass cultural icons on which the company's vast wealth rests are considered much too tacky to be displayed in the town it is building.

Celebration's civic place-making is intended to be a classy rebuttal of the cookie-cutter subdivision, the strip, and the mega-mall. At a time when urban contact is so often simulated in bogus portrayals of public space like Universal Studios' City Walk in Los Angeles (and now in Orlando), real places like Celebration that are built to champion public interaction are surely a step in a better direction. The planners of the town borrowed some of the high moral ground of the New Urbanist movement that wants to get things right in the belief that most other places are wrong. But what had struck Moore about Disneyland in 1965 was not just the sense that it worked as a public place, where the surrounding urban sprawl of Southern California seemed dysfunctional, or hostile to human intercourse. What thrilled him was the public indulgence of pleasure, the sense of "participation without embarrassment" in a place where the interstate chitchat of the visitors ("You're from Ohio?") flourished alongside the intergalactic geewhizzery of the attractions ("You're going to Mars?"). If you could get beyond the false fronts and the gimcrack stage sets, you might even run into a chunk of the future. At least Moore thought so: "There, on the Matterhorn, from the aerial tramway over the bobsled run on the inside of the plastic mountain, is a vision of a place marked out for the public life, of a kind of rocking monumentality, more dynamic, bigger and—who knows?—even more useful to people and to the public than any the world has yet seen."[2]

Was Moore half joking, in that arch, ironic way that would subsequently become the house style of the postmodern movement? Not exactly. For a brief, but significant, moment, the Pop attitude of the day allowed its devotees to imagine that, if you came to it with no prejudices or snobbish reserve, pop culture harbored impulses of progress that had stagnated elsewhere, especially in the Establishment's preoccupation with good form and paternalistic planning. In the mid-1960s, anything was still possible. In America, no one had put the brakes on yet, and the future, like the monorail, still looked futuristic.

But the sector of the future that gave rise to Celebration had little to do with the heady vision of scale and speed summed up in Moore's "rocking monumentality." Instead, it could be found, in embryo, on Main Street, and in the picturesque parochialism of Disneyland's versions of American history. Within a few years, the vigor of the urban ghetto uprisings and the opposition to the Vietnam War, followed by the flourishing of gay and women's liberation and the ecology movement, had shattered the innocent daydreams of the Mouseketeers and plunged the country into an orgy of national self-analysis for the next three decades. Historians' accounts of American settlement underwent a total overhaul, as the chronicles of genocide, slavery, ethnic exclusion, and imperialism sliced open and remodeled the official narratives about the past. The great ethnic revival—enriched by the pride of discovery for peoples, like African Americans, who had been denied their histories—was matched by a reappraisal of folk and vernacular arts. This protracted season of historical revisionism was long overdue, but it meant that the national culture would be focused more exclusively on the shape of the past than on the profile of the future. In a nation in imperial decline, like Britain, there were obvious reasons for this retrospective mood. But for a country like the United States, so long identified with progress and fast-forward motion—a country that had always been viewed as the home of the future—the backward-looking turn was as genuine and unlikely a heresy as this century has produced.

First of all, however, the look and feel of futurism had to wither on the vine, and it turns out that the Disney company played its own role in that story.

THE STRANGE DEATH OF THE FUTURE

Within a year of Moore's comments, Walt Disney had described his own short-lived blueprint for the future in a 1966 TV clip for "Disney's Wonderful World of Color" that announced plans for the company's newly acquired property in Central Florida. Walt's television manner in these years helped to define the term "avuncular." Running his pointer over a map that, in its current incarnation, still occupies prominent wall space in every Disney conference room in Florida, he casually outlined the plans for the 28,000-acre spread—twice the size of Manhattan—as if he were describing a carefree family vacation. The blueprint included a theme park, a Vacation Land (with the resort hotels the company had lacked in Anaheim), and an innovative transportation system, each of which was realized in the final design for Walt Disney World. The features of the plans that went unrealized were an Airport of the Future, an Industrial Park designed to showcase American industry at work, and the ur-EPCOT (Experimental Prototype Community of Tomorrow), a model city for 20,000 Disney employees with a radial hub design.

In the downtown area of ur-EPCOT, business and commerce would thrive in a climate-controlled center encased in a giant bubble, where "the pedestrian is king." This area would house offices, a thirty-story hotel and convention center, stores "recreating the character and adventure of places around the world," theaters, restaurants, and other nightlife attractions. It was to be surrounded by concentric zones allocated to High-Density Apartment Housing, Green Belt and Recreation (playgrounds, churches, and schools), and the outlying neighborhood and residential areas. Surface transportation would be primarily electrical, in the form of the Wedway people-mover, which never fully came to a stop, even at embarkation points (the modernist, industrial idea of the city somehow had to include twenty-four-hour-a day motion, if only to rival fully, and perhaps to surpass, nature). The auto routes lay underneath the city, again living up to Walt's solemn vow that "no stop lights will ever slow these automobiles." The professed goal of Walt's EPCOT was to build a model solution to some of the great urban problems of the day: blight, poverty, unemployment, traffic congestion.

Predicting that EPCOT would "influence the future of city living for generations to come," he spoke in the film of meeting the urban challenge

> by starting with the public need, and the need is not just for curing the old ills of old cities. We think the need is for starting from scratch on virgin land and building a special kind of community. . . . EPCOT will always be in a state of becoming. It will never cease to be a living blueprint of the future, and a place where people actually live a life they can't find anywhere else in the world. Everything in EPCOT will be dedicated to the happiness of those who live, work, and play here, and those who come from all round the world to visit our living showcase. . . . It's our hope that EPCOT will stimulate American industry to develop new solutions that will meet the needs of people expressed right here in this experimental community . . . a planned environment demonstrating to the world what American communities can accomplish through proper control of planning and design.

The urban utopia of ur-EPCOT was the ultimate modernist linear city and company town rolled into one. Being a Disney town, it was also for show. The showcase design had antecedents in the White City of Chicago's 1893 Columbian Exposition (where Walt's father, Elias, had been a construction worker) and the City of Tomorrow from New York's 1939 World's Fair, both of which had a hefty influence, respectively, upon the City Beautiful movement and the urban renewal of the postwar period. In the 1964 World's Fair, the General Electric pavilion featured "Progress City," a city of the future that was subsequently added to the end of the "Carousel of Progress" exhibit in Disneyland. It became the model for ur-EPCOT, code-named Project X.

As for the workers' town, Project X had a long list of predecessors among benevolent Victorian capitalists—Cadbury's Bourneville and

Lever's Port Sunlight in England, Krupp's Maragaretenhohe in Germany, and the Pullman town in Illinois—and many not-so-benevolent corporations. The United States produced hundreds of company towns (the first was established as early as 1645 by the Braintree Iron Works).[3] By 1917, as many as one thousand American firms provided some form of worker housing, whether in the form of model rural precincts, with cottage rows and boardinghouses, or as bounded municipal enclaves, where even the social behavior of workers' families was extensively regulated.[4] By 1938, with company towns in sharp decline, they still accounted for a total population of 2 million persons.[5]

Though not the final try at a superplanned modernist city, Walt's ur-EPCOT was the last gasp of the paternalist company town, which had provided planners (like John Nolen, much lionized by New Urbanists) with an unparalleled opportunity to design whole towns. But the most audacious detail of Project X lay in the idea that a large corporation would actually try to resolve the urban crises of the late twentieth century by creating its own, alternative version of urbanism—a city that didn't exist elsewhere—for its own workers. Hitherto, this idea had flourished only in the dystopias of science fiction. Only the "unacceptably optimistic" Walt Disney Company would take up such a challenge in the midst of urban renewal, with the ghetto uprisings in Watts, Newark, and Detroit just around the corner, and with political movements for community self-determination and grassroots participatory democracy sweeping through the inner cities and campuses of the nation. It was just as well that Walt died before the plans got under way. There is little doubt that the civil rights and political instincts of 20,000 residents (envisaged as temporary renters, who would therefore not be able to vote on the affairs of Disney World) would have been impossible to manage, even by the masters of corporate management. Hired as a consultant on Project X in 1964, Ray Watson, future chair of the Disney board, advised against a plan to closely regulate the residents' dress and behavior. A development veteran of the new California city of Irvine (and pioneer of the use of market research in consumer taste to plan and sell housing), Watson reasoned that if visitors were paying to see them in their utopian habitat, residents would need to be heavily subsidized to live like fish in a bowl.[6]

Ur-EPCOT had too much nineteenth-century residue in its gut

to give birth to a workable twenty-first-century urbanism, at least one inhabited by real people and not audio-animatronic puppets or lobotomized workers. In the course of the internecine Disney family struggles that followed Walt's death in 1967, Project X shriveled up, and when the nonresidential EPCOT finally opened in 1982, it was a perfectly schizophrenic affair—one half an extension of the World's Fair pavilions run by major U.S. corporations, the other half an international food court on a grandiose scale. Pictorial vestiges of Walt's plan lived on in a few of the pavilion rides, where the futuristic dioramas of floating cities, space colonies, and desert farms were already outdated in 1982, and were virtually museum pieces a decade later. To this day, these obsolescent futures are populated by many of the same audio-animatronic families that were satirized to death by the Jetsons. Nonetheless, it took the company until the planning of Euro Disney in the late 1980s to acknowledge that the space-age version of the future in the Magic Kingdom had aged beyond redemption. Euro Disney got around the problem by replacing Tomorrowland with a Discoveryland that features fantasy versions of the future according to French progenitors of science fiction like Jules Verne. After several attempts over the decades to overhaul the originals, Disneyland and Walt Disney World followed suit with versions of Yesterday's Tomorrowland. Geewhiz futurism was presented now as a retro period look, on a par with Frontierland.

The creators of Celebration tend to play down the legacy of Walt's ur-EPCOT. When I quizzed Michael Eisner about it, he almost shrugged off the original proposal: "It was like having an idea for a movie over dinner, and then dropping dead after dinner, and people saying that this was your fully conceived vision." Many residents, by contrast, still spoke religiously of "Walt's dream," and, on several occasions, I saw one resident use the phrase to remind backslidden TCC employees of the idealism behind the town. By the time the master plans for the neotraditionalist Celebration were drawn up in the early 1990s, what did they retain of Walt Disney's "idea for a movie"? Actually quite a lot: a community of 20,000 residents, built from scratch, "on virgin land"; an international showcase for technology, education, and medicine; and a macro-construction challenge that only a company with deep pockets, booming profit margins, and a financial need to expand and diversify would take on. There are even some unrealized ur-EPCOT features like the "Workplace," a manufacturing complex that would display work methods to visitors, that still appear in the undeveloped sector (west of I-4) of the plans for Celebration.

To be sure, this was no longer a company town, although many residents took jobs, conveniently, with Disney after moving to Celebration. In my estimate, as many as one fifth of the families in Phase One ended up in some direct (and many more in a less direct) relation to the company, even if the price points were well beyond the means of the vast majority of the company's 55,000 area employees. Above all, Celebration had retained Walt's promise to correct some of the wrongs of modern urbanism. But only some of the wrongs, and only for those who could afford the entrance fee. Then, as now, "urban problems" are a code word in American public speech for the expendable labor pool of the inner cities. When I asked him about the likely impact of the town on urban planning, Eisner volunteered: "I will say one thing. This does not address the problem of the underclass, like you have in New York or Detroit. It is not a panacea, it is not the model for the next city, nor was it meant to be."

THE VIRTUAL FRONT PORCH

In the twenty-five years between Walt's futuristic blueprint and the master planning of Celebration, the Disney stage set for urban utopia underwent a complete change of scenery. Instead of a climate-controlled bubble, we had preserved wetlands; instead of cloud-capped towers, we had relics of Americana. From the outset, Celebration would be seen by outsiders as a raw nostalgia trip down Memory Lane, or, at best, as a stark expression of the *Back to the Future* ethos that took the Main Streets of the past as its inspiration for the way forward. But this was only the surface, as Celebrationites were always quick to point out. Behind the twee facades, the billboards and sales brochures promised a state-of-the-art, "wired" community with its own intranet, serving the school and the health center and accessible to all residents through high-speed data access from every home. Here, in a largely invisible form, was the rapturous technological future that Walt's company had always been careful to honor.

For those residents who had been lured, in part, by assurances of a brave new wired world, the high-tech operation that greeted them and serviced their needs in the first two years was one of the bigger disappointments in town. The existing, buggy network, providing community updates and an activities calendar, Internet access, and limited bulletin board space for personal ads, was a thin shadow of what had been imagined. The online infrastructure was also dominated by a one-way flow of information from the company. You could send personal e-mail, access the World Wide Web, find out what movies were showing downtown, when the next PTSA meeting was scheduled, and generally stay abreast of upcoming events. But it was technically impossible to post publicly to the community at large, while the more interactive components of the network—operational access to the school and to physicians at the health center—were nowhere in sight. As for TV, Jones Communication, the local cable franchise, offered a community channel, where tapes of official meetings or forums were often broadcast, but, again, there was no provision for public access channels where residents could air their own content.

Over half of the pioneer residents already owned a personal computer, but most had not used it for Internet access, and so the advanced technology and access provided gratis to pioneer families as part of an AT&T survey were a great bounty for these "newbies." In general, they were happy to be guided through the portals of cyberspace. To insulate their future shock, the home page of the community cyber network was called The Front Porch and was designed graphically to comfort rather than disorient the senses. But for residents already familiar with computer tool basics, the oversold image of a town on the cutting edge of technology was a bit of a joke. These included residents who volunteered to maintain some aspect of the network. Scott Biehler, who had worked part time on the AT&T survey and who updated the Calendar of Events on the community network, was of no two minds about the hollow promises: "This is not a wired community at all," he pointed out, "it's not even a high tech town." Bill LeBlanc, who had previously worked in the University of Miami's computing center, observed that residents like himself had "taken a step backwards in moving here," and that "we've been hoodwinked technologically." Scott Fought, founder of a California computer company, who also helped out with the network, described the technology as "basically 1980s quality ISP." I had to count myself among the crestfallen, having expected a high-speed T1 connection in my apartment. I had also read about the open speech environments of other wired communities, like the Blacksburg Electronic Village in Virginia or the Infozone in Telluride, Colorado, and had hoped to see evidence of that "virtual republic" of free speech that Internet advocates have long touted as the new medium's contribution to the future of democracy.

Celebrationites were all too aware, and more than a little embarrassed, that the town and its school were being ballyhooed around the nation as twenty-first-century cyberpioneers at a time when both of their high-tech services were pretty basic and when "vaporware" (cyberproducts that do not yet exist) was the norm. Only part of the problem appeared to lie in the chronic mismanagement of the network. Willing and proficient residents like Biehler, LeBlanc, and Fought were discouraged from taking an active, technical role in improving or innovating the system. Nor had the facility been used in any way for active community discussion through an open list-serve, distributing messages and postings to all the network subscribers. Naturally, it was not in the developer's interest to encourage public discussion of this sort. Neither the company nor community managers were eager to see the proverbial "handful of discontented residents" air their views in an online forum. In July, in the first real instance of civic networking independent from Town Hall, an action group of "concerned parents" began to post their discussions about the school on one of the network's bulletin boards. In response to their call for a public meeting, 150 parents showed up in the school cafeteria. Biehler, who first posted the parents' notices, reported that he had to re-post them several times. The postings kept disappearing, according to network managers, because of a "bug" in the system.

Shortly thereafter, management of the network was transferred to a start-up company owned by a resident, Ken Liles. Liles promised to galvanize the interactive features of the network, including the virtual community forum it lacked from the outset. He was already thinking about the potential impact this might have on community life. "Would this displace the need," he wondered, "for a physical community center" of the sort that was already high on the residents' wish list for new amenities? "Which of the two would residents be willing to pay for?"

Would they settle for the electronic Town Hall meetings conducted by community managers or would they hold out for face-to-face meetings? Celebration—the first town to be built where everyone was hooked into the same server—might have been a good place to answer that kind of question. But not yet. In its fledgling years, at least, the electronic grapevine had been silent while the ears of the physical town—its streets and block parties—had been burning with rumor and circumstance.

When I last visited the town in January 1999, the network's Web site had been redesigned. The interactive component that Liles proposed was there, but it was not going to rock anyone's world. "Gatekeepers" from several residents' groups and organizations were now permitted to post their own information about group activities, at least after the content had been approved by the network manager. More interesting to me was a feature of the old Web site that had been dropped. The network no longer carried a virtual archive of previous pages. The town's history, as it had been documented on this depository, had been erased. The new management would not return my calls, but there was lots of talk about trouble at the cyber-mill. A week later, the company backed out of the contract, fired all its employees, and closed its doors.

Commercially curious about technology use, AT&T, one of TCC's corporate "strategic alliances," had decided early that the semi-controlled environment of the town would be ideal for market researching their communications products. The company hired a team of economists, psychologists, computer scientists, statisticians, anthropologists, and marketing professionals to undertake a behavioral study of the use of advanced technology among the first three hundred families. This expensive study was terminated after a year, with little to show for its efforts other than some flat-footed data analysis. "Strong evidence," the study report claimed, "shows that fax machine activity is positively correlated with long distance outbound voice calling." Apparently, residents using fax machines for the first time were sending recipes, greeting cards, and pictures, and then calling up the far-distant recipients to discuss the faxes. "This would suggest a bundling strategy," the report concluded. "AT&T could partner with a fax machine manufacturer and give machines to AT&T customers to incent Long Distance usage." The report also noted that "some teens are chatting [online] and using the phone simultaneously—Are they a potential target for Internet telephony?"

Celebration had been planned to host a fiber-optic delivery system for dispatching interactive multimedia to buildings on a fiber-to-curb network. The system would have a huge bandwidth capable of furnishing the myriad services—switched digital video, telephony, cable TV, and high-speed data transfer—associated with the much-hyped information superhighway. By 1996, when residents were due to move in, the immediate future of digital delivery had turned uncertain. Fiber optics were no longer being touted as the definitive industry standard. The company backed off and decided simply to future-proof the town, laying a network in the ground and installing multiplex outlets and empty conduits in houses to cover any eventuality. Amy Westwood, TCC's director of network development, explained the new timidity in terms quite removed from Disney's gung-ho trademark bluster around technological innovations: "Our approach has always been to take smart, small baby steps, and not take these huge leading edge–type of leaps, only to find out that potentially there's no value to the homeowner." As for "determining the future," she explained that responsibility would lie with Honeywell, AT&T, Jones Communication, and Vista United, TCC's alliance partners, or "coopetitors," as she put it, among the "stakeholders in technology."

The uncertainty surrounding these technologies was not simply the result of local teething problems. It reflects a general climate of doubt about how to create new markets at a time when corporate America sees high technology as the only vehicle for embodying and carrying forward traditional ideas about the shiny new future. R&D and short-range planning is a dog's breakfast of disarray and overcompetition, with scant attention to people's real needs. On the highway to the future, the signposts and road surfaces seem to change every year. The Disney company had been a veteran traveler along this road. But while the heady promise of cutting-edge technology has always been a staple billboard feature of the Disney profile (bolstered by the think-outside-the-box reputation of the Imagineers), the company's internal policy is mostly governed by the principle of "no field innovation." Disney has been more intent on advocacy, or "telling a story about technology," as EPCOT does, than on transforming any technical field itself.

The most notable exceptions have been aimed at worker and crowd control and at waste disposal. Disney's audio-animatronic puppets, as

Walt pointed out in a 1964 interview, "don't have to stop for coffee breaks and all that kind of stuff." "One advantage of mechanical animation," he elaborated elsewhere, "is that machines don't demand higher wages."[7] So, too, the Wedway people-mover and other means of transport are basically assembly lines for processing the movements of visitors to the parks. Walt Disney World's awesome underground garbage disposal system is as efficient at sucking away trash (at speeds of up to 60 mph) as the sales environment of the park is at sucking money out of visitors' wallets. Otherwise, the company, for the most part, has limited itself to offering a showcase environment for other corporations' products. In common with the other alliance partners in Celebration, technology specialists like AT&T and GE are primarily there to showcase their names and products—a marketing opportunity for which they pay millions of dollars—but they are not encouraged to innovate, either on their own or by working together, in response to community needs.

With so many technology-forward residents and companies in town, it is unfortunate there is so much resistance, on the developer's part, to allowing the town to become a living laboratory for interactive technology. As a highly placed operative in one of the technology alliances put it: "What we have is a snazzy display, designed to impress the casual visitor. Disney is building a library, with lots of plush cherry oak paneling, and all the right names are on the book binding, but if you take a book off the shelf, there's nothing inside it." Around town, even the most seasoned resident, on occasion, could still feel like part of the display shelf. As one of my neighbors put it to me, with more than a touch of *X-Files* brio, "I sometimes feel like we're like being harvested for outer space." But nothing so daring was afoot. Bold technological innovations that build on, or answer, people's needs and desires are seldom the product of large corporations. Indeed, corporations are more likely to patent such inventions and let them gather dust so as not to threaten the steady sales of their existing technologies. The future is a risky business, and is usually invented by people with nothing to lose.

4
MAIN STREET IS BETTER THAN ALRIGHT

"Americans work awfully hard to get such a raw deal. It's really not a good deal that's being dealt to these people. They're so hard-working—husbands, wives, sons—and for what? Crap food, second-rate shopping experiences, a second-rate public realm, and an automatic commitment to purchase of an automobile. That car costs six thousand dollars a year to run on average. You can go to Bali for your holidays for that, for God's sake. And it's not a choice, it's part of a contract. As an American, part of my contract is owning one car per adult. I think it's a raw deal."

—Andres Duany, interview with author

In media stories about Celebration, pioneer residents were occasionally typecast as nostalgia hounds, fleeing from the complexities of modern life to a picture-perfect past that never was. Sometimes, the stories took this impulse in the spirit of the latest retro mood, as indicative of a national, or generational, trend to revive the days of yore. At other times, they assumed that residents were sincerely escapist. Naturally, Celebrationites resented this kind of profile, regardless of its tone. While mostly cooperative with the press, they often took offense at three-minute stories that required reporters to offer some pat overview of their reasons for moving to town. On several occasions, I watched as a journalist or news crew interviewed a resident in front of her home or down by the lakeside. "Do people here feel that they are returning to a simpler way of life?" "Are you happy to have stepped back in time?" It was difficult not to empathize with the folks on the receiving end of such questions. When I winced, it was with the full knowledge that the resident under interrogation was unable to do so at that precise moment. The laborious task of correcting a stereotype would begin. "Well, it's not quite like that . . ." Clichéd questioning from the press was a cross to bear in this town. Many Celebrationites had become well practiced in giving interviews, and some had perfected the art of soundbiting, even lifting quotes from some previous media story and recirculating them. Teens, especially, were already blasé about having TV crews following them around.

Almost everyone was weary, if not intolerant, of the routine media banter about Mickey Mouse as mayor of the town, but the stories about the bygone days were especially galling. Celebrationites were right to feel this way, since few, if any, appeared to have moved there with the expectation that the town would be like a time machine, conjuring up a vanished world of affable tradesmen, welcoming mom-and-pop stores, and eccentric local characters like the batty widow in the crumbling mansion on the hill. Besides, the sales brochures had promised too many contemporary things to lock into illusions of yesteryear: ultra-progressive schooling, state-of-the-art medical technology, and enough high-tech razzamatazz to bring on a mild, epistemological headache.

A good number of the pioneers had been highly successful in their careers. They had not achieved their stations in life through the pursuit of escapist fantasies, and they proved as competitive within the affairs of the town as they had been in the business or professional world. Some had grown up in small towns, and wanted the same for their children. Many more had known only life in subdivisions, and saw the new town as a true alternative to the cheerless isolation of suburbia. Only a few were in classic "white flight" from cities like Miami or from suburbs where the racial composition had "tipped." Several, senior in years, acknowledged that the old-time decor brought out the child in them, although many of the retirees genuinely wanted to be around younger folk and children. Most nester parents admitted, in retrospect, that the school had been the main attraction. As Jackson Mumey, one of the first residents on the pioneer row of Teal Avenue, liked to put it, "we came for the school, and they threw in the house." There were also Celebrationities who privately confessed to me that a house in this town was an investment opportunity they could not pass up.

To be sure, I also met residents for whom the environment was a catalyst for their pet fantasies. John Pfeiffer, an ex-doctor, moved here from the Midwest to pursue his ambition (now realized) of becoming a monorail driver in the Magic Kingdom. John Sarantakis, an ex-businessman, raised in a cold-water flat in Lowell, Massachusetts, had settled on Celebration after searching high and low for many years for a Shangri-La village he had once seen in a 1940s movie. Maureen Rubel, lately from Connecticut, and sales manager of a medical technology company, was attracted by the frontier romance of subsistence rural living eked out by the modest crackers depicted in the Florida novels of Marjorie Kinnan Rawlings.

Whatever their story, or fantasy, they had entered the field of vision of influential people in the media, education, and design professions who would judge them guilty by association with the contrived traditionalism of the town's antique facades. Almost fifty years before, the first wave of war vets who moved their families to places like Levittown were subjected to the scorn of elite urban critics, for whom cookie-cutter suburbia symbolized a soulless haven for the conformist masses. When that same class of critics trained their contempt on neotraditional places like Celebration, sniffing out inauthenticity behind every picket fence, the target was more upmarket, but the charge of bogus living no less patronizing.

For some time now, it has been considered a feat of publicly minded heroism to save and restore old buildings. By contrast, constructing old buildings from scratch is considered a morally corrupt act of forgery. One enterprise is true and noble, the other is false and vulgar. According to this double standard, gentrifying urbanites are serving an admirable cause by restoring Federal townhouses, while well-heeled suburbanites who move into brand new neotraditionalist communities are fodder for the heritage machine that merchandizes a counterfeit past.[1] This is no small irony in a country whose most cherished public buildings are often ardent copies of ancient European originals (New York's lost Penn Station, cause célèbre of preservationists, was, after all, a copy of the Baths of Caracalla in Rome).

The good life, on Veranda Place. (Photo: the author)

To get beyond these moral judgments of taste, it may be important to grasp that the antique porches of a place like Celebration can symbolize things other than a sentimental craving for days gone by or a sorry lack of imagination about the future. They can be a conservative marker of status for their owners, and they can also be a radical criticism of the whole way of life that is associated with the present-day suburban landscape. The key to understanding this paradox lies in the great shifts in architectural thought and practice that separate ur-EPCOT's city of tomorrow from Celebration's community of yore. Three broad-based movements had helped to shape the neotraditionalism of this new town: historical preservationism, postmodernism, and New Urbanism.

LESS BUILDING, LESS HARM

The impetus for the first of these lay in the early 1960s, when preservationist advocates like Jane Jacobs began to take a stand against the bulldozers of city improvers and developers that were flattening decayed neighborhoods and frayed civic landmarks (like Penn Station) in an all-out war against urban blight. Urban renewal planners were busy condemning inner-city neighborhoods in the belief that residents would lead safer and healthier lives in those low-density "towers in the park" to which they were relocated, most often without their consent. Rejecting this "doctrine of salvation through bricks," in theologian Reinhold Neibuhr's famous phrase, Jacobs took an eye-level view of her bustling Greenwich Village neighborhood, and, in *The Death and Life of Great Cities*, wrote an exuberant defense of its rich street life. She insisted that her neighborhood's vibrant urbanism had taken shape organically, over many decades, and could not be summoned into being by top-down planners.[2] Her 1961 book convinced an entire generation of the environmental sanity of preserving the high-density urban neighborhoods that planners were itching to condemn as slums. Jacobs's legacy was equivalent to a giant "Do Not Disturb" sign. In her wake, respect was now extended to streets that had survived and evolved over a long span. But a moratorium would be declared on ideas about how to create new ones. It was a stark symptom of the cruel trauma of postwar planning that the status quo, however passive, would now be preferred to any new alternatives simply because it was less harmful than what had gone before.

Jacobs's immediate comrades-in-arms were community groups, bent on revitalizing or "unslumming" their own neighborhoods, not property speculators trading in nostalgia. But, over time, entrepreneurial offshoots of the preservation movement, ever on the lookout for value-added equity, created a lucrative market for the restoration or rehabilitation of old buildings. This enterprise took on a high commercial value in the 1980s, when run-down center cities attracted the realty interest of a new generation of young professionals in the urban service sectors. Among the budding yuppie ranks, a speculator's eye for brownstone row houses, industrial cast-iron facades, pitched or mansard roofs, gabled dormers, and other ornamental details helped to drive the juggernaut of gentrification. Combined with the rapid disinvestment in city neighborhoods by private landlords and federal public housing programs, the impulse of the monied to repossess a chunk of urban history and buy up some of that "urban lifestyle" resulted in driving away a neighborhood's poorer residents and thinning out the diversity that Jacobs valued. In an unintended irony, the preservation movement, forged to combat the planners' uprooting of poor populations, ended up displacing almost as many residents, unable to afford to live any longer in their old neighborhood.

In the meantime, other decaying urban sites, primarily harbors or old marketplaces, were sculpted into spectacular, sanitized re-creations of their own traditional forms—Manhattan's South Street Seaport, Boston's Quincy Market, Cleveland's waterfront, and Baltimore's inner harbor, among the better known. The use of historical recreation, whether a stimulus for residential property investment or for tourist power-shopping, was widely adopted as the key to reviving crumbling downtown areas. James Rouse, the master developer of these festival marketplaces and others, took his cue from the Imagineer theme masters. In a famous Harvard lecture, Rouse declared, following Moore, that "the greatest piece of urban design in the U.S. today is Disneyland."

Preservation in small-town America also took its cue from Disneyland. Anaheim's gingerbread version of Main Street helped stimulate a nationwide campaign to revitalize all these boarded-up downtowns that had become tumbleweed territory with the arrival of the interstate highways and Wal-Marts. Under the organized thrust of Main Street programs (like those of the National Trust for Historic Preservation, first launched in 1977), hundreds of small-town efforts to seed a downtown renaissance got under way, aimed at reviving a commercial core of locally owned stores and restoring a civic commons. Spruced up and smelling of fresh investment, the new "historic downtown" was usually less a focal point for community locals than a lure for tourist visitors, to whose shopping requirements its stores catered primarily.

To the seasoned eye, Celebration's own downtown core was not so much a copy of a prewar town as it was a facsimile of one of these Main Streets that had undergone its own Disneyfied preservation makeover. So, too, there were other odd ways in which the preservation movement had made its impact in a brand-new town like Celebration. Here were many residents, like Lise and Ron Juneman on Honeysuckle Avenue, who had moved several times in their married lives, often spending a good deal of time and money on repairing old houses. In Celebration, the Junemans say they were "able to buy an 'old' house which needed no restoration work," a solution that satisfied a number of well-defined boomer desires. Celebration cannot really pretend to be an idyllic, well-preserved, old town, but it can build in the expenses of restoration that would normally be incurred by gentrifiers buying into a close-knit urban neighborhood.

MIXING IT UP

Less direct, but no less important, in its contribution to the new traditionalism was the postmodern movement, which fostered most of the architects who designed Celebration's signature buildings: Michael Graves, Charles Moore, Robert Stern, Cesar Pelli, Aldo Rossi, Robert Venturi, and Denise Scott Brown. Defiantly cast as a revolt against the pleasure-denying reign of modernism's flat roofs, sheer facades, super-block slabs, and transparent cubes, the postmodernists pledged to bring back some of the banished sensuality of past historical styles. For added measure, there would be a new appreciation of vernacular architecture, especially that of the commercial strip, where Colonial and Tudor and Roman and Mission jostled for attention alongside the exotica of Pueblo and Congo and Polynesia and Babylon. This new inclusive attention to popular culture promised a fresh dialogue with the public, and, it was hoped, some new clients for architects who had played virtually no role in the building of postwar suburbia.

If the postmodernists set out to return the profession of design to a more democratic plane, the doors they intended to open were not exactly rushed by the masses. Their populist aims were largely thwarted by the 1970s recession and by the awkward but simple reality that architects, with no access to the purse strings, and with a bad rap from years of compliance with urban renewal and corporate patronage, were no longer in a position to effect any substantial changes in the design of the built public environment. Instead, the first wave of postmodern architects took the liberty of fashioning their own private medley of styles for mostly private clients, juxtaposing High and Low, Classical and Cartoon, Eternal and Everyday. All of architectural history became a supermarket of ingredients from which to concoct a new and daring cuisine. A postmodernist house could be a potpourri of international elements—

Mediterranean Villa, Italian Baroque, English Regency—melded into one bold composite.

For those who associated the profession with good taste, restraint, and decorum, the postmodernist foray into the funhouse was seen as an abdication of the architect's moral faculties. For those who had stood by the modern movement's commitment to building a better world, it was a nostalgic flight from present responsibilities. Critics complained that in the postmodernist funhouse, history and geography no longer had any *particular* meaning. Proponents of the widespread Greek Revival style of the early 1800s, for example, strictly copied the ancient orders—Doric, Ionian, and Corinthian—in the belief that this borrowed style best reflected the classical ideals of democracy and republican virtue embodied in the new American nation. By contrast, critics were hard put to find an equivalent for postmodernism other than that it reflected the anything-goes spirit of consumer markets. Yet style very rarely has a fixed meaning. As Gwendolyn Wright points out, the republican ideals expressed in Greek Revival columns and porticoes between 1820 and 1840 may have signified "civic virtue and social reform" in the anti-aristocratic Northeast, but were associated with "simple ways and democratic strength in the West" and with "the heritage of slavery and aristocratic leadership in the South."[3] Even now, the neotraditional styles favored in places like Celebration invite different interpretations. For some, they do indeed evoke the time-honored virtues of civic community; for others they represent a stark retreat from the multicultural reality of modern America.

Ultimately, the jaunty pursuit of postmodernism led its practitioners along the semiotically hot strip to a cool terminus—the gates of the Magic Kingdom. It was in the service of the Mouse that postmodernism found its most dependable employer. At a time when signature architects had long given up the prospect of finding clients among public or government authorities, a company with a commissioning power greater than that of some nation states, and with a vested interest in the inventive recreation of the past, would prove the ideal client for architects willing to serve up history without consequences. Clients who control the purse strings are usually concerned with service and marketable product, not aesthetic innovation. Disney was a client for whom the aesthetic impact of buildings was also the service and commodity component—a perfect solution for the postmodernist.

Almost from the day that Michael Eisner took over in 1984 and canceled contracts with the Tishman developers for their torpid hotel plans at Disney World, the New Disney became a bounteous patron of signature architects. There are very few elevated names in this profession who have not either worked on, or been invited to compete for, Disney projects.[4] At Disney World, the most lively examples of what Eisner called "entertainment architecture," and what critic Beth Dunlop called "mauhaus moderne," were Arata Isozaki's Team Disney building (the first to win a major American Institute of Architects award in 1992), with its mouse-ear entrance and Brobdingnagian sundial; Stern's Casting Center, a whimsical neo-Venetian hiring hall that sits in public view on the edge of the interstate; and Graves's Babylonian-scaled Swan and Dolphin hotels. In Burbank, there was Graves's Team Disney, with caryatids of seven dwarves holding up the pediments, and Stern's Feature Animation Building, topped by the Mad Hatter's hat.[5] Such buildings often featured Disney icons in the figurative manner with which biblical and pagan deities had been treated in great civic structures since antiquity.

The association with star architects generated oodles of cultural capital for a company that had captivated intellectuals in the 1930s with its vivacious cartoons, but had become a target of their disdain, if not the very symbol of inauthenticity, in the decades since. "The Art of Disney Architecture," chosen as the theme for the American entry in the Venice Architecture Biennale in 1996, marked a cease-fire in the hostilities and a milestone in the quest to reclaim a place for Disney in the landscape of high culture. Eisner began to compare the commissions of the Disney stable with the great public works of nation states, quipping, for example, that Aldo Rossi's office building at Celebration "is our own La Défense."[6] The offhand comment, at a lunch event, harbored an insider reference to Eisner's longstanding efforts to bring the Italian architect into the fold. A few years previously, Rossi had broken off discussions with Eisner about contributing a building to Euro Disney. Knowing that Bernini had once aborted his designs for the Louvre after disagreements with Louis XIV, Rossi declared, "I realize I am not Bernini.

But you are not the King of France. I quit."[7] The prize of their reconciliation was Celebration Place, an office plaza set back from route 192, its cone and cubes sitting on an empty surreal plain worthy of de Chirico. A cool, Leggo-style recollection of Renaissance piazza buildings from the Pisan original, it was Rossi's only design to be completed in the United States before he died in the fall of 1997.

Unlike the tradition-oriented postmodernists who celebrated the past through witty allusion or through meticulously imitating its forms, Rossi believed that good urban building should try to evoke communal memories of the past by reminding people of places, things, and ways of life that the cruel velocity of modernization and its market civilization heedlessly erased. This kind of memory is not fueled by the comfort of nostalgia for the good old days. It should come as a shock, as meaningful encounters with history do, reminding us that the present is not some inevitable outgrowth from the past. This is quite different from "Disney realism"—the term often applied to the work of the Imagineers, dedicated to creating ideal, "improved" places and histories, the way they should have been but never were.

All the prestige architects invited to produce Celebration's civic buildings—Graves's post office, Moore's preview center, Johnson's town hall, Pelli's cinema, Venturi and Scott Brown's bank, Robertson's golf clubhouse, Stern's health center and restaurants—exercised a quirky modesty in their designs. The point, after all, was to avoid self-indulgence in evoking classic civic forms. The results, though, are still quite at odds with the detailed period work of the residential housing. In the main, architectural critics pronounced these buildings as "disappointing." Todd Mansfield, former TCC president, acknowledged that the deference of Disney toward star architects in the early planning stages of the town was a significant obstacle to the work of the planning team: "We lost two or three years in terms of cost and time."

Visitors can follow the architectural walking tour recommended by a brochure from the Preview Center, and biographical vignettes of the star architects are prominently featured in the brochure. But the efforts of these architects are seldom commented upon by Celebrationites themselves. One exception is Philip Johnson's Town Hall, which residents seem to dislike universally. On occasion, Rossi's office buildings and Pelli's cinema are singled out for praise. In spite of their tributes to the past, they are often cited by residents as tasteful modernist contributions to the traditionalist palette of Celebration.

TRADITION, NOT NOSTALGIA

Once in Celebration, most townsfolk become acquainted with the term New Urbanism, although they are reluctant to grant its local relevance. Urbanism, after all, is associated with big-city life, whose density and anonymity are seen as undesirable for the most part. But everyone is more than familiar, in their daily lives, with the New Urbanist movement's basic principles of town planning: a mixed-housing, mixed-use, walkable town with small lots, interconnected streets, and an identifiable center and edge. Architects aside, there are a few nonprofessionals in town who actively sought out a New Urbanist community to live in. Jim Bailey, president of the Celebrators, the seniors' group, and his wife Shirley, looked at plans for New Urbanist towns in Colorado and Arizona, and decided on Celebration because it was further along in development. One of the most active citizens in the community, Bailey is a retired engineer who drives a Disney World monorail part-time, "for fun, and not for the money." His generation had lived through all of the fast-forward decades of postwar America. What was his response to the neotraditionalist approach of New Urbanism? Was it regressive, reactionary, and in cahoots with the conservative climate of the times, as some critics have claimed? Pondering the question on his porch one morning—Bailey is one of the town's most active porch users—he began to describe Celebration as a benevolent "glance back" and not a wholesale "return to the past." Thinking of a better way to answer the question, he slipped inside the house, retrieved a recent magazine interview with Penelope Leach, British author of the child-care bible *Your Baby and Child*, and read me her response to a query about the alleged "decline of the family" and the conservative resurrection of family values:

> Have these gentlemen on the right forgotten why this lifestyle vanished? Women didn't particularly like it: that's why it came to an end. I don't know why these people think we can go backward. . . . Single parents have been used as scapegoats both in your country and mine.

> Being an "alone" parent is seen as a disgrace and immoral as well—and not just sexually. . . . The vast majority of single parents don't fit that description.[8]

Soft-spoken and gracious, this was Bailey's way of pointing out that a literal embrace of the past is a dangerous thing, if and when it hankers for a time when women worked only in the home. But he also believed that the rediscovery of traditions was especially beneficial for those who had long neglected them. Judy Ziffer, a counselor, who had moved from picturesque Mount Dora with her retired doctor husband Al, agreed: "The 'Me generation' is a very lonely generation as it grows older." Referring to Ferdinand Tonnies's famous distinction between a traditional community of full and open relationships and a dispersed modern society of individuals in partial relationships with each other, she added, "This is a Gemeinschafte and not a Gesellschaft place." Not everyone would cite a classical German sociologist to illustrate a point, but such views were common among residents with a healthy romantic streak but who never sought to live in a time capsule.

Advocates of New Urbanism itself, the movement that has most influenced the planning of Celebration, also take exception to the charge of nostalgia. Glowingly feted all across the media, New Urbanism's panaceas for urban sprawl are being met with increasing approval by local and state planning authorities. They have been adopted by federal agencies like HUD, which has initiated a $2.5 billion New Urbanist public housing program called Hope VI, and they have even won a strong benediction from Al Gore.[9] Like the modern movement's zealous break with Beaux Arts and other historicist traditions, the moral clout of New Urbanism draws on its vigorous opposition to a sworn enemy—conventional suburban development.

The postwar formula for mass suburbanization emerged from the pressure of a powerful coalition of real estate, finance, and transportation interests. It also included the oil, asphalt, and rubber industries, tire manufacturers and dealers, motor-bus operators, parts suppliers, road builders, state highway administrators, service-station owners, and many other groups that pursued their common interests as the American Road Builders Association in 1943. Everyone remembers President Eisenhower calling attention to the evils of the "military-industrial complex" and its powerful lobby. Few know that Harry Truman characterized the housing industry lobby as the most dangerous in America.[10] After the war, the vested interests of these groups meshed with the federal need to create jobs and provide affordable shelter for over 16 million returning vets. When the FHA guaranteed bankers' loans to builders, and the VA offered low-interest mortgages as part of the GI Bill of Rights, vets could virtually borrow the entire value of a home without a down payment. Government subsidization of suburbia grew by leaps and bounds, whether in direct aid to white home buyers or in the financing of roads and infrastructure.

Social engineering was a crucial, and immoral, part of the formula. In the name of "neighborhood security," the FHA adopted the Home Owners Loan Corporation's codes governing racial zoning, especially its secret ratings categories for valuing neighborhoods and blocks according to racial homogeneity. The FHA's infamous Underwriters Manual recommended restrictive covenants that prohibited mixed-race developments and set in motion the practice of redlining neighborhoods and ZIP codes as off-limits to loans from banks and coverage from insurance companies. Discrimination in lending and selling continued well into the 1970s, long after it had been declared illegal. In one final twist, land and housing prices exploded at the very moment that minorities were allowed into the housing market, in the mid-1970s.[11] In the period of the New Deal coalition, between the mid-1930s and the mid-1970s, when the "good" federal government earned itself high moral credentials, official housing policy had been outrightly segregationist. Eighty-two years after racial zoning was banned, fifty-one years after discrimination in government lending was banned, thirty-one years after the Fair Housing Act outlawed all discrimination in housing, and after numerous related legal decisions, we still have a housing landscape that is highly segregated and subject to an essentially unfair distribution of services and life opportunities.

While the legacy of this racial engineering has left large footprints all over the place, the physical planning principles of the suburban formula are still legally enshrined in the zoning and building codes that govern the housing industry. The basic elements include maximum housing densities and minimum lot sizes and setbacks, the separation of commercial and residential space, and street hierarchies governing limited-access highways, arterials, connector roads, minor roads, and cul-de-sacs. Introduced initially as safeguards of public health for affordable housing outside of blighted cities, they rapidly became insurance against market risk and were institutionalized in local and regional planning codes all across the nation. Under these zoning codes and regulations, New Urbanist towns like Celebration are literally illegal in most counties.

With an evangelical zeal that seems to characterize architectural movements as a whole, New Urbanist advocates can often be found venting against the backslidden depravity of almost anything built since the 1940s. In the more extreme versions of this holy war, the modernist slab, the honky-tonk strip, the centerless subdivision, the freeway interchange, and the mass-market mall are all viewed as products of the same evil empire—a philistine bureaucracy that has laid waste to the landscape and sacrificed community life in its haste to serve the peddlers of tract housing and gas-guzzling automobiles. The result can often be highly moralistic. Commenting on a popular restaurant chain, James Kunstler, the most cantankerous of New Urbanism's enthusiasts, notes: "The Red Barn is an ignoble piece of shit that degrades the community."[12] The author of two wrathful jeremiads about suburban alienation, *The Geography of Nowhere* and *Home From Nowhere*, Kunstler's broadsides are stuffed with contempt for lower-middle-class taste, any kind of popular culture or avant-garde architecture, and most forms of urban behavior that deviate from his crotchety version of orderly civic conduct. But his spitfire grandstanding on the public lecture circuit is an important counterpoint to the careful packaging and politicking of Andres Duany and partner Elizabeth Plater-Zyberk, founding figures of the movement, in their efforts to loosen the stranglehold of prefabricated development.

The Congress for New Urbanism, founded in 1993 and representing "a broad-based citizenry, composed of public and private sector leaders, community activists, and multidisciplinary professionals," includes, among its charter principles, a program for the wholesale reform of urban policy. Many of its members (including Ray Gindroz and the Pittsburgh firm UDA, which produced Celebration's Pattern Book), have worked on infill projects in several large cities. But, to date, the proving ground of New Urbanism has been in suburbia and not the large metropolitan areas. Duany and others have campaigned tirelessly to reform the bureaucratic suburban formula in the belief "that the suburbs are the precursor of the twenty-first century city."[13] Their mission is moral and corrective—to recover the lost art of small-scale planning ("we don't have to invent anything, it's all been done") that created the compact towns of presuburban America, and to design close-knit communities that are more economically and environmentally sustainable. With the support of sympathetic planners, local authorities, politicians, and citizen enthusiasts, Duany-Plater-Zyberg (DPZ) and other firms have forged a working relationship with developers in the hope of rewriting the planning codes, public policies, and commercial habits that govern the housing industry. Where the will is weak, growth management legislation in states like Florida has thrown developers into the arms of dialogue.

Capitalizing on popular sentiment for the "lost community" of the small American town, New Urbanism adopted neotraditional style as a vehicle for its goal of restoring prewar planning. Mindful of the charges of pandering to the conservative taste for Victorian values, Duany insists that the traditional housing styles are simply a tool to promote the town-planning principles and have no particular significance in and of themselves. They are popular, and not just among well-heeled white folks: "When you really talk and listen to people in the black neighborhoods of Coconut Grove or St. Louis or farm-working Oxnard, you discover that they want ranch houses with little columns in front."[14] Nothing could be more sacrilegious to architects than the suggestion that style is simply an expedient vehicle, or a Trojan horse for smuggling in adversary forces. These "little columns in front" are an affront to architecture's avant-garde, whom Duany describes as "nostalgic for the future."

The struggle to prevail requires tactics: "You have to create your own enemy," Duany says, "you have to simplify your enemy and you have to attack your enemy on your terms." Fighting within the "belly of the beast" of the marketplace, which cares not for ideas but for profits, it is the commercial success of New Urbanist towns that will "induce the beast to swallow its own poison."[15] Half joking about his own Cuban-American background, Duany comments: "Instead of exhausting ourselves with endless frontal attacks, we capture the radio stations and the revolution is won. No bloodshed, exactly what Fidel Castro did."[16] In Duany's case, the radio station is the urban code, which regulates the building type and the relationship of buildings to public space. Pioneered at Seaside, the much-lauded resort town on Florida's panhandle Gulf Coast, this zoning code has evolved into a more complex set of regulations, adopted as some version of a Traditional Neighborhood Ordinance by many local planning authorities. Celebration's Pattern Book is an elaborate version. In the West Coast wing of the movement, which tends to argue for denser urban pockets linked by light rail, codes for the Transit-Oriented Development have been developed by Peter Calthorpe and others.[17] These codes, which are tailored to local conditions, climates, and regional variety, are written to wrest control over design from the large engineering firms that issue prepackaged templates for block developers.

Underlying all New Urbanist efforts is the bedrock belief that the design of a physical environment has a fundamental impact upon social behavior. No principle is more steadfastly upheld. This belief is expressed either through vilification of the enemy—"A modern subdivision is an instrument for making people stupid"[18]—or as a benign statement of purpose—"We wish to improve the world with design, plain good old design."[19] But the belief is still consistent with the old doctrine of "salvation through bricks," which set the bulldozers in motion in the understanding that top-down planners know best. While DPZ's charrettes typically involve several days of meeting with local officials, community leaders, architects, interest groups, and citizens, Duany is wary about *too much* citizen participation:

> After being a rigorous practitioner of the public process, I have lost some confidence in it. When given the chance to make decisions, more often than not, citizens will make palpably wrong ones. They are usually against mixed use. They are always against higher density; they love five-acre zoning. . . . Until confidence is restored by some real successes and planners are allowed to implement the difficult decisions, a mob often decides against its best interests. . . . The citizens will close the drawbridge, oppose mixed use and economic variety in housing, so we must fight them. I'm not the sort of planner that does what the citizens dictate. We are not secretaries to the mob. . . . Our

> democracy is a representative form of government, there are elected officials and planning boards, and we should speak only to them. The citizens themselves are a distorting influence because they are specialists, just like traffic engineers are specialists. Their speciality is their own backyard, and only rarely the community as a whole.[20]

THEIR OWN BACKYARD

For all of the hoopla about the movement, there have been few opportunities to gauge how residents of New Urbanism do actually live in "their own backyard." This was one of my reasons for coming to Celebration. Seaside, since it is a resort town mostly of second homes, is not a very good guide. Nor have other developments, like Kentlands, near Gaithersburg, grown sufficiently to deliver substantial results. Celebration already hosts the largest population of any neotraditional site in the country, yet New Urbanists are wary of accepting it as a bona fide member of the club. Initially, many feared the association with the Disney name—a byword for crass commercialism and blatant showmanship—would be damaging to the movement. Sardonic media commentary about "Mickey Mouse towns" would be unceasing. The Disney connection would bring unwanted baggage, charges of charlatanism, and a snicker behind every corner. Others believed that, far from being an embarrassment to the cause, Celebration might be the mainstream breakthrough for New Urbanism, spreading the good word far and wide and persuading businesspeople that such places are a proven investment. As Plater-Zyberg explained: "There was a segment of the development community that felt these ideas were too high-risk. Now Disney has mitigated some of that risk. These ideas are not radical anymore."[21]

Much like Disney management, New Urbanists were willing to claim Celebration as one of their own if it performed well, but were careful to keep their distance in case it backfired on them. They were one of the many groups of Celebration-watchers that expected high scores from the town's residents. I quickly realized that my own presence and likely findings in Celebration would be warily observed for signs of partisanship. Would my book hurt or help the New Urbanist cause? On occasion, when Duany was in town (Celebration serves as a good demonstration site for prospective regional clients) he would look me up, naturally hoping for a positive report, and always willing to recruit a strategic voice.

Officially, its developer does not promote Celebration as a New Urbanist town. TCC employees are quick to point out that the town does not correspond strictly to the New Urban purist's profile. There are several cul-de-sacs, some curvilinear roads, and many departures from the preferred gridiron street pattern. Because of the wetlands conservation areas, the developable land on the site consists of squirrelly pockets, to be occupied by relatively isolated villages, and the overall housing density is a good deal lower than New Urbanists strive for.[22] Nonetheless, Celebration would not have attained its current form without the persuasive example of New Urbanism.

DPZ were invited to submit ideas ("a continuous curved grid") to Disney for the initial planning discussion in 1987, along with Gwathmey Siegel and Robert Stern Associates. Other firms included Skidmore, Owings and Merrill, and Cooper-Robertson. While the team of Stern and Robertson eventually emerged as the master planners, the New Urbanist modus operandi—borrowing the best ideas from old towns—became the signature mark of the planning process.[23] Reprising the legendary DPZ road trip around southern towns that yielded the design ideas behind Seaside, the Disney development team visited the likes of Savannah, Beaufort, Mount Pleasant, Charleston, Forest Hills, Kentlands, Sea Pines, Seaside, Kiawah, Santa Barbara, and Coral Gables, and borrowed from a wide range of towns, from Mount Dora, locally, to East Hampton, New Orleans, and St. Louis, in addition to meeting with large community developers like James Rouse at Columbia and Charles Frazier at Hilton Head.

Until late in the game, however, other visions of the town were still being discussed. Indeed, when the Osceola plans were publicly announced in April 1991, the buzz was all about the blueprint for a 2-million-square-foot upscale shopping mall, to be designed by Helmut Jahn. One of the largest in Florida, it would have generated $10 million in sales taxes for the county. The residential component of town was to be built in four "themed villages," three of which would be grouped conventionally around their own championship golf course.[24] The 1994 development order issued to the company for a Development of Regional Impact approves the building and zoning of 8,065 dwelling units, 810 hotel rooms, 325 time shares, 3 million square feet of office space, over 2 million square feet for retail, and a 1.7-million-square-foot Industrial Workplace attraction for 15,000 daily visitors.

The approved application also made provision for what would become the Disney Institute, with a 5,000-seat performance center.[25] One guiding concept for the town had envisaged it as a center of learning, modeled on the Chautauqua Institute, near Jamestown, New York, where Eisner's wife, Jane, had grown up. Enormously popular in the nineteenth century for spreading arts education to the provinces (especially to women, excluded from most colleges), Chautauqua had become a cherished relic of small-town America, and so its revival, in the form of the Disney Institute, as the core element of a neotraditionalist community seemed appropriate. Indeed, Florida had its own well-preserved Chautauqua town, De Funiak Springs, in Walton County, which had been part of the charrette for Seaside. Over the next year or so, this and other plans were substantially altered. The Institute was moved to Disney World (too large-scale, too much traffic for Celebration, it was decided), the time share and golf-course resort concept was ditched, and plans for the shopping mall went on the back burner. An amended development order, reflecting these changes, also shows a slight decrease in retail, and an increase in office and hotel space.[26]

In all but the smaller details, the final conception for the town plan corresponds to the New Urbanist blueprint for a neotraditionalist community of permanent residence. What made Celebration so novel, for a New Urbanist community, was its prior establishment of a downtown retail core—a financial indulgence denied all other planned developments and one that eluded large-scale communities like Columbia and Reston for many years. Kentlands struggled with housing sales after its pedestrian mall plans fell through, and other developments like Haile Village Center, near Gainesville, are proceeding with great caution, one store at a time. If Disney could not sustain a downtown core—and the first several years would prove very rocky—then no one could. As Peter Rummell, former TCC chairman, acknowledged, "putting these stores in two miles from route 192 was always the biggest gamble." According to Eisner: "We were probably too aggressive. Our expectations were too Panglossian. It will work out eventually, though maybe not economically. Sometimes if your company is doing well, you can afford to take some risks."

Eisner was shrewd to recognize that issues other than the bottom line were involved. Renting initially to stores and restaurants that catered primarily to tourist custom, rather than resident needs, inevitably created the perception that the downtown did not "belong" to the residents and was clearly Disney-controlled property. This perception was underscored by the fact that all stores (and the public golf course) were required to offer a discount to Disney employees but not to residents (though several did informally). On my first visit to Celebration in November 1996, when the downtown paint was barely dry, the new merchants were clearly skeptical about the town's capacity to attract business, and were looking to Disney to funnel customers their way. Over the next two years, the shortage of custom, the high rents, and the long hours demanded by leasing contracts (merchants are fined by Disney if they close before 9 P.M.), took their toll on owners and managers struggling to break even. Two stores had already left town: New Generations, a children's speciality store offering unrealistically priced toddlers clothing, moved out very early, and M Fashion, owned by a Tampa socialite who had privately acquired a dozen of Princess Diana's cocktail dresses, stuck it out in a hostile sales environment until the spring of 1998. Neither was missed by townsfolk rooting for retail that would serve their practical needs. Several more merchants were on the verge of pulling out. The absence of Celebration from Disney's tourist maps of the region, and the company's withdrawal of its name from the town in the summer of 1997 (it was no longer "Disney's Town of Celebration"), did not help matters. For Tom and Karen Zirbes, who had moved their business precipitously from Honololu, the predicament was clear enough: "Who would have come here without the Disney name? There's not a businessman in his right mind who would move to a community with a thousand people in the middle of a swamp."

More outspoken than most, and certainly more iconoclastic (in a whimsical affront to the zoned taste of downtown retail displays, an undernourished E.T. sat prominently amid the pretty clutter in their window), the Zirbes still represent the majority of merchants who decided to bank on the Midas touch of the company name. But there are also a few retailers who see the Disney name as a liability. Greg Gentile, owner of Café D'Antonio, aims at building a regular clientele of "business travelers and discriminating diners. . . . We don't want Mickey Mouse people here," he admitted. These competing views are inevitable in a retail mix chosen for its diversity. But residents would still feel neglected, especially when they began to petition hard for a hardware store, fast-food outlet, and other convenience shops that could not be sustained with a small population, or that would upset the tasteful ambience of downtown. Among the four restaurants, Max's Cafe was the only one that could offer a truly affordable family meal. While townsfolk tried to support some of the other stores out of loyalty, their needs were better served outside of town, where they had full access to the strip's shopping facilities and yet suffered none of the aesthetic hardship of living with the strip. For the Christmas season of 1998, the town found a solution, albeit temporary, to the retail chill. TCC installed snowblowing machines on Market Street. Every evening, the streets were jammed as hundreds of locals and tourists flocked to see the showers of soapy flakes. Central Florida had finally discovered Celebration, as "the town where it snows."

Living in an instant tourist attraction could be taxing, especially when the steady stream of visitors cruised through the residential areas. Ironically, in a town designed to favor the pedestrian over the auto, a semi-serious traffic complaint was directed at the sluggish crawl with which tourists made their tour of the town, retarding all in their wake. As one resident joked to me, "what we need is a minimum speed limit in this town." The other traffic issue of relevance to New Urbanist design affected the narrow (usually 10 feet) alleyways that gave access to garages at the backs of houses, and were used as service roads for trash haulage. In many instances, it was difficult to park in the garages without running over the facing neighbor's property, trucks had a tough time negotiating some bends, and the longer alleyways on curvilinear blocks posed a problem for two-way traffic. Eventually, the developer decided to add a couple of feet in width to the alleys in future phases of construction.

Some of the more skeptical residents saw the narrow lots and alleyways as simply an opportunity for the developer to maximize profits by squeezing more houses onto the block. But most accepted the principles of social interaction behind the design, praising the ease with which they could meet neighbors while parking at the rear, and hail passersby at the front, thanks to the small setbacks and porches. Without extensive backyards, children were obliged to mingle and play in the parks and public spaces. With the small lots, relief from extensive lawn maintenance, especially in luxuriant Central Florida, was considered a boon. On the other hand, the long, punishing summer took its toll on Celebration's famous porch life, as did the Florida bugs. Some porch dwellers were unstoppable, and were renowned for doing the porch thing, greeting passersby as if it were a civic duty. But in most houses I found there was little porch activity or use. In an age before air conditioning, porches had been a physical necessity of life in the South, utilized until late in the evening when interiors cooled down sufficiently. Celebration's buildings had been designed to breathe, as if there were no air conditioning, but of course there was and everyone used it.

The physical design of the town meant it was virtually impossible not to get to know your neighbors. Most Celebrationites readily acknowledged their social lives had been altered appreciably by moving to the new community from places without sidewalks, where neighbors did not know each other's names, and mailbox meetings were the only social encounters. Rodney and Debbie Jones, local transplants from a gated Kissimmee subdivision of ten homes, had been told by a former neighbor, "it will be nice to get to know you when we both move to Celebration." Dumbfounded at the small lot sizes, friends had warned Bob and Diane Kupchak, owners of a distinctive mansion on Arbor Circle: "It looks like you're going to have to talk to your neighbors."

Some portrayed their first days in Celebration as akin to a conversion experience. "It's almost as if our neighbors had been chosen," remarked Ed Hinson, a military retiree. Jorge Comesanas, an ex-contractor, and one of the very first residents in town, wrote effusively in an early Town Hall newsletter about the day he and his wife closed on their home: "Mimi looked at the sky, it was one of those summer days where the sun, low in the horizon, made the few clouds glow in a million colors with the beauty and tranquility of the heavens. She looked at me and said, 'Look Jorge. Walt is even providing the clouds for our enjoyment!! This is a real Disney sky!' "[27] Sonny Buoncervello, a self-described "Italian-American from Miami Beach who acts Jewish," who manages a limo service and sells real estate, recalled his first walk downtown on the day his house closed. "I didn't lock the house, I didn't get in the car. It was the first time I had really walked in forty years." The experience of meeting many new neighbors in a short period of time was often compared to a first year at college. In their fondest moments, many residents imagined Celebration as an outsize, open-air version of the bar in *Cheers*, though no such bar existed in town, or anywhere nearby.

Virtually everyone had a story to tell about public sociability. Social intimacy was another matter. The closer people live to one another the more likely they are to guard their privacy, and Celebration was no exception. Estate homeowners on the largest lots were the most comfortable, socially, with their immediate neighbors, while those in apartments and townhouse rows maintained a formal distance from neighbors with whom they share an internal wall. Typically, I myself found it was easier to be friendly with neighbors two doors down than with those next door. Stronger friendships tended to be the outcome of socializing beyond the block, through religious organizations, the school, or one of the town's many community initiatives. Relationships of proximity to neighbors were most important only for those who were not very active in the community. These were the people less likely to develop relationships of affinity formed around common interests.

Is the social strength of the community a direct outcome of the physical design of the town, or is this strength due more to the activity and character of the residents themselves? This is the one question that goes to the heart of New Urbanist belief in the power of design, and I discussed it, often at great length, with all the residents I met. The answer is not a simple one. Drawn by the promotional appeals to join a community-minded town, many folks had moved here with the express purpose of making friends and becoming active pioneers. Given this glut of society-seeking residents in a fresh setting, the community's early vitality owed as much to pioneer gusto as to the streets, the lots, and the porches. The more involved residents became in the public life of the community, the less they were willing to credit the physical design for the richness of their social interactions. Naturally, they believed it was the residents, and not the planners or the street design, that made the community what it was. The emergence of a "real" or "authentic" community, they believed, would feel quite distinct from the planners' "sense of community" prepackaged along with the town and fostered through the town's community managers. In addition, the social shape of the community owed a great deal to the distinctive character of these self-selecting pioneers. While Celebration had attracted more than its fair share of energetic citizens, many of these Type A people were used to being "leaders" rather than "followers," and were as likely to be "competitive" as "cooperative" in their community participation and their claims on resources. This generated some conflict within the community that had nothing to do with the town plan or its design principles. As for the less involved residents, they were willing to concede that the high sociability of the community may be a result of the town's physical layout.

As Celebration's first "suburb" began to spring up—in the North Village, noncontiguous with the central Celebration Village—the pioneers' loyalty to the New Urbanist credo of mixed housing was plain to see. Those fortunate enough to locate in Phase One had already begun to develop a defensive, almost anti-suburban, attitude toward the future occupants of the outlying villages. Occupying a site bordered by a freeway, and close to neighboring tourist attractions, the North Village posed the largest sales challenge for the developer, and the site plan clearly reflected decisions directed at the market. Accordingly, the most affordable styles—the Garden Homes—were built in the least desirable location, next to the freeway, and the more expensive estate homes stand directly on the golf course and are clustered in an enclave set off from all the other houses, with a single approach road. Joe Barnes, the town architect in residence, assured me that the latter decision was determined by the land mass and the need to plan around protected trees and wetlands, but few of the Celebration Village pioneers saw these changes in design as anything other than commercially motivated. They almost universally regretted TCC's decision to compromise the mixed-housing principles and conform to a more conventional subdivision pattern that would render class differences visible.

Estate homeowners in the original mixed-housing settlement had learned to submerge their class status. "Early on, I stopped asking people about the location of their homes," explained Longmeadow resident Paul Collins, "in order to avoid any awkward appearance of privilege."

Residents were proud of the fact that no one owned a status Mercedes or BMW in Celebration Village itself. When North Village lots were first offered, David Tennant, an early pioneer, remarked to me that he had seen luxury cars touring that area of the development. Appealing to our shared country of origin, he made a wry analogy with New Lanark, the utopian Scottish company town of the nineteenth century (now restored by preservationists), where the mill owners' mansions ended up being segregated from those of the workers. The outer villages of Celebration, it was widely assumed, would be closer to business as usual and might even attract a more "suburban" kind of resident.

THE RULES

While the developer could alter site plans at will, no homeowner or builder could stray very far from the copious dictates of the seventy-page Pattern Book. TCC's single most original contribution to neotraditionalist building was the decision to revive the illustrated Pattern Book, which in the eighteenth and nineteenth centuries had provided architectural instruction to builders about how to maintain proportion and unity in the design of a town. A legacy of the architects' handbook first developed by Vitruvius in the Late Roman Empire, and resuscitated by Andrea Palladio in Renaissance Italy, pattern books (especially Asher Benjamin's 1827 *American Builder's Companion*) had an enormous influence in post-Revolutionary America on building in the classical style. The use of these books, as handbooks of styles and model plans, continued through the Victorian period—in classics like Alexander Jackson Davis's *Rural Residences* (1838), Andrew Jackson Downing's *Cottage Residences* (1842) and *The Architecture of Country Houses* (1850), Gervase Wheeler's *Homes for the People* (1855), and Calvert Vaux's *Villas and Cottages* (1857)—and were consulted as late as the Colonial Revival of the 1920s and 1930s. After the Second World War, it became increasingly common for lawyers, and not architects, to write the specifications for building codes and standards.

Celebration's Pattern Book is a comprehensive volume of recommendations for the placement and design of houses within streetscapes. The community patterns establish "correct" proportions for everything from massing and setbacks to the height and opacity of fences (3' 6" and

60 percent for Cottage homes, 6' and 100 percent for Estate homes), the depth of porches, and the recommended facade material and color, each laid out according to the size of the lot and house. Landscaping is also strictly regulated: precise percentages are decreed for the appropriate mix of grass, hedges, shrubs, and trees. The degree of variety is prescribed: "No more than 2 different species of canopy trees, 2 different species of ornamental trees, 5 different species of shrubs or hedges, and 4 different species of ground covers." "No synthetic or artificial plant materials" are permitted, and no palm trees will be allowed in the front or side yards. The architectural patterns are addressed to the integral unity of the house, and govern such matters as the spacing between its elements (dormers, doors, porches, columns, and bays), laying down additional rulings about the color of cladding material and other facade features for each of the six prescribed housing styles. For the Coastal style, for example, all windows, trim boards, columns and railings should be white, but they are to be brown in the Mediterranean; pale green, pale ochre, or pale blue in the French; and "a deeper shade of the body color" in the Victorian.

Like DPZ's Seaside code (only one page long, and specifying eight building types), the book is intended to be a guarantee of urban quality, governing the relationship between architecture and urbanism long after the developer has gone. But it is also a formidable marketing tool, lavishly illustrating the ambience of classical, civilized living for those in the market for good taste. With the planned addition of a chapter of patterns for the corporate campus, emphasizing a deco style called "Celebration Modern," it will be an irresistible model for neotraditionalist developers to follow.

The bureaucratic rigor of the Pattern Book's building and landscape codes regularly draws ridicule among locals and in the press. While there are few Celebrationites who regret the style policing—the rules are expressly intended to protect property values—there are many instances when deviations from the Pattern Book became a matter of dispute between a homeowner and Joe Barnes, the resident town architect responsible for reviewing and approving all building and landscaping plans. If a tasteful historical precedent for a deviation could be cited, then the homeowner had a good case to present, although mutual agreements about taste are a hard target to hit in cases where the detail is inconsistent with the vision of the Pattern Book. One dispute I came across involved the veto of large glass engravings of Victorian golfers on the front door of Al and Judy Ziffer's home on Canaan Place. A precedent had been found in a real Victorian mansion, and Judy was approaching the dispute as "a First Amendment issue, a question of civil liberties. If it had cost my whole bankroll for my retirement," she declared, "I'd have spent it." The engravings eventually stayed on the door, though they had not met with official approval. Donna Latour reported a long and stressful series of approvals for her house on Golfpark Drive, where many of the features she wanted, including twelve-foot ceilings and low bay windows, were vetoed as incorrectly Victorian.

Buyers whose houses have been rectified in this way closely scrutinize each new home for signs of an overly permissive review. Would anyone ever be allowed to put shutters on their Queen Anne? In the Pattern Book, the interpretation of "Victorian" draws on the Carpenter Gothic cottage style (characterized by "steep roof pitches with deep gables and dormers") and a style described as "a decorated Classical box with a full width porch." Interpretation of the Pattern Book's own definitions of historical style can be a complicated affair, and it is no surprise that the result often seems overly legalistic. Judgments about what is properly Victorian and what is not can only end up in the realm of farce, worthy of a Monty Python skit.

Residents who had experienced stringent reviews and inflexible codes in other developments felt the architectural approval process was moderate in comparison. Immensely affable, and in no way resembling the caricature of a stiff-necked, rule-obsessed bureaucrat (people, he says, "expect to find some mean guy behind a curtain with a big nose span"), Joe Barnes explained that the Pattern Book is intended as a set of "guidelines" emphasizing what a builder or homeowner "can do," rather than a set of rules prescribing what cannot be done. Not surprisingly, this distinction is often lost on residents in the heat of a dispute. As the buildout progresses, more leeway is being given to home buyers' plans for idiosyncratic designs. One ornate neo-Gothic pile on Arbor Circle—known around town as the Addams Family house—was permitted after the owners, Diane and Bob Kupchak, transitioning from twenty years of high-rise condo living in Fort Lauderdale, proposed building a replica of the Parrot-Camp-Soucy House, a famous 1885

The Parrot-Camp-Soucy replica on Arbor Circle. (Photo: the author)

mansion near Atlanta. The design was approved, and the Kupchaks moved in, appropriately, on Halloween (the builders erected a temporary "Bates Motel" sign). At an earlier stage of construction, Barnes admitted, this level of eccentricity might not have passed muster. Now it can be regarded as one of the town's landmark buildings. The construction of an especially vivid, olive-green Mediterranean villa on Hippodrome Park in the fall of 1998 caused even more of a stir. When asked, one neighbor hopefully mused, "It looks like a primer coat to me," but added, with more resignation, "I guess every neighborhood has to have one." Not surprisingly, many residents saw this sort of architectural license as bending the rules for the well-to-do. It was well known around town that the most expensive houses were proving the more difficult to sell, and so the palette of approved colors had been opened up.

Architectural styles have always been beholden to rules, but the coordinated orderliness of Celebration's classical styles is an entirely modern invention. For anyone truly interested in historical authenticity, the archives have a much more messy story to tell. Heritage-minded preservationists don't like to be reminded that Greek temples and English cathedrals were once brightly painted. As for the Colonial landscape, those picture-book houses painted white with black shutters didn't actually exist until well after the 1790s (they were stained red or green before). The idyllic village green, as J. B. Jackson reminds us, was a "bleak, uncared-for open space where cows and horses grazed, children played and where the militia drilled once or twice a year." Tree-lined streets did not become a feature of town landscapes until the 1800s, and "the smooth, close-cropped lawn was unheard of."[28]

But neotraditionalism is not an homage to historical authenticity. In its New Urbanist version, it is supposed to resurrect only the best ideas of the past, not the whole kit and caboodle. In this respect, it differs from the ethos of those preindustrial villages, like Rockefeller's Williamsburg, Ford's Greenfield Village, and Well's Old Sturbridge Village, painstakingly recreated by business tycoons to honor a way of life that their own industries, based on oil and automobiles, had destroyed. For the most part, Celebrationites are reluctant to view their surroundings as a historical rendering of the past, preferring to speak about the period decor simply as an emotional influence upon their daily lives. Almost universally, residents describe the traditional streetscapes as "warm," "cozy," "relaxing," and "friendly." Modern architecture, by contrast, is "cold" and "alienating"—"there's nothing to relate to." Asked whether they could imagine Celebration as a modernist town, most shook their heads vigorously. But a surprising number declared that it would make no difference to them; the period styles were less important than the way the town was designed for sociability and walkability. Some who had come to Celebration for a sole purpose—the opportunity, say, to enroll their children in the school—had absolutely no opinion about the housing styles. One such couple told me: "We could be living in stainless steel cubicles for all we care about the architecture."

There were even a few who actively preferred modern building styles. Younger parents like Lance and Karin Boyer, who had bought a townhouse opposite the school, were among them. Karin is a counselor at a Center for Drug-Free Living at a St. Cloud elementary school, and Lance shifted jobs, during the year, from Domino's Pizza to renting out time-share apartments. Several years before, they had made a checklist of items for their ideal town: liberal, open-minded, strong on education, remote from nuclear power, semi-rural, low on taxation, and blessed

The Boyer family and townhouses on Campus Street. (Photo: Jonathan Hayt)

with good karma. Independent spirits, the Boyers occasionally pay visits to a Buddhist temple on the Kissimmee strip. Lance, who led the residents' initiative for a Montessori school in town, praises the old modernist dictum that "form follows function" when it comes to building design. "Why have shutters on a house," he contends, "if you can't use them?" Better to plan "in a utilitarian way for the future," he believes, "than to copy the imperfections of the past." He also believed all the houses should have solar heating. As a confirmed "pacifist and planetarist," he regrets the flag waving and shows of patriotism that are associated with the small-town traditionalism of Celebration. Karin, accustomed to the liberal views of her fellow social workers, regrets that the rest of the county is so resentful of Celebration. She had wondered if her politics "would mean that we wouldn't fit in here," but she is grateful, as an "essentially private person," that she has been drawn out socially, way beyond what she thought was her own "comfort zone."

The Boyers had been attracted to Celebration by the promise of a town dedicated to thinking "outside the box." They relished the "non-judgmental" character of their fellow residents and worried, like all good pioneers, that the homesteader esprit de corps was beginning to weaken. Lance noted that "only a quarter of the population had showed up for the last Halloween pumpkin carving," and in the Phase Two homes being built in the North Village, he could see the steady infiltration of "isolationists" who "wanted to lock themselves away." Rumor had it (and rumor was a friend in need to all Celebrationites) that TCC would soon be allowing "snowbirds"—those fickle, continental shuttlecocks—to buy their way into vacation homes in the South Village.

5
OUR MUCH-RUMORED LIFE

"Gossip is news running ahead of itself in a red satin dress." —Liz Smith

On a warm evening in late November, the lake wildlife is burping and croaking in the foggy distance, and the midnight hour is setting in. I am making a quick exit from Celebration's downtown cinema, soporific from two hours of Hollywood's crudest militarist propaganda (*Starship Troopers*). A cluster of teens is huddled on the tiled paving outside the theater, heads bent, legs akimbo, and voices at a low and uneven pitch. The small throng is more like a ragged raver grouping than the cleanly arranged prayer circles that I have occasionally seen over in the park by the lake. It's a teenage hang, a fine example of a near universal genre. I recognize some of the seniors from school, where I've been helping out on their research projects, and I'm made to feel welcome in their circle. None of them has seen this film, and while I don't recommend that they do, I try to explain that it's a kind of nostalgic look back at the science fiction future that never was, not unlike the movie house itself—Pelli's futurist moderne picture palace of the 1930s. No one seems at all impressed by my analogy, but they take the occasion to quiz me about the book I'm supposed to be writing. Am I here simply to boost the town and write about how cute it is to live in *Back to the Fu-*

The Cinema (Cesar Pelli, architect). (Photo: the author)

ture Land? Am I here to celebrate Celebration or will I be sketching the whole picture?

It was an honest question, and one I had already been asked many times in one form or another by residents even in the ten weeks I'd been here. Outsiders are outsiders, after all, and any fly-by-night writer is in a position to inflict severe tire damage on this fledgling community. Several journalists had already done so, and most residents are gun-shy of the press, suspicious at the least, at times quite hostile, and generally persuaded that there probably should be a moratorium on speaking to journalists on hard deadlines. This had not made my life easy. But as a scholar and a book author who had made the commitment to live within the community, I'd been evenly received as someone likely to be fair in his appraisals. In fact, most people I'd met were relieved that someone was taking the time and making the effort to speak to everyone at length. Among other things, my book was expected to dispel some of the widespread media misconceptions about the town and its residents. As for the company, my presence in the town had inevitably become another publicity item—having a scholar in residence was one more mark of prestige to tout around the media world.

PERFORMANCE ANXIETY

But the option of being "positive" or "negative" about Celebration wasn't just a matter for outsider evaluation. It had permeated the daily lives of the residents. Earlier that week, Jorge Comesanas, a Cuban-Floridian from the 1950s *exilio* generation, and one of the disappointed claimants to the disputed title of Celebration's first resident, told me he wished that residents would accept each other for what they were, rather than for whether they were "for or against the school, for or against the builders, for or against downtown, or for or against the company." His comment spoke to conflicts that had deeply shaped the virgin years of this community, and had on occasion polarized the residents to a degree all but a few regretted. Seventeen months after Comesanas and other pioneers had settled in, this was a town on battle alert, its populace watching themselves move from one trial by fire to the next, all the while wringing their collective hands over the fragility of the community's immediate future. Prominent pioneer Jackson Mumey, who runs a distance learning business and also works as liaison for Celebration School, explaining its mission to prospective homebuyers, expressed some of this anxiety to me at our very first meeting: "I have to say as somebody who intends to live here for a long period of time that it's a little daunting to have folks writing books about what we're doing, because it doesn't give us much margin for error." This abiding concern about the *success* or the *failure* of Celebration trickled down all the way from the Disney boardrooms to the school rest rooms. Would it be possible to have anything like a normal life in a town subject to so much examination?

Planned with impeccably correct intentions, built with improperly low-wage labor, and sold on the basis of improbably lavish expectations, Celebration would be put to the test time and time again. Condemned from the outset to the journalists' wrecking ball and to a constant loop of public scrutiny and self-analysis, it was a place that might forever have to answer to our society's media-mulching mania for ceaselessly assessing its self-fashioned icons (Are they still hot?), its market leaders (Are their stocks still up?), and their performance scores (Are they still on top?). True to the ethos of the blockbuster box-office hit, would this town deliver on the promise of its business plan or its community plan? Or would it sidestep all expectations and play by a different script? Denied the small-town, bygone-days innocence it was planned to evoke, Celebration was a knowing soul from the beginning, and few of its occupants would be free from the performance anxiety that came with permanent residence.

Least of all these kids, for it is on their performance that a large part of Celebration's promise rests. Not long after I join the circle outside the theater, our conversation hits a patch of oil on the road and begins to skid onto the bumpy verge of youth disaffection. A little bout of hysteria breaks out, fed by the pressure they are feeling at the school, the tight vortex of all the town's anxieties. Many of the seniors have fallen foul of traditional education and this is their school of last resort. They are now trying to make rapid sense of an ultra-progressive form of schooling that had been under siege from parents almost from the moment it opened its doors. However unfair, their ability to perform—to achieve high scores and gain admission to prestigious colleges—is the benchmark by which the community will assess itself and be assessed. All of them know this, and while it gives them some sense of self-importance, most are beside themselves with anxiety. Among other things, they know full well that TCC's ability to sell houses depends directly on how well they and their younger siblings test. Teenage alienation and property appreciation do not make good bedfellows.

Heather Kinneberg, a rangy girl with long blond hair and the most famous smile in town, is in a blunt mood. Bent on a career in the fashion world, she recently moved with her mother and brother from Columbia, Maryland, the vaunted 1960s planned community, and, like many of her peers, she finds the pressure intolerable. "Everyone in this county wants our school to fail. None of us can handle it. Especially the rich kids," she adds, throwing in an uncharacteristic note of resentment, or was it empathy? "Everyone else thinks we're all rich kids anyway." Besides, the die is cast. "Disney has already decided to sell the town," she announces, lending her flip authority to the rumor of the month.

Andy Parsons, a charismatic hipster with lyrical blue eyes and loose brown ringlets lately shorn of their dreadlock weight, takes the gambit and leads the group onto his favored terrain—the rich lore of teen paranoia. Andy had been a temporary high school dropout in Massachusetts, and had taken his parents' invitation to come to Celebration to complete his credits at a school that seemed to agree with his liberal-minded philosophy. Socially confident and resourceful, he wants to study anthropology at college. Since he belongs to the tribe of Phish, nomad successors to the Deadhead subculture, rap circles like this one are his element. "Half the kids in the school won't come back next year. Their parents will pull them out, or else they won't be able to hack it." Another boy, with colored hair, broken teeth, and an air of shambling angst, has been on furlough for psychological counseling and has stories to tell about his adjustment therapy. Andy empathizes. He's been there, or at least knows what atrocities the shrinks bring down on kids when their minds don't match the regulation profiles.

We sit and smoke and commiserate. I feel pretty helpless. I try to point out that they are all getting a unique, firsthand look at how some educators try to work against the grain and against the odds. After all, it is a break-the-mold school and not a grade factory. Students are prompted to take personal responsibility in lieu of a system of constant assessment and surveillance by teachers and testers. They are not, in the anthemic words of Pink Floyd, just another brick in the wall. This doesn't fly, they've heard it all before. Alternative values at Celebration School are the new orthodoxy, and like any new Establishment, must submit to the unforgiving artillery fire of teen cynicism. "They're using us as guinea pigs, we're just part of a social experiment," insists a sleepy-eyed girl with an artful nose ring. "We all need grades and a GPA to get into college." Conflicted, I shrug and nod at the same time. "But do you really want to mesh into a society that evaluates everything by classifying and number crunching? Surely this school is offering something different." This is my last appeal, to no avail. It's an adult thing, a repressive tolerance, a paternalistic imposition of freedom. If the kids really had a say, things would be different, but they don't know how.

We sit till one-thirty in the morning. Cars draw up, members of the circle peel off, heading for the bright lights of the Boardwalk in the Disney village. Andy has the superior staying power and launches into orbit, spinning a web of conspiracy theory that draws on characters from the novels of Kurt Vonnegut, the creation of AIDS, government surveillance, extraterrestrial activities, and other stock components of slacker lore, all of it seasoned with knowing skepticism about the dark designs of authority. Some of the kids left in the circle smile, enjoying the rant, tolerating his native genius for this discourse. Others, perhaps more gullible, frown as if considering his theses more carefully. The evening falls apart, and we go our separate ways.

This could have been a group of white adolescents anywhere in suburban America at the end of the millennium. Disaffection is their lifeblood, and peer sympathy helps them get through the difficult days. In Celebration, their beef with paternalism takes on a special flavor. This is a town where rumor and conspiracy theory have a rich life, largely on account of the paternalism of the mega-company that built it. Rumors about the company's doings are a natural response to the immense power of the town's developer, its reputation for overcontrol, and its skittish reaction to sour publicity. Even when nothing much is afoot, speculation about Disney circulates among a population that hosts a sizable number of employees with varying degrees of insider knowledge about the workings of the company. Leaks are common, and it is virtually impossible to maintain the company policy of keeping a tight lid on its plans and intentions. Oftentimes, the rumors are a kind of defiance on the part of those who feel out of the loop, excluded either from the company's grapevine or from the active core of pioneer citizens who have taken a leading role in community building. Knowledge about what's going on is a precious commodity. It can be used to solidify or increase one's standing in the community. The town has already produced its quota of citizen leaders, fully involved in the community institutions and organizations, and who have more ready access to this knowledge. In the absence of elected township officials (Celebration is unincorporated), these are the people who will carry the morale of the community through its formative years.

TALES TOLD

From an early point, I decided to document rumors, even the most farfetched tales, in the understanding that residents have stories to tell only about places they care about. After all, a community without rumors is like a sleepwalker living a half-life through automatic motions and private rituals.

Among the celebrities rumored to be taking up residence in town were Julia Roberts (or her sister), Bruce Willis and Demi Moore, Tom Hanks, Michael J. Fox, Patricia Schroeder, and Tiger Woods. O. J. Simpson had also been mentioned. The film stars were anybody's guess. The ex-Congresswoman from Colorado made sense; she was judged by many to have the right "Celebration attitude"—caring, publicly minded, communitarian values. (For once, in her case, the rumor about her purchase of a house was true.) The golfer, while an Orlando native, would have satisfied the unofficial rule these days that every exclusive, and predominantly white, community host a minority sports celebrity. (In fact, Woods moved into nearby Isleworth, the elite, gated community that hosts Shaquille O'Neal, Penny Hardaway, Michael O'Meara, and Sylvester Stallone.) Stories about Christian fundamentalists percolated; they were infiltrating the town with the intent of "taking over." Then there was the Porch Police, an invisible band of style inspectors from whom you would receive a phone call if your public arrangement of chairs, potted plants, and hanging flower baskets wasn't just so.

There was much speculation about the Preview Center tower, closed off above the second floor. Walt Disney was alleged to be buried there. A related rumor placed Walt's head in Disney World and his body in some undisclosed location on Celebration property. But more than a few residents agreed with my own interpretation, that the tower was closed to thwart a would-be sniper from claiming the ideal vantage point in town or to preempt a favored suicide spot. In reality, it was sometimes used as a make-out spot by teens, ideally remote from surveillance. Another Disney World spinoff held that the rotunda of Michael Graves's post office was the top of a subterranean nuclear power plant (under the terms of its 1967 Reedy Creek dispensation, Disney World had the legal option, never exercised, of building its own nuclear facility). Yet another concerned a supposed system of underground tunnels beneath Celebration, the purpose of which would be revealed at some point in the near future.

Jaundiced stories about the town were legion among area residents, some of whom referred to us as the "Village of the Damned." Men, it

Sales Preview Center (Charles Moore, architect). (Photo: the author)

was alleged, were not allowed to have facial hair (another Disney spin-off). Children, all potential Huckleberry Finns, were hired to cast fishing rods into the lake. It was obvious to us that many tourist visitors to town wondered if we were paid to live there, or at least to make appearances on our porches and verandas every so often for photo opportunities. I was hailed regularly by visitors on Market Street as I emerged bleary-eyed, breakfast tea in hand, to greet the bright Florida day from my second-story balcony; "Look, there's a real person." Some kids in town got their kicks from miming the stiff, jerky movements of Disney's audio-animatronic figures for the benefit of these bemused visitors.

The local press had a heyday with Celebration stories. One wry classic came from *Orlando Sentinel* columnist Greg Dawson, who recounted the alleged testimony of one Allan Oakley, from the nearby Indian Wells subdivision, who was in the habit of taking his pure white hound dog for walks in Celebration. Only after several visits did he encounter another dog, a "purebred, all solid black and tall and groomed,"

ZIP code 34747; the post office (Michael Graves, architect). (Photo: the author)

walked by a nicely dressed couple. The gentleman said to Oakley, "Is your shift over soon?" On meeting his quizzical response, he told Oakley he was being paid to walk the dog around the lake. "It makes the town more real," he said. As Dawson pointed out, "whether or not the story is true, it sounds true," summarizing a prevalent belief among area residents that the town just looked too good to be true.[1] This story had stuck around, and some residents were still asked by visitors if they were the people hired to walk the dogs.

The rumors about Disney were a dime a dozen, among which was the widespread belief that the company had retained ownership of the land beneath peoples' houses, or would reclaim it in ninety-nine years. Several of the renters also gave lip service to a belief widely held outside of Celebration that homeownership here involved a lengthy and rigorous screening process by the company. A bizarre rumor circulated that

Detail of a highway billboard, before the Disney name was dropped. (Photo: Ron Dickson)

gypsies were taking up residence in town. It appeared to have originated in an internal Disney memo, lending the town the ambience of a medieval fairy tale, even though the memo's purpose was to warn of the thieving ways of gypsies. Most prevalent of all was the canard that the company was pulling out of Celebration after only seventeen months, largely because of the bad publicity generated in articles in major newspapers about "trouble in paradise" and the teething troubles undergone by the school. Recently, Disney had taken its name off the billboards advertising the community, and, most conspicuously, had withdrawn its name from the water tower marking the main entrance to the town from route 192. These signs had been closely read. The withdrawal rumor was given credence by all and sundry, including several Disney employees. For several weeks, hearsay flew fast and thick around town. There was talk of a strike among the merchants, distraught at the loss of sales that accompanied the town's divorce from the high-revenue brand name. There was talk among disgruntled homeowners about picketing the sales Preview Center to alert prospective buyers that the company was not vouchsafing the guarantees that went with its name.

All of this talk prompted Brent Herrington, the town's community manager, to address the rumor at length in his monthly Town Hall newsletter in November:

> Is Disney happy with Celebration? I raised these issues in a recent meeting with management and the answer was an emphatic "Yes!" . . .
>
> In terms of marketing strategy, the company has been eager for the public to begin recognizing Celebration as a real, thriving community with its own unique identity, separate and distinct from the entertainment-oriented images of Mickey Mouse, the Magic Kingdom, and so on. According to Leigh-Ellen Louie, Disney's Vice-President of Business Planning and Development, when she reads about Celebration in the future, she hopes to see "The Town of Celebration" in big letters and "Disney" in small letters—rather than the other way around. Thus, future advertising and marketing materials will include less emphasis on "Disney" and more on "Celebration." The company plans to vigorously market Celebration on its own merits, featuring all the special things that give the community its warmth and unique character. A recent example of this philosophy was the phrasing on the town's newest Celebration billboards. The difference? Celebration is not billed as "Disney's town." In the new campaign, the "Town of Celebration" is the star.[2]

At times like this, Herrington's handling of his intermediary role was difficult to read. His style was not to everyone's liking, though his was surely the most difficult job in town (with the exception of the school principal's). The genial patriarch hired to manage the town's affairs in lieu of an elected mayor, he was enforcer of the rules, tax collector, redresser of grievances, cheerleader of the community spirit, and signature father and resident. Many professed bafflement about who actually employed him; in fact, he and his staff were employees of Capital Consultants, a Fort Worth community management company, and their services were contracted by Disney. An imposing Texan, built so solidly he should, by force of nature, have been unflappable, Herrington bared his discomfort in his facial expressions, though seldom in his speech. Some disaffected townsfolk regretted his personal stiffness, which often lent an air of enforced hedonism to community events—"It's Saturday afternoon, kids, it's time to have fun." Those who knew him personally had a warmer appreciation of the professional smarts he brought to the job and its daily scrapes. Part of that job was to serve as a target for wronged residents. Most seemed grateful for his rhapsodic sobriety if only because it kept the town's sense of itself on track during the turbulent formative years, when support from the company itself appeared to fall off.

Hefty doses of boosterism were administered through his monthly newsletters and those sent out by Kathy Johnson, director of the non-profit Celebration Foundation. These communiqués were always underpinned by Herrington's own ardent testimony as a community member in residence. A high-profile veteran of the world of community association professionals, he assured me that "it is almost unheard of for someone who does community management to live in his or her own community. You're never off duty, so to speak." There were also numerous public occasions, emceed by Johnson and Herrington, the town's model Mom and Pop, for keeping up morale and stoking the flames of volunteerism. Town meetings held periodically to promote "stakeholder pride and the sense of ownership," as Herrington put it, were reassuring exercises in community therapy. One that I attended in the school gym was mostly a community update ("All the news that's fit to hear," announced Johnson) and was capped by a performance ("Feel the Rumble, Hear the Roar!" "Be Aggressive! Be Aggressive!") by the Pep Team, fledgling infant cheerleaders from the school. By midsummer, these meetings were scaled down to intimate chat sessions with Herrington, initiated in no small part with a view to dispelling corrosive rumors around town, but also marked by his own weary desire to avoid the standard gripe session, where as he put it, "some guy gets up to complain and everyone will hoot and holler 'By God, Disney ought to pay for this.' " Eventually, he introduced electronic town hall meetings, televised on the community TV channel, where he and Johnson took incoming questions on e-mail and addressed the populace through the camera.

But this time around, his handling of the Disney withdrawal rumor produced only ripples of reassurance. One close reader of the newsletter text pointed out to me that it did not actually rebut the rumor. Others said they saw only corporate smooth talking, and Herrington's emissary role reinforced a prevalent perception of him as a "hired gun." Was he in an effective position to arbitrate the interests of residents and those of the powerful developer? "So far," he told me at our first meeting,

> the interest of the developer and the interests of the residents have run parallel, and so there's very little tension in the system. The first time there's an issue in which that's not true, Town Hall will be in a very difficult spot. Reasonably, the residents will expect Town Hall to be an unflinching advocate for their point of view. This is exactly what the developer wants us to be. If I'm successful at providing residents with good communication, making them feel connected, active, and involved, then having Town Hall against you on a critical issue is not something to be looked forward to. But I think the developer realizes that Town Hall cannot function if it is otherwise. If the residents had to wonder about my loyalties, and whether I'm going to stand with them, then I have no credibility, and the developer would be guilty of what it's often accused of—a paternalistic, over-controlling, over-engineered approach to community building. So it's been made exceedingly clear that they see my job as to always take the residents' part.

If you went by the book, Herrington was probably right. There had been no clear-cut conflicts of interest so far, but his "loyalties" would be put to the test repeatedly in the course of the year (his last in Celebration, as it turned out). As a parent of school-going children, for example, Herrington was perceived to be an advocate of the school's progressive methods, and so its many antagonists felt he had taken sides on an issue very dear to residents. Nor had he enjoyed much more than a day or two of smooth sailing in managing developer-resident relations. Fractious in most new planned communities, these relations were complicated here by everyone's prior encounters with the pixie dust treatment. Residents who felt their interests were being neglected by the company were genuinely surprised to discover that Disney, as a developer, had limited liability in the matter. Conflicts with the builders? Not our bailiwick. Problems at the school? Our hands are tied. Retail sales hurting? We're not responsible. Tax assessment hikes too high? Don't look at us. Long before the Disney rumor circulated, many townsfolk and merchants had come to realize that far from enjoying the sheltering paternalism of the Mouse, their relationship felt more like that with an absentee landlord. For Celebrationites who wanted unmediated contact with Disney, Herrington could be only a poor substitute.

Many of the pioneers I had met so far cited the Disney name as a primary reason for their moving to Celebration: "they do things right." They had vacationed, year in and year out, at the theme parks and were accustomed to high standards of customer satisfaction. Some were outright Disneyphiles, although I never met one who clearly matched the profile attributed by others to this Magic Kingdom type—a near-delusional believer that the company's pixie dust would transform daily life into a wonderland where all cares are banished. But a large proportion of townsfolk felt they had been led to expect more attention and support from the company, and were dismayed when the Mouse was perceived as taking a back seat. For the company's part, there was a clear tendency, on the part of senior officials whom I interviewed, to attribute some of the town's troubles to the zealotry of the Disney fans: "we didn't quite understand how rabid some of the Disneyphiles might be," acknowledged one TCC executive. "They had watched too many Disney films and they expected too much perfection." From the Disney perspective, the more fanatical Celebrationites were a multiheaded monster of the company's own creation.

THE MAN AT THE TOP

One popular response was to write directly to Michael Eisner. Any number of residents told me they had done so, for one reason or another, usually in the form of a petition over some grievance. Only one said she had received a response. Margot Schwartz, one of the town's most vigilant citizens and a former employee of the American Institute of Architects in Washington, D.C., had written to suggest that Eisner stage a day of architecture appreciation for the residents—an event that did eventually take place. Others believed that although Eisner had not responded directly to their letters, he had solved their problems by putting a word in the right place. When I interviewed Eisner the following summer, he did not appear to have noticed the receipt of any of these letters. Internal sources told me it was standard practice for these letters to be rerouted to TCC officials within Celebration.

With his reputation as a hands-on mogul, Eisner was perceived as fully accountable, a godlike figure who, when all other avenues had been pursued in vain, could be called on to "lay down the law" and say, "I want these people to be happy." This, at least, was the perception of residents like Ron Dickson and the pastor Donald Jones, who had teamed up to lead the campaign against Town and Country builders. As part of their organizing efforts, they had written to Eisner about the problems with their builders:

> Walt Disney's dream of a model town has become a horrible nightmare for many home buyers in Celebration, Florida. For over a year, countless homebuyers have struggled with their contractors to remedy delayed completion dates, poor planning and supervision, defective building materials, poor workmanship, and other serious problems. The level of frustration and bitterness is extremely high. Some have said that buying a home in Celebration has been the worst experience of their lives. Many disgruntled home buyers have asked senior employees of The Celebration Company to come to their aid, but these employees have declined to get involved in dealings with the contractors.

The letter, sent by certified mail, contained suggestions for action and fair notice of the talk around town about impending lawsuits and whistle-blowing in the local and national media. There was no response from Eisner, though shortly afterwards he happened to be in town and his visit was followed by the first direct responses to their grievances from Town Hall (the promise of inspection visits by an engineer and the bettering of relations with the offending builder). Dickson and Jones believed Eisner had personally ordered these changes after "chewing out" TCC employees. This was the Eisner who during the same visit, according to Jones, had ordered all of the pillows in the Disney resort hotels to be replaced because they were "not right."

If Eisner was their last court of appeal for many townsfolk, he was also clearly a fantasy embodiment of power—the man who could get things done and make everything right. The desire for such a figure is palpable and extends well beyond Disney, although Walt had succeeded better than most in defining the model personality (with a personal connection to consumers) for the corporate one-man show. The legacy of Walt's intimate profile within Disney ranks was so strong that many home buyers could feel they had signed a personal contract with Eisner himself, and that he was responsible for keeping up his end of the deal.

Aside from the fantasy of the all-powerful man at the top, there were a few practical explanations for the direct appeals to Eisner. By the summer of 1997, most of the original development team had left TCC, and there was no one recognizably in charge at the company's Seminole Building across from my apartment. TCC was now being run out of California, and with a new emphasis on the bottom line. In addition, Celebration was regarded as Eisner's brainchild, in which he had a special personal stake. "I'd liked to have lived there," he told me, "if it weren't for the heat. Initially I didn't, because of the risk of being seen to have an unfair advantage in the lottery." Some residents, however, liked to tell stories that contradicted Eisner's intimate relationship with the town. At the opening ceremony for the town center, Scott Biehler—life and soul of the downtown apartment community—and a friend had approached Eisner as they waited for the official events to begin. "Where are you living?" he asked. Biehler said he lived in one of the apartments. "Are there apartments here?" the CEO responded in surprise. Whatever the extent of Eisner's real involvement, the smallest changes in the townscape were regularly attributed to decisions made by the man at the top.

What was the response from the Seminole Building to the Disney withdrawal rumor? Celebration, I was told by TCC officials, had been planned as a town whose residents, given all the right resources, would have to prove themselves as a community with its own characteristic identity. To do so, it would be necessary to downplay any dependency on Disney and to gently sever the paternalistic ties that went with this relationship. This version of the events is what Herrington's newsletter alluded to, and many of the pioneers favored it because it clearly offered them a more active role in shaping the community. These were the joiners and the doers who had answered to the tacit call for community builders in TCC's advertising campaign. Among them were folks who made a point of not identifying as Disneyphiles, and who vocally berated those who were infantilized as "Disney nuts" or mindwashed "Disnoids." Predictably, it was among the most highly educated and professional residents that the scorn for Disneyphilia was most pronounced.

Even so, there was little zeal in any sector of the population for the prospect of the company's withdrawal. No one wanted to see Celebration become "a ghost town," as one resident put it to me, laid waste by "social problems" and plummeting realty values. Too many of Celebration's pioneers had experienced communities hyped by double-dealing developers who had pulled out before the lots were all sold, leaving the infrastructure to crumble rapidly and at great cost to the residents. Nor would you have to look very far in Florida, with its reputation as the "most lied-about state" and as the world capital of the huckster real estate deal, for a landscape littered with warnings about sleazy land and community management. Whatever folks thought of Disney as a company, everyone knew his or her property values depended on the company staying put.

Why then was the rebuttal of the Disney rumor so widely disbelieved? Why was it necessary for people to continue to believe that the company was pulling out or distancing itself from the town? This response confused me at first, but over time I saw how and why the rumor might be helpful for residents. For one thing, it could be used as potential media leverage to persuade the company to get things done in town. Celebrationites quickly learned they could embarrass Disney with exposure by threatening to go to the press. In this regard, they wielded a kind of power over the developer that is not ordinarily available to residents. Disney goes to great lengths to avoid bad press, and public opinion in Celebration is a free agent that the company cannot ultimately muzzle. In December, a lengthy article appeared in the *New York Times* magazine, questioning the lack of "democracy" in the town.

The article suggested that Disney was not coping well with the needs and demands of real people, and was backing off from its commitment to the residents.[3] While widely interpreted in town as just another snide piece of Yankee journalism, the article still gave fresh credence to the withdrawal rumor. By then, some folks had begun to view me as an authority on the town's doings, and so I was often directly asked whether the rumor was true.

No less than Disney's allergy to bad press is its fear of a bad day in court. Many residents, especially those who had been beaten up by the builders, increasingly suspected that the company was backing out to avoid liability in class-action lawsuits, especially if a case came to a local jury trial in Osceola County, where cumulative resentment of Disney might take its toll. Whether this was true or not, the rumor helped spur on homeowners, like Dickson, Jones, and others in the more badly built houses, in their resolve to protect what might turn out to be a minimal return on their housing investment.

On other occasions, the substance of the rumor could be used to allay the prejudices of outsiders about the town. For example, just before the first (and last) Catholic mass was conducted in town in early December, an informational meeting was conducted among those interested in forming a parish in the Celebration area. One gentleman in the audience, who was not a resident, wanted to know about Disney's involvement in the initiative. From his tone, it was clear that he would view any such involvement as a bad thing. Rodney Jones, a leader of the Catholic group in Celebration, assured him that the company had played no role in the group's plans, and implied there was no longer a direct connection between Disney and the town. In a county where Disney's presence is resented as much as it was welcomed, any distance the town could establish from the company helped its residents counteract a local bias against Celebration. This prejudice was all too readily evident in encounters in supermarkets and in daily interaction outside the white picket fence. Joan Jones, ex-music teacher and wife of the pastor, summed up a very common experience for townsfolk: "People look you up and down when they learn you are from Celebration—as if you're not a real person and if you are, what are you doing shopping in Walgreens anyway?"

Whatever other uses, public and private, that people had for the rumor, it was born of an intimacy with the company that was quite different from these infamous rumors about the tainted products of large corporations that circulate internationally and that are often impossible to eradicate: Kentucky Fried Rat, horse-meat Big Macs, the "satanic" Procter and Gamble logo. These stories provide lowly consumers and disgruntled employees some control, however desperate and minuscule, over the workings of powerful corporations. The Celebration rumor was in an entirely different class, but I grew to believe it harbors some truths about the principles of subcontracting by which Disney and most other large companies have come to do business. Under this arrangement, liability and accountability are passed down along with the labor contract. While the needs of the parent company drive the chain of labor, the company does not consider itself responsible for what happens further down the chain. This is the principle that gives rise to sweatshops and exploited labor all over the global economic map. While the development of Celebration does not strictly adhere to this business model—builders and school boards and hospitals are not exactly subcontractors of the developer—it behaves in a way that is quite similar, providing the company with exemption from accountability: in home construction, in schooling, in the health facility, and in civic affairs. From the perspective of Disney's presence, Celebration may already be something of a "ghost town," its streets faintly echoing with the footsteps of Imagineers lately departed or long gone. Some part of residents' fantasies about Eisner surely stemmed from the practical desire to hold a paternal figure accountable to a local community, the way it once was in the era of large family companies, before subcontractors became prevalent, and before CEOs became technocrats, accountable only to their stockholders and hardened to the habit of picking up their cellular phones to order the transfer elsewhere of hundreds of local jobs.

There were a few more mundane realities behind the withdrawal rumor. In the fall of 1997, the company had opened Downtown Disney—an urban entertainment complex of restaurants, movie theaters, music clubs, and retail stores—within Disney World itself. There were internal worries that tourists would confuse Celebration—advertised hitherto as "Disney's town"—with the Downtown complex. Celebration's merchants were especially sensitive to the debate, knowing full well that the company's percentage of sales in town were meager compared to the revenue potential of Downtown Disney. Their written demand to TCC that the company start busing in tourists to Celebration from the Disney World properties was roundly rejected. Similar anxieties had plagued the design plans for a hotel in Celebration. Initially a quaint forty-room inn designed by Graham Gund, the hotel was redesigned, at considerable cost, with the aim of stimulating the sluggish retail sector. It morphed up to a size—115 rooms that would put it in competition with Disney's own resort hotels. Dominating the lake frontage on two acres, the contract for the new four-star hotel was eventually secured by Richard Kessler, who has the reputation of being the Donald Trump of Central Florida resort developers.

The internal wavering over these and other perceived conflicts of interest was complicated by the rapid turnover of management within TCC. Somewhere along the way, balls got dropped, threads got lost, memories got revised. Like any other complex organization, there were differences of opinion and knowledge recall within Disney ranks. In my interviews with management, I often heard stories at variance with each other. One TCC official told me that Disney's name was never supposed to be attached to the town, and that its appearance in marketing materials was actually an oversight. A similar confusion surrounded the decision to treat Celebration as a one-off project. Despite assertions to the contrary from officials, former members of the TCC team suggested that there had been expectations of further development projects, and that the momentum of the team's work had been arrested by the decision to close the company's development arm in Florida.

Lines of communication got crossed. Eventually, a consensus story emerged and was laid over the old ones, like a smooth new road surface. In November, at least, the story went like this: Celebration is to be developed as its own brand, distinct from Disney's, and so, from a business point of view, is being treated in a way similar to company products that are not branded with the parent name. The network TV shows produced by Disney-owned ABC, for example, are not Disney branded, and as such, protect the company from full accountability for their content. In the case of *Ellen*, which fueled a Southern Baptist boycott of the company's products, and *Nothing Sacred*, which provoked a Catholic League boycott, this arrangement provided some, though not enough, relief from exposure.

THE ELLEN EFFECT

The mere presence of Disney provided raw material for speculation, sometimes as baroque as the fantasies it has merchandised for much of this century. Some of the more bizarre centered on the sexual preferences of Disney employees. This had been a center stage focus ever since the Southern Baptist Convention and the American Family Association voted in 1997 to boycott Disney for its granting of standard company benefits to same-sex partners, for the "promotion of homosexuality" in some of its films and TV shows like *Priest* and *Ellen*, and for the use of its theme parks as the occasion for the annual Gay Days (an event that is not promoted by the company but is immensely lucrative, coming at a slow time of the year). As a result, Disney is now perceived locally as a "gay" company. Notwithstanding the prejudicial origins of this perception, Disney, as a media entertainment company, would be expected to have a sizable proportion of gay employees. As it is, the company, whom its gay and lesbian employees consider to be gay-friendly, was still the last major Hollywood studio to extend same-sex benefits.[4]

Christian boycotters against "The Tragic Kingdom," who occasionally leafletted the slow-moving traffic on route 192, just outside Celebration, put the consensus figure of gay employees at 40 percent. One of Celebration's own gay male residents acknowledged that he wasn't at all surprised by this estimate: "How many straight guys would do that kind of job? Having to be that perky and smiling all day long?" He was referring to the kind of emotional labor that is performed by many of the front-rank employees ("cast members") in the park. Another, who said that he had come to Celebration "to live happily ever after with my prince," remarked that "the straight guys at Disney, even those who are married with seven kids, are soft and gentle, and almost 'swishy' in the way they say 'Hello' to you in the street." As for the town, it needed more gay men: "Who the hell else is going to help with the decorating of all these houses?" "I'm so Disney," he informed me, and, laying it on a bit thick, "this really is the gayest straight town."

Interrupting an otherwise routine chat at Barnie's coffeehouse one morning, George Gleason, a resident with a good deal of time on his hands, leaned over to quiz me: "Now, you're a heterosexual man, aren't you?" He seemed to be hoping I would say yes. "I guess so," I replied. "But you've had homosexual experiences?" again hoping I'd say yes. "Well, of course, haven't we all?" Apparently comforted by my response, he recounted how his male neighbor, who was having proverbial marital problems, had come on to him on their porch one evening. Having your neighbor "bury his face in your crotch," as George put it, is not exactly the kind of Celebration experience he had been expecting. But the neighbor was a Disney employee, and, he added, "you know how they can be." Accordingly, relations between the two neighbors became a mite strained. It so happened that George's neighbor on the other side was also a cheater; she had been having an affair with a Disney executive—another woman, I was led to assume. All of a sudden, George was caught in a tightening circle of homosexual lust, besieged on all sides by same-sex tomfoolery. "As I walked downtown I noticed all of the buildings had these pastel colors, and I got to thinking that this town must have been designed by homosexuals. Then you go to the school and you have all these fancy methods that the gay teachers have cooked up. What the heck's going on here, man?"

Who knows what game George thought he was playing with my head on that particular morning? But it was not the last freakish conspiracy theory about homosexuality I would hear in this town so devoted to realizing the full potential value of the nuclear family, and not the last time my own sexuality was probed. Sometimes the anxiety about sexuality was a little more public. One of the many issues that embroiled the school during its first year was the choice of its mascot and logo. A Disney cartoonist had been commissioned to draw a barely truculent (and almost happy-go-lucky) winged lion, and the moniker "Pride" was proposed for the school; the intended reference was to a pride of lions. The student body as a whole had voted for the proposal, although the seniors, more mindful of the impact the mascot might have on the reputation of the sports teams, had voted against. Sure enough, Celebration's athletes were often taunted by other teams for the effete, or insufficiently aggressive, associations carried by the mascot—a fuzzy cartoon friend and not a would-be predator—and also by the

Insufficiently aggressive: the Celebration School mascot. (Photo: the author)

rallying cry of Pride, associated with the gay liberation movement. Not a few of the students came from deeply religious homes, and one of them explained the situation to me:

> One thing most kids are concerned with is the school name. I don't want to sound politically incorrect, and since you're a college professor, I'm sure you know what Pride means—it's a little club. But many people here don't like that sort of thing. They have suspicions about some of the teachers and their preferences. People from the South are not open-minded about that sort of thing, they don't quite understand it. Personally, it doesn't get to me that bad, because my Mom works at Disney and many of her coworkers are gay. It's something I'll

> have to live with and I really can face it, even though I'm Christian and we believe it's wrong. The Bible says it's wrong. One of my dad's bosses was gay and he was really good friends with him. But you want a really strong name, like the Eagles, or the Bears or the Tigers, not Pride. There's never been a recall on it—though many folks are opposed—so I suppose we'll have to live with it.

Others students said they didn't care whether or not someone was gay but still resented the taunts and accusations of "wimpiness" that went with being bearers of Pride. In a region that is heavily Southern Baptist, the sports teams had a tough time defending the choices. So did members of the school's advisory council who debated the issue for several weeks. After a certain point, the parents in this generally tolerant community had a more difficult time discussing the matter, as if drawing attention to the links would further inflame the issue. Not a few had made some skewed connections themselves, and, like George, were no doubt wondering, "What the heck is going on here?" But who could regret that such issues were matters of public discussion at all? The American landscape is peppered with small towns that gay people have famously made a culture of fleeing from. Celebration already boasted a sizable gay population, including several same-sex couples who happened to live on the same street, prompting the cute rumor that the neighborhood had been designated as a "gay ghetto" by the town's planners. While the town also hosted a smattering of religious homophobes, the prevailing ethos in a community so identified with families was one of inclusion.

Despite the initial efforts, happily curtailed, to provide the town with "background stories" in the Disney tradition, this was a place that had managed to evade the Disney policy of storytelling. But there was no dearth of storytelling among Celebrationites, some of it generated by the romance of the new town and the publicity it had garnered, and some by people's breathless efforts to keep track of fast-moving events. Gossip on the street was so lush it grew rumors like spring shoots. At times, I was witness to its raw, nonadult form, in full flow that evening outside the cinema, and on many subsequent occasions among the edgy adolescents of Celebration as they fanned out over downtown in nomadic bands after sundown, skateboards in tow and hormones at a barometric high. At other times, I saw the germination of the stories in public meetings, among socially prominent citizens, or in the heat of dialogue among company employees and anxious residents. But most of the time you could tap the rumor mill simply by taking to Celebration's streets, designed, after all, for high sociability.

Ten weeks into my residency here, my own dilemma was becoming clear. Would it be fair to draw any conclusions from these stories and the experience of residents about the future of suburban living? A number of writers had already declared, often grudgingly, that Celebration might hold the key to one version of tomorrow's world. But however representative in the range of residents it had attracted, it was unique in several respects, and in one above all: the high-profile circumstances under which it was evolving—almost every national and international media organ had run a Celebration story—were, from the outset, a dynamic factor in the growth of the community. There had never been a town so exposed to media attention, and I could not count myself apart from that scrutiny. But since I was not looking for headlines, I had at least pledged to meet people where they were, and not where I, or my editor, or my colleagues, would like them to be. I would take the stories I heard and the exchanges I saw on trust and in sympathy, if only because trust, while no guarantor of truth, is not always a willing accomplice of make-believe, and sympathy, more than urban design and planning, is the master key to community life.

6

RIDERS ON THE STORM

"THE GIANT PIZZA"
One day a giant pizza went to town. It crushed a car. It crushed another car. Then it crushed a building. Then it crushed a car. Then another giant came.
—Poem on a wall, Lower 3 neighborhood, Celebration School

In January and February, Florida is a rehearsal area for two kinds of events that see major league action elsewhere. One is baseball spring training (the Atlanta Braves and Houston Astros are Osceola stadium tenants), the other is tornado season. This year, tornadoes became the main event. With the lower branch of the jet stream sagging south of the Panhandle, and the Gulf of Mexico relaying and feeding the Pacific winter storm track, the clash of cold and warm air often creates pressure gradients sharp enough for twisters to touch down. They are typically weak and less likely to stay on the ground than those that fire up later in the season in Texas, Oklahoma, and Kansas. In an El Niño year (and this was the year when El Niño was blamed for everything), the energy levels of the storms are turbocharged. In late February, several killer tornadoes with wind strengths as high as 250 mph, or twice the speed of Hurricane Andrew, came to town, devastating Osceola neighborhoods just two miles to the east of Celebration and in all three counties to the north. Forty people died and hundreds were left homeless in the wake of the state's worst ever twisters. These counties, especially Osceola, had already absorbed record rainfall (six times the average) throughout my winter stay. Officials in Celebration had seen fit to praise the town's drainage system, which had kept residents high and dry while much of the county was under water. Winds from hell now joined the high water.

Before the tornadoes touched down, the storm machines lumbering in from the Gulf cranked out an unbroken flow of lightning—enough to make the ground seem continuously floodlit from the night sky. My cats, Hamish and Molly, who are curious weather observers as a rule, nosed their way beneath the bed sheets (and spent days after in Zen repose, staring at their litter box for long stretches on end). We willed ourselves to sleep, knowing that wicked things must be happening somewhere. As the downtown bakery opened its doors in the morning, "Riders on the Storm" was being featured, inadvertently but bizarrely, on the Muzak piped into Market Street below. While Celebration was spared, many residents wondered how their homes, many of which had developed bad leaks during the long winter rains, would have stood up to a direct hit from the funnel winds. Typically, it was the poorest area residents, in manufactured mobile homes accounting for 20 percent of Osceola's housing stock, who were hardest hit. Expressing her sympathy with the victims, one of my neighbors repeated the popular myth that tornadoes are somehow attracted to the thin aluminum dwellings of the trailer parks. Esoteric beliefs have always been attached to extreme weather. This one offers a pseudoscientific refuge for people's remorse. The alternative—God's mercy—got a good airing, too, in the aftermath of the storms. But a few months later, televangelist Pat Robertson cited God's wrath as an explanation for Central Florida's record winter rains, record early summer drought, and extensive brush fires. Disney's Gay Days and the hanging of rainbow flags in downtown Orlando to acknowledge Gay Pride, were to blame for the end-days weather, according to Robertson: "I would warn Orlando that you're right in the way of some serious hurricanes, and I don't think I'd be waving those flags in God's face if I were you." More, he promised, would follow: "Terrorist bombs, earthquakes, tornadoes and possibly a meteor."

As with mostly everything in Celebration, the emotional core of the

Built for battle: the Celebration School (William Rawn, architect). (Photo: the author)

response to the tornado damage could be found at or around the school. Like the county's mobile homes, the school had attracted and braved more than its fair share of storms and squalls since its doors opened, somewhat prematurely, in the fall of 1996. From the outset, the staff and their teaching methods had been besieged and assailed by vexed parents. In the course of the year I spent observing and making myself useful in classes, the number of riled parents and the volume of their discontent grew exponentially. By midsummer, the turbulence mushroomed into a general uproar and brought the long-simmering discord to a flash point.

BUILDING FOR LEARNING

On this somber February morning after the tornadoes, the drama, for once, was not turned in on the community itself. In its second year of operation, over half the pupils in the school were drawn by lottery from county areas outside of Celebration, and several of their homes had sustained direct damage. The atmosphere in Upper 3 (grades 8 and 9) was bluntly subdued. Jackie Flanigan, an ever-popular teacher ("learning leader" in the school's often painful alternative jargon) in this multi-age classroom ("nurturing neighborhood," in the same jargon) describes this group as "Hormone High," with an adolescent energy mood "you can cut through with a knife." Eric Nelson, the science teacher, characterizes his charges as "squirrely as heck." This particular morning, the teen buzz is at ground zero. Sensitivity training is about to begin. Each of the four teachers in the 109-student neighborhood addresses his or her own quadrant, or "kiva" (an American Indian term), and then "grand kiva" is convened for the entire group. Flanigan recounts some of her own tornado experiences in Indiana and Kentucky, and advises pupils to go easy with the tornado humor.

Twister stories are shared. An infant was found lodged high in a tree, trucks had been moved 250 yards and sustained no damage, a diving board was driven through a brick wall, and pieces of straw had been forced through a two-by-four. One student "has someone's car in his front yard, and has no idea who it belongs to." Mr. Nelson, also a Midwesterner, from "the middle of East Jesus nowhere," seizes the mood: "It's OK to be amused and dazzled by force, because people are attracted to force, and the power of nature is awesome. We're all looking around and saying 'Wow, that's really cool,' but people lost their lives, so be sensitive." Flanigan invites anyone who feels "more affected than they think" by the storm trauma to approach teachers discreetly in the next few days.

Nelson, in standard Celebration gear—casual, green, short-sleeved shirt and chinos—clearly is itching to explain the science behind the tornadoes. On a revolving stool, he sets up an experiment that will generate a baby twister. A lump of Sterno—gelatinous with an inflammatory core to produce a slow burn—will be lit to provide the warm air conditions for a mini-tornado to develop inside a makeshift cardboard armature. But first Nelson demonstrates with his own body. He starts to gyrate, simulating the circles of wind formed by a supercell storm, and quickly gathers speed. "Soon you've got a Ho Ho of air going. Instead of a wall of air, it's being bent like a coat hanger, and this log of air is beginning to spin in on itself. The air is running around in a tight circle," he brays, and at this point, so is he, hurtling around the room, his blond hair swept skyward. "Are we safe? Are we insured?" queries Flanigan, who likes to offset Nelson by presenting herself as the most "anal, logical-sequential guy on the team." Nelson charges ahead, "When you multiply two forces, you create a new force at right angles," and he is now a whirling dervish, almost out of kilter, his arms windmilling like Pete Townshend on a wayward guitar riff. The Sterno is lit, and the stool is abruptly rotated. The flame flexes into a loopy vortex and funnels upward, arching hopefully toward the top of the chicken wire that encloses the experiment. No one has said a word for twenty minutes. I have never seen this group of students in a more attentive mood, with the exception of Sex Ed classes, and even then they cut their questions with bittersweet cool: "How many calories do you burn during intercourse?" (Answer: 65–70 cals) "Why do old people still do it?" (Answer: Sheer pleasure). Today, they seem more impressed by Nelson's antics than by his would-be tornado, which never really amounts to much. Their patience is finally exhausted, and, with the first rowdy hubbub of the day, they set off, in Brownian motion, to occupy each sector of the sprawling space that Upper 3 occupies.

These multi-age classrooms are immense, 6,000-square-foot omnibus environments that contain a variety of different spaces, some open, some self-contained. A central "hearth area," evocative of the family living room and large enough to congregate all 100-plus students, is furnished with couches, often facing each other like a hotel lobby. The hearth bleeds into an open "wet area" and a multipurpose work-study area, and is surrounded by a couple of traditional, enclosed classrooms, one or two smaller conference and group rooms, a teachers' planning room, and two unisex restrooms. Each neighborhood is customized, in consultation with the students (the spaces of Upper 2, my favorite, are remapped as The Beach, Atlantis, Coral Reef, Riptide, Octopus's Garden, and the teacher's planning area is the Burial Grounds). The furniture is all movable, except for the banquettes that line the walls, keeping company with the "old media"—sparsely stocked bookshelves (textbooks are rarely used) and the world globes (even less used) perched on top. Boom boxes and TV monitors are more central, and computer terminals are ubiquitous. Without having to trek to a separate computer room or media lab, students can call up media resources or make Internet links from all over the neighborhood ("computing anytime, anywhere"), using one of scores of data ports and video connections.

The neighborhood, like all other spaces in the school, is clearly designed for optimum flexibility. It can host integrated team teaching and traditional whole-group instruction, cooperative learning in groups and individual study and research. In fact, its builders say this is the first school in the country to be physically designed with the needs of progressive educational methods in mind. The design team, led by Boston architect William Rawn, included educators who had worked on the learning design for the curriculum. The result was a building that would make it easier for teachers and students to meet the demands of one of the most nonconformist schools on the national education map. Improbably for a town built to evoke old-time values, this school has been frontloaded with every last bell and whistle from two and a half decades of progressive educational reform.

In this light, Nelson's gyrations were not the usual antics of the resident whacko science teacher. One of the steadfast principles of this school is to base teaching and learning methods on performance and exhibition. This is a flat rebuttal of the passive methods of the traditional classroom, and the rote memorization of facts and digestible info bits that passes as preparation for the constant diet of tests forced upon students these days. "We've got better things to do," observes Charmaine Gabel, Upper 3's math instructor and teachers' union rep, "than preparing students for tests." (In addition to national tests like PSAT, SAT, ACT, and NAEP, the state requires FCAT, the Florida Comprehensive Assessment Test, Florida Writes! and HSCT, the High School Competency Test.) As an alternative to standardized testing, students here are assessed "authentically"—that is, more in line with how they would be judged in a real-world context. Grades and test-oriented curricula are eschewed (along with student desks, textbooks, period bells, daily schedules, report cards, and other ritual features of traditional education). The preferred methods of evaluating student achievement draw on a variety of activities—problem-solving tasks, community-oriented group projects, content-based portfolios, and public exhibitions and performances. Some part of student learning is self-evaluated (the most authentic form of assessment), while a written assessment appears in narrative reports prepared by teachers.

Later in the day, Flanigan introduces a new project to her Human Expressions class (or "domain"). Students will be using Hyper Studio, an Apple presentation program to build an autobiography along the lines of "This Is Your Life." The completed work will be presented orally to peers, parents, and mentors later in the spring. Recent projects included "Homeless and Alone in the Great Depression"—where students were given $20 a month to survive and wrote a diary that demonstrated credible emotion while highlighting the historical causes of the Depression. And the Cassini project, in which NASA's controversial space probe (with plutonium on board) was the topic of a forum between students assuming the roles of scientists and officials from the EPA, agents of Florida state, stockholders from corporations invested in the space mission, and NASA employees.

For "This Is Your Life," as for every project, students are asked to create their own rubrics for the evaluation of their work. "What do you expect to achieve and demonstrate through the project, and how do you expect it to be assessed?" The idea is for students to have a clear sense of their individual goals before they begin. They break up into groups, spontaneously but adroitly selected by Flanigan to match personality and skill levels, and begin to learn the computer program from the most technologically savvy pupil in the group. Cooperative learning, another of the school's methodological principles, is now being put into action. Instead of competing against each other, students are expected to learn from, help, and motivate their peers.

Methods like authentic assessment and cooperative learning are not exactly new, but for many Celebration parents—trying to make sense of the school's full deck of nontraditional methods and the accompanying mouthful of educators' jargon—they could just as well have been lifted from a therapy manual for psychiatric counselors. I quickly learned that virtually everyone in town felt he or she had some bone to pick with the school's innovative learning design. But it was clear that the teachers' opposition to grading and test preparation—cramming and drilling in the "basics"—was the chief source of parental discomfort. Later in the week, another one of those many media-seeking national surveys appeared, showing American pupils testing worse in math and science than almost every other industrialized nation. Another weary round of hand-wringing and doom mongering commenced among politicians and pundits of every persuasion, long addicted to the seductive but irrational habit of equating school test scores with the nation's ability to compete in the global economy. Captains of industry squeezed out dire warnings about the decline of standards in our schools. Around town, the school's critics (dubbed "negative parents" at the outset and "concerned parents" as time went on) took heart. Their distress, it seemed, was shared by the country's political and business elites, if not by the teachers of their children. "Who," they were asking, "knew better what their children needed to get on in the world?" The most successful achievers in the nation, or a group of lowly paid public schoolteachers in the rural South, tipsy from swigging at the faddish brews of reform?

THE PIPER'S PAYMENTS

Like most science teachers everywhere, Nelson protests that he is strapped for resources and so is always on the lookout for an extracurricular laboratory. Using the Winter Olympics events as a prop, he offered physics lessons through the town's community TV channel for two exhausting weeks, and currently has an eye on a role in the Animal Kingdom, Disney's new theme park, where he will be presenting "random acts of education." After the tornado traumas subside, he leads Upper 3 on a long-awaited field trip to the Magic Kingdom, where basic principles of energy and gravity will be demonstrated on some of the park's rides. I am to accompany the students as a chaperone. The evening before, there are numerous UFO sightings all over the county. A farmer claims that twelve of his chickens have mysteriously expired overnight, but no radiation burns have been detected on the dead fowls. I conclude that the mood is surreal enough for a visit to Mickey's own backyard.

Early on a chilly winter morning, columns of mist are coursing up from the theme park's tepid lakes and swaddling the walls of crenellated châteaus and palace hotels. We enter the Magic Kingdom well before it is open for business. Without the busy throngs (paying customers in the parks are called "Revenue Units"), features of the park's design are all too visible in clean detail. From certain angles, it does seem to resemble a townscape more than an empty amusement park, or is it that townscapes more and more resemble Disney World? In a small amphitheater off to the side, a fully garbed Pinocchio and some other cast members from his story are rehearsing their swaggering moves. I know that they are probably lucky if they are being paid much above the minimum wage and that Pinocchio's nose grows longer with each quarterly statement of profits issued by the corporation (which amassed $22.5 billion in revenues for 1997). But for a brief moment, without the mass of visitors and hawkers, it is possible to imagine this jolly boy-toy and his bulbous friends having the run of the park, as if it really were their own playground, the way it should be and never is.

"This is the ultimate classroom for me," interrupts our guide for the day, Michelle Thomareas, a profoundly perky teacher who left Celebration School after the first year to work in Disney's Youth Educators program. But education through Disney does not come cheap. At $30 a pop, it is a pricey outing for the students and several have been unable to afford the trip. No one is in line at Space Mountain—a rare sight at the most popular ride in the park. We are to brave the roller coaster twice, once with all the lights on and once, as riders ordinarily do, in the dark. The aim of this is to test our powers of observation and deduction when our sensory perceptions are altered. Students are asked to collect their observations and estimate the average speed of the car, the highest drop, and the time traveled during the ride. For Nelson, Space Mountain is also a grand opportunity to illustrate the difference between two types of energy. Sitting behind me in the car, he bellows "Potential Energy!" as we start to ascend the slopes, and "Kinetic Energy!" as we hurtle down. "Work! Work is being done!" By the end of the day, after repeated demonstrations on different rides, even the least attentive in our party will have grasped the distinction. Later, horizontal and vertical gravity are measured on the Big Thunder Railroad ride, and for an optics lesson, we go behind the glass screen in the Haunted Mansion to see how the images of the ghouls in the banquet scene are projected. It turns out to be nothing high-tech, just the old stage trick of Pepper's Ghost gussied up on a grandiose scale. But the euphoria of being behind the scenes is palpable.

In common with all the pioneer parents, teachers like Nelson had expected that Celebration students would enjoy regular field trips like this to Disney World, as well as daily access to the educational resources of EPCOT and the Disney Institute. As it happened, today's outing is a rare event, and no special privilege at that. Any school in the region can participate in this program if parents are willing to pay for it. This was not what had been promised to Celebrationites. The original blueprint for the school had envisaged far-reaching Disney input. "A Day in the Life of a Celebration Student," a promotional video from July 1996, just months before the school opened, shows Eddie, a model Hispanic student, visiting and learning from the EPCOT staff's environmental experts as part of his personal learning plan. Eddie's day also included a lesson, beamed by satellite from Paris and delivered in French, on the mathematics of medicine, a video seminar on African contributions to American music, and participation in a series of cross-age interviews about the psychology of physical injury. The blueprint stipulates that Disney experts in animation and film and video production were to be master visiting faculty, serving as career mentors in the performing arts and entertainment business. Disney "teachers of the year," from Florida and around the nation, would be on staff, and the EPCOT facilities would be easily accessible to students like Eddie.

Virtually none of the prized access to Disney resources materialized, nor did the teachers of the year. Underresourced and underprepared, the school was never able to implement Eddie's personal learning plan, though to many parents who saw the video and read the brochures, it was perhaps the single most attractive feature of the efforts to promote the school. What was Disney's involvement in the school? The company had "donated" the land and chipped in several million dollars to help fund the construction of a building that ended up costing over $24 million, in the estimate of one school board member, $17 million of which had been public monies. Even at that, Disney's contribution was offset by a waiver of the $4.1 million the company would ordinarily have paid the county in impact fees to develop the Celebration site. Under the twenty-year contract with the school district, the company shares stewardship of the school's Board of Trustees with Osceola County and Stetson University and is committed to helping with student mentoring. In all other respects it is a public school in the Osceola County system and is prohibited from enjoying fiscal privileges from Disney not available to the other schools in the district.

From the very first discussions about the school, board members expressed concerns about equality with other district schools, and in a county where Disney's money and power is resented and envied, the funding situation at Celebration was guaranteed to be politically explosive. Even before it opened, it should have been clear that the company could not freely extend its largesse and resources to the school as promised or open its facilities to the teachers and students unless the rest of the county was included. So, too, there would be no way to compensate for the extensive overtime that teachers had to put in to master the innovative curriculum. Even an effort to give teachers passes to the theme parks for educational purposes blew up a ministorm of bad publicity. The same fate befell an earlier trip to the parks for Upper 3 when Disney buses were used to ferry the students.

Most controversial of all, an enhancement fund of $5 million had been set aside by Disney to assist the school in its start-up period. In a district where school funding is about $3,460 per pupil (as compared to the national average of $6,564), the idea was to show how much educational worth could be squeezed out of a moderate hike in funding. At our first meeting, Terry Wick, TCC's liaison officer at the school, explained the gambit: "TCC then and now believes that the purpose of the enhancement fund is to show the county that by paying $300 more per pupil, the board could say to taxpayers, 'Look what you can do with a few extra dollars.' This is a good model for making the case to taxpayers for more money." Those in the know, including school board members, alleged that a good portion of these funds was being used to pay Disney's administrative employees like Wick and her staff, and so it was perceived that this money was not directly benefiting the Celebration students or anyone else in the district. Ratification of the use of the remaining enhancement funds lay in the hands of the school board, and its members exercised stringent control over the approval process. Consequently, the Celebrationites felt the school was clearly being underfunded by both the county and the company. As the only K–12 institution in the district (indeed in all of Florida, with the exception of a school plumb in the middle of the Everglades), it was allocated a budget equivalent to that of a middle school, an underestimation of the additional resources necessary for both a high school and an elementary school.

In the planning stages and in the first eighteen months of operation, the deliberations of the school board were a source of intense frustration to Celebration parents, teachers, and administrators. Here, raring to go, was the "school of the future," breathlessly promoted in TCC's sales literature as the model home of the best ideas to emerge from the leading centers and superstars of educational reform. Starved of resources, its growth was being retarded, in their view, by a petty school bureaucracy, rooted in the cracker mentality of cattletown Osceola. As one prominent Celebration citizen advised me early on, "our school is way above the thought bubble of Osceola County." In the rest of the county, the Celebration educators were seen as snooty neighbors who thought they had all the advanced ideas and wouldn't share them. One vice principal in Kissimmee told me she didn't think "Celebration School wanted to be friendly, they never invite us to anything, they think they're so far advanced, they couldn't care less about the rest of us."

Many townsfolk suspected the company might welcome any external excuse to distance itself from a school it had no control over and that had generated more than its share of embarrassing headlines in the national press during its first eighteen months. Some, like Larry Rosen, a Stetson University professor who had been involved in the planning of the school and its curriculum, were convinced that the controversies around the school had been a decisive factor in Disney's "withdrawal" of its name from the town. Players like Rosen, who had observed the shift in management policy close up, had seen the company freeze, as it were, in midstep, survey the pitfalls ahead, and step back. "I always thought of [the school] as a chance to leverage the opportunity with Disney to do something of real consequence," Rosen recalled. "In retrospect, though, they used us very effectively for marketing. There's no question about it. They used me very effectively, and I was willing to be used if this could be an exemplary, nationally renowned school."

Despite Rosen's and Wick's efforts, the partnership between Disney and Stetson had soured. The jewel in the crown of the partnership had been the innovative Teaching Academy, adjacent to the school, which they both had planned as a national center for forging new ideas in education. It was currently being used to train Caribbean Cruise Line employees, and would soon lose the original lettering over its facade.[1] Rosen contends that Disney could have smoothed over the board's equity concerns if only it had been willing to give some additional money to the district (for schools attended by the children of Disney employees, in effect). But the company had stood firm. Chastened by his close encounters with Disney politics, Rosen had turned down an offer to be the school's principal when Bobbi Vogel, the first incumbent, left after one rocky year on the job. He was now assisting the district in developing curricula in other county schools while helping to plan a new progressive school for Orange County. While Rosen took a sabbatical and eventually left town, the teachers who stayed, and who called themselves "survivors," felt they were fighting battles not of their own making or choosing. "We were thrown to the wolves," Charmaine Gabel coolly declared, "we had all the Disney pressure, but none of the Disney support."

Nor did they benefit financially. Teacher salaries in Oscoela County are appallingly low. A typical hourly rate is $16 for thirty-seven and a half hours, but most teachers put in ten-hour days, and then some. The workweek often stretches to sixty hours when it includes preparations for this novel curriculum and the multi-age classrooms, not to mention hours of laborious, extracurricular "communication" to ease the anxieties of parents who have laid down a small fortune for a stake in a community where very few teachers can afford to live. Most have taken a pay cut to move here, for the chance to teach in a nontraditional school. The odds on their surviving from one year to the next at Celebration School are less than fifty-fifty. Oscoela school principals can decide not to renew teacher contracts without so much as a word of explanation, a fate suffered by several Celebration teachers in the spring and summer.

TINKERBELL HIGH

The majority of residents—thirty- and forty-something parents and their children—told me the school had been their chief reason for moving to Celebration. Given the lowly reputation of the county's public schools, Disney had to put on quite a show to attract the kind of families that would buy into an upscale development. Early on, it was decided that a "school of tomorrow" would be the prize bait for luring prospective home buyers. It was easy to be smitten with the promotional package that was presented to parents.

A well-known supporter of nontraditional education, Eisner consulted Disney board member Reveta Bowers, director of the innovative Center for Early Education. The company quickly assembled a glittering array of star support for their plans, including some of the nation's best known educational theorists and gurus: Howard Gardner, director of Project Zero at Harvard and the theorist of multiple intelligences; Theodore Sizer, founder and director of the Coalition of Essential Schools at Brown University; David and Roger Johnson, from Minnesota's Cooperative Learning Center; and William Glasser, from the Institute for Reality Therapy, among others. Many of their ideas and methods were adopted into the learning design.[2] A consortium of universities—Stetson, Johns Hopkins, Auburn University, and the University of Central Florida—agreed to provide interns and teaching assistants, and professorial faculty from these colleges were to pay regular visits or be in semi-attendance at the school. With the collaboration of the National Education Association, these faculty were slated to participate in the Teaching Academy to train Osceola teachers and test new methods and ideas for the nation's schools. The school would thus have a sophisticated professional development institute on its doorstep, and the district would be able to showcase it to the nation as a model teaching laboratory. In addition, Celebration's technology alliances—Apple, Rauland-Borg, Claris—pledged to deliver a state-of-the-art multimedia environment with truckloads of donated hardware and software packages. Above all, the Disney touch would ensure quality support.

Only Tinkerbell was missing, and for many parents razzle-dazzled by the advance publicity, she could just as well have been waiting in the wings to work some magic on their little ones. Expectations of a quick fix could not have been higher and could not have fallen further. Jackie Flanigan speculates that the school became a "freak magnet" for many dysfunctional families who believed that Disney would make it all right. Other teachers, like Donna Leinsing, head of curriculum, confirmed that the first crop of students included many with a ruinous record in traditional institutions and whose parents viewed Celebration School as a last resort. Flanigan herself did not seem to mind, ever eager to meet some new challenge—in this case, teaching more than her share of "exceptional" children. Some other teachers were less charitable, resenting the kids' problems and comparing themselves to "punching bags" for parents whom they perceived as overwrought and over-privileged.

While most of the promised Disney resources turned out to be inaccessible, teachers and parents continued to view the company's sponsorship and backing as an opportunity to be mined. I could see their point but I wondered, as any educator might, if the use of such resources wouldn't inevitably affect the shape of the curriculum. Doesn't the payer of the piper always end up calling the tune? Over lunch in the Starlight Cafe during our Magic Kingdom outing, I put the question to the ebullient Nelson. As an elephant muppet in a tuxedo crooned nightclub standards from the stage, he explained that he could much better teach marine biology if his classes had access to EPCOT, or environmental preservation at the Animal Kingdom, or the physics of sound and light at MGM. A visit to Cinderella's Castle would illuminate the principles of Romanesque architecture for his students' group project on the history of castles. (Task: Compare and contrast the ways a medieval and a modern labor force would be organized to build your castle.) I acknowledged that there are precious few good copies of medieval architecture in Central Florida, although I pointed out that there are no shortage of large castles—Medieval Times, King Henry's Feast—on the commercial strips outside the theme parks. So, too, there are many other non-Disney amusement rides, much more affordable, where physics lessons could be demonstrated, if need be. As for environmental conservation, the Osceola School District owns a fine nature preserve fifteen minutes away in Poinciana, where I had spent many an educational day, but which no one at Celebration School appeared to know about. Aren't these cheaper, more available alternatives? Nelson reluctantly agreed, but it was clear that he was himself drawn to the romance of the Disney spectacle. Celebration, I expect, will be a stepping-stone for him to a better paying job in the parks. The school, in general, has had the most trouble retaining science teachers, largely because of better paid opportunities elsewhere.

By the end of our day in the park, the rides had murdered my neck (would I sue the school or Disney?) and I made a beeline for Muhammed, the deep-tissue masseur at Celebration's Fitness Center. A kung fu expert at the Wah Lum Temple in Orlando, Muhammed gave me my last lesson of the day in potential and kinetic energy. I reflected on the questions I had asked other teachers and parent volunteers about the educational virtues of our trip. Not one had doubted the "quality" of our Disney experience. Indeed, several observed that this was the "most authentic" environment of its kind in the area. If schoolkids could learn something from such visits, it would be better to learn it here, because Disney World was "the real thing." In other circumstances, these might have been bizarre comments and likely to chill the hearts of educators across the land. Disney, after all, is a catchphrase in our culture for the commercial falsification of real history, real experience, real knowledge. When Disney is the most authentic game in town, surely we are in serious trouble. But six months in Celebration had taught me to temper such judgments with the benefit of some local understanding.

No doubt, part of the response was due to the simple jubilation of parents and teachers at having gotten access, otherwise denied, to the educational component of the parks. But it was also clear that Disney offered some of the better job possibilities in the region's dominant industry. Its lowest paying positions, while pitiful in compensation, exceed other service worker wages in the local tourist industry, thanks to union contracts that increase hourly rates faster than at rival attractions like Universal and Sea World.[3] Management squeezes the unions at every opportunity, but the very existence of the Service Trades Council, which negotiates the largest union contract, covering 22,000 employees, is unusual in a right-to-work state like Florida. Courtesy of "Donald's Deals," cast members also enjoy a wide range of discounts from area retailers. Upper-level employment is well represented by Celebration's own coterie of Disney executives. Somewhat more glamorous to kids are the Imagineers, who combine technical proficiency and artistic flair. So from the point of view of the school (and the state's school-to-work initiatives), Disney World is not there to be *consumed*, nor is it perceived as a process (Disneyfication) of sanitizing culture or history. It is a career opportunity for students looking realistically at job possibilities in the region.

Celebration School is not a "Disney school" in any real sense. Neither its staff nor its mission have any relationship to the company's own educational programs. But it does serve a community with many Disney employees—where Disney culture is omnipresent—and the quality of things Disney, at least compared to other companies in the region, is respected. More to the point, perhaps, the school's performance-based methods lean toward the modes of exhibition and self-display that have become prevalent in a society where everyone has to advertise him or herself to win attention. We are viewed more and more as people with something to sell—our own brands—and our capacity to dramatize and showcase that product is a primary survival skill. If we cannot show how and why we count, then we will be cast as extras or as backdrop, at best, and passed over, at worst. Disney has played its role in the growth of that kind of society and those expectations, although they did not originate with the storyboarders who drew Mickey and Minnie Mouse. At Celebration School, it is easy to imagine, if you really want to be conspiratorial, that the classroom modes of performance are part of a systematic training in how to be good Disney cast members. In truth, such rituals of character acting and self-advertisement are much more widespread, and have become habitual in many zones of our daily behavior. As one parent noted to me: "There's not much structure in life anyway these days. It's all role-playing out there. So why do we need structure in the school?"

All the same, Disney ways were not entirely absent from the school. In several neighborhoods, I found that storyboarding was a favored technique of learning, as was reworking fairy tales. On a February visit to Lower 3, at that time the most tightly organized of the six neighborhoods, students were beginning a new group project that would amalgamate and update tales like Goldilocks, the Three Little Pigs, and the Three Wishes. Tom Vitale, the remarkably industrious team leader, told me that some parents had recently objected to the teaching of *The Devil's Arithmetic,* Jane Yolen's book about a Nazi concentration camp in Poland: "The subject matter is too grim for 8, 9, and 10 year olds," one parent had written. "There are so many nice books out there, why not choose some fairy tales?" Given that the original pre-Disney versions of so many of these fairy tales were the splatter movies of the Middle Ages, it was an ironic complaint. Whether or not today's project was undertaken in response to the complaints, Vitale's students were busy weaving familiar characters into new plots: Cinderella has her precious coat stolen at the school, allegedly by three pigs. She chases them home, and blows their house down. Three billy goats arrest the pigs and bring them to trial. The Wolf is the presiding judge.

This project is a springboard for a social studies exercise that examines the countries of origin of fairy tales. Some months later, the project became a full-fledged play, combining Cinderella, Sleeping Beauty, and Snow White, set in Celebration itself, with the town's landmark buildings as backdrops. Cinderella leaves one of her roller blades behind at the stroke of the clock on Skate Night, and she is wooed by a prince rapping hip-hop rhymes. Elvis is the fairy godmother, and pizza is the feast of choice. The new version did its fair share of reworking some gender stereotypes. A month later, Upper 3 students were producing "politically correct" fairy tales.

EDUCATION WARS

As an educator, I thought I had been around the block. But nothing had really prepared me for Celebration School. I learned my three Rs in austere Scottish schools, steeped in traditions of common education that date back before the eighteenth century. My secondary school enrolled everyone in my hometown. Latin conjugations were recited out loud in some classes, and corporal punishment for stray behavior was administered in all classes from a leather strap with long fingers called "The Tawse." For most of the boys and the gutsier girls, peer pressure required that we take a good beating from that instrument with some regularity. (Not so long ago, the barbaric practice was outlawed by the European court of justice.) The British Empire had lately dissolved, but the maps on the wall still displayed its greedy dominions spanning the earth's surface in pink swatches. In my last year, a teacher set an essay topic about "the Third World." None of us appeared to know what the term meant. The teacher smiled wanly and proclaimed that "the Third World is whatever you want it to be." In my final weeks, I discovered anthropology, the only curricular clue that had been offered to suggest that any societies outside of Europe mattered at all.

For college, I went north to Aberdeen, one of the "ancient" Scottish universities, a stronghold even then of the moral philosophy that had guided the Scottish Enlightenment in the eighteenth century. In the age of late hippiedom, it was modish to live and study (by the spirit if not the letter of Rousseau's Enlightenment) as far away from campus as possible, in communal farm cottages, where we grew our own vegetables and cannabis leaf in a noble rural setting. In the course of my graduate studies, I finally got to learn a few things for myself, first at a modern English "red brick" university—Kent—and then at a lavish American state "multiversity"—Berkeley. A peripheral casualty of Maggie Thatcher's war on the British intelligentsia, I took my chances in the rough seas of American higher education and embarked on a career teaching the great works of American culture, high and low, that had drawn me across the Atlantic. Leaving a job in Kent instructing English as a second language to cosmopolitan European teenagers, I set off to teach corn-fed farmboys and urban homegirls at Indiana University and Illinois State, and moved on to instruct the elite student ranks at East Coast institutions like Princeton and Cornell. In 1993, I left Princeton, after a stint of eight years, to head up a graduate American Studies program at New York University.

By the time I got to Celebration, I had been a college teacher for over fifteen years. These had been the years when higher education became a fierce battleground, ceaselessly targeted by conservatives who saw it as a vulnerable flank of the New Deal legacy they were so intent on putting to the sword. The contemporary form of a liberal arts education, partly focused on the teaching of multicultural justice, was a red flag to the monocultural New Right, and therefore had to be vandalized by their foot soldiers. Winning easy points with a compliant, scandal-seeking press, conservative detractors, from Reagan-Bush appointees like William Bennett, Chester Finn Jr., Diane Ravitch, and Lynn Cheney to reactionary professors like E. D. Hirsch and Allan Bloom and right-wing foundation hirelings like Dinesh D'Souza, ran a massive campaign of dirty tricks to discredit every socially relevant idea and program advanced in the nation's colleges. As a progressive teacher, writer, and public lecturer, I found it impossible not to be drafted into the Culture Wars that battered and bruised higher education during that time. For myself and my colleagues to be cast as "tenured radicals" was one thing. To be judged a threat to national security for holding to our progressive beliefs was a bizarre and chastening experience.

There is a sad lack of communication between those who work in the lower and higher sectors of education, and, with no children of my own, I had had no firsthand contact with schools. Embroiled in our own collegiate battles, it was easy to neglect the much greater trial by fire undergone by the public school system over that same period of time, much of it orchestrated by the same conservative forces, using the same tactics of disinformation and defamation. In particular, we did not have to deal with parents from the Christian Coalition on our school boards and in our classrooms, spreading fire and brimstone in our path. For all of our tribulations, higher education is still seen, even by its conservative detractors, as a great American success, attracting foreign students from far and wide. By contrast, the country's public schools are branded an abject failure. As a result of the New Right's campaign, by the mid-nineties virtually every ill in the nation was being laid at the door of public schoolteachers, and moves were under way in almost every state to privatize some element of the system.[4]

In the absence of a national religion or shared cultural traditions, the public school has long been held up as the unique source of American national unity. It has ended up serving too many agendas as a result. Since its mid-nineteenth-century advent, the common school has been viewed as the repository of democratic virtue for the republic at large, the principal medium of Americanization for immigrants, the guarantor of economic prosperity, the salve of inequity and intolerance, the wellspring of efficient workforces, the arbiter of all civil strife, and the supposed solution to a staggering range of social maladies, from teen pregnancies to voter apathy. Some part of this hopelessly overburdened status was begot by progressive educational thinkers like John Dewey, who believed that schools could replace the family, church, and community as the primary means of socializing children into the responsibilities of a democratic citizenry. But I would attribute the lion's share of these unreasonable expectations to the dearth of public criticism of an economic system that awards us with the grossest inequalities of any industrialized nation. In the absence of truly sustained critique of our market civilization, the public school system is an easy scapegoat for all the anxieties aroused by people's thwarted hopes and ambitions.

When public schools are invoked these days, there's a good chance that the speaker is not really talking about education at all. Public schools have simply become the default for sounding off on every grievance, wrong, injury, or prejudice afoot in the republic. Not that these injustices have no impact on the shape of the public education system, which is as uneven and unequal in its access to resources as any other institution in American society. Indeed, a wholly privatized system of competition could barely have produced a more unequal result, given the vast disparities between the funding of predominantly white suburban schools and inner-city schools largely populated by minorities. The federal taxing system that allows each school district to levy taxes on homes and businesses to fund its schools has directly reinforced the high segregation that existed before *Brown vs. Board of Education.* Jonathan Kozol has diagnosed the outcome:

> According to our textbook rhetoric, Americans abhor the notion of a social order in which economic privilege and political power are determined by hereditary class. Officially, we have a more enlightened goal in sight: namely a society in which a family's wealth has no relation to the probability of future educational attainment and the wealth and station it affords. By this standard, education offered to poor children should be at least as good as that which is provided to the children of the upper middle-class. If Americans had to discriminate directly against other people's children, I believe most citizens would find this morally abhorrent. Denial, in an active sense, is however, rarely necessary in this nation. Inequality is mediated for us by a taxing system that most people do not understand and seldom scrutinize.[5]

Under this local taxing formula, schools in wealthy suburban areas are allowed to enjoy funding levels that are often twice as high—up to $5,000 more per pupil—as those available to schools in low-income urban districts. Largely as a result of this formula, it remains the case that the color of your skin, the income of your family, and the location of your home will determine what you are likely to achieve in life.

As it happens, Florida is relatively untouched by this plague of unequal funding. The school districts are countywide. As a result, any funding gaps between the urban, rural, and suburban schools that often coexist within these large districts (Osceola has an area of 1,506 square miles) are nominally slight. This is why Celebration School is barred from access to additional Disney and county funding, despite the high tax base of the town. So, too, the Florida Education Finance Program, passed in 1973, allows for little disparity in per-pupil expenditures from district to district, basing its funding formula on the number of students, local tax base, cost of living, and program costs. The state ends up providing about 50 percent, local property taxes about 43 percent, and the federal government 7 percent. Florida's chronic problem is not unequal funding, but an overall funding famine resulting from the fierce anti-tax sentiments of its residents (many of them retirees) and its increasingly Republican legislature. With no state income tax, and with a legal cap on the percentage of property taxes that can be spent on education, the system faces a nigh impossible task in meeting the needs of its mercurial population growth unless there are some sweeping tax reforms. The equivalent of a 60,000-student school district is added each year, and, like the nation's other most populous states—California, New York, and Texas—these include a disproportionate number of poor, immigrant children. One in four of Florida's children lives in poverty. There is no greater disparity between a state's wealth and its children's well-being. While Florida ranked twentieth in the nation in per capita income in 1997, it finished above only Mississippi and Louisiana on the Casey Foundation's annual assessment of children's well-being.[6] Classroom overcrowding is a serious problem in the majority of districts, and above all in the Central Florida counties, where runaway growth and development has far outstripped school capacity. Some schools in the region are already almost 300 percent over capacity and may have as many as 5–7,000 surplus students in the next few years.

The relatively unpopulous Osceola (with an estimated 170,000 residents by 2000) still adds almost 3,000 students a year, will need twelve new schools by 2007, and is well on its way to becoming the portable classroom capital of the nation. Yet district voters routinely vote down penny or half-penny increases in sales tax to fund school construction, and housing developments are approved with no guarantee that the local school can enroll the new intake. Teachers' salaries are severely deflated, starting at about $23,000 in a county where the average teacher's salary is under $30,000. This makes it doubly difficult to recruit more talented educators to teach the county's diverse base of new residents—more than 45 percent are minority—so different from the white, cattle-ranching community that predominated only a decade before. The bustling Osceola High School, home of the state champion Kowboys, which I visited just after the tornadoes, has students from twenty-two nationalities, speaking almost sixty languages, with an annual turnover rate of almost 40 percent owing to the transience of the new tourist workers.

At Osceola High, Chuck Paradiso, whose principal's office is adorned with steer horns, was developing a limited program based on the Celebration methods ("if it plays in Peoria . . ." he quipped) in a school already vocationally aimed at the area's occupational niches like sports medicine and the hospitality industry. Popcorn was being sold outside to raise money for library books. Just down the road, at Thacker Avenue Elementary, 73 percent of the students qualified for free or reduced lunches in a county with a fifth of its children below the poverty line. Some of these students attend three different schools in one year as their families move around seeking marginally better paying jobs at area attractions. One school in Kissimmee, I was told, had a turnover rate approaching 90 percent. Pervaded by the smell of mold and sewage, decrepit, crumbling buildings with leaking roofs and rotting floors are not uncommon. What were once known as barefoot schools are scarcely less so today in a bedroom community district that faces daily challenges to its education system as formidable as anywhere in the nation with the exception of the most abjectly poor inner-city institutions.

All the schools in the district I visited are designed on the factory model to host seven hours of consecutive, self-contained classes. The formulaic factory school was created to accommodate the shift from an agrarian to a manufacturing economy that required neat, punctual, and disciplined batches of line workers. Schooling methods were devised to facilitate the efficient transmission of knowledge, through chalk, text, and test, to passive, pre-factory trainees. How relevant is this nineteenth-century model to today's more complex economic landscape? For over twenty years now, educators and policymakers have insisted that the postindustrial workforce requires skills that differ from the rote memory functions associated with drill sheets and standardized testing. Employers, we are told, are looking for self-motivation as well as self-discipline, teamwork as well as individual initiative, problem solving as well as functional reasoning, troubleshooting as well as maintaining technology, and attitudinal skills that rest on self-esteem, personal responsibility, and sociability. Of course, these are primarily for the higher-paying positions. The bulk of the new postindustrial jobs—in clerical, data-processing, hospitality, janitorial, and in-person service industries—are chronically low wage and carry no benefits or security. There is little incentive to seek or to retain such secondary labor positions—they lead nowhere because the rungs above are missing—and even less to learn the basic skills that entry-level positions require if it turns out that your employer and your workplace affords you no respect, let alone the prospect of advancement. Indeed, for a large percentage of these jobs, all that is required is a pleasant demeanor and a visible aspiration to please customers.

PLATE SPINNERS

First-time visitors to a neighborhood in Celebration School, especially those who associate classrooms with visible order and discipline, are usually baffled, and I was no exception. "It's like a three-ring circus in there," was a typical parent comment in this vein. On my first visit to Upper 3, I could see what they meant. If you were expecting the familiar, Hollywood tableau of schooling—a teacher in front of rows of desks—it was easy to conclude you had, instead, entered education's equivalent of the Twilight Zone.

Every conceivable kind of interaction and learning activity seemed to be going on at the same time, from seminar groups in high-energy discussion to individuals slumped on couches in a sullen, meditative torpor. A cluster were working on computers in the hearth, talking through a chat room to students in Scottsburg, Indiana, about a joint Web site the two schools are building to explore alternative scenarios in world history. A lively throng nearby were debating the male double standard in gender relations. They became too loud and had to relocate. Another small pack were working in the wet area on the soon-to-be defunct Lake Project, aimed at stocking the town's lake with catfish. (Disney, I was told, was pulling out for fear of being sued by fishers attacked by alligators.) A scattering of students were practicing their hopeful Spanish in the conference room. Several individuals were stretched out on the banquettes, reading books. Two bad boys, one of them my own skatepunk neighbor, were sitting in silence, side by side, and were clearly being disciplined. Another group was gathered around the work-study tables, sketching a presentation board for their History Fair project on immigration. Individuals were surfing the Web for research on the Castles project. There was a constant movement of bodies across the hearth area, and every so often, pairs of students retreated to vacant corners of the neighborhood to exchange confidences. If you knew what everyone was doing, and if you were familiar with the day's loose curricular schedule, then all of this made sense. If not, the place looked like a free-for-all.

At the center of it all was Jackie Flanigan, in a blue denim shirt, white jeans, and Keds, with none of the Disney accessories she sometimes sports in an apparently irony-free way (but, with Jackie, a tail-end boomer who earnestly describes herself as an "idealistic throwback to her generation," you could never be sure). Right now, she is "facilitating" several groups all at once. Teachers at this school are like the plate spinners on the *Ed Sullivan Show*, frenetically keeping things going on several fronts. More like a mother in the home than a teacher in a classroom, she is responding to multiple requests and situations in various parts of the neighborhood while directing her own groups and talking to me. At some point in the day, she says, she has "to go lift weights or go psychotic." Hailing from a family with classic Italian-American credentials—Mulberry Street, Providence, and Boston's North End—Flanigan, who spent most of her life in the Midwest, is one of the few teachers who did not take a pay cut to join the staff. One of the town's early stay-at-home moms, Flanigan decided to replace a teacher who left, and then stayed on staff to lead Upper 3's second-year effort at establishing good communication with its anxious parents. To that end, it helped that she was also a mother who lived in Celebration, the only teacher in the school who fell into that category. In the regular information meetings with parents she often emphasized the continuity between the school's standards of assessment and those used to manage a busy household. From month to month, I watched Flanigan, Nelson, and Gabel try to perfect the psychology of communication. Through e-mail, voice mail, Web home pages, live TV broadcasting, phone hot lines, newsletters, articles, and other print sources, Upper 3's parents were bombarded with information about assignments, methods, and assessment rubrics. Gabel joked that it was all about "bringing the enemy into your own camp." It almost worked.

7
THE SIEGE OF THE SCHOOL

Mi Kid iz a Honner Studant at Sellibration Skool

—Bumper sticker, Summer 1998

Nothing could fully allay parents' anxieties about the school, and it would take a palace revolt, or a bloodletting, for the enemy psychology on all sides to dissipate. The storm around the school had started early, claimed many casualties, and showed no signs of moving out to sea until it had inflicted more losses. Watching the toll rise from month to month was by far the most dispiriting experience of my stay in Celebration.

In any new community, the school is likely to be a flash point. Differences in beliefs and values among residents are more liable to surface there than anywhere else. These days, the odds are that the source of conflict will be a result of pressure from conservative Christian groups, especially active in the local public school system. Who could forget Ralph Reed's exhortation to his legions, when he was executive director of the Christian Coalition? "The future of the country is determined in the principal's office, not the Oval Office. I'd rather elect a hundred school board members than a single president." The resulting battles over school board elections, multicultural curricular reform, school prayers, creationism, secular humanism, and super-morality consumed the energies of a whole generation of parents and teachers.

No such religious agenda embroiled the stakeholders of Celebration School. Among residents, there did exist a branch of Moms in Touch, an organization that encourages Christian mothers to meet and pray for their children's schools. This prayer group met on Monday mornings. Individuals occasionally raised moral issues with teachers from a Christian angle. One succeeded in preventing the observance of Halloween festivities in a lower neighborhood. Others complained when "the Noah story" was taught in a class where every culture was shown to have its own creation stories (and still others petitioned the grocery store manager—unsuccessfully—to stop selling alcohol). But for the most part, there was no substantially organized Christian pressure group in town, nor in the Osceola district itself, at least not compared to neighboring counties like Polk and Lake. Celebration School's antagonists had different fish to fry.

FIRST BLOOD

Along with the first principal, Bobbi Vogel, several teachers in the starting lineup had been recruited from an innovative program at Highlands Elementary in the Osceola district, but most had been trained in traditional methods. An elaborate book-length document of principles and "essential learnings"—known as the "DNA_2" design—had been hammered out by Vogel, Donna Leinsing, head of curriculum, and other senior teachers in the year before the startup, but very little was ready to go by the time Celebration School opened in the fall of 1996 (contrary to the advice and desire of the school board). Classes commenced not in the school's own (unfinished) building but in the neighboring Teaching Academy, designed for quite a different purpose. The resources were simply not there, especially for the senior school, and many teachers were ill-prepared to team-teach or to interpret such a nontraditional curriculum. Everything was makeshift. The new residents, some of them still living out of suitcases in nearby hotels, were about to live through Celebration's first trauma.

Accustomed to getting customer satisfaction without delay from Disney, many pioneers were already facing long waits to move into their houses, and were in no mood to be told the school would need a few years to come up to speed. Why sacrifice a few years of their children's education on what some were beginning to perceive as a social experiment? Within several weeks of opening, a group of distressed parents were loudly assailing the school, its staff, and its methods. Their children, they alleged, were not progressing, but were actually regressing under these methods, and with no apparent discipline to stem the decline. The group included one of the new town's poster parents, Rich Adams, an ex–fire chief from Pennsylvania, whose family had been showcased ("Residents begin to Arrive!") in TCC's promotional newsletter, the *Celebration Chronicle.* Since the town was crawling with journalists and TV crews, Celebration's first genre story about "trouble in paradise" was catapulted into the public eye as Adams and others made their dissatisfaction known in several interviews with TV and the press. In a flash, MSNBC and other national media outlets had superheated the story. Even if they had anticipated the fishbowl effect of living in Celebration, few residents had bargained for this kind of media attention so early on.

Overnight, the swampy air was rent with accusations on both sides. Beverley Neff, a parent actively involved in the school, noted how quickly people became polarized: "Even in the first two weeks, parents were asking me, 'Well, what do you think?' and very soon we were being persecuted and guilt-tripped if we were not in there fighting the teachers every week. We were being asked, 'How can you feel that way when this affects your children so much?' " In order to plan a response to the accusers, an emergency parents' meeting was called, as Sara Mumey recalled,

> over Founder's Day weekend, and was called in a matter of an hour, by word of mouth. We sat there for three hours, and everybody had a chance to say what they thought we should do. There were people who wanted to call a press conference. But by the time we left the room there was a consensus, which is how this town has operated, so far. There was a consensus that we would work within the community, and let the press do what they wanted to do, and say what they wanted to say, but that it was more important for us as a community to make sure that the people in the community who were going to the media didn't get their way in terms of changing the way things were here. And that's really continued to be the way that we operate.

As for a plan of action, three initiatives emerged from the parents' meeting. One was to circulate a petition in support of the school and its staff, another was to stage a teachers' appreciation picnic, and the third was to create the Dream Team, a parental support group. The first two further polarized the community. Many residents told me that the pressure to sign the petition and attend the picnic made them uncomfortable. They were not entirely happy with the school either, but decided to go along with the program of support. Terry Neff, Beverley's husband, paid for a plane to fly over the picnic with a banner message of support: "Great Job, Bobbi, Teachers & Staff of Celebration School." He also opened the first bank account for the Dream Team, in the name of the "Positive Parents," a spontaneous decision he regrets, in retrospect, because of the divisive connotations it took on. "I wouldn't have done it if I had thought it would mean that others were seen as 'negative.' "

No matter, the incentive to be "positive" in most things related to Celebration was already firmly established and well seasoned by a mix of Disney's compulsory peppiness and Middle America's native boosterism. Above all else, loyalty to the "positive" program was virtually guaranteed by residents' concern for their property investment. In such a climate, loud dissenting is likely to be seen as a betrayal, rather than a measure of the strength of the community. The opinionated quickly become spoilers, or threats to a common investment. On the other hand, the flap over the school meant that, all of a sudden, Celebration's much-hyped "sense of community" became something real to be fought for. Like any real town, it would now have its share of strife, scandal, and vendettas. But the "positive" and "negative" labels would die hard. Whenever I was asked, as I frequently was, whether I was writing a positive or a negative book, and replied that it would be a truthful book, the response was often one of mild disappointment.

In November 1996, however, there was far too much at stake for the boat to be rocked. All homeowners, whether they had children or not, could see that the value of their property was going to be tied to the fortunes of the school. Realtors will attest that the value of homes in this region can vary by over 15 percent depending on the test scores of the local school. No one was about to give the naysayers too much leeway. It was hardly surprising, then, when Adams and the other critics began to believe they were being ostracized, perhaps even encouraged to leave. They numbered no more than six or seven families, but at the time their opinions had a sizable impact on a tiny population. While some pioneers alluded darkly to the "personal problems" that these families had brought with them, others spoke of them in retrospect as martyrs who were hounded out of town—the Adamses decided to go back to Pennsylvania, the Burtons returned to Illinois, and the Thompsons, Summertons, and Bilentschuks moved elsewhere in the Orlando metro region. Like many others who figure in this book and who have left Celebration, their names, like the unquiet dead, are still on the bricks around the flagpole in Founders Park and in front of Town Hall.

Whatever drove them, individually, to leave, a ruinous decision was made by the developer to hush things up. TCC agreed to help these families sell their homes on condition they sign a confidentiality agreement amounting, essentially, to a prohibition against speaking to the press. Inevitably, the existence of the gag order became public, generating a new round of bad publicity for Disney and confirming some residents' worst fears about the company's controlling instincts. Despite the public embarrassment, the spirit of the gag order was not entirely lifted; as the teachers were preparing for their second year in the trenches, they were "advised" by TCC's communications officer not to speak to reporters. In the interim, the *Wall Street Journal* had spoken, running a stinging front-page article about the school's troubles.[1] While Celebrationites were learning to disregard the press, Disney's executives and major stockholders could hardly ignore what the *Wall Street Journal* had to say.

Media reports had interpreted Disney's heavy-handed response to this early crisis as a confirmation that the company's interests would ride roughshod over the liberties of residents. From the outset, outsiders took great pleasure in viewing Celebration as a company town in civilian clothing. Yet I found, to the contrary, that these events had jumpstarted the engine of civil debate among townsfolk, and set the machinery of opinion into motion more rapidly than any formal political process might have done. Since there was no provision in the town for public assembly or representative political opinion, and since the press was so heavily mistrusted, the town lacked a designated forum, for at least the next two years, for focusing the debate about the school. But a Pandora's box had been opened, and the messy outcome served to politicize the community, early and abruptly. These first loud disagreements not only marked the end of Celebration's microscopic age of innocence but also determined that the school would be the chief medium for registering opinion in town. As in the nation at large, when Celebration's parents recorded their general dissent with the way things were, they would invariably use the school to do so. Since it was in the public domain, the school was considered a legitimate target of public discussion, unlike, say, the problems with housing construction, which lay in the private domain. Besides, the response of Adams and others, however intemperate and ill-timed ("We were promised caviar, what we got was dog biscuits")[2] established the perception that there *might* be something "wrong" with the school. Henceforth, open season would be declared on its teaching staff, their methods, and their educational credentials. Many of the "positive" parents got fed up waiting for their "world-class" school and found themselves in the opposing camp a year and a half later, pleading for a more traditional curriculum.

ON THE FAULT LINE

The first task, however, was to repair the damage, or, as Brent Herrington put it, to "prevent scar tissue from forming, and dividing the community." Margo Schwartz, one of the founders and first officers of the Dream Team (who would later become a fierce critic of the school), confirmed that the actions of the "negative parents" prematurely created solidarity among the new residents: "Rich Adams brought us together," she explained. Rosemary Cordingley, a parent on the other side, who pulled her son from the school but stayed in town, put it another way: "These events made the town real." Schwartz, a former teacher herself, from Maryland, was typical of the pioneer cadre that ran the Dream Team, the embryo of the PTSA. Few were outright boosters, and most had their own concerns about the educational methods but thought they could best be met by getting involved, rather than by sniping from the sidelines. Stuart Devlin, a retired Long Island fire chief and two-term Dream Team president after it became the PTSA, saw the organization as a potential "conduit for correcting the flight of the plane," and ran it accordingly. By contrast, the first president, the more loyalist Cyndy Hancock, had described it as a "support group with no political role to play."

The most immediate need was to improve communications between the school and incoming residents, many of whom seemed not to have gotten the right idea about the school. It was perceived that TCC's housing sales agents, some of whom had transferred from selling Disney vacations and time shares, had been ill-equipped to educate prospective home buyers about the school's nontraditional curriculum.

So, too, the crisis at the school had fractured lines of communications with parents, and created a siege mentality among teachers that would assume an air of permanence over time. Many felt personally attacked and became overly defensive to the point of insularity. When the education gurus—the Johnson brothers and the Project Zero people from Harvard—were flown in for an instructional meeting with the parents to dissipate the first crisis, several of the teachers who were present felt neglected and professionally slighted. The Ph.D.s commanded respect from the assembled parents that the grunts in the classrooms could never expect to earn. Teacher turnover would be brisk during the first three years, despite the support efforts on the part of the "positive parents." In the course of my year—the school's second—an extensive program of education about the teaching methods was launched by the PTSA Dream Team's communication arm and by the school's second principal, Dot Davis—a formal, firm-headed Alabaman with a genteel bearing who had taken on the one job in town that no one coveted.

The campaign to communicate the school's mission and methods was arduous for all involved, but it felt like a Sisyphean task for teachers especially. Teacher-parent meetings I attended in several neighborhoods were dominated by exasperated complaints (usually from male parents) based on badly digested information or opinion. Seemingly oblivious to the reasoning behind the teaching methods, parents posed the same questions again and again: "Why aren't you teaching my son the basics?" "How is he going to know your basic history, your basic geography?" "Who's teaching my child to diagram a sentence?" "Isn't there a better way of evaluating their work?" "How do I know if my daughter is a B or a C student?"

Among all the residents I talked to, there were few who did not reiterate several of the many half-truths in circulation throughout the community. The most common of these wedded together expectations drawn from traditional education with misconceptions about the new. Our children are being held back because of the multi-age groupings; are not getting the basics, especially in math and science, because of the integrated curriculum; are getting the wrong ideas about authority because discipline is virtually nonexistent in the "chaotic" classrooms; are not being challenged because of the lack of competitive incentives; are not being prepared for the rigors of testing that will determine their careers; are unlikely, without grades, to get very far with college admissions; are less interested in being "friends" with their teachers than in learning something from them; are not motivated enough to choose or determine their own education; are simply not learning as much as they were at their last school. Among the openly antagonistic, there was much talk about research showing the "failure" of some of the progressive methods, while others were routinely described as fads. Celebration was ploughing ahead at a time when every state in the nation, it was alleged, was backing off from the changes implemented in the wake of the reform movement. Even Brent Herrington, a "positive parent" by dint of his office, acknowledged to me that the school was "pretty far-out for Middle America."

In the course of the year, children, some of them from prominent families in town, were pulled sporadically from the school. Trying to make the best of a bad situation, the previous administration had let it be known that "this school is not for everyone." More than anything else, this formulation made parents livid. Public education, after all, is supposed to be for everyone, and there were few alternatives for families who had exhausted their credit on their homes in order to be assured of a Celebration education. They felt they had been promised a "public school, with a private school education," and had not budgeted for private school fees. Disgruntled chatter dominated the town's dinner party conversation, street-corner talk, and phone time. In time, individuals made loose attempts to organize the opposition. In December, Joseph Palacios, one of the school's most outspoken opponents, brought together a posse of the dissatisfied parents under the aegis of a meeting for a MENSA group, established for the purpose of getting access to a town facility. At this point, most parents were still too nervous at the prospect of being blacklisted in some way if they called for an open forum. But the covert nature of the MENSA meeting alerted the School Advisory Council (SAC) to the desire for a public forum about the school, and in January SAC scheduled the topic for discussion at its monthly meeting.

People I knew well in Celebration were amused by my passion for SAC. Among the many groups whose meetings I attended regularly, I never tired of listening in on the council's deliberations. On one occasion, during a slow meeting, Jackson Mumey, a council member, gestured toward me. "Look, Andrew is over there, taking his notes, and there will be a chapter in his book about this, so let's pay attention." SAC was nothing if not attentive to the media and outsider opinion in general. The council, representing parents, businesses, teachers, and students, functioned like a think tank on the school's behalf. Notwithstanding its minifactions, SAC often felt like the Praetorian Guard, recruited to protect some inner sanctum of power. Councils like SAC are mandated by the state to guarantee public involvement in the school system. They do so by advising the principal, evaluating decisions about the allocation of funds, and administering a self-assessed school improvement plan. By its second year, SAC had attracted many of the major players in town, who clearly viewed it as a power forum. Its membership was largely male, compared to the predominantly female participation in the PTSA. The PTSA's mass gatherings were informational and inspirational. SAC's much smaller meetings were quite polemical, featured verbal sparring contests, and they occasionally took a philosophical turn.

While SAC meetings were open to the public, they were sparsely attended by parents, at least for the first twenty months. Residents occasionally showed up to voice a grievance, as they did on the first evening I attended in November. By that time, dissatisfied parents were beginning to question SAC's objectivity, insisting that its members were too close to the school to see the warning signs. At the meeting's outset, council member Brent Herrington expressed his opposition to SAC being viewed as a "tribunal for complaints," especially if they were "unfiltered, unsynthesized problems." But having two angry parents, the formidable Linda and Tom Dyroff, sound off a few feet away put paid to that suggestion. After an hour or so of patient listening to the proceedings, they let fly: "We were promised everything would be hunky-dory here this year, and our high schoolers are still not getting what they need. This is Celebration School, and we expect better. Please help us before we take our children away." The Dyroffs had been ardent participants in every Celebration event I had attended, and I was not surprised to see they were as outspoken as they were physically active. Tom, a pharmacist and a weekend hockey coach for the town's kids, told me he "worked hard for twenty years, seven days a week to get here," and he clearly was going to ensure that all of his time and effort had not been wasted.

On this occasion, the Dyroffs' specific concern is with the shortage of math and science teachers at the upper school. Herrington, shifting gear, decides that these complaints may be an appropriate SAC matter after all, since they involve the allocation of funds. Dot Davis, the principal, slowly tilts her lean Modigliani profile and summarizes the difficulty she has had recruiting teachers—"there are no warm bodies willing to teach for this kind of money." Terry Wick, TCC's energized liaison officer, explains that "this is frustrating for us all, and we are trying to push the legal limits to additionally fund the teaching staff. It was only two years ago that the company discovered it could not pay more than an Osceola district wage." But the Dyroffs are not about to be placated softly. Linda launches into a second rebuke against "inappropriate reading material" on a teacher's reading list. It depicts "homosexuality and rape in graphic detail that would make you all turn white." (The offending text, I later learned, was a novel called *Kaffir Boy* about a black male youth's coming of age in South Africa.) "This is out of order," she protests, and demands a better system of "checks and balances." The response to this second outburst is less sympathetic. No one on SAC wants to get mired in morality talk, and the meeting diplomatically winds down.

The Dyroffs believe they are delivering a wake-up call, and there will be many repeat performances from them and others. The desperate tone of their appeals is typical of the climate of fear and frustration that has worked its way into many parents' lives. By the time the discussion of the MENSA group's concerns comes around in January, some SAC members are of a mood to debate the issues. Herrington, again, is a key voice, arguing that there are "folks in the community who feel that they are not being heard, that no one is listening. . . . We can't let these people feel they are underdogs, or they will run to the media." Charlie Rogers, the SunTrust bank manager, regarded by many as the town's alternate "mayor," agrees: "If we don't allow the forum, this group will bring in the press, and Dot will be subjected to all hell." "If it is advertised as a public forum, the press will show up anyway," suggests another member. At this point in Celebration's history, the prospect of press coverage enters into almost every discussion of the town's affairs.

Leonard Timm, an especially active citizen (he had successfully petitioned TCC to redesign bridges, sidewalks, and playgrounds to meet federal requirements for the disabled), is more belligerent: "We will always have splinter groups with philosophical differences. The philosophy of this school is more or less set in stone, and we all bought into it. If folks don't like it, they should go elsewhere." Appreciative of Timm's fighting spirit, Herrington raises the stakes: "We have to have the courage to stand up and defend the curriculum. It's not a flaky religion thing that can't be defended." He reminds us that SAC's job is to "uplift, and not to encourage trashing, along the lines of 'This school sucks!' " Jim Whelan, SAC's sole friendly witness for the MENSA group, takes exception to this remark: "You won't hear comments like 'School Sucks' from members of MENSA." Herrington reaffirms his support for the forum, suggesting that it will give the school's critics "an opportunity to stand up and evangelize. Just like the Oprah Winfrey show." Whelan strenuously objects again, this time to the spirit of the Oprah reference: "These people are sincere, as sincere as you and me, and they speak for a majority." The council concludes with a loose consensus to convene some kind of forum, and to commission a survey of parents, teachers, and students' attitudes toward the school to help with the school improvement plan.

This forum did not take place, largely because there was no appetite for it on SAC and not enough push, at this early date, from MENSA. The survey at hand was conducted, however, and came up with mixed results. Most teachers and students who responded were fairly comfortable with the methods of instruction and assessment. Only a fifth of the parents responded, and almost half registered strong dissatisfaction with the school. The rumor mill alleged that some of the more damaging returns had been pulled by SAC. But the results suggested a gap between parents' and teachers' perceptions of the school. Not even SAC members, widely perceived to be "in denial" about the scope and depth of parental unrest, could ignore this evidence. Among my interviews with residents in their own homes, I had already found widespread discontent with the school, presumably among the silent majority who did not respond to the surveys.

Increasingly all-powerful in public life, survey polls are drastically limited in the information they offer, especially about changing the status quo. They tend to tap into people's short-term interests, but are less worthwhile when it comes to gauging opinions about complex issues. Regardless, their results are easily spun into the weave of given wisdom. A year before, a controversial national survey conducted by Public

Agenda, a public interest group in New York, suggested a fundamental gap between what teaching professionals think and what the public thinks about education. The professionals are more concerned with the process of learning itself, and see the classroom as a place where teachers and students are active, collaborative, lifelong learners. Getting the right answers is much less important than making habitual use of the cooperative methods. By contrast, the public's priority is safe, orderly schools that will graduate students with basic skills and work habits. The gap is greatest between education professors—resolutely opposed to methods of competitive testing, reward and punishment, and memorization—and parents interested in quantitative results and discipline. Teachers, on the front line, are naturally torn both ways, philosophically in step with the professors, but bound in practice to the will of the community where they work. Among the public surveyed, there was little enthusiasm for knowledge that offers no immediate practical use. Some part of this response can be attributed to the native pragmatism of American life and some part to the notorious anti-intellectualism that often goes along with it. Most parents surveyed thought that well-educated people are socially clumsy, impractical, merely "book smart," and generally just "too big for their britches."[3] The survey results suggested that, in matters of education, a deep split ran through American society. Whether or not it corresponded to the same division indicated by the survey, there is no doubt that Celebration School was sitting directly on a fault line. The tremors that shook it were violent, and the damage was amplified by the local geography. The only surprise was that, so far, the carnage had not been greater.

THE LAST STRAW

Before the school year ended, the contracts of several teachers were discontinued. Among them was Troy Braley, a dynamic science teacher in Upper 4, who had found favor among dissatisfied parents by distancing himself from the nontraditional methods. Braley was not afraid to voice his skepticism—"We've been lying to students all along"—or to register his impatience with what he called the "verbal diarrhea" of the teaching mission and the "touchy-feeliness" of the teaching methods. His dismissal was perceived as a rebuff to the concerned parents who were more and more persuaded that their concerns were falling on deaf ears. At the end of June, a group of residents met to discuss the continuing problems faced by the school and to urge concerted action. To avoid being labeled as "bad parents," they gathered outside of town, at the Radisson hotel across route 192. Two nights before, irate residents had met with Town and Country, the builders, and there was a strong sense around town that residents' pent-up frustrations were finally breaking out into public showdowns.

As I entered the meeting, I could see that some of Celebration's most notable furies were present, cooking the air inside the hotel conference room. Pinned to the walls all around the room were lists of grievances against the school collected over the past two years. Scott Biehler, who had boldly organized the meeting, announced that it was unfortunate such a gathering could not yet take place within Celebration, and urged a free and frank airing of views. Among those not present were several parents who had expressed their interest privately but, as Disney employees, did not feel they could attend, or speak openly. The opinions of those who were present ranged widely, from those who fundamentally opposed the school's philosophy to those who simply wanted some cosmetic reform. There were hotheads who had personal grudges to settle and friends of the school who believed things had gotten off track. Larry Rosen, surprisingly, had been invited. As the architect of the school's philosophy, he was regarded as an enemy by several in the room. But the Stetson professor, speaking first, conceded that the curriculum had not been fully developed, owing to lack of resources, and that it had been further hamstrung by Disney's decision to "back off": "Normally, 65 percent of parents are happy with a school," he reported. "We always said that if we had more than 10 percent unhappy here, we'd be in trouble." With this crowd, Rosen was coming in from the cold, but the parents needed his professional credentials to mount a credible opposition, and this was his chance to reestablish a personal connection with the school he had conceived.

Among the thirty-five who attended, accumulated bitterness at being ignored welled up:

- "There have been too many attempts to divide and conquer us."

- "Why have we spent so much to get in here and still have no power?"
- "We do have some power, but we don't know how to use it."
- "We're tired of hearing people say that they are ready to leave town, and of being told to leave if we're unhappy."
- "SAC is in profound denial that there is a problem. They think we don't get it and that this is a reflection of our intellect."
- "The only thing that interests Disney is whether the school is good for the bottom line. They just want to sell houses and hush everything up."
- "We're well-off, we live in Celebration, we should be able to do something about this for our children."
- "The teachers should stop whining about being underpaid. They knew what the salary was when they took the job."
- "We can afford to live here, they [the teachers] can't."
- "These teachers are kids. Kids are teaching our kids."
- "We've been too nice for too long. I say, 'No more Mr. Nice Guy,' it's time to be loud and public."
- "We're pissed, we're mad as hell, and we're not going to take it anymore."
- "If we call the press and announce a massive protest, it will destroy Disney. If a hundred 'For Sale' notices go up on Saturday, we'll get their attention."
- "When they spin and lie, what are we going to do, will we sue?"

These last two sentiments fed into a plan of action based on threats that no one really intended, or wanted, to follow through on. If enough parents in the community could be mobilized behind a list of concerns, the group would threaten to embarrass TCC by taking their concerns to the press during the upcoming events surrounding the launch of Disney's Caribbean Cruise Line. Talk of a class-action lawsuit was more muted, but circulated anyway. In the first use of the cyber network for an independent communitywide initiative, Biehler posted several memos on the general bulletin board, including, "What Brought Us Together," an explanation and summary of the meetings, a long list of "Parents' Concerns," and a call for an "Open Meeting with Parents and Concerned

Citizens." A committee, comprising Rosen, Biehler, and Jack Howard, a sweetly reasonable Herman Miller furniture salesman drafted from nowhere to chair the committee and keep the peace, met with principal Davis and vice principal Ruth Christian. They happily discovered that the school's summer teaching and planning workshops had been aimed at many of the same objectives and reforms favored by the concerned parents. Less fortunately, they also learned there would be strong resistance among some of the teachers to implementing the full diet of reforms.

On July 9, over 170 parents showed up for the open meeting in the school cafeteria. Residents were used to attending meetings called by Town Hall, the Foundation, or the PTSA, but this would be the first independently organized public assembly in Celebration, and attendees were more than aware of its historic significance. While this was an open forum, and while it gave parents a chance to vent in full, it was also skillfully managed by Biehler and Howard, who had shaped the outgoing message: " 'Concerned parents' are those of us who support the school's progressive model of education, but want to see a number of traditional measures adopted." Apparently, the school's administration wanted the same thing, but one obstacle stood in their way, and many of those present seemed to know all about it. At the outset of a long speech that surprised many by its diagnostic candor, Patrick Wrisley, the town's imposing Presbyterian minister, went straight to the point. He denounced the "parading of educational fundamentalism" among several key teachers at the school, and expressed his "concern that there are faculty that do not understand their own principal's and their own administration's desires. Why do they have that much weight?" This question, backed by the minister's authority, was taken as an open invitation for others to berate the teachers in question. Margo Schwartz declared that her "biggest concern is that there is a non-inclusive clique that still runs the school and we are not getting through to them." Others fixated on the resistance of this clique to change: "No clique is going to stand in the way of the mass of parents. If the clique stops us, if Dot Davis can't stop them, we'll go down to the grand opening of Caribbean Cruise Lines and confront the top brass." Very soon, names were named. Prominent among them were Donna Leinsing and Carolyn Hopp, two of the original shapers of the school's mission. More than a whiff of sacrificial bloodletting lingered over the proceedings as the meeting drew to a close. It was a chilling spectacle to witness, not least for a fellow educator like myself. For this community to heal itself, some of its number would have to be cast out.

Within a week, three teachers, including Leinsing and Hopp, had been "reassigned" for budgetary reasons and effectively informed, in their account, that it was in the best interests of the school for them to consider leaving. Hopp was the charismatic team leader of the much-assailed senior neighborhood of Upper 4. I had been following, and occasionally assisting in, her classes throughout the year, and had watched her hold up under immense pressure from parents. Her doggedly loyal students considered her the emotional and intellectual core of the upper school, and, as a non-Osceola teacher, recruited from the Northwest, she had brought national clout to the faculty. She was also the only African American teacher left on staff (the other, her daughter, Wanda Wade, had been let go in the spring). Hopp was clearly startled at the alacrity of the decision, but had rationalized it. "We took a stand, and there was no room for disagreement. We were perceived to be the people with a conscience, and therefore would always stand in the way, and so integrity and honesty would have to be sacrificed." In a less personal vein, she noted, "It comes down to a dollars and cents thing. It's easier for the company to sell houses when they can say that the school really does listen to the community."

Rather than stay on part-time, Hopp resigned and entered a doctoral course of study at the University of Central Florida. Her departure, along with other teachers of color who had earlier resigned or been terminated, meant that the school's faculty would now be virtually all white. For her part, Leinsing expressed less shock at her reassignment (to in-house suspension duties), noting that she had been viewed for some time as a "resister." Rather than stay and "play the martyr," she had accepted a teaching assistantship, also at UCF. Now numbered as official casualties of the Celebration School wars, both veteran teachers were convinced that the administration had reneged fundamentally on the school's bedrock principles.

Members of SAC, the PTSA, and other parents close to centers of power were aware of the "dismissals," some even before the teachers themselves. Among the folks I spoke with, the general attitude was, "I don't want to know too much about it." The departures were seen as the price to pay for peace in the community. In addition, many of these parents had privately harbored their own criticisms of the school, but in their public stance as "positive parents" had been unable to voice them. News like this usually spreads fast on the Celebration grapevine, but I found that, in this case, the details took several weeks to circulate generally. Truly, this was information that no one really wanted to hear about, nor was there any enthusiasm for being interviewed about it by me. While I picked up some general dismay at seeing more teachers let go, there was no mistaking the consensus—this was for the good of the community.

A few days later, another mass meeting was convened at the school by Dot Davis to announce the curricular revisions in the upper school that resulted from the summer workshops. She thanked the staff "for being true to our beliefs" and described the changes as being "in the interests of efficiency." Most of the reforms concurred with the concerns of the parents' group: rigorous test preparations for SAT and HSCT would be introduced along with an Honors Track, textbooks would be bought and issued (though the curriculum would not be "text driven"), discipline would be seriously upgraded, and classes would be taught on a modified block schedule with a focus on basic core course work. Assessments would be aligned more with county procedures, although the school would still not issue letter grades, preferring a numbered system: 4, 3, 2, 1. In the course of the first two years, reform of the grading system had come a long way. Initially, it comprised very soft categories of "extending," "proficient," "developing," and "not yet," which had met with a visible reaction around town. Most parents saw this latest attempt to distinguish numbers from letter grades as a last desperate holdout on the road to normality, but were willing to accept the distinction as a way for the administration to save face.

Hostilities lingered on in some circles, but the July meetings marked a truce of sorts and ensured peace in time for the school to open its doors for the 1998 fall semester. Pressure from the concerned parents' group had been decisive, though the leaders were keen to downplay their impact. "At the very best," Biehler dryly observed, "I hope my son gets an average education." As for the threats of media exposure, Howard explained that the "sabre-rattling helped to make our point and to empower us. We would be the very last people to allow the press to take shots at us." Above all, it was important to avoid the perception that parents had simply walked in and gotten what they wanted. "The changes were already under way," Howard added. "We gave them the strength to implement their plans." While there was considerable relief around town that parents' desires had been heard loud and clear, no one in Celebration wanted to believe its institutions could bend too easily to pressure from residents. That would be a bad precedent, and besides, it was too close to the Disney training philosophy that "the customer is always right."

As the school readied to open for the new year, only one member of the original development team—mild-mannered media librarian Paul Kraft—remained. Hopp, Leinsing, Vogel, and the others had all gone. Terry Wick was being reassigned to Disney's education programs in California, and Larry Rosen was moving out of town for good. In the course of one year, Celebration School had lost twenty-five of the fifty-three faculty on staff, and several more would leave in the first few weeks of classes. On my first return visit to the school, in early September, it was clear that the personality of the upper school, most affected by the reforms, had substantially altered. The sofas had been removed from the hearth areas in the senior neighborhood, and along with the changes in the furniture, there was a sense of detached formality in the movements and interactions of students and teachers. The introduction of fifty-minute class schedules had dispersed the fluid communal environment of the neighborhoods and made interdisciplinary teaching impossible. The schedule, and not the learner, was now driving the day. Faculty were edgy and visibly daunted in response to the official directive that "the slate had been wiped clean." An air of mute discipline prevailed. Many of the students whom I knew had thrived under the old model appeared to be in shell-shocked mourning. Several were "borderline depressed" and having trouble sleeping.

One group, who styled themselves "concerned students" after the parent lobby, had prepared some talking points for discussion with the administration. After all, they were "stakeholders" in the school, according to the mission statement, which assigned power to the "student voice."

> We feel corralled around like livestock. All day it's rush here, hurry there, all within three minutes. We would like personal time—to just BE a human. Where is the time for us to interact on a personal level? We want to feel a personal connection with our teachers. We are wondering why we aren't spending time building personal relationships first. . . . We are wondering how the time will be found for all of us to

> sit down together and speak in depth. Even if we did find that time—we aren't sure that our teachers really know us anymore anyway. . . . We thought that as we grew, the "nurturing neighborhood" concept would be a buffer zone so we could still feel known—really known. The really scary thing for many of us: We were not successful at our old schools. You could say we had fallen through the cracks. Many of us already feel those old thoughts and behaviors creeping back into our minds. . . . That's scary. We liked the new "us" and we want to continue to grow in the direction we were headed.[4]

The talking points got short shrift and the rebuffed students fell into line. By January 1999, on my last visit, their resignation had hardened into indifference. Senior Rachel Binns, a picture of enthusiasm the year before, summed up the new apathy: "We put up blinders, put on sunglasses, do what has to be done, and then go home." Lamenting the loss of the neighborhood's extended family spirit, she confessed that "those of us who saw what it could be like are miserable. We got to learn the how and the why, and now that we just sit and take notes, we're not so interested." As we sat and chatted, it was getting on for four o'clock, and Rachel pointed out that everyone was clearing out of the neighborhood. She reminded me how the year before, students and teachers used to stay and work until seven or eight, and often showed up on weekends. Any link with the past, even my own reappearance in the neighborhood in January, was an occasion for exuberant reminiscences on the part of students like Rachel.

Celebration School now had its own "lost community" for veterans like Rachel and myself to recall with nostalgia. There was some hopeful talk among teachers and positive parents about the pendulum swinging back. "Next year will be different." But I suspect that this kind of togetherness is always lost in time, unsalvageable. Even principal Davis conceded, in an interview on my last day in Celebration, that the compromise she had approved—"to get students on track with their transcripts"—turned out to be "a more extreme swing than we wanted to do. We've lost some of the neighborhood feeling," she acknowledged. "We'd like to reclaim it, and get that common time back." Seated in her scrupulously neat office, filled with plaques and trophies, it was an uncharacteristically wistful comment from Davis. But she must have been a little raw, having survived the mother of all SAC meetings the evening before.

In the previous few months, SAC's monthly meetings had become the target for a renewed assault on the school's methods from the ranks of concerned parents. After the upper school reforms were implemented, the summer group's momentum had stagnated. Convinced that the changes were merely cosmetic, four of the ten committee members pulled their children, and the leadership fell apart. Parents around town began to "partially withdraw" their children, home-schooling them in academics, and sending them to the school for arts classes and wellness activities. In November a new round of public meetings, this time directed at reforming the lower school, took place, cosponsored by Palacios's MENSA group. Organizers noted that several residents who were Disney employees showed up to speak strongly in support of the school. Accusations about a planned "cover-up" circulated. A new note of paranoia was creeping into the opposition camp. Anyone with ties to the company was now suspect. SAC was increasingly being pressured to open more and more of its agenda to public comment from the floor. Everyone was expecting fireworks at the January meeting, thus the video cameras and a full house were in attendance.

As the meeting gets underway, Davis takes a full twenty minutes to read an autobiographical essay. She begins by recalling fondly her time as a principal of "the first, break-the-mold magnet school in Alabama," where a very mixed community of affluent and welfare families "refused to allow disappointments and broken dreams to divide us." It is a barely veiled parable about the quite different atmosphere in Celebration, where earlier that day, the Reverand Wrisley lamented to me that the school's troubles "were destroying the fabric of the community." Davis's eulogy to her past is beginning to sound like a resignation speech, but to the relief of the teachers sitting around me, it segues into her State of the Union address, describing how far she thinks the school has come and how far it has to go. Professionally upbeat as always, Davis cannot resist one censorious reference to the recent loss of teachers "due to pressure from parents who make unreasonable demands." It is her own foretaste of what is to come.

At every subsequent agenda item, the concerned parents in the audience make their presence felt, with pointed questions and comments.

They are clearly determined that this time, finally, the town's education establishment will have to sit and listen. Mike Robinson, a UCF professor who spends part of his week in Celebration neighborhoods, is introduced to report on his survey of studies on multi-age education. He begins by reminding everyone that "there is a much longer history of multi-age education in this country than single-age education." Of the four hundred studies he has consulted, most show there is no difference in academic achievement between multi-age and single-age, some show that multi-age is superior, and all show that multi-age is overwhelmingly superior in nonacademic areas, like student development of social skills and peer relationships. This is a tense moment. MENSA leader Palacios has long mobilized residents against the school on the grounds that there is no research to prove the successes of multi-age education. "I seriously question the validity of the research," Palacios proclaims, rising from his seat, and launches into a sustained interrogation of the basis, span, and age of the studies that will go on, intermittently, for much of the evening, despite the valiant attempts of the chair to silence him. It is clear that he has lost face, however, and some of those parents who have been persuaded by his line on research concede as much when I question them after the meeting. (Others feel insulted that a Ph.D. like Robinson had been wheeled in to set them all straight.)

All is not lost however. Stuart Devlin, the PTSA president, picks up a loose thread. "What I hear is that multi-age education works well for most children, but not for all. So what are we doing for the kids who don't do well?" Danny Bumpus, the nonchalant chair of SAC, observes that there will always be children who "fall in between the cracks." Devlin's question and Bumpus's response appear to sum up the problem for the aggrieved in the audience who are here to vent. The door to full frontal discourse is now wedged wide open. For the next ninety minutes we hear a long string of passionate testimonies from parents, fighting back tears, about how and why Celebration School is failing their children. One refrain is constant: "Disney promised us a world-class education." Off to the side, where I am seated, the teachers boil and fume, pass each other unutterable comments on Post-it notes, and occasionally rise to express their sense of injury or defend a point of principle. SAC members sit impassively in a semicircle, rather like coconuts on sticks at a county fair sideshow, as parents take potshots from the floor.

Finally, the response from some teachers on SAC begins to turn rancorous. Kathy Gross, a teacher who left the school two years before and is now home-schooling her own children, darts across the floor and pounds her fist on the SAC table: "You are not hearing us at all." Things could get physical in a flash. Instead there is a collective recoil in the entire room, perhaps from the prospect of open aggression. Some teachers get up and leave, others present an ultimatum: "There is a negative current running through this community, and that has to stop this evening." An official from the district points out that since the original visionaries of the school mission have left, it might be appropriate to bring in a fresh set of Ph.D.s to address some of the parents' concerns. Dot Davis agrees to chair a committee, including outside experts, teachers, parents, and students, to consider the grievances. Two and a half years after the first blowup at the school, Celebration's concerned parents finally get their public forum and a response from the top that offers the inkling of a way beyond the stalemate. As the meeting breaks up after a draining four hours, one teacher, an old hand, confesses to me that she had expected it would be a lot more bloody. Outside, a confrontation between a parent and teacher almost does turn violent. The next day, combatants can read a blow-by-blow of the meeting's verbal scuffles in the *Orlando Sentinel*, which begins: "It was not a good day in the neighborhood that Disney built."[5]

Nor was it a good week, five months later, in June, when TCC and the school district suddenly announced some new plans. A brand-new 2,000-student high school would be built on fifty acres of Celebration swampland, and the existing K–12 would turn into a much expanded K–8. With 50 percent of the students coming from the surrounding county, these schools would go a long way toward meeting the district's overcrowding problems, but would not sit well with any of the factions among the townsfolk. Celebrationites had not been consulted at all, and in spite of all the tribulations they had been through with the school, the hornet's nest stirred up by these plans looked as if it might be the last straw for many of the pioneers. Ironically, the Hatfields and McCoys of the town's warring camps were temporarily unified in their common opposition to the plans, and so the siege of the existing Celebration school was relaxed for the first time in almost three years.

8

OIL AND WATER

"JAMES BOND"

Once upon a time there lived James Bond. He had to go to the mzeum but he dint have a car, so had to call a taez. The taez didined come, so he wockt 2 days to get there. But the museum wasn't there. It was burnt, so he called the police. And the robbers ran away and never came back. . . . The next day he saw the museum built and James Bond got very happy, with his mother, he went to the museum. James was very happy now. —Poem on a wall, Upper 3 neighborhood

In the year I spent attending Celebration School, I must have thought more about education than I had done in fifteen years of college teaching. Until then, the one sure thing I thought I had grasped was not to expect to see immediate results from my teaching. The most valuable lessons are absorbed and utilized five or ten years down the road when students find themselves in circumstances where the insights make sense. Very little of this can be evaluated in the short term, and least of all by testing. I pointed this out one day in conversation with Marvin Ashmen, one of the town's ex-military residents. Skeptical of the school's alternative methods of assessment, he nonetheless agreed with me. He had been an instructor in the army, he said, and acknowledged that teaching, by contrast with instruction, probably should be aimed at lifelong learning. "But," he added, "we do have to live in the real world."

Most educators don't agree. We contend that education serves best when it shapes the world anew rather than tailors itself to the status quo of the "real world." There has been too much tailoring of late, especially now that schools are cutting their curricular cloth to fit the high numbers game and to meet the cost-benefit analyses of would-be privatizers. Few teachers will deny that the quality and breadth of education suffer when it is approached as a private investment in a competitive market, or when the classroom is treated as a marketing arena in return for corporate-sponsored teaching materials. As for the obsession with testing, colleges are mostly to blame for perpetuating the SAT and GPA system in the interests of boosting their own prestige. Every year, my own employer—the largest private university in the world—touts an increase in SAT scores among applicants. In some other college there is an equal and opposite reaction. Scores have to be decreasing elsewhere. Statistics are a grifter's game: you might win some, but mostly everyone will lose in the long run.

The reforms in the upper school at Celebration felt like a loss, in a short time, and it was disheartening for me to watch the novel energy between teachers and students dissolve and get realigned in more orthodox ways. The iron law of the GPA stifles other forms of learning. Parents moving into town often asked me, as an educator, what I thought of the school. "It will make your child a much better person," I used to say, "though it won't necessarily get him or her into Harvard." The upper school now seemed to be headed in a direction where it would not do either of these things; it would be neither fish nor fowl. For a small number of students, these two goals are not mutually exclusive, but for most they are, and the majority lose out when the pressure to compete kicks in and drives out the rest.

From what I could see, Celebration was a public school besieged by parents' consumer-driven demands for a private school education. "Fix my child" was a prevalent demand. The school's association with Disney did not help. As a result, many parents expected brisk consumer satisfaction. It was also easy to see how Dot Davis could believe that she was "one of the few residents who did not have these expectations." From the vantage point of her principal's office, she had heard the discourse of entitlement loud and clear: "I constantly hear, 'What is Disney going to do for me? What is the school going to do for me? What is the

Health Center going to do for me?' That is not my paradigm. My paradigm from birth has been about helping others. What can I do for others?" Davis was presiding over a school where the public—the realm of rights—was regularly confused with the private—the realm of privileges. This was not a dilemma unique to Celebration, though there were local details, like the Disney factor, that exacerbated it. It is a condition that is more and more common in a society where market dictates are all-pervasive.

IN THE FIELD

The fresh, blue Florida spring had dissolved into a very early summer blur by the time I went on my second field trip with the school, in late April. The mosquitoes were back in business, and the pine groves and palmetto thickets already had a seared and punished look, as if rehearsing for the onslaught of high summer. This time, we were headed for a not-so-magic kingdom in Apopka, just to the northwest of Disney World. As the bus rolled into the Lake County farmtown, we passed shabby two- and three-room shacks sitting squat on the land. Pickup trucks, washing lines, overgrown weeds, and trailer homes lined the thin country roads. A crooked sign announcing "Chikens 4 Sale" was stenciled on the side of a rickety apartment block. We pulled into the lot next to our first port of call, the Apopka branch of the Florida Farmworkers Association, and were greeted by officials and volunteers—Sister Ann Kendrick, Jeannie Economos, and Tania Rosado—who would brief us for our day in the area. Two and a half thousand farmworkers were about to lose their jobs, and we had come to find out why.

This was a field trip I had helped to organize for the students in Upper 4, the senior neighborhood in the school. The intensively farmed lands around Lake Apopka, once Florida's second largest lake and the country's prime mecca for bass fishing, had become an object of great controversy. After decades of pollution from phosphorus and pesticide runoff, the lake was so hopelessly choked with algae that it showed up bright green on high-altitude photographs and the local passions provoked by its cleanup were second only to the bitter public struggle over plans to restore the Everglades. A local environmentalist group, Friends of Lake Apopka—composed of businessmen, attorneys, chamber of commerce politicians, and small landowners—had successfully lobbied the state to buy 14,000 acres of the surrounding muck farms and restore the lake to health. The farmers who had bought their land, drained from the lake, for 25 cents an acre during the wartime Victory Gardens effort were about to walk away with $91 million of state and federal money. The farmworkers, who had been the backbone of Central Florida agriculture for over fifty years, were about to lose their livelihood and their Farmers Home Administration housing. As a result of new immigration laws, most would not qualify for public assistance. From a distance, it looked like a case of environment vs. jobs, the kind of simplified conflict favored by our news media.

But things were much more complex on the ground. Through the research students had done for this trip, they had learned there was no ultimate guarantee that the cleanup—which involved a large-scale plan to filter the water and restore marshland on the lake bottom—was going to work. All told, the regional economic impact of the loss of agriculture would amount to a staggering $120 million a year, and it looked like the cleanup would benefit those (well represented among the environmentalist group) with their eye on the lake as a site of tourist development and luxury subdivisions.[1] As a result of the NAFTA agreements, the site of this agricultural production would now simply move to Mexico, where the lack of environmental regulation allows farmers to treat fields with human sewage.

Lake Apopka had also become infamous after a 1980 pesticide spill caused freakish mutations in its alligator population. Young alligators had shrunken penises and deformed ovaries, and the egg hatching rate plummeted, as it has done more recently in many other Florida lakes. High on the food chain, these prehistoric creatures do not stop reproducing easily, and a sudden decline in their health makes them a sentinel species for all of the state's wildlife.[2] Louis Guillette, a University of Florida biologist, had argued that the DDE spill was the cause of the population crash. His study of Lake Apopka persuasively demonstrated the long-suspected link between pesticides and hormone behavior.[3]

Clearly, there was more than enough to keep us busy at Lake Apopka. That morning, we heard about the plight of the farmworkers, who, for the most part, had been sacrificed in the farmers' scramble to make a deal with the state. Hispanic, Haitian, and African American,

Apopka farmworkers before the last harvest. (Photo: Sister Ann Kendrick, The Last Harvest project, Crealdé School of Art)

many of them elderly, illiterate, and unable to speak English, they would have little chance of finding new jobs in the region without extensive retraining. So far, the state settlement had provided little more than a batch of computers to help them locate new jobs online. This was a world where a Mexican mother rises at 4 A.M. to make lunch and dinner because she will be too exhausted to cook after her long shift in the fields. Later, we visited some of the fields and a packing factory and listened to the owner grumble about the $10 million price tag on his farm. A visit to the lake provided water samples for analysis back in the school's biology classes. At lunch we heard presentations from Jack Amon, former president of the environmentalist group, and John Conner, the director of the St. Johns River Water Management District, charged with administering the cleanup. Each offered earnest accounts, but there were some rough edges. Amon suggested that the workers had not done a great job of representing themselves. Conner reassured us that the environmentalists were "not a bunch of screaming lunatics."

I wondered what the lunatics would have done. From what we had learned, the Lake Apopka settlement was a missed chance to do the right thing for the environment and the workers alike. It could have been a golden opportunity to create a model of sustainable agriculture. A marsh flowway created by Conner to filter the lake water and retain the phosphorus had begun to show results, and further cooperation from the farmers might have led to some creative solutions in the fields themselves. Instead what we got was a corrupted but increasingly common form of environmental politics, where the polluter does not pay and the cleanup boosts the land value of property owners and primes the pump of luxury development.

The students on the trip had responses as varied as their diverse backgrounds allowed. For most, it was their first encounter with migrant workers, while others had parents who had once worked the fields in Puerto Rico. Some instinctively identified with the businesspeople, many more empathized directly with the workers, others were simply glad to have a day out of the classroom. Several told me they felt uncomfortable at being voyeurs of the workers. The next day in government class, students were asked to do some role-playing, representing the opinions of the different groups we had met in the course of our visit. In the course of the debate, the farm owners got short shrift, the workers got high respect, the government agency was coolly received, and the lobbyists generated a good deal of cynicism. With the exception of a few grandstanding males, with a knee-jerk reaction to bleeding hearts who stood in the way of growth and development, students were mostly agreed that justice should be done both to the environment and to the workers. But they clearly doubted that anything quite so fair would ever happen.

The government class was led by Melissa Rodriguez, aided by Debbie Delevan, a popular intern from the Johns Hopkins University. Rodriguez had been recruited as a social studies teacher from the upper Midwest in January, and had hit the ground running. She was the first Celebration teacher whose style I instinctively relished. Socratic and provocative, she pushed buttons, raised hackles, and rabble-roused from the get-go. In return, the students erected a solid wall of complacency. It was a familiar game, and a delight to watch it unravel, even in her first class a few months earlier:

"I grew up in a two-room log cabin without running water in Wisconsin. Part of your complacency is about how easy it is to access everything you want. I need you to come up with something you're going to get riled up about."

"I can feel the passion in this room," one student quips dryly.

"I'm a dyed-in-the-wool Democrat, marched for NOW, went on a hunger strike, and boycotted our junior prom because the district wouldn't provide services for non–English speakers."

A deep pool of silence swallows up this last remark.

"Don't you want to make a difference here?" she asks.

Finally, the dawn of dialogue.

"At the beginning of the year we were vocal, but the administration paid no attention to us."

Rodriguez takes a more direct approach:

"Give me an example of someone who acted against the law, because of their beliefs."

"George Washington, he acted against slavery."

"Harriet Tubman, she helped free slaves."

"Rosa Parks, she stood up for her rights."

"Only three names, in all of American history?" Rodriguez asks.

"Nixon, he broke the law, and lost our trust."

"Where is that bright shining face that wants to be president?"

"Talk to the elementary kids, we know too much about the government's lies."

Rodriguez moves briskly through the classroom, picks up several backpacks, and starts to look through them. Voices are raised in protest. She explains she has the right to do this, and that no student has the right to stop teachers searching their bags, lockers, and cars. "When you enroll in school, you check your rights at the door." Are students full citizens? Maybe not. "I can violate your individual rights to protect others from you." Of all the rights, however, the most important, she declares, is "the right of the governed to start a revolution." One student considers this suggestion to be "mutinous." Another says it "makes for weak government." They are given four weeks to come up with their own "quiet revolution" as part of a service-learning project. The results are mixed. One group opts to find out whether Town Hall has installed surveillance cameras to watch over teen behavior around town. Nothing tangible can be found; all evidence turns out to be anecdotal. Another chooses to petition the school administration to allow students to plan the graduation ceremony. The student council has no effective presence in the school, and this ad hoc group has little chance of holding sway. But they do finally prevail and graduation is organized, this time around, with full student input. A third group is organized to initiate an AIDS Awareness Day in Osceola schools. A much more ambitious undertaking, it slowly dissolves.

Just before the Apopka trip, Upper 4 had successfully completed a project on simulating a local government system. Nominations were made, campaigns were run, and a mayor and city council were elected to preside over mock meetings. The mayoral choice, Marcel Zahner, was already a legend around town. An exchange student from an elite school in Switzerland, Marcel was the walking definition of precocious. As part of an earlier class project on Wall Street, this wunderkind had invested $10,000 of play money in the stock markets and within a month had apparently racked up over a million dollars in returns. Word got around about this feat, and area investors asked him to repeat his performance, which he did with ease. A stock market player since the age of five, his senior project was a business analysis. While Marcel and I were quite friendly, he was cagey about letting me read the research paper, "in case it got into the wrong hands." Some of Marcel's classmates referred to him, rather enviously, as "The Capitalist." At times he adopted the finely tuned politics of a European-style Social Democrat, and at other times inveighed, from the right, against American-style liberalism. He quickly became a model of character building for other parents to judge their Celebration children against. As one put it to me,

"Marcel sees a challenge and makes a beeline for it. My son senses pain and moves away. That's the problem with this school."

In time, the government project yielded to one focusing on utopian communities—the last topic of the year. Students convened into self-selecting groups to draw up the founding principles of their ideal societies. The political spectrum was well represented. On the right, Marcel's all-male group came up with following: security/crime prevention, rights of ownership, small government, limited welfare, no drugs, individual rights, free education, and no laws that violate the founding principles. On the left, a coed group, led by culture rebels like Aimee Ramos and Ryan Frith, had a wish list of neo-anarchist principles: freedom of choice (anytime, anywhere), no censorship, equal opportunity (regardless of sex, age, sexual orientation, and social class), full media publication of all government transactions, free education, free health care, freedom of religion, firearms are prohibited. The other groups were centrist, the exception being a New Age–oriented female cohort, led by the formidable duo of Sarah Fields and Rachel Binns, who listed evident and relevant love, words with meaning, giving (money-free), and equality in numbers. How did Celebration match up? "Diversity is not happening here," claimed the anarchists. The law-and-order group wanted more "structure." The New Age group argued that the school, in particular, could not be an "ethical" institution because its administrators were too authoritarian and hierarchical in their mode of government.

At year's end, Melissa Rodriguez had weathered the storms well. She stole a march on everyone by persuading Patricia Schroeder, Celebration's own resident celebrity politician, to deliver a cheery graduation day speech. A Hispanic-Jewish mother of two, with a keen scholarly interest in the Holocaust, Rodriguez had taught previously in Kenya, in barefoot village schools where paint was applied to the wall to illustrate lessons. Unlike other, greener recruits on the staff, she took everything with a grain of salt. Besides, by the time she came on board in January, Upper 4 was functioning, as she put it, more like a "normal high school in a different building." Given the pressure on seniors to collect graduating credits, classes even then were reverting more and more to single discipline teaching and to traditional whole-group instruction. Teachers had less and less need to draw on those break-the-mold skills for which their recruitment interview had involved questions like "Have you ever broken a law?" (The correct answer, of course, was yes.)

But the turmoil of the summer reforms and faculty departures took their toll, even on Rodriguez. When the fall semester began, she encouraged her students to open a dialogue with the administration about their concerns. She reported that she was issued with a verbal warning for "unprofessional use of student alliances." When this was explained to her by a district official as "inciting students to riot," she could see the writing on the wall. Rodriguez taught her last day of classes, and, with a dramatic touch, wrote her letter of resignation on the blackboard for all seniors to read, before heading back to Wisconsin. At that time I was back in New York, but students were so stunned by this turn of events that they let me know all about it. In retrospect, Rodriguez explained that she had not come all the way to Celebration to teach in "a regular high school," but had left comforted by the knowledge that many of her students "had got it." In her mind, they had understood the goals behind the school's methods and had participated in their own education in ways that are rare for a teacher to witness.

One month later, Charmaine Gabel, the union rep and Upper 3's unflappable mathematician, also called it a day. Worn down by parent harassment and unwilling to watch Celebration become a "prep school instead of the nurturing, creative body it was intended to be," she concluded: "This was no longer the school in which I was hired to teach." Tired of hearing about "bright young people getting out of teaching because of parents," she said she was considering writing a book entitled *How to Eliminate the Teachers from Your Child's School.*

SELF-STARTERS

I first visited Upper 4—the school's sticky spot—at the invitation of team leader Carolyn Hopp, and ended up spending more time there than in any other neighborhood. Trained in the performing arts in North Carolina and France and a veteran of several school start-ups in Washington state, Hopp was a member of the original DNA_2 planning team and hailed from a family of educators. Leroy Walker, her father, had been chancellor of North Carolina Central and, later, president of the

U.S. Olympics Committee. Snapshots of him with Bishop Tutu, Bill Cosby, and Al Gore lined her personal space in the teachers' room.

It was the afternoon of portfolio night, when students show their parents a selection of their work from the past nine weeks. In the classroom where Hopp was teaching, an American flag hung limp by the blackboard, while smaller flags of other nations lined the back wall. Beside Old Glory was a faded snapshot of a pre–Civil Rights multi-age classroom of black children. Off to the right were a picture of Martin Luther King Jr., arms crossed patiently across his chest, and a defiant if goofy John Lennon flashing a peace sign in front of the Statue of Liberty. Ranged around the walls were presentation boards from student projects about anorexia, bulimia, depression, and other phobias and obsessions. By the end of the year, these would be joined by large displays on constitutional rights and amendments, healing the world, and starting a revolution. The hearth area featured a *Combate el Racismo!* sign and tourist posters for Spain, France, and Puerto Rico. Pictures of Geraldo Rivera and Tito Puente hung in the Spanish language classroom, and in the science area, a mockup of the HIV virus posed alongside a depiction of the electromagnetic spectrum. There was little chauvinism in evidence here—I never once saw a pledge of allegiance observed in any Celebration classroom, and the school's dress code was rarely in evidence. These images were not set up as multicultural icons to be idolized. They were matter-of-fact details of the environment that students would simply take for granted.

Hopp and her team were expecting portfolio night to be a highly charged drama, with parental frustration at this new ritual running into the red zone. Many parents would not be satisfied until the school sent a senior to an Ivy League college (and they doubted that "portfolios" would help). An Ivy League admission may happen in time, but it was not a goal emblazoned over the entrance to the senior neighborhood. Hopp had become well aware of the consequences. She took more direct parental hits than anyone else, and her resolve to stand by her, and the school's, principles gave her the scent of a martyr. She considers herself "an educator, not a black educator," and modestly makes the case for "thinking outside of the box" of the bichromatic mentality governing race in America. Regardless, she often underwent a special scrutiny. Months after the fact, she was still rankled by the memory of her encounter with some visiting college educators from the Holmes Group who had tried to take her to task for being a "token" black teacher in the white-bread Celebration environment. "Does it bother you that I teach here?" she had retorted, turning the issue into *their* problem.

The school owed its diverse student body to a decision to draw 20 percent of its enrollment from outside of Celebration. Larry Rosen's original blueprint for the school cited a Diversity Plan, which proposed that the company "through its marketing procedures and approaches will create incentives for individuals to move to Celebration Center who represent a range of ethnic, racial, and socio-economic diversity. This would require a wide range of financial options for prospective residents of Celebration."[4] Rosen recalls early enthusiasm among some TCC team members for low-cost, even public, housing, but these plans fell by the wayside. In this first full year of operations, the student body would be at its most diverse, since residents came nowhere near to filling their 80 percent quota. Nine hundred and four county students had entered a lottery for five hundred places. Hopp was not alone among the teachers in applauding the clear successes the school had registered with many of these students from nonprivileged backgrounds. Angie Morales and Edwin Jo Mrosek, Puerto Rican newcomers to the region and bright lights of the Drama Club, had been overwhelmed in their first weeks in Upper 4. By the end of the first quarter, they clearly had undergone a conversion. "It's like a jack-in-the-box," mused Angie. "Once you're free, you don't want to go back." Aimee Ramos, who had come to Celebration via the Bronx, had worried about being "the loner, the poor girl," and had been astonished at the "new doors that opened" for her among "open-minded peers." She sat between students who lived in low-rent apartments and $300,000 houses, but had met none of the social cliquishness she expected.

From lower-income families, many of these kids were consciously seizing an opportunity that their Celebration peers would take for granted. If anything, they were more responsive to, and supportive of, the progressive methods, and they worried at evidence that classes were reverting to traditional ways. Rachel Binns, one of the most socially confident and articulate of the senior class, had found a perfect fit for herself here: "I went home to St. Cloud smiling each day—a dream come true." A self-starter, she deeply regretted signs that the school's mission was slipping and was glad she had enrolled when things were still fresh and innovative. As for her peers who lived in town, Rachel had a surefooted analysis: "People use their residency for status but many can't afford their monthly bills. It's an instant utopia that they can't afford, and it messes their kids' minds." For other county kids, things had not clicked so well, and they had opted to transfer to another school. All of those who left seemed to have learned something for themselves about their personal educational needs, recognizing that they were not sufficiently motivated to take advantage of Celebration or that they needed more traditional instruction in platoon schools. Here, perhaps, was confirmation that the school "was not for everyone." Some Celebration parents had a different reaction to their departure: "If county kids are not being 'challenged' at the school, then my kids certainly won't be." Months after the lottery, I still came across the rumor that a large number of "problem kids" from district schools had been entered into the competition for places. It was assumed, in other words, that the county had used the lottery to offload its problems much the same way that Cuba had used the Mariel boatlift to export its undesirables.

On the other hand, Upper 4 also boasted many students from within Celebration for whom the looseleaf curriculum had delivered clear benefits. Andy Parsons, the charismatic Phish fan who had held sway over our rap circle outside the cinema back in November, was a case in point. The countercultural foil for Marcel, the clean-cut, stock-buying school mayor, Andy was an alternative mayoral figurehead among the town's teens. After his years as a Massachusetts dropout, he had gambled hard in coming to Celebration, and his arrival in town in August, dreadlocked and dressed for decay, had garnered immediate attention, not least from the police. A staple presence on the streets, he took on a nurturing role for some of the more troubled kids, ran soccer clinics, and kept the peace without forfeiting any of his native gusto. Against the odds, and surprising even himself, he became a valued moral adviser to his peers and reconciled famously with his long-suffering parents. A week before he graduated, he acknowledged that he had been wrong in his dire forecasts about the school. "They didn't mess up my education, but I was a guinea pig." Andy had been self-started by a curriculum that required students to take personal initiatives. But still, he was less sanguine about many of his peers. "Half of the kids don't learn a thing because they lack motivation. They don't belong here, where they don't have worksheets thrust in their faces, or where chapter three follows chapter two." For himself, he was looking forward to an adventurous pre-college year. Through a foundation in Boston, he hoped to be working at a dolphin center in Hawaii, a sheep farm in New Zealand, a greenhouse in Thailand, and in an East African community in the Great Rift Valley. By Christmas, however, Andy was back in town. The world tour had fallen through, but a familiar substitute had kept him busy—Phish's national tour.

BAGELS AND GRAPES

Against the civil rights backdrop of Upper 4's classrooms, it was a little surreal to hear Celebration parents talk about their own "rights" with respect to the school. When I mentioned the Ocean Hill–Brownsville battles over parents' rights in New York in the late 1960s (where mostly white teachers in the New York City public school system were pit against mostly minority parents) to Hopp, she responded that these had been struggles over the power of the school board and not a direct challenge to what teachers were doing in their classrooms. Celebration's teachers had felt the full brunt of parental disrespect in their own workplace in a way she had never imagined possible. "Whose rights," she asked, "are being reduced here?" With a weak union, teachers' grievances had little in the way of an organized outlet and often took a curt and embittered form. A typically resentful comment came from one teacher in the lower school, weary of close scrutiny by the barrage of parent observers and visiting educators' groups: "I feel like a monkey in a cage—'Look, they chew their food.' Leave us alone, and don't make us live here with all the freaks, just pay us more. I'm not here to ruin your child's life." Even the support from "positive parents" got a lukewarm reception from some teachers: "Our spouses are leaving us, our families are falling apart, we can't pay our bills, and all we get is bagels and grapes"—a reference to the appreciation picnics thrown in support of the teachers by the friendly parents.

Resentment of this sort thrived among teachers who felt that their credentials were being slighted by parents who believed that they knew better. This was surely a sign of the times. All across the country, affluent, suburban parents of high-achieving children have strenuously resisted school reforms like detracking, noncompetitive learning, and alternative assessment. From their perspective, reform is unnecessary. The SAT testing system, after all, has evolved into a highly efficient delivery mechanism for propelling their children into elite colleges while relegating the less fortunate to less distinguished points of the compass. Why would such parents support changes in a system that successfully awards their children labels of distinction at the expense of others? If their kids are doing well under this system, they do not support reform. When their children flounder under a reformed program, then that program is likely to be sabotaged by the influence of parents' money, opinion training, and political clout.[5] Something like this was clearly happening in Celebration.

Another part of the story lay in the need for new parents to have some kind of outlet for their opinions that was otherwise denied in town. After all, boomer parents are accustomed to having their say. They had learned the liberating value of voicing their opinions in the course of their own college years, and much of that training arose from questioning the relevance of education itself as a result of the student movements of the 1960s and 1970s. It's no surprise that this generational experience has carried over into strong parental opinions about their own children's education, and that these opinions are viewed as an exercise of rights.

I didn't have to look far in Celebration for a generational profile of the outspoken, credential-conscious parent. Joseph Palacios, one of the school's chief antagonists, was a prime example. A Venezuelan in his early forties who moved to the United States for "security reasons," he had transferred from Boston University to Stanford because he had not felt "intellectually challenged." In the course of our first conversation, Palacios lost little time in presenting his credentials, which included consulting for the Venezuelan Ministry of Education. He was confident about his opinions: "I always give ideas, most of them unsolicited." Neat, energetic, and a self-described "white Hispanic," he early ran foul of Bobbi Vogel, the first principal, and several of the Celebration teachers when he enrolled his daughter at Highlands, their previous school. Somewhere along the way, Palacios's offer to the principal to volunteer his expertise (in Internet technology) had been rebuffed, and a personal enmity had developed between the two: "Vogel was like my high school friends who never advanced beyond what they needed to live locally. She was a local bumpkin, on top of a mountain, who didn't know diddley." He took some personal "credit for getting rid of Vogel," alleging to me, among other things, that she had fixed the ballot for the first SAC elections (for which he had run unsuccessfully). Above all, Palacios believed that Celebration's concerned parents were "better educated" than the parochial Osceola educators who had designed the curriculum, and, once they were out of the way, the parents would have their day.

Although he had given credence, initially, to the school's progressive methods, his skepticism had hardened in the same measure as his dissent had been ignored. Over time, he became an embittered foe of the school and its more prominent defenders, none more so than the education maven Jackson Mumey, who lived directly across from him on Teal Avenue. From the perspective of Palacios, who felt marginalized for his outspoken views, Mumey was the consummate insider—commercially tied to the school, intimate with the powers that be, and, to Joseph's mind, rhetorically endowed with miraculous, but mendacious, spin-doctor skills. Palacios's discontent extended to other features of the town, but he was always careful to distinguish between TCC and the Disney experience. He still went to Main Street, in the Magic Kingdom, to have his hair cut, "for the magic."

The rest of Celebration swung uneasily between the poles of Mumey and Palacios. Closer to Palacios but more open to dialogue was SAC member Jim Whelan, in semi-retirement from a New Jersey career in psychological counseling, who took a very active, scientific role in examining claims about the school. He was especially interested in the behavioral impact of high levels of ambient noise in his son's neighborhood, Upper 3, and cited to me scholarly papers contending that noisy classrooms raise children's blood pressure so that they tend to give up more easily. Whelan even had a pop psychologist's explanation for the defense of the school's methods by the town's establishment: "Just as Finland, when it perceived the Soviets as a threat, began to identify with them, and just as Patty Hearst began to identify with her captors, so too we increasingly identify with what is perceived as a threat here. We begin to question whether the linear approach is the right one, whether rote memorization of anything, even periodic tables, is any good." What exactly is the threat you are describing, I asked? "The unpredictable outcome of this progressive education." Whelan had shrewdly summed up the anxieties of many parents, unwilling to reject the methods that had "done them no harm" in their own schooling.

Among his other volunteer activities around school, Whelan was a highly vocal advocate of E. D. Hirsch's "core knowledge" textbooks, and had stumped at PTSA meetings for parents to use them as home tutors. Indeed, in many of the homes I visited, I saw copies of Hirsch's *What Your 2nd [or 3rd/4th/5th] Grader Needs to Know*. This was a highly conservative approach to learning, viewing pupils as empty receptacles into which digestible bits of knowledge can be poured. Hirsch's methods are aimed at the passive absorption of discrete facts, selected as the crucial information for all citizens to absorb. They ran directly counter to the methods espoused by the school, and must have confused children faced with pressure to respond to both. Whelan's was not the only effort at alternative education. At least one resident, Lauren Adams, was preparing a different course of home tutoring. The "spiritual aspect" of her children's education had been lost when she moved them from the First Baptist Church school in Orlando, and so she was busy coauthoring a guide for parents to teach biblical doctrine entitled *Discipling Your Children*. "Once children have accepted God, what do you do with them then?" she queried, adding that her book would fill a market need. When I asked Adams if she believed Celebration School was too liberal, she thoughtfully made a distinction between "progressive methods" and "liberal content," implying that she was, in principle, comfortable with the former.

There was no doubt that many parents believed the school was too far "to the left of what was natural" and that it was clearly a by-product of liberal thinking that had driven the reform movement in education. Ironically, ever since the milestone year of 1983—when the Reagan administration's infamous *Nation at Risk* report was published—most of the educational reform movement has been far from progressive. The appearance of that speciously alarmist report ("if an unfriendly foreign power had imposed our schools upon us we would have regarded it as an act of war") tethered the nation's economic crisis to the state of the public school system. The anxieties of the day about corporate competitiveness were answered by a nationwide crusade for school improvement by introducing more rigorous competency testing and implementing state and national standards. Most of the time, it was an invitation to cheat and doctor statistics and to squander the potential for learning knowledge that was not forgotten the day after the tests.

In the meantime, the call for reform was also taken up by "education entrepreneurs," who believed that the discipline of the marketplace would force public schools to brave the same kind of restructuring undergone by industry in recent decades. With corporate management rhetoric already entrenched in many education sectors—the public as customer, education as marketable product, learning as efficiency tool—it did not take much to draw public schools into the orbit of the movement for deregulation and privatization.[6] Corporate advocates of reform insisted that if schools were liberated from being monopolies of the state, they would innovate more productively and efficiently in partnership with the private sector. Shortly before becoming secretary of education, Lamar Alexander declared that Burger King and Federal Express should set up schools to set an example of how the private sector would run things.[7] School-business partnerships opened the door not just to Total Quality Management but also to every corporate huckster looking for ways to promote and build brand loyalty in "the K–12 marketplace." Tax-supported school vouchers and union-free charter schools were introduced and were seen, respectively, as the fast and the slow track toward privatization. Every CEO worth his or her salt intoned that corporate reform would bring schools more in line with the needs of industry, and thereby provide solutions to the nation's economic problems.

Fortunately, most educators, and enough policymakers, cannot afford to declare that schools exist solely to meet the industrial needs of corporations. They know that the concept of public education is historically tied to the training of a democratic citizenry. Yet the encouragement of independent, critical thinking among youth—the mark of an active citizenry—does not lead to the compliant workforce desired by corporations. The questioning of rules, traditions, and authorities is deemed undesirable except among "responsible" elite students being prepared for entry into the professional-managerial class. So how do progressive educators justify their reforms? One of the easiest ways is to appeal to the "new" industrial skills of cooperative problem solving. Progressive schooling, then, is often presented as a response to corporate managers who say they want employees who can work together in groups rather than compete against each other as goal-achieving individuals. Dot Davis repeated this standard defense to me, implying that, these days, no one had any use for fact-ingesting robots: "That's not what business and industry wants. It's a lot easier to sell what we do because of the demand of business and industry for people to work together as a team, who can write grant proposals, who can construct things. We used not to teach children to do these things, we taught children to fill in the blanks."[8]

While they may pay lip service to "the demand of business and industry," principals like Davis know that this does not serve the cause of public education, at least not for the mass of students for whom there simply are no problem-solving jobs out there in the service sector. The ideals of nontraditional education make much more sense if you relate them to a democratic rather than to an industrial training. From this perspective, competition in the classroom is socially damaging. It stigmatizes those who fall short and habituates the majority of children to thinking of themselves as failures, rather than as active participants in society. The healthier and more democratic alternative is for students to learn from, and work alongside, their peers in pursuit of some common goal. As the story of Celebration School shows, this alternative is on a collision course with what "academic excellence" usually means for parents—rewards for the best and brightest, as determined by the numbers game of high-stakes testing.

Privately labeled as the "keeper of the vision" by her colleagues, Donna Leinsing, the school's poised director of curriculum, had a reminder from Einstein mounted on her office desk: "Not everything that counts can be counted, not everything that can be counted counts." She also had Warhol's silkscreened "The Art of Mickey Mouse" on her wall. One was a dignified rebuttal of the number-crunching mania that presides over public education and so much of public life. The other was a gently ironic tribute to her school's chief sponsor. Until she was ousted in the summer, in what she termed "a hostile takeover," Leinsing's confidence in the mission of the school—"we changed the paradigm . . . it had to happen all at once"—was as steadfast as her underestimation of the power of parents to change it back. When I first queried her about the dissatisfied parents, she asserted that they were simply "unused to change" and that the hubbub around the school was nothing more than "small-town politics."

Leinsing's ouster proved otherwise. The fact is, schools like Celebration are few and far between in upscale suburban communities. Andres Duany likes to point out that in urban planning, "one must never experiment with the poor; they are already under stress. Experiment with the rich because they can always move out."[9] This principle is exactly the opposite of what prevails in the planning of education. Savvy policymakers will tell you not to "experiment" too much with a Celebration-type population. Nontraditional education is more ordinarily tried out in depressed, central city areas where there is "nothing to lose" from the perspective of educators. One couple who had pulled their son from the school in the first year curtly described the Celebration curriculum to me as a program more appropriate for "keeping inner-city ghetto kids off drugs." It was not uncommon around town to hear talk of the school's "inner-city curriculum."

In the search for existing educational models for the Celebration School, handpicked county principals and administrators had undertaken a national tour, including stops at inner-city schools. According to Candy Parker, one of those county principals, they were hard put to find high schools that fit the bill. She recalled only one, Schomburg High School in the Bronx, a school for students who had been expelled at least twice from other schools, where the team found that integrity and commitment to "habits of mind" had shown outstanding results. They also looked at Central Park East, the East Harlem school most often cited as a reference point by Celebration's teachers, which was pioneered in 1974 in one of New York's poorest communities, with test scores, at that time, "that placed it last out of the thirty-two city districts."[10]

While concerned parents saw their children as part of an "experiment," and repeatedly used this term, teachers insisted that Celebration was not an experimental school. Its methods (or "best practices," in TCC's corporate jargon) had all been tried out elsewhere, some of them in Central Park East two decades before and many more in the schools (over a thousand nationwide) affiliated with Theodore Sizer's Coalition of Essential Schools, the progressive alternative to E. D. Hirsch's Core Knowledge Foundation. While the methods may not have been experimental, at least three aspects of Celebration School were highly novel: its location, in a community of parents accustomed to getting what they had paid for (including high test scores); the nature of its corporate partner, from whom parents had expected much more than they thought they had gotten; and the rural profile of the school district, still grappling, as one school board member put it, with a crippling "inferiority complex."

KOWBOY COUNTY

In Osceola County, the school's methods might well have been branded as communistic not that many years ago. Would they have met with a similar reception if they had arrived in Kissimmee without a Disney copyright attached? How did the school figure on the county map? The politics of the school board more or less reflected a county that had transferred its seasoned Dixiecrat loyalties to the Republican Party over the last decade. This had produced some strange fruit.

Deena "Dee" Stevens, the crankish board representative for the western end of the county, which included Celebration, had run in 1994 as a moderate Republican against a Democrat whom she openly described as a "redneck." One of her tasks, as she presented it to me, had been to stave off the efforts of the Christian Coalition to control the party and the school board, although no one I consulted could offer any evidence to substantiate her claim. She prided herself on her New York degrees in education and her passing familiarity with the latest ideas, and lost few opportunities to put down her board colleagues and her numerous public detractors, as hopelessly provincial—"I'm too sophisticated for them down here." After I had met with Stevens a few times, she called one evening to warn me "not to get too involved" in the affairs of the county. "Don't ask too many questions. The Klan is active here." I was curious to know what kinds of questions would bring the hooded ones to my door. "You don't want to get involved," she warmly counseled, "a lot of things happen in this county."

If I had been talking to any other elected public official, I might have been alarmed, but Dee Stevens was truly a world unto herself. As one county principal confided, "Dee comes from a long line of Osceola County crackpots, just this side of sanity." Recently, she had been in the newspapers a lot, on account of her numerous lawsuits against fellow board members (one had cut her "maliciously" during a meeting by handing her a sheaf of papers), the board attorney (for checking up on the veracity of her educational background), and, most infamously, a citizen who had launched a drive to petition Florida's governor, Lawton Chiles, to recall her from office. As Dee put it, "They always put me in the headlines because my name makes news. I can understand how Jackie Kennedy felt." On occasion, she had been escorted from school board meetings by a deputy for too zealously pursuing her complaints. Celebration School had not escaped Dee's litigious fervor. A lawsuit had been entered against two officials who, Stevens alleged, had conspired to keep her name off the ceremonial plaque in the school office lobby.

Her appetite for justice aside, Dee presented herself as a friend of the school—"I'm a true believer." With something of an arty background (a degree from the Fashion Institute of Technology and a brief sideline as a fashion show radio host in Kissimmee), she liked to identify with the avant-garde spirit of Celebration School and with the "creativity" of Disney. But she had mastered enough of the art of local populist politics to deride, at the drop of a hat, the principles behind its curriculum: "The teacher and the learner are related to one another. It took them thirty years at Harvard, and that's what they came up with. I mean, anyone can tell you that. You're the teacher, they're the students, they're the learners and you're the teacher, right? If that's the most they can come up with, then I don't know. I'm not an expert, but . . ." Dee could yuck it up with the good old boys when it came to putting down the fancy stuff out of Harvard. Oddball that she was, she knew a thing or two about lobbying for votes in a county unreceptive to anyone putting on airs and graces.

These days, when people decide to move somewhere new, they scan statistical profiles of the district to find out if the schools are actually as good as the real estate brochures claim. They also want to know about the composition and agenda of the local school board. Captivated by the Disney promotional literature, it's unlikely that many Celebration residents gave more than a passing thought to the makeup of the Osceola board. They had been led to expect that the new school would be "world class," and Disney all the way. Charmed, perhaps, by all the CEO talk about corporate school reform, they had pictured a school that would have nothing in common with the county system's low test scores and undistinguished educational record. Those who had a passing acquaintance with the workings of the Florida public school system might have had more foresight. But no one could have foreseen the impact on the town of several years of battle-hardened negotiations between TCC and the board, both before and after the school's opening.

Much of the early friction revolved around the opposition of Martha Anderson, a fairly liberal Democrat and the sole board member to vote against linking the school to the district. Anderson believed the school would drain resources from other county schools. She was uncomfortable with the use of the school as "a marketing centerpiece for the town of Celebration," a "Disney promotional opportunity for which other county schools would have to make a sacrifice." In Anderson's opinion, other schools did suffer once the Celebration contract was signed. A planned wing of a Kissimmee school was sacrificed, and already crowded classrooms overflowed when student stations were assigned to Celebration, a site at that time without any population. Some of the district's leading professionals became fixated on the intellectual romance of the Celebration curriculum, anxious to make their mark on an institution in a way that would enhance their CVs. Other schools were treated like "neglected stepchildren." The cost, Anderson acknowledged, was difficult to measure in dollar amounts, but the psychological legacy was clear enough to see in the countywide prejudice against Celebration.

Anderson was defeated in her, by now, Republican district in 1994, but other members' bipartisan concerns about equity in funding persisted long after the school opened in 1996, generating no end of friction between TCC and the county. In an emergency measure in the fall of 1997, the board finally allowed the school to use a major portion of its enhancement funds to meet its staffing problems. These funds had originally been designated to support the school's innovative programs, and, in keeping with the school's contract, were not supposed to be used to subsidize regular staff recruitment. Among Celebration stakeholders, the board's approval was seen as a victory and a turning point. By February 1998, Jackson Mumey was able to declare in a SAC meeting that "relations with the District have seen a 480 percent turnaround from last year. A year ago we were more like an oddity to be punished—a group under siege from, rather than a part of, the district."

By that time, however, many pioneers saw that Celebration might be better served by having its own representation within the county government. At some point, it was assumed, townsfolk would be active in seeking public office. Much sooner than expected, Celebration would field a candidate in the very first election to be held since the town was established. At the end of March, after much consultation among the town's elite, Mumey announced he would be running as an independent in the school board race in November 1998. Even before he threw in his hat, he admitted to me that he didn't "hold any illusions that a white male businessman from Celebration with a law degree is the people's choice in Osceola County." But Mumey's family had long been in the education business—his Vermont ancestor was Justin Morrill, who sponsored the seminal Morrill Land Grant Act of 1862, establishing over seventy land grant colleges in the Midwest and far West—and he had already made a favorable impression by serving on one of the district's education commissions. A highly articulate liberal, Mumey's candidacy would be an early test of how Celebration was going to play in county politics.

Like most of the school's friendly stakeholders, he was an advocate of the role played by private corporations in sponsoring public schools, but worried that the district's stingy treatment of Celebration had not set an attractive precedent. "A lot of private companies right now are reluctant to partner with this school board because of Disney's experience of being kicked in the teeth. Some of these companies have looked at Disney's experience and said, 'We're not sure that this is an environment where we'd want to get involved, without a school board that's going to be more supportive.' " Mumey dismissed any concerns that corporate funding might influence educational content: "No company really wants to be in the education business. If there was a company that was really interested in control, the epitome of that would be Disney. They are the most controlling, and if they've been willing to back off and say we're not controlling the school, I certainly don't see Quaker Oats saying we need to control the school to contribute to it." On the other hand, he believed that any company that wants to earn

The Mumey family and their Cottage home on Teal Avenue. (Photo: Jonathan Hayt)

community goodwill "needs to do more than have their plant manager become the chair of the chamber of commerce." Mumey would advocate a school board putting strong pressure on developers and companies to build a school on any site with more "than a handful of homes." In line with the Celebration model, Mumey believed that a percentage of the places in these schools (20 percent in the case of Celebration) would be open to all children in the district and would disperse their influence accordingly. The goal was to build schools without raising taxes.

Acknowledging that Mumey may be an "enlightened candidate," Anderson judged his views as "politically naive." "He doesn't have a prayer," she added. An orchid grower, she was a businesswoman herself ("I believe in the capitalistic system"), but had learned a lesson, from her experience with Disney, that a "line had to be drawn between private commerce and public education." Indeed, at an early meeting between the board and TCC officials, she had warned the company, "You really don't want to deal with us. It's like mixing oil and water. We're more trouble than it's worth." Anderson, an ex-teacher, was referring to the potential conflicts between private and public interests. Disney, after all, had had very little experience with the public domain. Never once, she maintains, did she worry about the company's interference in the school curriculum. Other companies in the county would be a different story: "As for some of these developers, I wouldn't want a penny from them. . . . They're not enlightened enough to trust with preserving the freedom of educators."

All the current board members (who, in Florida, enjoy a salary greater than that of an entry-level teacher) and many of the district's school principals shared Mumey's view that corporate partnerships were relatively benign. "If they want a better product," said board member Judy Robertson, who raises emus in her family business, "it's in the company's interests to contribute." Was she worried about the potential for using the classroom to promote company products? "People are bombarded by commercialism," she replied. "Why should schools be any different?" Pete Edwards, chair of the board, as well as of the St. Cloud/Greater Osceola County chamber of commerce, recalled a failed, and admittedly shameless, attempt to interest companies in advertising in county schools: "We would have had final review of the ads, and they would have been tasteful." A Republican, Edwards was generally keen on corporate partnerships, but, in light of the Celebration experience—"the enhancement funds caused more trouble than it's worth"—he thought that public authorities would need to come up with much stricter rules about the use of additional private funding to ensure fairness.

This last point was a relatively minor fiscal matter, but it had become a politically charged issue, resonating throughout the county system. Several school principals whom I interviewed confirmed the intensity of feelings about the subject. Mike Smith, head of Ventura Elementary, verified the countywide perception that all of the rules, from funding to busing, were being bent to accommodate the new school.

"Local folks had started out thinking, 'We're building a private school for Disney, and that's not right,' " (the district took hundreds of calls to that effect) and pointed out that public relations had not improved much now that the school was built. Along with others on the board, Smith predicted that, in time, it would become a charter or private school.

As a member of the county's design team for Celebration School, Candy Parker, principal of Pleasant Hill Elementary, agreed that the concerns about equity had hindered progress, and regretted that some of the initial vision and planning—especially plans for personalized learning and vocational training—had also fallen by the wayside. As for the involvement of the private sector, Parker was of no two minds that "education has shot itself in the foot by shying away from corporations." Resistance to privatization had been "massively detrimental" and "it's all coming back to haunt us now, with the charter school movement."

Gary Mogensen, head of Hickory Tree Elementary and ex-principal of St. Cloud High, was plainly sympathetic to the aims of Celebration School. He himself had been forced to abandon authentic assessment because of parental opposition among his school's poor rural residents. Nonetheless, he acknowledged that the promotion of Celebration had come off as high-handed: "It was like the Ugly American in the 1950s, landing in Costa Rica and saying to the locals, 'Look, we have all these wonderful things we're going to sell to you.' " In particular, the school's promises about access to advanced technology had ruffled many feathers. Thanks to its corporate donors, Celebration had up to six high-speed T1 Internet connections by now (plus a host of Sun Unix servers and Java stations), while most county schools barely had access to one. But Mogensen reserved his real frustration for the policies of Florida state legislators, devoted to a senseless regime of testing and standards, and for an economic system that had taught children to accept educational failure, poverty, and minimal expectations about their future. If anything, Celebration had the chance of being "a haven of intelligence in the hostile world" created by these legislators. Fond of drawing analogies to fascism, Mogensen felt more and more trapped in the "Nuremberg problem": "Your leaders are mad and bad, and the more you comply and follow orders, the more you are personally responsible."

None of these administrators was opposed, in principle, to corporate sponsors. Even Mogensen had twenty-eight small business partners who contributed, in what he felt were benign ways, to his school. Smith, who personally dislikes advertising, confessed: "If I have to put a Pepsi sign at the entrance to my school, I have no problem with it . . . as long as there's no strings attached." Among the county principals who worked on the Celebration project, only John Beall, the principal of Kissimmee Middle School, drew the line at private sponsorship. He had turned down an offer of Pepsi ads in his school: "I don't feel comfortable going cap in hand to Home Depot."

Donna Hart, the only Democrat on the board, playfully described these other county schools as "bratty older sisters," envious of the younger Celebration, and explained that a board member was like "the mother of thirty different children all competing for your attention." Insisting that county support for the Celebration methods had always been firm, she recalled the idealistic "fire in the belly" of the Disney development team: "They had wonderful dreams, but things didn't always work out that way after they discussed things with California, when they were told to look out for the bottom line." Acknowledging that corporations' involvement in schools can be dicey—"they are like guys on a date who pay for dinner and think, 'What am I going to get out of it?' "—she has a different angle on corporate support of education. For her, anti-tax sentiment among voters is not a selfish evasion of the obligation to fund public institutions: "I don't see it as a shameful resistance of people to paying their taxes. The whole system has been borne on the backs of workers. People are saying 'We've paid all these taxes and corporate America has gotten fat. It's time they paid their due.' We'll end up paying for it all anyway, through an increase in sale prices."

In the last twenty-five years, corporations have become fly-by-night entities, devastating communities when they decide to relocate in search of cheaper labor, better tax treatment, and higher profits. In the course of the corporate era, and especially during the postwar period of stable union wage employment, workers came to expect a level of infrastructural support for social and community life from large employers in town. These expectations dissolved with the cruel advent of capital flight, downsizing, and rapid restructuring. The new industrial landscape is populated by companies willing to locate only on the condition that they are handed preferential tax exemptions and wage concessions.

In turn, these corporate tax breaks weaken the tax base for public education. The result is an environment—here today, gone tomorrow—in which management sees no obligation, or any real incentive, to invest in the social life of a community, and so very few do. Locally, there's little chance that a company like Disney, with its capital fixed on the land, will uproot, but it remains the case that all such decisions are answerable to market swings and stockholder anxieties. Every page of corporate history reminds us that even the "cloud-capp'd towers" of Disney World could melt into air if the price was right. If education is to remain a matter of public trust, why hang that trust on an itinerant peddler of fairy tales?

Like others, Candy Parker was enthusiastic about her experience with the original members of the Celebration development team—"they were on exactly the same page as us"—but regretted their departure—"we never imagined it would be turned over to managers," referring to the shift in TCC management in the summer of 1997. The "strong trust level" she had felt was a turn of good fortune in working with individuals who had approached the task with passion and commitment. But what of the near future, and the long term, when the bottom-line managers have erased any memory of the creators' aspirations or benign will? Should company stockholders be expected to care? What do Pepsi, McDonald's, General Mills, and Campbell's Soup have to gain from helping students to become broadly educated citizens as opposed to loyal consumers of their products? Nothing, nor should we expect them to. Entities geared to opening up new markets for private profit cannot and should not be expected to cater to the general welfare. Too many educators already use teaching aids and packets of materials, "donated" by companies, that are crammed with industry propaganda designed to instill product awareness among young consumers: lessons about the history of the potato chip, sponsored by the Snack Food Association, or literacy programs that reward students who reach monthly reading goals with Pizza Hut slices.[11] There could hardly be a worse way of guaranteeing the public interest in education than by turning it over to corporate hucksters, or even by entrusting it to temporary corporate executives, however sympathetic, who see a way to boost the PR ratings of their employer by doing a few good community deeds. In the corporate world, allying with a well-known brand name is like hitching your wagon to the brightest star in the firmanent, at least until the next stock market swing, leveraged buyout, or disappointing quarterly statement. But public trust needs the support of earthly bodies, in an orbit that is dependable, for the long run. When a society allows public education to be dependent on lottery funds or the passing benevolence of toy manufacturers and soda producers, it has already walked away from its democratic obligations.

THE FIRST HURRAH

When Jackson Mumey first announced his run for the school board, few people outside of Celebration were willing to give his candidacy much of a shot. Mostly everyone paid lip service to the axiom that "you can't get elected as an independent in this county." But Jackson, ever big on data, had done his homework and hired a polling agency to estimate his chances. The animosity to Dee Stevens's antics was so widespread that there seemed to be an opening for him to run. Others had seized on the same idea. Within two weeks, five candidates had declared, and Dee was having second thoughts about her own plans for reelection. In any event, she had already put her finger on what she hoped would be Jackson's weak spot. "Where does he get his money from?" she asked. "Nobody owns me," she added. Just before she opted out of the race, she alleged that Celebration PTSA was being "run like a political machine" on his behalf. At the next PTSA meeting, each of the candidates had a chance to stump, and Mumey made his debut speech in front of a home audience. Streets ahead of his opponents on every count—speaking skills, issue relevance, common sense, and sheer persuasion—Mumey concluded by pledging to hand over his $25,000 salary, if elected, to the county's school advisory councils each year in the belief that board membership should be a public service and not a paid position. It was a bold move, calculated to attract the kind of media interest he needed to bring in votes. Risky, too, since it fed into the perception of Celebration as peopled by wealthy individuals who could afford to forgo a substantial source of income as if it were a peppercorn rent.

In Celebration itself, Jackson had a mixed constituency and could not be certain of too solid backing. He was bitterly disliked by the school's antagonists—one referred to him as an "educational thug"—and had caused a stir when his company was engaged to do SAT preparation testing for students at the Celebration School. Disney funds, in effect, had been used to pay him without the approval of the school board. In addition, his critics alleged that in his capacity as a paid liaison between the school and home buyers, he was in a position to "screen" prospective residents on the basis of their attitudes toward the school. Aside from the ancillary positions he held at the school, Jackson was perceived to be powerful because of his verbal skills. Several residents referred to his "ability to manipulate words"—the signature of the slick lawyer. In this capacity he had wielded his influence in opposing, decisively, a groundswell of support for school uniforms. In his PTSA speech, his Republican rival spoke of trying to mend the rift between Celebration and the rest of the county, a feat that Mumey would have a tough time replicating. One resident compared Jackson's chances to "eating an ice cream in hell." Nonetheless, the town's establishment got firmly behind him and put up some solid backing for his campaign. He would run on an empowerment ticket, speaking to countywide concerns that the school board wielded too much power.

Within Celebration, Jackson faced the task of persuading residents that he was not running as an advocate of the school itself. By his own admission, this was an "ugly task." "In this town," he confessed, "I've been dragged from pillar to post." At fund-raising receptions hosted in residents' homes, he encountered a fair share of ill will directed at the school. The goal, as he put it, was to convince "those who don't necessarily agree about the school to wear my button in the interest of rallying around a candidate from Celebration." In the county at large, he also sought to distance himself from the school and from Disney, though the press would inevitably run cartoons of Celebration candidates, present and future, wearing mouse ears. Independently wealthy, he took no corporate or PAC money, and put a cap of $250 on individuals' contributions to his $50,000 campaign—an unheard-of war chest for a school board candidate. His campaign sent out thousands of mailings, put up hundreds of yard signs, ran a battery of newspaper ads, and won hands down the endorsement wars by earning the backing of the Teachers' Association and several powerful county figures. By the time he had collected enough signatures for a place on the ballot, Mumey had appeared in enough flea markets and shopping malls to win extensive name recognition around the county.

But nothing could break the stigma carried by his place of residence. Anti-Celebration sentiment helped his Democrat rival win the day in the final polling. All the same, Mumey took 21 percent of the vote, the highest ever recorded by an independent in a county election. More significant were the patterns set by Celebration voters. The precinct had a little over one thousand registered voters, of whom 551 were registered Republicans and 219 were Democrats. In all the other races, Celebrationites pretty much voted along party lines. The Republican bloc, in particular, had quite an impact on one or two of the county races. In the home race, the majority of residents pulled for Jackson, but the strength of the anti-Mumey faction within town also took its toll. A substantial number of residents voted for Democrat Mike Harford, who never once set foot in Celebration to campaign. Mumey was bitterly disappointed, and sounded like an exhausted presidential campaigner: "I don't want to put my family through that experience ever again." Soon, however, he was being approached to run for county commissioner. His first run for office had proved that Celebration would have a colorful and not at all predictable career in local politics.

9
IT TAKES A VILLAGE

The sable slave, from Georgia's utmost bounds,
Escapes for life into the Great Wahoo.
Here he has left afar the savage hounds
And human hunters that did late pursue;
There in the hommock darkly hid from view,
His wretched limbs are stretched awhile to rest,
Till some kind Seminole shall guide him through,
To where by hound nor hunter more distrest,
He, in a flowery home, shall be the red man's guest.

—Albery Allson Whitman, 1884, from *The Rape of Florida*

The DJ is cranking out dance classics—every one a winner—but it's slow going on the dance floor of Southern Nights on a rainy Tuesday evening. Jeff LaMendola and I are on a mission at one of Orlando's oldest and most popular gay clubs. The first gay mixer in Celebration—a historic, though unofficial, milepost in community building—is set for Friday, February 13, and we are on the lookout for a bartender to keep everyone happy. Toward midnight, the go-go boys climb on their pedestals and start winding their waists around the booming bass and drum beats. None of the bobbing hunks Jeff asks can work this weekend, and he won't invite the one who can because he doesn't seem quite right for the job—too much attitude, and a little too butch. I suggest we hold out for a nonprofessional, and so we decide to stay for the Amateur Strip Contest. The winner, Rick, is surely our man. Superbuff, with a bashful smile and a level blonde tuft on his cropped head, he reminds us of Ed Harris's John Glenn in *The Right Stuff,* and who better than a glamorous astronaut to please the gentlemen of Celebration? Jeff wants him to tend bar in a snug Cupid outfit, but we figure—accurately, it turns out—that Dave Eaton, our discerning host, will favor a more discreet profile for the weekend's guests—the smattering of gay men who live or work in town, plus a swelled party list of male friends from the metro area.

Indeed, it's not until late in his shift at the party that Rick gets to take off his formal gear and work Dave's kitchen bar in his black jockey shorts, combat boots, and suspenders. In the course of the evening, he has learned how to mix a martini, and we have been regaled with stories about his skills as an animal trainer, recently hired at Disney's new Animal Kingdom theme park to train Pocahontas's raccoons and skunks to strut in front of crowds and wave. Among the guests are Cary and Bruce, also Disney employees and Celebration's very first gay residents, obliged finally to leave town because they couldn't afford a house, and after their apartment had to be rebuilt when the walls collapsed. They confirm a suspicion long held among this party crowd. Disney's gay employees do indeed group themselves in particular areas of the theme parks—in the Magic Kingdom, it's Tomorrowland for butch men and lesbians, Space Mountain for the not-at-all butch, and, in EPCOT, the Horizons and General Motors (Ho-Mo) pavilions for everyone. Among the other guests, there's much shoptalk about same-sex partner benefits at Disney and other area companies. Everyone in this group has stories about their dogs, substituting for the conversations about children that are obligatory in straight Celebration.

There is a polite consensus that this will be the first of many gatherings. Jeff, the manager of the town's antique furniture store, knows the evening has gone well, but is still miffed that several of his friends hadn't shown up. Dave, our host, is clearly relieved to have pulled the whole thing off. This is not his first effort at community building in

Dave Eaton, president of Celebration Players, raises a glass. (Photo: the author)

Celebration. As president of the Celebration Players, he has had community theater up and running since his first weeks in town. The play list has included Neil Simon one-act comedies, *Ten Little Indians, Steel Magnolias,* and a British sex farce, *Run for Your Wife.* Retired from treading the boards after a career in dinner theater and children's TV (for a spell he held the role of Bozo the Clown for an Ohio network affiliate), Dave now owns a chain of Magic Stores on the Kissimmee strip and in other parts of the country. Described to me early on by the company communications officer as a model citizen, there was no doubt about his reasons for moving to Celebration from rural Polk County—he has "a passion," he says, "for the town's aesthetics." Dave has been trying for months to coax me (a stalwart of the drama society in my college days) into the troupe, but *The Fantasticks,* currently in rehearsal, is not my cup of tea. Before my year was out, he successfully persuaded me to don a theatrical costume. In my last volunteer capacity in Celebration, I played the role of George Washington, leading the town's 1998 July the Fourth parade down Market Street. Apparently, my per-

July Fourth, 1998. Mike Turner debates a fine point of military history with Lise Juneman and the author (aka George Washington). (Photo: Elyse Cheney)

formance was less than convincing. I overheard at least two spectators in the crowd explaining to their children, "Look, it's Benjamin Franklin!" Another, no doubt hallucinating in the hundred degrees of midsummer heat, hailed me as Abe Lincoln.

At the end of the February evening's festivities, Dave sees me to the door. It's damp and chilly, Longmeadow is shrouded in mist, and the white townhouses off to the right in Savannah Square are a Victorian phantom from some operatic demimonde. A Gilbert and Sullivan devotee, he sighs on cue, "It's almost like London."

Dave and I had discussed hosting a weekly talk show with selected residents on the town's community TV channel. Both of us knew it wouldn't fly. Town Hall wasn't quite ready to risk putting Celebration's dirty laundry on display. But we would have made a good team. In common with many residents, he had, at one time, speculated I would be writing a book like *Midnight in the Garden of Good and Evil.* No doubt he secretly coveted the role of Jim Williams, the Savannah bon vivant who is tried for a crime of passion. I assured him and others that if there were a scandalous homicide, I would try to do it justice in writing. While Celebration had been physically modeled, in part, after Savannah, it did not have the Georgia town's pedigree, nor its libertarian morals, but there was a general small-town hunger for scandal here. Besides, many residents are convinced that a nut with a gun—probably a disgruntled Disney employee—will march into town one day and open fire.

So far, the scariest intrusion had been a car thief who took a wrong turn into town and hid out in the wetlands while police helicopters buzzed the skies all night. The story was quickly embellished. The felon, it was alleged, had been living in the boiler room of the school for several weeks, just a lunge away from every mother's son. Later in the summer, the town saw its first home invasion. With one hand in his pocket, allegedly clasping a pistol, the perp held up a Lake Evalyn resident and then apologized for robbing him. True to form, the story, especially the part about the apology, ran well in the national and international press.[1] But my trip to the Osceola Sheriff's office revealed that this model community had run up quite a crime sheet in its short life span. Larcenies (bicycles, construction tools) and burglaries numbered about one every two weeks. There had been several drug-related arrests, some battery charges and attempted suicides, and a number of child abuse cases (including complaints lodged against a summer camp counselor who made a child sit in the hot sun for five minute intervals as a form of punishment). It was widely known that there had been several incidents of spousal abuse where the victims had not pressed charges. Celebration had also hosted one violent traffic death owing to road design of an interchange that links I-4 with Disney World on Celebration Boulevard. A series of accidents at the intersection culminated in the drowning of one driver in a retention pond that had claimed other automobiles catapulted from the curb.[2]

PARTIES FOR THE PEOPLE

The evening after the gay mixer saw the only other social gathering at which children were conspicuously absent. On Valentine's Day, the more prominent residents of Celebration and the town's many corporate friends turn out for the Red Rose Ball, the big event of the season. A lavish, black tie affair at Disney World's Yacht and Beach Resort Club, the ball and its silent auction raise money for the nonprofit Celebration Foundation. The top corporate tables command a two-thousand-dollar tag. A volunteer worker for the evening, part of my job is to set out me-

mentos beforehand on the tables—Oscar de la Renta perfume for the ladies and a lite jazz compilation tape for the gentlemen. It is a little awkward to circulate at this event without a date, and so most of my volunteer coworkers are drawn from the sizable population of single women (all mothers) in town. There are several single men in town, but with few exceptions, they are not all that publicly visible in Celebration and unlikely to show up here. In any event, I am also lucky enough to have a date, the sparkling Dawn Thomas, who is Celebration's most fashion-forward dresser and gregarious soul. Formerly from Trinidad and Brooklyn, she used to run a halfway house in Orange County for violent felons before her mercurial rise in the Disney ranks from the sales staff to assistant community manager at Town Hall. Dawn, it is fair to say, has seen it all, yet she is still as buoyant as a fresh recruit.

The Red Rose Ball is an event to be seen at, not an occasion to let your hair down. Especially active citizens are honored with community awards, and snapshots and footage of a year in the life of Celebration are shown on a big screen. After the compulsory dance rituals of the Electric Slide, the Macarena, and a few slower standards, the crowd is homeward bound in a hurry. In the adjacent ballroom, a wedding party is in full swing, and the guests are seguing into bump-and-grind dance numbers to the accompaniment of stripper tunes. I am not the only Celebrationite tempted to linger.

There are much better parties in Celebration. Every so often, Town Hall or the Foundation throws one down by the lakeside, like the surprise party in April, where a block party trailer was unveiled. Brent Herrington and David Pace from TCC management took to the stage to exhort residents to turn the town over to an orgy of reveling. "We want Town Hall flooded with complaints about the noise." Events like this draw an intergenerational crowd. Kids and young teens try out the latest hip-hop moves alongside the rocking parents and jiving elders. The DJ makes some concessions to contemporary sounds, but the preferred standard is usually precounterculture rock 'n' roll, a direct link to the boomer age of innocence, just before the life of youth in America got seriously complicated. The R & B and doo-wop classics also rule at Max's Café, downtown's central eating institution, and they are broadcast into the street during the waking hours of the day to compete, bizarrely, with the piped TCC Muzak. When the school band plays at picnic gatherings, the Beach Boys are a sure bet—the early, pre-druggy Beach Boys, at least. In a town devoted to the rearing of its young, it is often the parents' own youth that is referenced most in the community's social gatherings. The generation that invented youth culture seldom misses an opportunity to remind its offspring of this achievement. For visitors, the town also hosts a variety of concerts in the park and by the lakefront, and the restaurants have jazz, reggae, and Latin music performances, but the official soundtrack is *Grease*, *Happy Days*, and *American Graffiti*, and the area's vintage Cadillac owners often provide a drive-in backdrop at the festive events.

Celebration's own *Grease*-aged teens are not likely to show up at these definitively uncool events. They have their own music wars that need to be staged out of the public, or at least the adult, eye. In a valiant attempt to meet teen social demands, Sarai Cowin, the vivacious Parks and Recreation manager, raised Nuyorican in the Bronx and a Jewish convert by marriage, occasionally puts on Teen Nights in the school cafeteria, where adult chaperones are in close attendance. On at least one occasion, an open-air dance was permitted in Lakeside Park, but the anticipated attendance of rowdy outsiders drew a heavy security presence that soured the party mood.

Like generations of their forebears, Celebration teens are fiercely devoted to their accursed exclusion from the mainstream life of the community. The proverbial complaint that there is "nothing for us to do" is the vital, low-calorie diet of youth culture in suburbia and small towns. In part, the complaint is self-affirming. After all, "doing nothing" is a crucial feature of teen life, and it actually covers a wide variety of youth activities and rituals. In Celebration, this protocol was not confined to the street hang. The school's loose scheduling had actually made room for some of this dedicated nonactivity. To the parental eye, flex time in the neighborhood hearth areas could resemble a festival of indolence, with limp bodies clumped inside the sofa squares and conversation in apparently random holding patterns. In fact, a good deal of peer socialization occurs in these communal moments. Youth learn how to interpret and identify with each other in an unplanned setting that is not separated from their work or study environment, as it is on the street. This quality of bonding is lost when students are running from one fifty-minute class to another—classes where they learn to

Town teenagers at the end of the millennium. Jason and Andy. (Photo: the author)

compete against each other in relative isolation. Seniors testified to the loss of this connection when block scheduling was introduced in August. Simultaneously, a great sigh of parental relief could be heard all over Celebration. In school or on the street, the spectacle of youth inactivity was an irksome, if not subversive, affront to the town's self-image as a place where community health was pursued *actively.*

On the other hand, there really were no outlets for youth activity. Teenage needs are almost always the most neglected item on the planner's agenda. It was so in Columbia in the 1960s—where the kids called the town "Endsville"—and it still is in Celebration today. Much of this is due to thoughtless planning, although when push comes to shove there are few blueprints for activities that respond so little to planned forms. Attempts of adults and town officials to build structured activities for youth (at times, Cowin's singular mission was "getting the teens away from hanging out") are likely to meet with a cool reception. Teenagers need amorphous spaces they can customize for their own purposes. Failing that, they will choose two kinds of places to gather:

those that are as remote as possible from adult surveillance—to make out, get high, and otherwise self-indulge—and those that are directly in view of the community—for the purpose of posing, provocatively. The proximity of Celebration's downtown to the lakeside and wetlands provides ideal locations for both kinds of hangout. The main retail area of Market Street is off-limits because of friction between teens and merchants and because it is the domain of tourists, but a teen cluster can usually be found camped out near the theater and the ice-cream parlor on the immediate downtown margin. Slightly more secluded spots can be found by Lakeside Park and behind Town Hall. For a truly clandestine rendezvous, there are always the wetlands, off-limits to adults. Regardless, the town's security force—county sheriff's patrols supplemented by hired off-duty cops—can follow with ease the telltale trail of cigarette butts. With one voice, teens spoke of their desire for a skate park, at minimal cost—a half-pipe and some rails at least. But the specter of attracting outsiders—"kids with baggy pants"—was too much for most adults to bear. Town Hall's solution was to create another layer of management, this time composed of teens themselves. Members of Town Teens were handpicked to organize activities and negotiate with their peers' concerns.

In the spring, some teens were up in arms over rumors about Town Hall's possession of photographs of kids smoking pot, allegedly snapped by surveillance cameras. Belief in the existence of these cameras—while unproven—was persistent. There was talk of illegality on both sides. Some parents held meetings to push for community curfews, and there was much strategizing about how to get youth off the streets. "Everyone is in your business here" is a common grievance of young people, who, next to the criminally institutionalized, have fewer rights than almost any other group in society and who are thrown back on a desperate quest for private autonomy as a result. In a small town like Celebration, with its ethos of intimate community bonding, the sense of surveillance is acute, especially for those who already have one foot outside the White Vinyl Fence (the town's much-commented-on polymerized boundary fence) and are counting the days until graduation.

A milder version of this complaint circulated among single women in town, extra-conscious of scrutiny, although more than one insisted to me, "I give them nothing to talk about anyway." Traditionally, it is the mixed blessing of life in small towns to sacrifice confidentiality on the altar of community, and yet what was this complaint but the flip side of the town's much vaunted "sense of community," where it is your civic duty to know other people's business? After all, surely only the deluded would move to Celebration if they were truly seeking privacy. Promotional literature had promised an alternative to the Lonelyville of suburbia (especially for women). Here you would get to know everyone faster than almost any other place on the face of the earth.

For teenagers, there was little to be done. Parental concern about their waywardness has been a constant since the early days of the republic, and in every conceivable form of settlement, rural and urban alike. Like Columbia in the 1960s, which bore the imprint of Rouse's Christian devotion to the nuclear family, Celebration was planned with young families in mind, and arguably worked best for those nesters. It is primarily a place for rearing, where a typical compliment paid to a fellow citizen is that he or she is "totally into their kids." In general, Celebration families are outsize, many with four children, and therefore well above average for thirty- and forty-something American parents at the end of the century.[3] For single women with children, the town is considered "a safe place" to move to, where the community might easily function as a coparent. Many parents told me that they knew of ten, even twenty, houses where their children could sleep over without generating anxiety in either parental home. "It takes a village," in Hillary Rodham Clinton's adage, to raise a child, and certainly, in an earlier time, before the cult of domesticity in the nineteenth century established the Currier and Ives stereotype of the woman as guardian of hearth and home, it could be said that many children were raised as much by communities as by families. For a town that is often glibly touted as utopian, there are no truly alternative approaches to childrearing (househusbands notwithstanding), and certainly none on the scale of the utopian communities of earlier centuries, which radically rearranged the functions of the nuclear family along communal lines. Yet, for all its showcasing of the single family Dream Home, the interfamily fabric of Celebration has a fluidity that is easy to see, in the streets, the parks, the block parties, the holiday events, and other social gatherings. I have no doubt that some part of this resilience owed to the school's emphasis on group activity and emotional cooperation, which circulates, through students, into the social lifeblood of the town as a whole. It is no small irony that the only genuinely utopian feature of the town—its noncomformist version of schooling—was widely seen as a troubling, even disastrous, experiment.

MR. MOMS

If Celebration is, in part, a postmodern town, it is not because its architects sprang from the postmodernist movement or because its developer has tried to recreate the feel of days gone by. More important is that many residents believe they have taken a step out of the frenzied pace and sequence of modernity by choosing to move there. Figures from an informal AT&T phone survey of the first pioneer pool showed up to 40 percent of residents working, in some fashion, from their homes. My own, no less informal, estimate would be about one-quarter less, a figure that nonetheless reflects the real impact of telecommuting. But I also found that a sizable number of Celebrationites had taken the opportunity to scale back their workloads, along with, perhaps, their career ambitions in order to downshift from high-powered jobs. For many, their lucrative stock investments in the bull market of the 1990s had cushioned this switch from a formal workplace. Celebration provided an ideal haven for what I would call the "affluent downshifter," weary of the corporate rat race and generationally attuned to the spiritual value of alternatives.[4] So many middle-aged men were in semiretirement that residents like Ray Chiaramonte, who hailed from a Chicago-Tampa working-class background and who commuted sixty miles daily to his own workplace, expressed worries about the effect on their children of growing up in a town where "the American work ethic was not pronounced." While their own parents, of whatever class, may have felt bound to a rigid career path where early retirement was an anomaly, these late boomers operate in an economic environment where there are no fixed expectations about the shape of a working career. When flexibility rules in the workplace, it is a boon to those who can afford to benefit from the loosening of custom, and a cruel regime if you have no guarantees about the source of your next paycheck. Celebrationites mostly fit into the first category, although many assume that if they fall on hard times they will have a caring community on their doorstep to soften, if not fully absorb, the blows.

Since dual-income families are the norm in Celebration, and the physical plan makes it easier for couples to share the duties of work and child-rearing, the town boasts more than its share of "house-husbands." Some of the more prominent Mr. Moms have indeed given up their high-profile jobs with large corporations. Mild-mannered, forty-something Paul Collins kept house on Longmeadow after his career as a CFO, most recently in charge of Pepsi's Florida division. He resigned after realizing he "wasn't ever going to enjoy being a middle manager for a large corporation" if it simply involved "getting paperwork shuffled at me and then pushing it on down the line." Just as important was his philosophical discomfort at being in a position that required him to eliminate jobs. Transitioning (a favorite word in Celebration) to the home had brought him "spiritual relief" from corporate routines, and he feels his work in the home is embedded in community rituals that are more personally satisfying. The role reversal has not been easy, since he feels his wife, Valerie, an executive with Darden Restaurants, still presumes an overriding responsibility for the children. Nor, he confesses, does he feel comfortable enough to participate "as the only male parent in the playgroup." Collins says he has come to realize that the efficiency of modernization is not necessarily desirable or progressive, at least not if it entails the erosion of the personable, social relationships he has encountered in Celebration. "After my family moved to suburbs," he explains, "I couldn't understand why my father still went to the local garage to buy his tires, rather than get them much cheaper at the big chain store. I finally realized it had something to do with the fact that the proprietor still called him Mr. Collins."

Marc Miller, who is Collins's sometime golfing partner—"half of what we talk about is how to cope with executive wives"—had no qualms about being the only male at the playgroup. Big-boned, blond, and boisterous, and sporting the only adult male earring in town aside from my own, he too had left the world of corporate finance, and employers like Arthur Andersen, Montgomery Ward, and Speedo, to look after the toddlers. After a year of homemaking in a nearby suburban development, where he had "to drive twenty minutes for a carton of milk," he suffered a mild case of "lost personal identity" and took a part-time teaching position. "It's important," he reported, "to allocate yourself some money to make you feel good about yourself." Feeding off the bright bonhomie shared by two men discussing housework, Miller coyly explained to me that it is difficult to get "positive reinforcement" for his efforts from his wife, a Disney VP of merchandising who is "more interested in the four or five things I haven't done than in those I have." If he had begun his house-minding career while in Celebration, things would have been a little easier.

Recently, he had begun to set his sights on graduate school and some kind of a career in academia. As a friendly caveat, I drew his attention to the local newspaper, currently running a series of Doonesbury cartoons about the desperate plight of low-wage adjunct professors in the rapidly downsizing academy. Confronted with the bad edge of the economy, where labor contracts can sour or dissolve overnight, Miller's buoyant mood subsided. Designing New Urbanist towns to ease the job of child-rearing was a step in the direction of stability. This was just as well, since the prospect of job stability out there, even in the formerly secure, tenured precincts of the academy, was disappearing fast.

THE COMMUNITY SOFTWARE

At a Community Update town meeting in mid-February, organized by the Osceola Chamber of Commerce, Brent Herrington warmed up the early-morning crowd in his signature cheerleading style. "Wake up, Celebration, this is the only community in America with a special deed restriction that requires all residents to be perky." No one could ever be sure of the exact degree of sincerity in Brent's voice when he addressed townsfolk in this manner. Savvy and accomplished in his thinking about his own profession, he had not yet found the common touch, nor had he mastered the slick repartee of a corporate master of ceremonies. Many found his performances a mite sophomoric, especially the happy talk that filled the pages of his Town Hall newsletter, regularly punctuated with gag makers: Wow! It Was a Blast! or Pretty Cool! On this occasion, however, he had deftly tapped the rich vein of what passes for gallows humor in Celebration. Upbeat community spirit was so much a mandate of residency that townsfolk had developed their own cute jokes about the culture of boosterism. Many residents felt a little patronized by the pressure to be involved, especially the more educated professionals. Compulsory good cheer was too closely associated with the world of the theme parks, and Celebrationites, in general, wanted their community to be recognized as real and distinct from the fantasy of undiluted happiness in nearby Disney World. People got divorced, lost their jobs, fell sick, and died in Celebration, and, occasionally, all hell broke loose.

In the course of the meeting, residents posed questions to a panel of representatives from the company, the school, and the Osceola County Commission. One retiree wondered if there were plans to build a cemetery. After all, no small American town is complete without its graveyard. Tom Sunnarborg, TCC's director of commercial real estate development, explained that this was a complicated business decision, owing to the high cost of the land, and that nothing had been resolved on the matter: "Should the right opportunity come along, the company will consider it." His response generated a new round of sick humor around town. It is a common perception that officially no one is "allowed" to die on Disney property, even though visitors expire there with regularity and as many as thirty-one animals notoriously died of various causes in the months before the recent opening of the Animal Kingdom. A rich mythology surrounding the preservation of Walt's own body had arisen from the promotion of the Magic Kingdom as a Never-Never Land of eternal life. Celebration itself had been actively promoted as a model of community health where people would live longer and more robustly than almost anywhere else. Ground would soon be broken for an assisted living center, but so far the sound barrier of mortality had not been broken. On the face of it, land value did not appear to be the obstacle. Cemeteries are one of the most profitable uses of land. Indeed, Charlie Rogers, the bank manager, told me he had once heard it estimated that plots would sell like hotcakes to the thousands of Disneyphiles around the world who were literally dying to be buried on Disney property.

In time, the town will probably get its cemetery, as a result of some private commercial initiative, but it was considered noteworthy that the company had made no provision for it in the early phases of construction. Nor had an adequate space been allotted for a community center.

The spaces that did exist for community events—Lakeside Pavilion and the Golf Course tavern—were diminutive and all too soon swamped by the crowded community schedule. The only place available for a sizable public assembly was an open-air pavilion in the North Village, remote from the town center and contingent on fair weather conditions. Again, not a few townsfolk saw this planning omission in a vaguely conspiratorial light, as a surefire way of discouraging large public meetings, and there were jokes about this, too.

If there was any real basis for this perception, the same could not be said of the planners' approach to community building itself. Celebration's creators had made a special effort to build in community initiatives, lest the residents' team spirit proved weak. Beyond the personal sacrifices required of all members of a planned community, and the pioneer zeal that propels residents of any new town, the company had laid down a professional infrastructure to ensure that community ties would be staunch from the outset.

In talking to members of the original development team—Peter Rummell, Todd Mansfield, Charles Adams, Chris Corr, Joe Barnes, and Don Killoren (all now gone their own ways)—it's clear that they each had an unbridled passion for the idea of Celebration. Recruited from the community development profession to create something quite different from a boilerplate Florida golf-course or prestige community, this was a group, according to Rummell, "for which Celebration was a favorite child." Rummell was careful to downplay the physical planning and talk up the community plan: "The town plan is the hardware, the grid, the alleys, the streets, the setbacks, the architecture. That's all hardware. My concern has always been that as people come and try to get lessons from Celebration, they get all obsessed with the architecture. The architecture is about eight on the list as far as I'm concerned with what was experimental about this place. What was much more important to me was the software—the things that we tried to make it into a place, make it into a real town."

One of the more uncommon features of the software package is the Celebration Foundation, a nonprofit institution that fosters and facilitates community initiatives among the residents. Funded with startup grants from Sun Trust Bank, TCC, and the Kohler Company, it would soon file for designation as a public charity, eligible for tax-deductible contributions. Heading up the Foundation was Kathy Johnson, an ebullient Minnesotan with twenty years of experience in fund-raising, government, and nonprofit program development for youth, the disabled, the working poor, and the aging in Duluth. Her mandate was to jump-start the pioneer phase of residential life: "Most foundations have been created after a problem emerges and people are trying to solve a problem. The notion here was to start out with an organization that can help to build positive responses, and to try to address problems as they come up—but to build it into the civic infrastructure. Most foundations are strictly a pool of resources that you regrant out, or are operating foundations where you only run programs, or grant-making foundations, which only award grants. We're a mixture of all of those."

As a result, the Foundation has been active on many fronts. Among its functions, it runs a Volunteer Center, recruiting and placing resident volunteers; provides seed money for community groups, clubs, and branches of national organizations; runs orientation programs for new residents; organizes community picnics and yard sales; and does its share of outreach work in Osceola County, including volunteer service to institutions like Help Now, the county's domestic violence shelter. These endeavors "to stir the pot," as Johnson puts it, showed clear results. Initially, volunteerism ran high, and the town's clubs and community groups got off the ground rapidly. The Garden Club, The Celebrators (for retirees and semi-retirees), the Rotary, Chamber of Commerce Council, Children's Playgroup, Scouting, and Indian Guides were all well established and thriving in the first two years. A barbershop chorus and the theatrical group, Celebration Players, both had two seasons under their belts. Other initiatives, like the stamp club, had a tougher time attracting interest. Aside from its municipal character, Town Hall also hosts the Parks and Recreations Office, which sponsors a raft of sports clinics, activity classes, and children's groups. Between the Foundation and Town Hall, the town's daily "event calendar," listed on community TV channel 12 and the community cybernetwork, is chockabloc and requires careful coordination among the many groups to avoid chronic conflicts.

For some purposes, the community clubs can take on civic service functions, and even act as lobby groups. One unexpected example of this featured the popular Garden Club in an activist role. In April, its members got wind of a rumor that the weekly downtown Farmer's

Saturday morning in downtown Celebration. The Farmers' Market. (Photo: the author)

Market—a trinkety, boutique affair—would be phased out for reasons of poor economic return. However ersatz, the market served as a communal meeting point and was an especial favorite of the Gardenites. Twenty club members banded together and entered Town Hall to protest the market's impending closure. It was Celebration's first "march on City Hall." So, too, the Celebrators, (fifty-five years and over, and comprising a representative 12 percent of the town's population) are much more active than as a strictly social group. The monthly meetings to which they invite speakers—many of them from Disney—are rare occasions for residents to have their questions directly answered in a public forum. The Celebrators actively lobbied the county to start a satellite site of the public library in the school, and their members are consistently among the most outspoken attendees of any public meeting. Of course, retirees are habitually the bane of developers. Highly vocal, with lots of time on their hands and living on fixed incomes, they are much more likely to affirm their rights and question decision making. Attending their meetings, I felt I was in the presence of the conscience of the community.

By the time I arrived in town, the Foundation was no longer offering an elaborate orientation program known as "Celebration Traditions." The initial program had run for several weeks and covered the biogeographical history of Central Florida, from the time it was part of the African portion of Gondwanaland, through the period of the Caloosa Indians, and the Seminoles (who moved from Georgia in the mid-eighteenth century), the postbellum Homestead Act of 1866 (which gave freedmen and "loyal whites" eighty-acre tracts), to the flourishing of cattle ranching in the area and the advent of Disney. Researchers on the development team had taped a series of local interviews that resulted in a patchwork oral history of Osceola oldtimers—trappers, cow hunters (Florida's term for cowboys), ranchers, and loggers. Before it was Celebration, this spot was known as John Dan Bend. The researchers had traced the name to an alligator hunter, John Dan, who frequented the gator hole in a bend in Reedy Creek. The tract was named for him after he accidentally shot his arm off in a confrontation with his prey. A century and a half before, this whole area had been a strategic sector of the swamplands from which Chief Osceola led his guerrilla warriors on hit-and-run raids against the U.S. Army in the course of the long Seminole Wars.

The orientation program was conducted by volunteers coached to initiate new resident groups by using, for no evident reason, the American Indian institution of the Talking Stick. *The Volunteer Trainer's Guide* explained how the program was designed to resolve the dilemma of creating an instant community that had no real past: "Most places around the country that exhibit a strong community spirit have a long history. Here we're starting from scratch with no past or traditions. . . . How could we give newcomers a common history that in some way begins the process of weaving our individual lives into that tapestry we call community? The answer to this question turned out to be right under our nose." For what it's worth, history offered some striking parallels. Centuries before, on this land, the Seminoles had welcomed runaway slaves—Indians and blacks—from southern states into their communities as maroons. The result of this loose sanctuary policy was the free mixing of Indians and blacks in the region. In Eatonville, the nation's first incorporated black township, just to the north of Orlando, Zora Neale Hurston would later quip, "I am the only Negro in the United States whose grandfather on the mother's side was *not* an Indian chief."[5] With or without a Talking Stick, it is unlikely that the methods of initiation for these earlier Florida newcomers hastened their socialization into the community as much as did the threat of recapture. Then, as now in Celebration, community building drew strength from adversity as much as from the seasoned customs and best-laid plans that greet the parvenu.

Those who attended it remembered the full Traditions program as a little hokey, and joked about the "indoctrination" sessions. One volunteer described the orientation and welcome gatherings as "an unnecessary form of brainwashing" because the pioneers bonded well enough anyway. Too closely associated with the company's employee training programs at Disney University, called Disney Traditions, the program was renamed and eventually segued into an eight-part seminar called the Discovery Series, focusing on topics like "The Legend of the Florida Cracker and Early Ranchers" and "Celebration's Environmental Legacy." By that time, of course, the town already had some authentic (and much reported) history of its own.

From the moment newcomers attend their first orientation meeting, Kathy Johnson acknowledges, "there's a constant message that we expect people to get involved, we want them to get involved, we encourage them to get involved." No one questioned the goal behind "being involved," but for the most part, residents agreed that "community" had to be earned, and not purchased, for it to be real. Everyone, of course, had his or her own idea of what "real community" was, rooted in an idealized childhood or drawn from the yellowed pages of American mythology.

Phyllis and Paul Kleinman, for example, had grown up in the tight-knit Bronx in the 1940s, where "no one was well-off, everyone was in the same boat," and where stickball, stoopball, and other street games like Johnny-on-the-Pony and King Queen required little more than a sawed-off mop handle to play. "Now that was a real community," they ardently declared. The Kleinmans, who own a military surplus store in Orlando, still subscribed to *Back in the Bronx*, a nostalgia magazine devoted to the proposition "You Can Go Home Again!" which features wedges of warm reminiscing about the old neighborhoods, candy stores, picture palaces, plots of grass, and the El. Celebration, by contrast, was a place where "they are developing community artificially, and it will never have the same warmth." Of course, the Bronx of legend, like any "real community," was lost in time. Paul was not the only senior male for whom Celebration had triggered the child within him, offering a safe but thrilling form of regression. Several others, more Disneyphilic, spoke wistfully of reactivating the emotional link with their childhood—the "Mickey within us"—through their newly intimate association with the company name.

As with the Kleinmans' Bronx, fifteen years from now Celebration veterans will be lamenting the loss of the "real community" that existed in the early years. As the pockets of the site's residential land were developed, some slated for as far away as four miles from the downtown area, the bounded solidarity of the population would inevitably erode. The Foundation would have a tough job providing the glue for this archipelago of island communities, not to mention the sundry expectations of what a real community feels like. Among the initial pioneers, it built a broad and spirited volunteer base, but aside from this core, the pool increasingly drew upon retirees and empty nesters. Some residents, like Debbie Lehman, shrewdly observed that Celebration's much-vaunted "Type A" population did not necessarily translate into a selfless volunteer pool. "There are too many Type A people in this town. They thought this would be a ground-floor experience, and they could be in control of something—'I'll move there and be boss of something.' It's a little scary because there aren't enough positions, everyone is vying for them, and it's very competitive. Type A folks can't just be members, they have to be leaders, and since there's no real boss, you can't fire any of them. So we have a town full of bosses, and not enough followers or team people." Sporting a tie-dye T-shirt reminiscent of her 1960s youth in Madison, Wisconsin, Lehman, a doll maker who lives on Golfpark Drive, sees the problem crystallizing in the debate over the school. Soured by the memory of how her own artistic proclivities had been suppressed in a traditional school, she explains: "We have so much trouble from parents who want 'competition' at the school. They point out that they are very successful in their own business, but if we don't learn how to be cooperative then this town will fail. Being Americans, we have much less of a sense of cooperation or teamwork than other countries. As a society, especially at this moment, we are very self-centered."

After all the talk about its Type A population, I was surprised to discover that Celebration actually had a large share of nonjoiners. Over half the residents I interviewed were not particularly active in community or volunteer initiatives. More startling yet, I came across people who were confirmed "loners," even hermits. That the loners did not feel threatened by the compulsive pressure of Celebration's peer sociability was a tribute to civility, though it ran against the grain of the town's official self-image as Participation Central. One such loner told me that even if he were not a recluse, he wouldn't volunteer because a wealthy town like Celebration didn't need additional help. Another was even more cynical. "Everyone here wants to be your friend. I'm basically anti-social and pathetic, and don't care, as long as they don't infringe on my rights." Others had a vigorous sense of entitlement and approached community life as clients or consumers, expecting prompt attention to their needs. Having paid "an expensive entrance fee" to live in town, they tended to view the management professionals in Town Hall and the Foundation as service workers, often treating the Foundation, as Johnson admitted, "like an adult day care service."

FIGHTING FOR COMMUNITY

Of all the amenities Celebration would offer—summarized in the five cornerstones of Place, Health, Education, Community, and Technology—the promise of a "sense of community" is the least easy to plan, guarantee, or put a price on. Hiring professionals to deliver the promise and ensure its upkeep is the natural offshoot of a corporate society where layers of experts are added yearly to monitor and manage activities that people used to do for themselves. The corporate concept of a community manager would have been as bizarre as a bug-eyed Martian to the idealized small towns of yore, whose close-knit civic virtue and neighborliness Celebration was designed to restore. Nowadays, there are managers for everything, even things that are supposed to have been lost, like our fabled sense of community.

"Community" is one of the most emotionally ubiquitous and versatile touchstones of American life. As a result, it is one of the more overused words in our daily lexicon, relentlessly mined for all sorts of social, religious, and commercial purposes, and in most instances no more meaningful than a sugary advertising cliché. Of all the things that can be acquired in a market civilization, it is supposed to be one of the most elusive. Like religious devotion or public service, it is not something we can easily put a price on. According to the given wisdom, community takes decades or centuries to build and then is rapidly eroded by the impact of modernity—usually in the form of a new technology like the automobile, or the TV set, or the Wal-Mart. Yet, in a modern society, people can create a sense of community very quickly if they are united around a common cause or can identify common concerns and affinities. A ninety-minute disaster movie can persuade us that close, altruistic ties emerge among complete strangers in peril at sea or in a burning tower block.

To be sure, community consciousness is accelerated in the face of threats: war, disease, impoverishment, discrimination. More and more, community in our time is associated with groups identified as endangered. People discover they belong to a community when it is suddenly at risk or jeopardized. Community, in this sense, is discovered at the very moment it is seen to be fragile and on the verge of disappearing, and then its true strength is put to the test in the struggle to survive. Ethnic or single-issue groups that are marginalized through discrimination also unite around a composite identity. "The African American community," "the gay community," "the Arab American community," are all shorthand summaries of very diverse populations united as much by external disrespect as by common pride. The very composition of American civil society is the legacy of communities seeking protection from threats: Indian communities surviving prolonged decimation, immigrant communities fleeing religious and economic persecution, ex–slavery communities resisting disenfranchisement, and political refugees of all stripes.

In the last twenty years, "community" has become a competitive feature in the consumer housing industry, where developers bundle it into the package of amenities on offer. Customers can buy into a "strong" community where others appear to be weak or disorganized or in decline. Community then acquires value as a therapeutic asset that can be purchased by those who, among all the groups in society, probably have least need for its restorative virtues. Celebration's planners set out to raise the bar in the industry by offering a deluxe, next-generation version of the all-inclusive community package, far beyond the "enclaving" model that promised a safe retreat from the hustle and bustle of the city, and the "lifestyle" model that threw in golf and other sports. Celebration's packaging was expected to set the new standard for community-in-depth models of marketing. The demand for such a place rests on the perception that community is everywhere else an endangered species, especially in the nowhere of suburbia. Move to a real town, goes the pitch, and you'll see the difference it makes in your social life.

Thirty-five years ago, the sociologist Herbert Gans took up residence in Levittown, near Philadelphia, to find out what difference a place really makes. GI suburbia had become the preferred punching bag of critics of the mass-produced life in the postwar years. To its critics, this new crabgrass frontier was an unrefined and soulless place of refuge, where individualism was stifled, where the fluid vibrancy of city community life was squeezed into the box of conformity, and where the nation's husbands, among other things, were being emasculated. Suburbia, they concluded, was creating social automatons that were a threat to the health of democracy. Lewis Mumford, the influential architecture critic, typified this stance: "A new kind of community was produced, which caricatured both the historic city and the archetypal suburban refuge: a multitude of uniform, unidentifiable houses, lined up inflexibly, at uniform distances, on uniform roads, in a treeless communal waste, inhabited by people of the same class, the same income, the same age group, witnessing the same television performances, eating the same tasteless prefabricated foods, from the same freezers, conforming in every respect to a common mold, manufactured in the central metropolis."[6] Gans's classic study, *The Levittowners,* took issue with this view, which he characterized as an elitist perception on the part of urban intellectuals.[7] Levittown represented the promise of the good life to working- and lower-middle-class families, and was disdained as cheap and vulgar by the well-heeled urbanites who had long enjoyed access to good taste, privacy, and security. Besides, weren't the urbanites' Victorian row townhouses identical, too? Gans's findings disputed the stereotype that suburban environments had a life-draining effect on the people who moved there from city neighborhoods. The new environment, he concluded, had a negligible effect on community life, and it certainly had not created the new kind of social person that the critics of suburbia had sketched in caricature. Residents carried on their old ways in new settings. They kept intact their ties to ethnic, religious, and cultural groups, and their interactions continued to be shaped primarily by the social class of residents, who ranged from moralistic blue-collar workers to conservative managerial executives and liberal cosmopolitan professionals. If anything, sociability increased among Levittowners because of the homogeneity or, rather, compatibility of their immediate neighbors. Above all, Gans noted that the changes in people's lives—most were happier than in the city they had left behind—were due more to aspirations to improve their lives than to the physical environment of suburbia.

In the time between the building of the Levittowns and the founding of Celebration, the middle landscape of suburbia has sprouted a hundred different species of development and undergone some significant population shifts. By the time of the 1990 census, a third of all African Americans—blacks were excluded, initially, from places like Levittown—had suburban homes. But despite the findings of Gans and others, the view of suburbia as an oppressive and alienating environment has prevailed. Those who are especially critical of suburban sprawl continue to assume that its physical disconnectedness produces residents with low moral or civic fiber. Today, the association is almost taken for granted—housing and traffic patterns determine civic personality—but it still is largely unsubstantiated. Do cul-de-sacs, half-acre lots, and houses with garages in front automatically produce mediocre citizens?

The answer may depend, ultimately, on how you view citizenship. But those who believe that the buildings we inhabit determine our civic behavior too often put the cart before the horse. Citizens are like the communities I discussed earlier. They often discover how to be active only when they feel their own rights are threatened or when they see others befouled by injustice, as in the civil rights struggle. Active citizenship has to be learned, long after it has been learned about in civics class. It can be learned from others, and it is undemocratic to assume that life in a suburban villa precludes such an education any more than life on a neglected inner city block does. Much more important is to see what the villa people do with their citizenship once it has been activated. Do they use it to protect their own resources and privileges or to help remedy the neglect of the city block dwellers? Celebration is the kind of place where active citizens were already well represented in the population. Their zeal was further energized by perceived threats to their property value and their children's education. But would this citizenly vigor ever extend beyond the town limits, and if so, how far? At this point in time, the center city was barely on their map, least of all on their minds.

Earlier suburban newcomers like the Levittowners had moved from urban neighborhoods, and were more likely to empathize with those left in the inner-city neighborhoods. By the 1990s, this would no longer be the case. The majority of Celebration residents had lived before in suburban places and few had any extensive familiarity with center-city life to draw on, outside of jaunts to enjoy the museums, restaurants, and nightlife. In addition, the widespread perception of Celebrationites that they had sacrificed greatly to come to town did not help arouse their will to sacrifice for others. Celebration was the last place that Osceola County folks would associate with sacrifice, let alone trials and tribulations, and yet I would discover this was the self-image of many of their new neighbors in ZIP code 34747.

10

KINDER, GENTLER GOVERNMENT?

"Government, like dress, is the badge of lost innocence."
—Thomas Paine

"Walt wasn't against people voting; he just didn't want them hanging their dirty laundry out. . . . I don't agree. I don't disagree." —Michael Eisner

Everyone has made a sacrifice to be here." This belief was an article of faith among Celebrationites, and everyone paid lip service to it. Sacrifice was seen as a built-in condition of pioneerism, stressed routinely in Town Hall newsletters and drummed home in the annual speeches by clergy and managers on Founder's Day.

This perception of selflessness had even helped persuade some retirees to come to Celebration rather than to one of Florida's adult communities. In this category were Jim and Jane Clayman, whose home on the pioneer row of Teal Avenue was crammed with art and artifacts from their working lives in Peru and Brazil and whose porch rockers had once stood on Jane's mother's porch in Kentucky. The Claymans had been attracted by the many young parents they saw at the lottery who seemed willing to forgo creature comforts for a worthier cause.

"We'll be eating peanut butter and jelly," one of them had said to the couple, "but this is what we want for our children."

Conveniently, perhaps, from both the residents' and the developer's point of view, the pioneer spirit could be invoked to explain away encounters with adversity: the hardships endured by residents while waiting, as long as two years, to move into a finished home; the Pyrrhic victory over the builders; separation from kith and kin in other parts of the country; the financial burden of stretching for a mortgage and meeting all the bills; the frustration of living through the growing pains of the school; denigration from the press; and resentment from locals prejudiced against Disney. Witnessing at public meetings, especially school related, often began with a proviso like: "After all we have been through . . ." In this town, everyone was expected to show some evidence of personal sacrifice, and not just as a gesture toward community spirit. One refugee from an upscale condo canyon north of Miami explained to me that she "had learned to live without Neiman Marcus" (though she was still within shooting distance of Saks, at the Florida Mall). The upside was that she had found that the "civil servants are more civil here than in South Florida." One parent, especially active in the PTSA, told me she believed the school "should recruit teachers who had the kind of value system that could embrace the personal sacrifice" that came with their low salaries. In response, I found the schoolteachers often wore their taxing workload like a badge of honor, while at other times they used it as a shield to deflect the reproaches hurled by parents. Especially deep sacrifices were professed by single parents who had given up the kernel and pith of their personal lives for the sake of their children's education and betterment.

With all of this talk about sacrifice, I might have been excused for inferring that I was living in a training camp for humanitarian workers rather than one of the wealthiest towns in Central Florida. I thought I had surrendered a fair chunk of my own life to go and live in Celebration (among other things, my year out took a fatal toll on the relationship with my girlfriend), but this noble impression would have to be downgraded. Compared to the ordeals of my fellow citizens, my own burdens were a trifle. Living amid so many accounts of great hardship, I needed a regular reality check. Every so often, I would motor out of town in pursuit of places where poverty and hardship were as conspicuous on the ground as Spanish moss was on the trees. In Osceola's trailer parks, Orlando's ghettoes, and all the twilight districts in between, people might have thought they had gotten a raw deal, for which they might have paid dearly. Yet they would probably not have chosen to describe their lives as a condition of self-sacrifice. Sacrifice goes by other names when it is not buttressed by the sense of entitlement that often percolated through Celebration.

But Central Florida's less privileged had one dubious advantage over the Celebrationites. If you do not have the option of living in a pricey, planned community you do not have to agonize over whether to restrict your freedoms in order to abide by the rules. Of all the sacrifices faced by Celebrationites, this was the one that generated the most commentary from outsiders, and the least reflection from residents themselves.

The hundred-page "Declaration of Covenants, Conditions, and Restrictions" signed by all homeowners, and the less weighty, but substantial, document signed by tenants like myself, were generally referred to as "standards" implemented to guarantee the physical upkeep of the houses and streets of Celebration. If these restrictions were of negligible concern to residents, they loomed larger for folks who decided not to move to Celebration, including some who had placed highly on the original lottery draw, and many others who had investigated residency through Celebration Realty. In the course of the year, I ran into several who had decided that the rules and restrictions were too much of an imposition on their personal land use. (Small lot sizes, lack of privacy, and the jitteriness about the school figured among the other reasons.) The chance to build this community would effectively be limited to those willing to regulate their conduct, and perhaps curb their liberties, to safeguard their property values.

One resident, a middle-income manager from a working-class background, explained to me one day that working-class people "don't share the same civic culture as us" and "because they value their freedom of expression too highly, they would not tolerate the deed restrictions." He figured he must "sound like a jerk for saying so," but his comment was little different from the nightmare neighbor scenarios conjured up by-many others of unruly, low-class folks with trucks, rundown '83 Buicks, and washing lines in the yard, not to mention garish colors on their window frames.

The "Covenants, Conditions, and Restrictions" are common in planned communities (these days, many bankers will not issue loans without them), but, true to form, Celebration's rulebook got special attention in the media and was widely cited by outsiders as evidence of the company's totalitarian control over residents. One section, in particular, would become quite famous in its own right:

> 6a) Unless the Board of Directors otherwise agrees, the only acceptable coverings that may be affixed to the interior of any windows visible from any street, alley or other portion of the Properties are drapes, blinds, shades, shutters and curtains. The side of such window coverings that is visible from the exterior of any improvements must be white or off-white in color.

Town Hall clocked more phone calls about this one rule than all the others combined. Brent Herrington reminded townspeople, in a Town Hall newsletter in the fall of 1997, that he intended to implement the rule: "I have noticed a couple of residences where the owner has installed colored window coverings, and, unfortunately, these will need to be corrected." For once, at least, the derisory response around town partially echoed the mockery of the media, especially since the warning was accompanied by Herrington's opinion that the colored drapes in question were "icky." Most residents knew that one highly visible window, in a Longmeadow home, had been in violation of the rule for several weeks, and the owners' initial decision to hold out had become a cause célèbre. Since the rule was regarded as a little excessive, many townspeople saw this resident's red drapes as a flag of liberty. In general, however, Celebrationites were quick to fault Town Hall for not cracking down sooner on offending residents. In this town, the developer was perceived to have better taste than the residents, and so homeowners were not happy when management was lax about enforcement.

In response, Herrington encouraged residents to take pride in Town Hall's personal touch. In most planned communities with homeowners associations, negligent residents are sent a formal letter of warning. In kinder, gentler Celebration, they receive an informal phone call. This technique belongs more to the code of friendly customer relations—Disney's field of expertise—than of an inflexible bureaucracy. As far as governance went, everyone understood that the basis for the town's restrictions, perhaps even its "sense of community," lay in the bedrock desire to maintain and promote the value of property investments. It was in bad taste, and antisocial, to remind anyone of this, and besides, it was unnecessary to do so since in Celebration this belief was as natural as breathing.

COMMON INTERESTS

Levittown, as Herbert Gans pointed out, was neither a town—which would offer employment—nor a community—which suggests a desire for sharing values. The Levittowners moved there to own a home, most of them for the first time in their lives. Celebration did not yet feel like a town, but it was conceived and populated with the aim of becoming a community as quickly as possible. Between the era of the Levittowns and this new place in Osceola County, the idea of building self-contained communities evolved into a staple of the housing industry in Sunbelt states like Florida. Today, most developers will say they are building communities, not subdivisions.

Historically, most communities were not designed by professionals at all, let alone planned in any systematic way. Community design was the outcome of piecemeal building by artisans, craftsmen, townsfolk, and peasants. Celebration's neighboring lakeside towns of Kissimmee and St. Cloud are typical, modern examples. Most of the great European cities so admired for their urbanity are haphazard hybrids of aristocratic pleasure grounds, sober bourgeois quarters, merchants' commercial enclaves, and proletarian holding tanks. It was not until the onset of rational urban planning at the turn of the century that professionally designed communities would see the light of day as an industrial enterprise.

Originating in Britain, in Ebenezer Howard's blueprint for the Garden City (which rested on cooperative ownership of the land), this planning concept was translated into the American private housing landscape in the form of common-interest developments.[1] Today, we know these as planned unit developments, condominiums, or co-ops, where private developers offer buyers commonly shared land. Oftentimes, they are governed by covenants and deed restrictions that "run with the land" and forbid alternative uses of the land in the future. These covenants, which date back to twelfth-century England, protect property value, and, to ensure further protection, homeowners associations offer a form of community governance, at the behest of fellow residents' votes and assessments, which assumes many of the public responsibilities of local government. In the United States, the evolution of these interlocking institutions has given rise to what Roderick McKenzie calls "privatopia," which he describes as a condition of private government currently enjoyed by over 40 million Americans, or about 17 percent of the population.[2] By the year 2000, it is estimated that a quarter of a million homeowner associations will exist, exacting restrictions to guarantee members' property value, and where the only form of participation for homeowning shareholders is to satisfy their contractual obligations by maintaining their mortgage payments.

The privatopian community has become the preferred development for builders of nonurban housing in the last two decades. Lenders are increasingly unlikely to issue mortgages for planned developments unless they have a homeowner association.[3] The flourishing of walled and gated communities—a natural extension of privatopia—arouses widespread concern about a rampant "fortress mentality" in late suburban America, signifying what Robert Reich termed the "secession of the successful" from all public contact with, let alone obligation toward, their less fortunate fellow citizens.[4] One of the most common outsider misperceptions of Celebration is that it is gated, or that its managed ambience is "gated" even in the absence of a physical gatehouse and uniformed guards. On the contrary, the creation of this town is a highly visible counterpunch to the prestige ethos of the gated community. Virtually every resident I met, including many who had lived behind electronic gates before, took pride in the town's open public access and resented the mischaracterization. Should some calamity occur as a result of this openness, the decision about whether to keep the town open will be a real test of residents' commitment to retaining its cherished public character.

In principle, the concept of the homeowner association promises self-government to residents, and in its most shrewdly promoted ver-

Celebration's first polling day, September 1998. Precinct #73, Town Hall. (Photo: the author)

sions, conjures up the sanctity of ultra-democratic Town Hall meetings, New England–style. In Celebration, Town Hall's information sheets about governance describe membership in the association as "a representative form of government similar to our federal system." Yet voting in the association, unlike in the federal system, is restricted to homeowners (not renters), and to one vote per property unit. (In addition, a supermajority of 75 percent is needed to carry any motion.) In most developments like this, the developer will retain control of governance until two-thirds of the lots are sold, and often exercises voting rights thereafter based on continued ownership of parcels of land or other residual rights. When homeowners eventually do take on elected positions, regulating in accordance with the developer's original rules, their zeal often marks them out as "condo nazis," and residents pine for the professional management of the fledgling years.

The governance of Celebration is not exceptional in this regard. The company controls the homeowners association until 25 percent of the units are sold, at which point one out of three board directors are elected by the residents of the town's several villages. After 50 percent, the residents elect two of five directors, and after 75 percent, three of five. One year after this initial "control period" lapses, six of seven directors are elected, and a year later, the developer withdraws all official representation on the board. The 75 percent deadline is nullified if the buildout has not reached this level after forty years. The developer can also withdraw before the deadline at its own discretion. But the "Covenants, Conditions, and Restrictions" also record that nothing can be changed without the decree of the "owners of at least 75% of the total number of Units within the Properties and by the Celebration Company." The latter clause is particularly notable. So long as TCC owns any property or developable land in Celebration, it has veto power over all changes in governance. While they had all read and signed the covenants, the vast majority of residents were unaware of this veto power until an article in the *New York Times* magazine pointed it out. When I asked Herrington to clarify the matter, he professed that although he thought he knew the document very well, he too had not been fully cognizant of this veto power. "In practice," he ventured, "using those kinds of residual powers is a little bit like setting off an atomic bomb in your own underwear," especially for a developer who, at that point, would be "contributing zero to the budget, and has nothing at risk."

For the most part, Celebrationites were content with what they often called their "benevolent dictator" (a phrase that originates in Walt's comment that he wouldn't want to be U.S. president but would "rather be the benevolent dictator of Disney enterprises"[5]). Though if things got too "Orwellian," as one of my tennis partners observed, that would be another matter. It was expected that the company would maintain good order, and so long as the decision making remained benign, TCC would serve residents' private interests better than would any office-bearers elected from their own ranks. Among the townsfolk, I ran into several former presidents of homeowner associations who swore that Town Hall's administering of the rules was much kinder and gentler than in the associations of housing developments they had known, some of which had the power to enter private homes and to restrict the stay of guests. The deed restrictions were no more, and in some cases less, severe than those they had helped to administer elsewhere. Terry Neff, who had served as an association president in nearby Hunter's Creek, even alleged that helicopters had been used there to survey residents' backyards for infractions of the rules, though no one I questioned at Hunter's Creek could confirm this.

If anything, Herrington's light enforcement of the rules drew complaints about the laxity of regulation—"things are not being kept up." Aware of media scrutiny, it's likely that Town Hall sometimes chose to waive some of the micro-rules rather than risk public ridicule in yet another boilerplate press report about the company's suppression of civic liberties. To compensate, residents exercised their own scrutiny, building a groundswell of hearsay that Town Hall could not easily ignore. Many townsfolk were vexed, for example, when homes were not lived in. An ornate, ochre Mediterranean estate home had been lying vacant on Golfpark Drive for as long as I could remember. This violated the residency rule (a home should be occupied for at least nine months of the year), and reinforced conjecture that there was one rule for the wealthy and one for the others. The rumor around town (other than that it belonged to Julia Roberts) was that a rich businessman had bought the home for his wayward son, who decided never to occupy it. On the other hand, there were some decrees that disgruntled residents were happy to see annulled. The rule, established as an antispeculation deterrent, that no one could profit from sale of a home within one year of closing, was routinely waived if the seller could prove "hardship."

For myself, I was guilty on two counts. I decided that Hamish and Molly, my capricious cats, would live illegally in Celebration rather than observe the renters' rule requiring them to be declawed. As a result, I lived in abject fear that my furry charges would be found out, especially when they made a periodic run for freedom, padding and loping along the Market Street balconies in full view of passersby below. Aware of their clandestine existence, my neighbors never turned them in. In addition, I had reluctantly invested in an array of large potted plants for my balcony. On Market Street, balconies festooned with plants were a prime element of the downtown decor, and I did not want to be the odd one out. Never having had any luck in keeping flora alive, sadly my efforts fell short again. A notice distributed to apartment residents drew attention to "unsightly plants on balconies," and I assumed, as the guilty do, that it was for my eyes. In a slender act of rebellion, I allowed mine to decay visibly for the next four months before I bid them farewell.

One evening in April, the Osceola County Planning Department called a meeting in Town Hall to solicit residents' feedback for its reappraisal of a comprehensive plan adopted in 1990. Poorly advertised and ill-timed at the dinner hour, the meeting attracted only three residents (it would take a while for residents to feel that their input in county affairs might be a priority). In attendance were myself, Jim Bayley, president of the Celebrators and an inveterate presence at all community events, and Ray Chiaramonte, the Tampa urban planner. It was mostly a red-tape affair for county bureaucrats, but at a late hour, we were asked whether we thought residents would eventually vote to incorporate the town. From the outset, this prospect had been widely discussed among residents, although very few seemed to be aware that the state requires all Community Development Districts to hold a referendum on incorporation when they reach a population threshold—about 9,800, in the case of Celebration.

In response to the question, Bayley summarized the majority view of the "benevolent dictator." If nothing goes too badly amiss, Celebrationites would probably be happier living with the rules laid down by Disney, as interpreted by residents on the board. I summarized another view I had found on residents' lips. Since it had attracted more than its share of independently minded citizens, hungry for true self-government, Celebrationites, I predicted, would incorporate sooner or later. For his part, Ray declared that residents were "more interested in pragmatism than politics," and suggested they would actively resist incorporation for that reason. Of course, there was much more to be said on this topic, and we had not begun to cover the views of all the townsfolk. But these three positions were fairly representative. Jim's opinion displayed a concerned tolerance of the status quo and a general desire to hold the developer to its obligations. Mine was based on evidence of residents' pushing already for more input in decision making, and on their general frustration with outsiders' perception of the community as a Disney-controlled "puppet state." Ray's comment reflected the conviction of many residents who had moved here, in part, to escape from local government politics. It may have also reflected his own professional relish for utilitarian order. Civic politics have a tendency to get in the way of planners' designs.

In truth, none of us had hit on the most likely factor to influence votes on incorporation—the cost of government. Most planned communities figure out whether they will have to pay more or less to assume control over their own destinies. Gary Moyer, the manager of the Celebration Community District, was not able to estimate the financial feasibility for Celebration, but he cited the example of Weston, an Arvida development to the south, where his company is also contracted. Residents there had recently incorporated, and had established what Moyer called "an almost 100 percent contract city," with only three full-time employees. The services of everyone else were contracted. Weston had no mayoral governance structure; it was pure management all the way down.

Many Celebration residents felt they had been promised a "town," with all the municipal trappings that term evoked, but, when the time came, the Weston model might just offer the preferred privatopian alternative—a township with no real public representatives. In the meantime, one sure thing I had learned is that Celebrationites were very defensive about any suggestion—a favorite in the media—that they lived in a less than democratic environment. They knew that they enjoyed the same rights as any other citizen of the republic, and, far from considering the deed restrictions to be an erosion of these rights, they saw the maintenance of community standards as an extra layer of privileges that local government could not otherwise afford. On the other hand, I interviewed several who made a point of speaking passionately about their dislike for "democracy." What could this possibly mean?

John Pfeiffer, the doctor who had moved from Ohio to fulfill a childhood dream of driving a Disney monorail, offered an explanation:

> I'd rather live in a civil than a political society. Here we have a contract with TCC that defines our property rights, and we are not frustrated by bureaucrats with their own agenda. I don't have a contract with politicians. . . . What we have here is a deconstructing of government, a roll-back of politicization. In a civil society you feel a desire to fit into a community and satisfy your neighbors. In a political society, under the heavy hand of government, you expect your neighbors to satisfy you.

Pfeiffer, who looked preternaturally young for his age (he and his wife had fully adult offspring), and who wore a baseball cap backwards to Town Hall meetings, was satisfied that his "contract" gave him more rights than one that was not based on property rights: "We have more self-determination here under a nonpolitical regime than in a political society." His views offered the purest statement of a vision of governance entirely based on property rights. Nor did everyone's property rights appear to be equal. For Pfeiffer, who owned an estate home, there seemed to be a sliding scale, on which owners of smaller lots might have a lesser contract. "If you have less expensive houses, you lose the sense of sacrifice," he explained, adding a new spin to the Celebration ethos of self-sacrifice.

However chilling to behold, these were hardly crankish views in the world of Florida's planned communities. Yet for all the security represented by Pfeiffer's "contract" with the developer, there was little residents could do to stop the company from obtaining a zoning variance to alter its plans for the site, or from blocking a majority resident initiative. As Ray Chiaramonte pointed out, "the developer could decide to put in a Saturn manufacturing plant." At a meeting in June, when TCC unveiled plans for the commercial corridor, several residents loudly expressed dismay at the prospect of twelve-story hotels rising up to obscure their westward views: "We feel it's no longer a small town," one grieved, "it looks like a city, with big buildings." They must have forgotten that they had signed a raft of disclaimers at closing, among which was a waiver of their rights to a view. Pfeiffer's contract could easily turn into a raw deal, and homeowners' rights could often seem like thin, self-addressed envelopes.

Given the legal maze of the "Covenants, Conditions, and Restrictions," it's small wonder there was a general fuzziness in residents' understanding of their internal rights. Most Celebrationites confessed they did not really understand the town's system of governance, and habitually flunked when examined on details regarding the fiduciary responsibilities of entities like the Community Development District. Unlike most master-planned communities, Celebration had as many as four entities of governance: the Residential Owner's Association; a Non-Residential Owner's Association, which represented retailers and owners of apartment parcels; the Community Development District, a quasi-government entity which provided services and was responsible for maintenance of infrastructure (water, sewage, roads, drainage, landscaping) and utilities; and an Enterprise Community Development District, responsible for services to the commercial campus. An overarching Joint Committee governed all four, and Town Hall functioned as a one-stop home for the whole kit and caboodle. Celebration actually enjoys more of a working distinction between public and private sectors of governance than in most communities with homeowner associations. Here, the municipal functions of government relating to infrastructure are handled by the Community Development District, a unit of special-purpose government created by the Florida Land and Water Adjudicatory Commission, and whose board of supervisors, currently all Disney executives, will eventually be elected by landowners in the district. By contrast, the homeowner association's realm is limited to more private matters such as those relating to architectural review and community standards and restrictions.

Naturally, residents tend to take more of an interest in matters of governance when their property values are on the line. Jim Whelan, the canny psychologist and dedicated cyclist, confessed to me one day: "I didn't think for one minute about the governance structure of the town until I decided to sell the house." After less than a year in town, he and his family had decided to move back to Mahwah, New Jersey. He had only recently discovered that homeowners are not permitted to erect a "For Sale" notice in their yards. In Whelan's view, this helped give the developer a virtual monopoly over the housing market in town. He had begun to suspect that the residency rules helped reinforce the monopoly while masquerading as a deterrent against speculators. Whelan's suspicions in this matter were unconfirmed, but it was significant that his property interest was the factor that galvanized his concern about governance.

In the course of my year in Celebration, at least one hiccup in governmental process did occur, and went entirely unnoticed by residents. The chronic problems caused by the narrowness of the back alleyway increasingly demanded a resolution. At a Community Development District meeting in December, the board members decided they would consider a "one-way" designation for alleys if a majority of the residents on the block petitioned and voted for the measure. There was some discussion about the percentage of votes required: would it be 51 percent, 65 percent, or 75 percent? At several such meetings I attended, no residents were present, and this one was no exception. The meetings were tedious and mostly technical in content, although a period was always set aside on the agenda for public comment. The board decided to implement a 65 percent rule. Several weeks later, residents on Campus Street and Greenbriar were informed in a letter from Town Hall that their alleyways were now one-way streets. No formal votes had been taken, and no one I talked to on those streets had noticed the oversight. It was a small measure, and by all accounts a popular one. Nor was it likely to affect the value of anyone's property. But this had been the first time in Celebration when a residential vote was endorsed, in principle, and yet it had not been solicited.

UTOPIA ACHIEVED

Advocates of homeowner associations often argue that their method of community rule keeps at bay the messy intrusion of "politics." Yet there were some Celebrationites, like Larry Haber, a founder of the town's Jewish Council and the Jewish Congregation and whose family had been the town's first official residents, who saw the management structure as a perfect embodiment of their own partisan politics. A busy pioneer, Haber was active in United Way and saw himself as a George Will kind of Republican—social libertarian, fiscal conservative, religious liberal, and fierce opponent of big government. In addition, he was a Disney employee who had no great affection for "big corporate paternalism," a trait shared by many Celebrationites I knew who were also company employees. Haber believed Celebration to be the ideal Republican state in miniature, without government's layers of elected officials to stifle the process of self-determination. In fact, Celebration was pretty close to what Haber saw as a "condition of direct democracy." He said he had liberal friends in town who saw their own politics reflected in Celebration's community values, and he liked to tease them by declaring they were simply "closet Republicans." I never met any liberals who could match Haber's view with a counterclaim, based on their own principles, but it was not inconceivable that they existed in Celebration. In addition, there were residents like Pat Breck, a pro-choice Catholic who attended Presbyterian services, who believed that Celebration was a conservative community in a cultural sense. Conservatives, in her view, are "people people," a "tribe that looks out for another," and she associated liberals with "working mothers and latchkey children."

Haber's view of the town as personifying his own ideal of a pure political utopia was probably exceptional. When people loosely referred to Celebration as a "utopia," they generally meant that it was a good place to start over again, where other places had failed, or that it was a place of general happiness where no one had reason, other than his or her own personal misfortune, to be disenchanted. The use of the phrase had little connection to the venerable American tradition of utopian communities.

In the fanciful European mind, the New World had always been imagined as a utopian place, with apocalyptic dimensions—the end of the world as we know it and the beginning of a new order. The early Puritan settlements, with their own form of community *covenant*, including a New Urbanist–type rule that required residents to live within a mile and half of the meetinghouse, established a model for hundreds of utopian religious communities to follow. These were founded in the seventeenth and eighteenth centuries on the principle of the communal ownership of property by sects like the Shakers, the Rappites, the Moravian Brethren, the Zoar Separatists, and the True Inspirationists of Amana. Some survived for hundreds of years, and a few are still extant. The nineteenth-century versions were mostly secular, like Brook Farm, New Harmony, Fruitlands, Skanateales, Nashoba, Oneida, and the Phalanxes, and were heavily influenced by the anarchist and socialist ideas of Robert Owen and Charles Fourier. More than a hundred sprang up before the Civil War, each with its own polished vision of a new age to come where inhabitants would be truly free to pursue a rational form of the good life.[6] The equivalent in this century were the thousands of hippie communes founded in the late 1960s and early 1970s as living laboratories of a communal freedom that the materialism of consumer society promised but could never deliver. However short-lived, these were all intentional communities, planned as pocket-size correctives to the corruption and inequalities of dominant society. All of them, from the religious to the countercultural versions, experienced the tension between freedom and order that is intrinsic to the planned utopia.

While Celebration was living through the same tensions, none of its creators or residents saw the town as a descendant of these earlier utopias. More important were the utopian ideals of the Dream Home and the Main Street town. Also relevant, perhaps, was Florida's own utopian backdrop, having built long and hard on its early reputation as the site of the Fountain of Youth. Under Spanish rule, it had offered religious sanctuary to runaway slaves from the southern states. In its self-promotion as a frontier haven for settlers, it lured Civil War veterans, black and white, to a "soldier's paradise" by offering free land.[7] More recently, Florida had flourished as a resort and vacation utopia, and, thanks to Social Security, a retirement utopia where 25 percent of each generation of Americans now come to live out the rest of their lives, free from northern taxes and chills.

In the historical utopias, community was an intentional goal shared by individuals with allegiances to commonly held beliefs. In today's planned development, community is mostly a marketing term, aimed at a consumer niche to be attracted and recruited through effective advertising. True to the gospel of the "clustering of America," TCC had done its share of niche-market research. But the company had also staked its brand name on the premise that residents would forge common bonds that exceeded the mere "sense of community" featured in advertising for the town. This was something of a gamble, since the outcome of overly zealous community building can easily threaten the property interests of residents and the developer. But the genius of the marketing concept would override any potential conflict. In Celebration, residents would be protecting their private interests precisely by building strong community bonds. The more community-minded the town became, the more its property values would improve, since its homes were built to attract buyers who wanted to come and be community builders. Of course, since no one wanted any single group or initiative to overreach itself, Town Hall and the Celebration Foundation were there, in part, to manage and channel the zeal.

Between the two, community management had become a fine art. The Foundation, staffed entirely by women, kindled the flames of volunteerism. Herrington's checking role at Town Hall was decidedly more paternal, though he lamented to me on more than one occasion that his job was mostly restricted to "housekeeping duties." Professionally ambitious, Herrington was a leading light in the national association of community managers (the Community Association Institute), and while his Celebration job was highly prestigious, he was clearly hungry for responsibilities that would give him a more active role in designing communities.[8]

This personal drive was reflected in the Town Hall newsletter that always carried the stamp of his own opinion. While the force of this opinion was powerful, it did not always sway residents. One good example appeared in the January 1998 issue, where Brent implored residents to kick the habit of referring to different parts of town as West Village or North Village, and even worse, Phase I and Phase II. These, he argued, are developer's short-term labels, and

> tend to reinforce parochial thinking, stratification and division ... words that do not currently come to mind when I think of Celebration. In adopting the "town" model, Celebration is committed to an entirely different ethos than is found in a typical residential subdivision. At Celebration, we are all stakeholders—whether apartment residents, estate home owners, cottage home owners, garage apartment residents, retail merchants or office building workers. We all have a stake in the future of the town. As fellow stakeholders, our shared goal should be to build a sense of community, shared responsibility and civic pride that runs through the width and breadth of our town. Somehow, dividing ourselves into "villages" seems to run counter to what Celebration stands for.[9]

The proper frame of reference, he observed, should be traditional towns like Savannah, or Cambridge, or Kissimmee, where residents say "I live on the north side just off of Exeter Drive," or "I live near Waterford Park." In his next newsletter, Brent recorded that a majority of the respondents to his cause expressed agreement, but this one really was a losing battle. Around town, I found that most folks had taken the advice with a grain of salt, and were lacing their conversation with heavily ironic phrases like "In what used to be called North Village . . ."

In September, Herrington abruptly announced his resignation. Those who knew him personally did not seem surprised, but the community as a whole was stunned. There was much speculation, though no real evidence, that he had been fired by Disney. Some residents viewed his resignation as an act of disloyalty, as if his duties had been bound by an oath of public office. Others surmised that he had been in a tight political corner, both as a Town and Country homeowner facing possible litigation with the builder and as the father of the only two children in town who could never be pulled from the school. He left for a plum job at DC Ranch, in Scottsdale, Arizona, where the developer DMB was building a similar, but larger, master-planned community. Recruited to Celebration after the rules and governance structure were established, his job description had indeed been confining. With DMB he would have a more integral role in community planning, a business he considered more like a "cause." In the course of our last conversation, he acknowledged that Disney's connection to the town did not always help the advancement of this cause: "As wonderful and fun as it is to be a part of Celebration, it is a one-project deal, and, quite honestly, as powerful an asset as the Disney organization is in getting this project done, its sponsorship of the project to some extent colors the world's perception of whether any of this is replicable, or meaningful in real terms."

Herrington joined the steady exodus of planners, managers, and teachers from the Celebration project, reinforcing the impression that a job in this town or at the school was simply a career stepping-stone. The name was like gold leaf on a job résumé, and he acknowledged that there was a "constant drumbeat of opportunities for everyone" associated with it. Herrington had done more than anyone to build morale, yet his abrupt departure did little to diminish residents' perception of management as a corporate revolving door.

TWO FROM LEFT FIELD

Celebration had not witnessed anything on the scale of a community "barn raising," but there were myriad small, interpersonal efforts that marked it as a caring community where people pulled together. Word spread very quickly about illnesses and personal difficulties, and the casualties were often deluged with gifts in the form of food and goodwill packages. More than one Celebrationite observed that they initially thought they had moved to a community with a high proportion of misfortunes, accustomed as they were to the anonymity of suburbia. It was clearly a place where residents could feel that they would be supported in the event of some personal mishap, and in ways that went far beyond neighborly expectations of mutual help.

Even so, several community initiatives had taken on an organized life of their own. There were two—quite different in nature—that I chose to follow closely in the course of my year. The first was a plan to start a Montessori school, undertaken by a small group of residents against all odds. The other evolved out of the time-honored institution of block parties.

The Montessori initiative grew out of residents' dissatisfaction with the day-care services provided by Children's World, a local company awarded an exclusive franchise by the developer. These services were widely perceived as overpriced and underattentive to young children's needs. So, too, there was the dissatisfaction with Celebration School, originally planned to include a preschooling component, until the funding ran into complications. Several parents met to discuss an alternative—"a much better school at a fraction of the cost"—with the potential, eventually, to provide K–5 education. This group included residents with a wide range of incomes and was spearheaded by the resilient Lance Boyer, the Domino's Pizza employee with a wry wit and a healthy instinct for independent equality of opinion. It began to meet regularly in the fall of 1997 to investigate all possibilities, and by the early summer had succeeded in launching plans for the school. It became the first truly successful independent initiative in Celebration.

As the group built confidence in its efforts, the reception of my own attendance at meetings shifted. I progressed from being ribbed as a "spy in our midst" to being listed in Lance's minutes as "scribe" and finally "historian." This wasn't simply a twist of Lance's mischievous spirit. The first several meetings were marked by a decidedly conspiratorial air, as if the attendees were contemplating a coup against Disney. In the course of one of them, a mother in the group thought out loud, "If we could only get our foot in the door," adding, on reflection, "Isn't that silly? We live here." Whenever someone made a disparaging comment about the company, my presence was acknowledged: "Did you get that down, Andrew?" No one was sure how the developer would react to an alternative educational initiative that intended to go all the way, and group members assumed, from the outset, that TCC would not be terribly helpful at all. The group was already disheartened by a flat response to their initial overtures. At Town Hall, Lance had been told that "surveys show that everyone wants a Montessori school, but it usually doesn't work out. It's the same with a hardware store." The reference here was to the store that everyone in town wanted to see happen, but that the population was not large enough to support.

Convinced that there was a big difference between a school and a hardware store, the group pushed ahead. They were now faced with the Herculean tasks of fund-raising and finding a suitable site on Celebration's costly land. At that time, the going price was $330,000 an acre, almost three times the price of land outside the White Vinyl Fence. Over the course of several months, the group doggedly explored every possible site within a feasible radius of the town, and made loose contractual commitments to a Montessori principal in the region. The initiative might have fallen through at several points, but it was driven by a visible passion for the children's well-being, and also, in some part, by the view that residents should have more than "a foot in the door" when it came to creating institutions independent of TCC. In due time, Lance and others learned the tactics of approaching Disney from other residential contractors in town, and eventually won over key TCC employee residents who decided that their own children might benefit best from a Montessori education. By late spring, the group had secured a site and a floor plan, teachers, and the registered interest of about forty families, and they laid down a deposit on a three-thousand-square-foot French estate home in the area to the east of downtown, where residents are permitted to run a business from their homes.

The only serious setback occurred over internal disagreements about financing. Some members felt that the seed investors in the school would, in effect, be subsidizing the education of others, especially much wealthier parents who could easily afford private tuition for their kids. Would it not be fair, then, for these investors to expect a fair market return, by raising the tuition rate and charging market value for use of the space? This gave rise to a heated debate about the principles behind the initiative. What should be the goal of the group? To open the school at the lowest cost to everyone in the community? Or to make a reasonable return on a for-profit institution? Questions like this stirred up a small hornet's nest, as the group factionalized for several weeks, one side pleading "from the heart" their simple cause of furthering education, the other adopting a more hard-nosed business approach. Amy Gould-Pilz, director of the Children's Playgroup in town and an active Montessori participant from the outset, regretted the intrusion of class resentment in the discussions, but was hardly surprised. "There's a reason why suburbs are divided into different income levels," she joked. The specter of class friction faded when a pragmatic business plan (seven large investors with limited return on their investments) eventually prevailed over the more egalitarian proposal (many small stakeholder investors in a not-for-profit corporation). On September 3, the building broke ground, only a year after the group had first met, and the school opened its doors to fifty students in June 1999.

Low-intensity class friction will flourish in any mixed-income community, and though muted, it was hardly absent from the social life of distinct neighborhoods in Celebration. Each block consisted of the same lot sizes, and so block parties, inevitably, took on a local, socioeconomic flavor. Residents in the middle-income homes took pride in the fact that all the townsfolk, including apartment tenants, were welcome at their potluck parties. Those in the newer and less central neighborhoods, like Lake Evalyn, which hosted the least expensive, detached homes, made a special effort to attract the rest of the townsfolk. It did not escape notice that residents on blocks of estate homes often had their parties catered and that the guest lists were more carefully zoned. In April, Town Hall launched its "block party trailer" (outfitted with barbecue grills, stereo system, ice chests, hula hoops, and water sprinkler games) for general use. Since every act of Town Hall was closely analyzed, the chuck wagon was perceived by some as an intervention in the "block party wars" and as a subtle invitation to keep these events nonexclusive and noncompetitive.

Competition aside, one street had already achieved an unsurpassable record for its potluck performance. On Honeysuckle—an early pioneer row with middle-range Cottage lots—the zest for neighborliness was running far ahead of expectation. Regular monthly parties were slated at residents' houses for almost two years in advance, and

An early Honeysuckle potluck gathering. (Photo: Jonathan Hayt)

each was announced with ornate invitations. The driving force on Honeysuckle was the home team of Darlene and Fred Rapanotti, who supervised the soirees with cosy precision. Originally from Garden City on Long Island, with a "five-and-dime on every street corner," the Rapanottis were one of the town's many (ex-)military couples, long accustomed to the regulated environments of military housing. In addition, theirs was one of the houses decorated as a teeming shrine to Disney memorabilia. Shelves, tables, and wall space were lined with figurines, pictures, and sculptures of Walt's entire entourage, including an awesome rendering of Cinderella's Castle. The Rapanotti home was also a fount of hospitality, and I was always received there with uncommon largesse. Of Chinese-American descent, and with a culinary range to match, Darlene's no-nonsense efforts at pioneering the potluck circuit were justly famous and had been lovingly archived. An attendance book registered residents' comments at each event, a photograph album recorded past gatherings, and a range of custom invitations from each party were preserved. Darlene, who worked at Disney's Caribbean

Cruise Lines, had also been active in exporting the potluck protocols to other neighborhoods and had aspirations to link the several circuits together in an annual, communitywide bash. The Honeysuckle potlucks had hosted votes on block adornments—coordinated Christmas decor on the mailboxes—and Darlene wanted to organize discussions on how best to represent the town to visiting journalists in hopes of dispelling the media cliché that "we are all mechanical puppets and Disney mannequins."

Each of the several parties I attended had its own flavor, where hosts would invite their own friends from other parts of town. One event in late summer took the form of an elaborate hayride to the North Village. Attendance varied. There were regulars and not-so-regulars. To be sure, there were some on the block who found the monthly regimen to be a little more sociability than they cared for, and the Honeysuckle model, while much admired from a distance, had set a pace that no other block in town tried to match. In some ways, it represented the tolerable upper limit of community bonding in Celebration.

There were many blocks in town where neighbors, lacking willingly active organizers, preferred to socialize informally or loosely attach themselves to the party circuit of an adjoining block. If anything, the pace of community building that had been set here had resulted in partial burnout. Several pioneers acknowledged there was too little time for their own families. Religious leaders, partially in competition with the community professionals at Town Hall and the Foundation, expressed concern that overcommitment to community activity was in danger of producing dysfunctional families. In Celebration, there was such a thing as a little too much community.

Besides, block solidarity was an uneasy feature of social life in a town where Town Hall encouraged residents to identify with the whole of Celebration. In his newsletter item discouraging the use of village labels, Herrington warned against "the tendency of new developments to fracture into separate districts rather than functioning as dynamic, cohesive communities." Officially, at least, community was intended to be synonymous with the entire town, and professional help was on hand to ensure that community building kept its course. A subtle reward system was in place very early, where especially active volunteers enjoyed the gratitude of the professionals. Each year, the Foundation handed out Community

Service Awards and ran a "Tattle Tales" section in its newsletter in which residents were encouraged to inform on their "do-gooder" neighbors. Town Hall had established its own impromptu practice of awarding certificates for community-minded acts, and Herrington rarely missed a public opportunity to comment on "the incredible organic juice that flows up from the residents."

There was lots of evidence of this juice, but it was still too early to say that the residential fabric had developed the truly organic texture that is the Holy Grail of nostalgic mythmakers and community management professionals alike. Community pride among Celebrationites was a heady cocktail, mixed with equal parts of performance anxiety, property angst, and pioneer exuberance. Professional community management, on the other hand, had already proved itself as a well-seasoned vintage. Beyond the machinery of management, however, the battles being fought in town had fashioned community bonds that were arguably stronger than those brought on by the physical advantages of New Urban neighborliness or the Foundation's culture of volunteerism. This was a sense of community forged out of conditions of adversity, and however much outsiders snorted at the mere idea of Celebrationites suffering, these internal struggles had worked their way into the guts of community building in ways that offered some lessons for the outside world.

11

GOD'S HOUSES, A PICTURE OF HEALTH, AND THE COLOR OF OUR MINDS

"Eat fresh fruit, nuts, and vegetables. Get plenty of rest. Exercise. Get plenty of fresh air and sunshine. Avoid meat, high-fat and high-sugar foods. Get a good night's sleep. Don't smoke or use alcohol. Reduce stress. Learn to relax. Enjoy life."

—"The Corn Flake Connection," Celebration Health

Patrick Carrin, the pastor of Celebration Community Church, had delivered his Mother's Day sermon on the gospel of love with vigor and dash. It had been international in scope, ranging from the Vietnam War to the crisis of faith in the old Soviet Union, and had touched, in some depth, on the novels of Fyodor Dostoevsky. Assembled in the school cafeteria, where the church met regularly, members of the congregation were asked to stand, individually, to pay tribute to their mothers. Several rose and testified in turn. Joan Jones, retired schoolteacher and former tenant of my apartment, spoke passionately of her mother's kindnesses and good deeds, and went on to praise "all good Christian mothers." As she sat down, she leaned over, patted my knee, and added, sotto voce, "and Jewish mothers, too." It was a characteristically thoughtful act, though Joan, who had quizzed me on my background at our first meeting, hadn't quite got it right. It was my father who had been Jewish (though he had chosen not to be a Jewish father, as Holocaust refugees in out-of-the-way places sometimes did). My siblings and myself were brought up in my mother's Church of Scotland at the sober Presbyterian core, a world away from the emotive witnessing of the Bible Belt. In making this inclusive gesture Joan was doing the Celebration thing. But there was already a trace of local history attached to her kind words, in a town where two Protestant congregations coexisted uneasily, each courting favor with the non-Christians and other potential recruits.

Whatever Bible Belt energies pulsed through the veins of this town met here in Carrin's nondenominational congregation, conceived as a church in the spirit of Celebration where people "leave their labels at the door and worship together." Carrin, a shrewd Honeywell executive with his name on four patents and a graduate of Louisville's Southern Baptist Theological Seminary, spoke to me of uniting the Christian faiths. "As we enter the second millennium," he predicts a "new paradigm" that "will see a tremendous wave of people integrating the Church, seeking commonality, and enjoying diversity together through agreement on fundamental issues." In addition to several different kinds of Baptists, his congregation already included Methodists, Catholics, Lutherans, Mormons, Episcopalians, worshipers from the Assemblies of God, and various independents. Regardless, around town it was referred to, often with disdain, as the Baptist congregation. To set up in town, Carrin's church was sponsored and backed by Jim Horton, the much respected pastor of the College Park Baptist Church and the moderate Cooperative Baptist Fellowship. Horton, along with other prominent Orlando pastors, had vigorously opposed the Southern Baptist boycott of Disney. Sinners were to be befriended and recruited, not shunned.

Establishing the several houses of God had been one of the thorniest issues faced by the developer. The Baptist boycott was the least of the problems, though it had probably scuttled the prospect of an overtly Baptist ministry on Disney property. The town had been planned with one small two-acre site for ecumenical worship, classically located across the street from Robert Venturi and Denise Scott Brown's bank building. Small-town architectural convention demanded a neoclassical, steepled, clapboard building, and the cultural expectation was that it would be occupied by a mainline Protestant church. In spite of Walt's own distaste for organized religion, stemming from an overdose of pulpit zeal in the Congregational Church of his childhood, the Disney company had a de facto Protestant identity—Catholics cannot be married at Disney World. In all prudence, however, the company could not make a decision to allot the site to any one faith, and so they hosted discussions among Celebration's pioneer religious leaders about establishing an interfaith center. But who would program the services and manage the use of the center by so many different groups? TCC officials did not relish taking on that prickly task. When push came to shove, the bottom line was the decisive element. Someone had to come up with cash for the site, and the Presbyterian Church got their act together first.

Flush with a quarter-million-dollar gift from Walt's niece, Dorothy Disney Puder (who announced, "This money was not our money, but the Lord's money"),[1] their bid not only secured the site but also determined that the Presbyterian church would become the town's alpha-male "community congregation." For a while, both Protestant congregations (each headed by a man named Patrick) met at different times on Sunday morning in the AMC theater, and some confusion resulted, with residents mistaking one for the other. Carrin's group eventually removed to the school cafeteria, leaving the larger space to the now-burgeoning congregation of the other Patrick, the Rev. Wrisley, who had been appointed as the only full-time religious leader in town. Yet the rivalry continued. In a letter to prospective church members, Carrin boldly pleaded: "Leave your prejudice at home and come take part in what will become the most watched new church in modern history." Everything that was new in Celebration was prone to an overkill dose of publicity.

Wrisley had been recruited from a ministry at Peachtree in Atlanta, where he and other pastors had built a mega-church—the largest Presbyterian church in the country—with about 11,500 members. The "church of the next millennium" he was assigned to build here was a "national church," since it had been voted up and approved by the Presbyterian General Assembly. In accord, he claimed, with the precepts of the New Urbanism—it was to be a "New Urban Ministry"—Wrisley envisaged a site with embedded religious themes:

> The church will be surrounded with loggias, porches, gardens. It's going to be a sensual environment in that it will stimulate the senses. Not only the eyes and ears, but also smells—we'll have a fragrant

> garden. Jesus spent most his time in four places. The sea, the mountain, the desert and the garden. So what we want to do architecturally is to develop a movement where you experience vegetation from the desert, then there's this long stream to represent the river or sea—a giant rock will have water coming out of it—and then you have plants and vegetation that are germane to the Garden of Gethsemane. So you experience the Gospel sensually, before you even go in to hear it. It's an environmental imagination.

If there was more than a touch of Imagineering to this vision, plans for the interior sounded not unlike a Virgin mega-store. "We want it hot-wired, with cable, media, electronics. It's our notion that the stained glass of tomorrow for the church is electronics and technology, not glass. . . . In our culture, we're moving from page to screen, and the church needs to be there with it." Burly, bearded, and jovial, Wrisley did not have to strive hard for his downhome image (his e-mail name is "DisneyPope"), and his agenda was firmly in line with the precepts of a postmodern Gospel. He was completing a doctoral dissertation on the concept of a New Urbanist ministry with Drew University's Leonard Sweet, a "church futurist" and entrepreneurial author of works including *Quantum Spirituality*, *FaithQuakes*, and a devotional called *Soul Café*, which spelled out the "ten commandments for the postmodern church." Wrisley's reformed liturgy laid him open to some congregants' criticism that his God was too much of a "buddy" and not enough of an authoritative or transcendental force. He was nothing if not an evangelist for relevance, insisting that "the church has been doing American Bandstand ministry in an MTV 'Grind' culture." As in Celebration proper, the church's laptop- and circuit TV–driven infrastructure would be treated, on the outside, to a neotraditional skin. Its Welcome Center on Celebration Avenue was to be housed in a Victorian home, fully equipped with a porch, and its sanctuary was planned to seat eight hundred people, by far the biggest meeting place in town. Despite a second gift from the Puders, redeemed from Disney stock inherited from Walt and Roy, initial funding for the $11 million site was very slow in accumulating, but when Wrisley launched a local campaign, $800,000 was collected from congregants within a year. Even so, "value engineering" forced a reduction in the scope of plans for the site, rescheduled to break ground in September 1999. In the meantime, the congregation had come up with some ideas of their own. One member wanted to donate a full pipe organ—not exactly MTV.

On the national religious scene, there was some skepticism about placing a large house of God within the bosom of Mammon, or at least a Lord of the Marketplace. Wrisley responded in the press, "If you want to play cynic and say Disney represents American capitalism gone exponential, then I'd say there's no better place for the church. I don't care how fast your Pentium processor is, people die and get divorced; and kids get head lice at school here. You can't buy happiness, and you're going to have hurt. . . . The mere presence of a church here blows the notion of Disney illusion out of the water. You don't build a church in the land of make-believe."[2] The Rev. Roger Richardson, executive president of the Central Florida Presbytery in Orlando, who had brokered the Celebration ministry, was not at all sobered by the prospect that his church might some day be at odds with Disney. "A faithful church doesn't have to be a fearful church," he declared. "We've seen kingdoms rise and fall and we're still going forward, and we'll be here long after Disney is here and gone."[3]

As the Celebration congregation ramped up, its social justice ministry was soon active, perusing Habitat for Humanity plans to build affordable housing in Orlando and Kissimmee, and actively competing with the Foundation for many of the same burned-out volunteers. As Wrisley noted, "You can only effect change if you're inside." Around town, of course, there was a different concern. Members of other denominations naturally felt a little sore that the Presbyterians had stolen a march on everyone else, and inevitably, there were suspicions about backstage deals. In Central Florida, Presbyterians numbered a mere 4 percent of church members, and so Celebration was a real coup to have pulled off. Before long, however, Wrisley had built a three hundred–strong congregation, and he credited a trend among boomers of rediscovering their faith. Indeed, many folks I knew in town mentioned that they were much more religiously inclined than they had been ten years before. Wrisley saw a challenge in responding to these returnees, who had been "shaped by a sound-bite world, where everything has to be sensual and engaging." Two-thirds of his congregation were non-Presbyterians, including lifelong Catholics and a few charismatics, who decided they wanted to commit to a church within the community rather than travel to worship. Melding this group culturally was a challenge. Wrisley's casual style and dress helped, but he sometimes adopted a more direct educational strategy.

One such attempt occurred in late May, when Wrisley put on a service based on the bagpipe-heavy ritual called the "The Kirkin' O' The Tartan" to teach the Scottish heritage of the Presbyterian Church. This ritual was an entirely American creation, introduced in Washington, D.C., in 1941, but not untypical of the image of Scotland abroad. The tartans, after all, were associated historically in Scotland with Highland traditions, and therefore with a Catholic heritage that had been fiercely at odds with the lowland Reformation. But that was all in the bloody past, and the Highland regalia had long been co-opted into the official national symbology of State and Kirk, and packaged for export overseas. For the Celebration service, the Orlando Regional Police Pipe Band lent their wobbly bagpiping talents. Wrisley briefly covered the history of the Scottish Reformation and the founding of a church governed from the "bottom up." In his sermon, he inveighed against "complacent American Christians" who have grown "spiritually fat on spiritual junk food, a feel-good diet that doesn't burn any spiritual calories." This "couch potato spirituality" makes us forget the "blood, sweat, and tears" of those who suffered and died for the history of the Church. The Scots Presbyterians, Wrisley told us, came to this country, like other immigrants, in order to practice their faith free from persecution. To be sure, there were other groups who had suffered much more persecution than the Scots Presbyterians, but Wrisley's theme of different immigrant groups drawn by a common purpose was one that would be easy to identify for a congregation composed of many different religious backgrounds and especially attentive to any petition on the topic of pioneer sacrifice.

Many Catholic families preferred their own devotions, and they organized early to start a parish in town. The Catholic organizers included some of the town's most active citizens—Lise and Ron Juneman, Rodney Jones, Robin Delany, and Ray Chiaramonte—and, given the pioneer drive, nothing seemed impossible to this group. At one meeting I attended, in which they rehearsed what they might say in their first meetings with the bishop from the Orlando diocese, their spirit was clearly resolute: "We feel we are on a mission here, and that we were chosen to do this, and will continue, whether you help us or not." With kids being pulled weekly from the school and sent to parochial schools, the group also hoped TCC might welcome a private alternative in town and would help them set it up.

In the course of the next several months they learned a good deal about the company and about their church. TCC, it turned out, was unwilling to discount the price of land sufficiently, not even for an initiative to found a crucial communitywide institution. For his part, the bishop decided the residential demographics showed that a parish could be sustained in the Celebration area, but he was unwilling to pay a million dollars for the three-and-a-half-acre site that residents had selected—just east of downtown, across from the planned Presbyterian church. One would-be parishioner described the hardball negotiations between the diocese and TCC as "one corporation going up against another corporation." Mary, Queen of the Universe, a shrine across from Disney World frequented by tourists and locals, had cost only $30,000 an acre, and the bishop did not want to see attendance there depleted by an area rival. In addition, the diocese ruled that a new parish has to serve as a mission of an existing church before it could be licensed on its own—an eternity of waiting if you are on pioneer time.

The group held the town's first Catholic mass in the Lakeside Park pavilion in December, but was discouraged by the diocese from holding any more. They had run up against a brick wall in town, even though Rodney Jones reported that the group had built a support base of five hundred area families who would have been willing to pledge the million dollars required to buy the land. By way of compensation, the bishop committed informally to a parish within two miles of the town. Though it would be several years in the making, Celebration residents, with a higher proportion of Catholics than most southern towns, would play a leading role in the formation of that parish.

As with the Catholics, Celebration's Jews had been jump-started by the Presbyterian initiative. According to Larry Pitt, a high-ranking Disney lawyer and legal secretary of TCC, they had also hewed to the spirit of the old Jewish joke: "How many synagogues are there on an island of shipwrecked Jews? Three." A Hebrew school met twice a week, a Jewish Council was established for social and cultural representation in civic affairs, and a Jewish Congregation put on a service and Shabbat dinner in the Golf Club tavern on Friday evenings. The Council was a political compromise from the beginning. One or two Orthodox members, strongly vocal, were opposed to a synagogue that they knew would be Reform. Lacking any consensus as a result, the Council was mostly inactive. Pitt and Larry Haber, a business director with Disney's TV department, had both helped to start a conservative temple in South Orange, just to the north. Trained in Boca Raton as a community Jewish leader (a "SuperJew," he quipped) by the Wexler Heritage Foundation, Pitt pushed for a Reform congregation in Celebration so as not to conflict with the South Orange synagogue. He had chosen the first seder Haggadah carefully—a politic blend of traditional references spliced with modern commentary about the condition of the Jewish faith around the world.

Passover in April was swelled by the addition of the tornado-ravaged Osceola congregation, one of whose elders, seated opposite at the table, tried earnestly to recruit me to the Poinciana temple. "We need young blood," he pleaded. I noticed that there were no gentiles from Celebration in attendance. Neither had the Orthodox members shown up, partly because gentiles had been present the year before. Several Jews in town told me they found the Orthodox presence to be off-putting. They preferred to attend the merely social gatherings and steer clear of the low-intensity religious friction. Haber and Richard Cowin, the presidents of the congregation, clearly favored a more inclusive profile, and eventually won the adoption of a Reconstructionist identity for the synagogue. Pitt was less enthusiastic about this development: "The message is being muddled and watered down to the point of being Jewish in name only." This kind of sentiment was shared by the town's fundamentalist Christians, like Donald Jones, the evangelist pastor who believed that "there's too much here that goes under the name of Christianity that's not at all Christian." Jones was active in Carrin's congregation, but he saw the religious scene around town as more of a "country club, or social occasion" than as a serious Christian environment.

Its identity aside, Pitt acknowledged that the founding of the Jewish congregation had been an important form of publicity, especially for attracting prospective residents: it was "like putting up a lighthouse to say 'Jews are here' in Celebration." A high mark of visibility had been the erection of a large menorah by the lakefront next to the Christmas tree during the long holiday season. A Christian group had lobbied for a nativity scene, and there was some heated debate about whether the Christmas tree was a sufficiently Christian symbol. Ron Dickson, the merry prankster from Campus Street, made his own intervention in the name of religious pluralism when he showed up at Herrington's Town Hall office in full Druid regalia—white shirt and pants and a broad-brimmed, white sailing hat—to request permission to position a Druid wreath between the menorah and the Christmas tree.

In late fall, other symbols, with a less direct religious origin, had begun to dot the landscape. Pink flamingos were appearing mysteriously in backyards and on porches and balconies. Given Celebration's official canons of taste, and the unofficial surveillance of the semi-mythical Porch Police, this was a highly questionable item of decor. In November, Rev. Wrisley had declared that the birds would henceforth be an "anchor for prayer" around town to remind residents of those "throughout the world who are persecuted for the faith they hold." They were "planted" overnight in residents' yards and were supposed to be moved every few days, circulating around the congregation. Whatever were you thinking, I asked him? Wrisley explained that he had chosen the trophy bird—the tackiest object of outdoor Florida furniture—because it is supposed to "represent reality" in a town where the aesthetic regulations are often viewed as an artificial imposition, even by residents. His iconoclastic taste for the offbeat had embraced the postmodern appetite for kitsch. Town Hall tactfully turned a blind eye to this violation of the rules. "When we take ourselves too seriously, we're in trouble," Wrisley observed earnestly. He joked that his next scheme for the kitschification of Celebration might be to sponsor a "tacky Christmas parade."

WELLVILLE

There was another church that exerted its influence in town, in quite another way. Out near the I-4 interstate (which bisects the Celebration site), Celebration Health, a massive 260,000-square-foot "wellness center" had been designed by Robert Stern in the red-tiled, Spanish style. It is owned and operated by Florida Hospital, health-care home of the Church of the Seventh-Day Adventists, and it boasts an octagonal tower that symbolizes the Adventists' eight principles of health Creation. Bodily health and purity had been a staple of Adventist doctrine since the evangelizing of Ellen White in the 1860s and the founding of Battle Creek health-care center in Michigan, where W. K. Kellogg held sway with his strict, natural-fiber dietary regimes. The Creation-based, Adventist health credo has now been retread as a forerunner of today's holistic approaches to disease prevention, emphasizing fresh air, exercise, and whole body maintenance as a fillip to spiritual upkeep. The Sabbath Rest Principle, a cornerstone of church doctrine, is part and parcel of a creed that sees Christ as a physician as much as anything else.

Florida Hospital itself has grown from a small, restorative haven for wintering northerners into the second busiest hospital system in the United States, and the recipient of the nation's largest Medicare check. But it has never had the opportunity, which Celebration now offered, to integrate a planned town, founded on the principle of community health, with a health-care doctrine based on bodily and spiritual holism. More to the point, this concept had not promised a life of profits until recently. Now, with the escalation of self-care and nonallopathic medicine, and the gathering crisis of managed care, the conditions were ideal for a commercial venture of this sort. As Des Cummings, director of Celebration Health, put it to me, "society was not ready before to reward the holistic approach." Cummings saw a lucrative opening for bridging the gulf between the New Age holists and the Machine Age surgeons, viewed by each other until recently as quacks and mechanics, respectively.

The Adventist credo of "creating health" fits seamlessly with postmodern concepts of promoting organic wellness, so opposed to the medical industry's prevailing view of the body as a machine that needs a technical fix after every illness crash. But Florida Hospital had not exactly turned its back on machines; it still embraced the full spectrum of advanced medical technology. The challenge behind Celebration Health was to forge a mission in synch with TCC's blend of tradition (community or family doctors doing the rounds) and futurism (high-tech magic bullets). Consequently, the building was designed to resemble a grand Mediterranean hotel—a "hospit-el" where patients would feel like "guests"—and a huge portion of its facilities was given over to rehabilitation and fitness centers. Some of the medical industry's top names—GE, Johnson & Johnson, GlaxoWellcome, Hewlett-Packard, Hoffmann-Laroche, Astra Merck—were recruited as corporate partners, contributing big bucks for the opportunity to showcase their products in the Disney corporate tradition and duly underwriting the construction of the building. All the latest toys, from state-of-the-art imaging to telesurgery, were lined up to be showcased. It being Celebration, the facility was loudly touted as a laboratory for the "health care delivery system of the future."

The lavish grand opening in November 1997, replete with the release of a cloud of white doves, also featured a two-day symposium of podium voices offering hosannas of praise more befitting the coronation of a monarch than a new hospital. Leland Kaiser, a silver-tongued futurist, who is a consultant to Celebration Health, spoke breathlessly of Celebration as the "start of habitat redesign. If it works here, it will work in other places. This is the epicenter." Mindful of the assembled corporate partners in his audience, he was more direct: "What we have created here is a possibility. Not since the Middle Ages have we had one language system that can bring together science, spirituality, and business and we have done that here. We have entered the Quantum Age. . . . For the first time, the businessperson, the clinician scientist, and the spiritual person sit at the same table, use the same words, and are engaged in the same business. What we see here is a new kind of capitalism, a capitalism with consciousness, with the resources and the vision to create a better world." I was not so comforted by the prospect of these three groups sitting at the same table and speaking the same language, whether in the Middle Ages or in Osceola County. The table, for one thing, probably ought to be a lot bigger, with a much wider circle of conversants. This new rhetoric of body-mind-spirit was a training seminar for the corporate titans of the medical industry, whose junior reps filled the seats around me. They were studiously learning how to survive the ratcheting down of the welfare state and, in particular, how to poach some of the direct fee-for-service action from the huge boom in self-care and alternative medicine. The language made perfect sense for an industry bracing itself for a life of profit beyond managed care where premiums would lie outside the insurance orbit.

Florida's HMOs had started to hemorrhage money, and Florida Hospital's own Medicare HMO, Premier Care, would go belly-up before the year was out.

Kaiser had offered a rather different angle in an article he wrote for the first issue of a promotional publication called the *Celebration Journal.* "The investment-owned health providers trying to dominate our current marketplace will fail," he predicts, because the "for-profit industry is opportunistic, it comes and goes with the fortunes of Wall Street." "Empowered communities" with their own health plans will come to the fore, collecting the premiums from the enrolled population and the profits will go back into the communities. "Dollars will not leave the community and gravitate to Wall Street while children in the community go without basic services." Self-care and nonallopathic treatment will help this system keep costs down, but Kaiser also advocates tapping the "gift economy" whereby retirees will volunteer their time and talents, in addition to working people who will "tithe their time." Pretty soon, the "gift economy will be larger than the money economy."[4]

However stirring as an agenda—Cummings, the hospital's director, described it to me as "universalistic and socialist," and impractical in a "mobile, capitalist society"—Kaiser's vision of an "empowered community" was not likely to be realized in Celebration. With poised understatement, Brian Haas, a physician who lived in town, observed, "It's not exactly a community hospital." Haas, a partner in one of the metro region's top ophthalmology groups and a crack ex-Navy surgeon, had been passed over initially by the hospital in favor of a group headquartered in Tarpon Springs, eighty miles distant. When contracts with this group and others fell through, Haas was asked to direct the opthalmology unit, but declined. By then, several doctors within the community had left the staff, as had some units, including pediatrics, and the hospital's business plan was in disarray. It had dropped the $25,000 fee required of all participating physicians but was still taking 50 percent of all revenues. Unusual for a medical center, Celebration Health was strictly in the subcontracting business, with no permanent physicians on staff and none at all who functioned within the community in the bedside manner. So far, what existed of the hospital's holistic component seemed to be pretty upmarket. A center for holistic evaluation was gearing up to offer luxury package weekends to corporate executives in need of a life booster. In the meantime, Celebration Health had already become a regular on the conference circuit for organizations like the Christian Medical and Dental Society.

Haas, who still uses the facility on occasion to see his patients, offered a clearheaded analysis of the economics of the facility. Getting into the wellness business, he pointed out, was the future of industry profit because "preventive care is fee-for-service, and it is much more profitable to run a wellness center with healthy people who pay their own way than to run a hospital for the chronically sick." Indeed, fitness centers within hospitals are the fastest growing trend in medical real estate in Florida, fast displacing the independent gym sector. Haas saw Florida Hospital "maximizing a marketing niche in a competitive milieu," and predicted that the ultimate source of its business would lie in the international tourist facelift market. Affluent world travelers could linger under lasers while their families enjoyed the theme parks. Sure enough, Florida Hospital had already embarked on an extensive campaign of international marketing in countries that service the Orlando tourist market. The facility's brochure for selling itself to physicians promised that "Celebration Health will develop major channels of international business targeted at the following regions: Central and South America, Caribbean countries, United Kingdom, Mexico, and Germany. Contracts will be developed with international governments, physicians and insurance carriers to provide medical services, educational conferences and clinical demonstrations through teleconferences. . . . Many other strategies are planned to capture international and tourist business."

For a while, it looked as if Celebration Health would be a hospital with no beds. In a highly unusual sequence, the $150 million facility had been built before a certificate of need was issued by the state. Indeed, the application was turned down twice by the Florida Agency for Health Care Administration on the basis that the area, where occupancy rates averaged less than 36 percent, did not need more hospital beds, especially acute-care beds at a cost of almost $2 million each.[5] The agency had concluded that Celebration Health would draw wealthy patients away from other area hospitals, leaving these hospitals with an underfunded responsibility for indigent patient care. Initially, Florida Hospital had submitted no plan for indigent or Medicaid care.[6] But no one seriously doubted that the combined lobbying power of Disney and Florida Hospital would not prevail. Sixty beds were approved in January 1998—they would be moved from the group's Kissimmee hospital—and, as part of the agreement, a Community Health Improvement Coalition was established to fund innovative health care for women, seniors, minorities, and children in the county. But the agreement was a costly one for Florida Hospital. Under its terms, the nearest rival hospital, Orlando Regional Healthcare System, would have an option, after five years, of buying half of the facility.[7]

Of all the town's institutions, the wellness center seemed the most remote, and not simply because it was located out near the corporate campus. Few talked of it as an integrated community limb, although about half the residents had initially joined its fitness center. Perceptions of health among Celebrationites were focused more on the benefits offered by the town's physical layout, its walkability, parks, and trails, and the highly *positive* psychological environment promoted within the community. The pastoral virtues of exurban places have long been considered a beneficial moral influence on the population. Far from the vices and vexations of urban life, and secure from the physical hazards of the central city, there would be no excuse for ill health, and indeed every incentive to avoid it. Celebration had been designed to cultivate healthy people, and its capacity in this department, as in every other, would be promoted and boosted before its performance was proven. For my own part, I had a mixed response. I exercised more than I had done in twenty years, but I also became a regular smoker for the period of time I lived in Celebration.

For practicing health professionals, the boosterism was not always easy to stomach. Haas's wife, Diane, a critical-care specialist at a clinic in Lakeland, found an overly moralistic streak in the constant inducements to be healthy. Involved daily in keeping people alive, she was nonetheless dubious of the American obsession with living as long as possible, and had a robust skepticism about community expectations that "you must cut all of the bad practices out of your life." Professionally in a position to joke about the Health Police (even more mythical, but no less diligent around town than the Porch Police), she believes that a wellness regime may only defer for a little while the high cost of keeping people alive for the last few years of their lives. The real problem, she feels, is that "death is morally unacceptable in our society." Until that taboo is broken, all talk of the economic prudence of cutting

The Haas family in their estate home, on Longmeadow. (Photo: Jonathan Hayt)

costs is a sham. Health care, she regrets, will continue to be seen as "a consumer commodity, and not as a community right."

These were candid, though unorthodox, thoughts in Celebration, but then Diane and Brian were exceptional residents. Ardent cosmopolitans, and Ivy League educated, their tastes ran somewhat against the cultural grain of the town. The walls of their Longmeadow home were lined with prints from Japan, Sri Lanka, and Greece, German Expressionist and Russian Futurist posters, and contemporary neorealist photography. Devotees of the opera, fine arts, and international cuisine, subscribers to magazines of opinion, and victorious survivors of many tennis matches with the author of this book, they started an informal film club toward the end of my stay. At these exclusive monthly gatherings, discussions of the films, shown on home video, took place over a leisurely dinner. The first few screenings were cerebral foreign fare: Nanni Moretti's *Dear Diary* and Pedro Almodovar's *Labyrinth of Passion*, followed by an arty Italian vampire film and Dusan Makavejev's *Sweet Movie*.

Diane Haas was not the only medical professional in town to acknowledge the perils of health moralism. Cummings himself painfully recalled a Rotary Club meeting when an insensitive visiting speaker had wisecracked about a local member's weight. "How can you be so fat in a such a healthy community?" The Celebration resident had slunk away, shamed and mortified. Cummings also conceded that the denial of death was a great obstacle, but assured me that the massive costs of dealing with the coming geriatric bubble could be sliced by attending to chronic diseases long before they occur. Through stressing "the individual as the primary care-giver," he insisted, "we can reduce the number of disabled years, and increase the enabled years."

In public, Cummings had the profile and style of a health evangelist, and was fond of pithy maxims: "I want you to die as young as possible as old as you can," or "I want you to go out like a light, and not a campfire." He was seldom short of anecdotes about witnessing the power of rejuvenation: a ninety-one-year-old resident who had asked for a Fitness Center membership, or a seventy-year-old woman who wanted braces for her teeth because "lately she was being more social and wanted to look good." Anecdotes were all very well, but TCC and hospital officials had come up with an actual plan for quantitatively testing improvements in the health of the community. A five-year research study, called Accelerating Community Transformation, funded by Astra Merck and run by the Health Care Forum, in San Francisco, was already under way. It would establish a database of indicators of health in the civic, physical, political, and spiritual aspects of the community. In addition to the greenfield site of Celebration, five other sites had been chosen for study: Bethel, Illinois, an inner-city neighborhood in Chicago; the small southern town of Aiken, South Carolina; the semi-desert city of San Bernadino, California; the metropolis of St. Louis, Missouri; and a four corners region of Nebraska, Kansas, Missouri, and Iowa. The goal of the study was to synthesize the six sets of data about community behavior into a software toolkit that clients around the country could use to measure and improve the overall health of their communities.

The research study team collaborated with a group of forty stakeholders handpicked by Town Hall and the Foundation. The task of this panel was to come up with attributes of a healthy community based on their own experience of Celebration. As a result of their meetings, the panel reviewed how well the town was living up to the principles behind its planners' five cornerstones—Health, Education, Place, Technology, and Community. It also diagnosed the problem issues that persistently came up around town: the high cost of living and housing, poor construction quality and quality assurance, bad retail mix, destructive internal criticism and rumors, lack of economic and ethnic diversity, media and outsider misperceptions, tourist crowding, and, of course, a panoply of issues relating to the school, including the problematic us-them divisions it had created among residents.

For some members, the stakeholders panel was yet another level of scrutiny—albeit self-scrutiny—for a community that had already been studied, surveyed, and analyzed almost before it had a chance to breathe. Since I myself was a professional scrutineer, I cheerfully compared notes with some of the others: Maureen Kersmarki, Brian Crawford, and Ernie Claxton on the Astra Merck team, and Christine Herzog from the AT&T survey. Brent Herrington did his own surveys of community behavior, based on performance indicators approved by the Community Associations Institute. TCC collected data on residents (which they would not share with me), as did the various real estate groups in town. Academics and urban planners whizzed through town, pursuing their own analyses. At times, it also seemed as if half the population of Celebration were in on the act, appraising and assessing the growth of their own community at each step of the way. In passing encounters with residents I knew, I was often grilled about my own findings. How are we doing? It was more than community pride that drew residents to identify so strongly with the data gathering and critical inquiry of others like myself. Self-scrutiny was a heady narcotic in a town that had been designed to perform, above par if possible.

Then there was my own competition. Another couple had moved to town to write a book about Celebration. I tried to extend myself socially, and suggested that we get together for dinner or a drink. After all, we were fellow writers living in the same small community. Their editor in New York, they said, had told them not to meet with me.

SURE TRIED

The draw for the Phase One lots in 1995 had attracted a crowd far exceeding the company's expectations, but there was one big letdown. As Peter Rummell recalled: "I remember when we had the lottery for the first homes, people were camped out. One of our guys came back, reporting on the crowds, and he was shaking his head. There were five or six hundred people camping out and I think there was one black family in there. We were all disappointed. Sure tried." Following the advice of James Rouse, who had worked hard to integrate Columbia in the 1960s (and who once served as a consultant for Walt's ur-EPCOT), TCC had advertised in minority publications, and had produced promotional literature that portrayed families and students of color going about their business in town and at the school. The video shown in the Preview Center for prospective home buyers focused disproportionately on nonwhite residents. There was nothing the company would have liked more than to see a diverse population in Celebration. But it flourished as a largely white-bread town during the pioneer years, and was likely to remain so for the near future. This had not been a foregone conclusion. Central Florida has its share of middle-class minority families living in upscale suburban communities. But they were not choosing to come to Celebration. After two years, the town had attracted only one African American homeowning family, while three single women were living in rented apartments (two of whom moved away shortly after I left town). Dawn Thomas, Town Hall's assistant community manager, and her son Eddie were full participants in the community, and were among the town's most popular residents. So, too, was Dorothy Johnson, an ex-teacher and librarian, who was a drama and opera fan and a regular attendee of the Celebrators retiree group meetings.

The third renter, Wanda Wade, a young teacher laid off in April, had virtually no involvement in the community: "This town's too interesting for me," she joked. She rarely went out at night, at least after she had been stopped and questioned by police on more than one occasion. "I don't pass GO, I don't collect two hundred dollars, I go straight home to my little house, and hole up." Wade says she hates labels—"I tear labels off beer bottles after I buy them from the store"—but was quite clear about why the town's aspirations might not be appealing to African Americans: "For a majority of us, this concept of perfection is not reality, it's not a realistic outlook on life. We haven't grown up like this, we haven't had exposure to it, and we're not comfortable with what's not real. African American parents wouldn't want to sugarcoat their kids' perception of reality in this way." Referring to the common sight, around town, of bicycles unfettered by lock or chain, she conceded that she had "never been in a neighborhood where people felt they could leave their bikes out in the front yard."

The only black homeowners, Bob and Mountrey Oliver, had built a solid brick Colonial Revival mansion at the top of Longmeadow. They had moved from Torrey Pines, an exclusive development in the Dr. Phillips area of Orlando, where there were several black families. From the look of the promotional literature, they had expected at least 30 percent minority population in Celebration, especially since the range of advertised housing prices was so broad. The Olivers, who moved partly because they did not want their children to grow up "too bourgeois," faulted the media for portraying Celebration as all white, but reported what several of their black friends had said: "Why spend $300,000 for such a small lot?" Forgoing a larger lot, it was implied, was an extravagance that white folks could more readily "afford" to do. Materialism for the black middle class is harder to come by and thus more difficult to compromise. As for the Olivers themselves, they retained most of their friendships outside of the community, especially through their ties to their church in Orlando.

They had almost been joined in the ranks of homeowners by Beulah Farquarson, a feisty, self-described "Harlem child," who withdrew her children from the school and herself from the town after signing builders' contracts. Farquarson, who sells time shares, had run twice for the school board (and once for county commissioner), and was collecting signatures for another bid, unsuccessful as it turned out. Described to me by another resident as a "negative black person," Farquarson had little good to say about the reality of Celebration, although she praised some of the planning behind the town. When her children turned sour on the school (they "signed themselves out"), there was no reason to stay, especially in a town that lacked black residents. She blamed the inflated price points. "Black people aren't stupid. Folks here are starving their behinds off just to pay their utility bills. We are not a cash-flow people. Once we've made it, we stay put in our mansions and don't think about starting new communities. Besides, we aren't interested in a 'community.' Black folks grow up in a 'culture,' and it's a noisy one. Celebration's downtown is noiseless. It's a joke for us." Since she moved down from New York City nine years before, Farquarson had become active in the Republican Party: "All my friends grew up on welfare, but I had a different attitude. I wanted more, so I didn't need to be a Democrat." In Osceola County, she had found the Dixiecrat good old boys to be much like the Republicans in the North, and felt more welcome in the GOP. In the school board election, she was planning to campaign against Mumey by exploiting his association with a school that she had no love for: "There's no American flag, no dedication to country . . . and all of the teachers are gay, so there's no sense of right or wrong at that school."

Celebration also had a sprinkling of South Asian physicians and a range of Hispanic residents—Cubans, Dominicans, Mexicans, Puerto Ricans, and South Americans—but none of them (with the exception of MENSA kingpin Joseph Palacios) figured among the town's most active citizenry or had forged a prominent role in the community. Minority students from Osceola County had a much more visible presence in and around town, and so it was the school, again, that provided the active ingredient of diversity in Celebration.

In my interviews with the mostly white residents, I always asked why they thought the town had not attracted more minority residents and whether their relative absence was a source of concern. These interviews were informal conversations, lasting for ninety minutes or longer, and mostly took place in residents' homes. I tried to ask the questions about race in a way that did not put anyone on the defensive, but they often did.

A few retirees were clear examples of "white flight" from urban areas that they considered to have "declined." For one couple from Miami, the "last straw" had been a DEA agent at their door asking to park a car in their driveway because he anticipated a shoot-out across the street—"This was not the ghetto," they explained to me. "It was not Overtown, or Liberty City, it was a nice middle-class suburb, where Jackie Gleason lived." "We are so happy to have been delivered," they declared, adding, "We're not racist, but some people are used to living at a lower level of life, and what can you do? You try to be a model and hope they will follow." Other stories from elderly residents about Miami typically distinguished between the good *exilio* Cubans and the bad new immigrants, starting with the "social deadbeats and psychos" who came with the Mariel boatlift, as one prominent resident put it. "Florida's public schools," he continued, "teach to the bottom third of each class, and these are mostly the Hispanics. The rest are bored to tears as a result, and they are the ones with the talent."

Some residents' perceptions of Osceola County were not exempt from that notorious white rule that divides the good minority from the bad one. One Celebration businessman spoke of the recent "Latin influx" in the county. "These are not Latins from Long Island, mind you, they are from south of the border and Puerto Rico." Slighting "the Oriental families who own all the small hotels on 192," he praised "the original Osceola County folks, the white folks; they are good people, who put down roots, they are *hamischer* people." Despite the locution, he himself was not Jewish. Another woman, who *was* Jewish, observed that "Osceola is a low-rent county with too many ethnics—it's basically a bedroom community for hotel domestics." In the same vein, a resident with a Ph.D. commented that "comparing us to Osceola County is like comparing us to retarded children." Route 192, running along Celebration's property line, was perceived by one resident as "full of racial gang activity" that "we cannot let in here." Apparently, these were the same gang activities that had determined him to move his family from their former home in Maryland's Columbia (several Celebrationites had moved from Columbia). Another resident described that same town as an "LBJ Great Society–type experiment in integration" that had failed miserably.

Younger nester parents, born after the civil rights era, were less likely to make bigoted comments, and many felt they had moved from communities riddled with prejudice to a town that was much more tolerant. Several regretted the lack of diversity here—"We need to be diluted"—

and confessed to being embarrassed that there was "very little coloring in town." For a small number, usually those who had a spouse with a Latin background or who were Jewish, diversity was an aspect of community life that did register on their scale of priorities. For the majority of white residents, it did not. Most felt "it was not natural" to identify others by skin color, and so it was not something to which they gave much thought. "We don't really notice it." Those who acknowledged that they did notice race, believed, however, that it was "not natural" to try to integrate communities. In general, it was assumed that integration had been "artificial" because it had been done "for show" and had not happened "naturally." Diversity, as one put it, was "good for the right reasons, and bad for the wrong reasons." A typical pattern of response was to acknowledge outright that race was "not an issue," to be followed by some qualification that veered way off track into the subconscious hinterlands of white, propertied America.

- "I'm not prejudiced, though my parents were. I look at people as people. But I don't like to hear people complaining about slavery and all that, or using their color as a crutch. Though I know what it's like for them to feel left out. If I go out with my husband and his friends and they talk about football, I feel left out."
- "We don't really notice the color issue, but let me tell you, we resent people hanging clothes over the balcony, and that can happen in fancy homes too, but luckily it doesn't happen in Celebration."
- "I don't look at people as colored one way or another, and I don't think it's natural to do social engineering. You can't mandate an idea. Bussing screwed up in most cases. But you shouldn't have to be stepping over homeless people in order to feel like you live in the real world."
- "90 percent of us wouldn't mind. I don't know what Arabs or Hispanics or Blacks want, but they're welcome to live next to me. Here Christian, Jewish, and Muslim kids play together. Besides, the black people have progressed so quickly. I may have set them apart at one time, but since 1970 or so, they are like us."

- "I don't care myself, although this is a white ghetto. I would welcome more diversity as long as it doesn't drive the prices down."
- "We don't like the fact that this town is so unbelievably white, but we don't lie awake at night thinking about it. People are not willing to move out of their own culture just to experience other cultures."
- "It"s just not an issue for us. We don't see it in terms of minority this or that. We're from Miami."

For the most part, white Celebrationites were politely stumped when asked why the town had not attracted more minorities, but there were several theories offered. The architecture of the town, some of it directly evoking plantation houses, was perceived to convey the feel of an all-white community of yore and might be off-putting to nonwhites. Disney, some said, was also considered the essence of white-bread family values and not very inclusive in its approach to the marketplace or to its own corporate culture. The theory of black middle-class materialism was echoed by at least one other resident: "Blacks are smarter with their money, they work hard for it, they want a big lot, and a good-sized shelter, and don't want to plop down $300,000 for something that's so . . . small." Other views aimed at being more sociologically acute:

- "Members of ethnic groups don't often move freely from state to state because of their close-knit families and communities."
- "Minorities lose more of themselves than they gain when they move to places like this. They give up a lot of their own culture."
- "African Americans don't go out of their way to invite risks. This is a test community, and they already have enough tests in their lives. Their culture is less receptive to change or risk."

Black tourists sometimes commented, when I asked them, that the town seemed a little "scary," but this was a common observation on the part of many first-time visitors, of whatever racial background. Whatever distillation of "white fear" resided among townsfolk was strangely reflected by a "fear of Celebration" evinced by outsiders. But fear, I concluded, is not the signature mark of whiteness in Celebration. Indeed, liberal guilt about the community's demographics is widespread enough among residents to generate a veneer of regret. Instead, I found that the key to whiteness lay in the many comments I heard about the invisibility of race: it's "not natural" to view people in terms of their skin color. In truth, nothing has ever been *natural* when it comes to race in America. What seems natural at any time and in any place usually corresponds to what white folks feel comfortable with seeing. At the end of the century, whites seem increasingly comforted by the notion that race is becoming invisible, once again. It had been so, for different reasons, before the ferment of the civil rights era, when minorities had simply been eclipsed from the public eye. Recently, the force of conservative opinion that a "level playing field" has been achieved for all races has prepared the way for a new kind of colorblindness. Today, white people are often at their most white when they believe that consciousness of race is not natural. In many ways, it is a belief that most defines us as white. Seventy years ago, what united whites was the perception that their racial designation was an outcome of biological nature, in the same degree as, but superior to, other ancestral groups. It is much less acceptable now to believe that biology is responsible for the differences between people. But white-skin privilege abides and goes unexamined when it's no longer "natural" to think about someone's racial background and is perceived to be racist to do so. As Malcolm X pointed out, "racism is like a Cadillac. There's a new model every year."

It has been well over three decades since racial discrimination was publicly outlawed in housing, education, and public transportation. While no longer chronic, the patterns of segregation by race and income persist. Residential census maps still betray the grisly story of racial isolation. Every day, in the thousands of housing developments under construction, suburban white communities inch farther out from the increasingly diverse populations of the inner suburban rings. The ending of redlining and racially restrictive covenants, it turns out, did not make a truly radical difference to demographic patterns. The free housing market has produced an outcome today that is not so terribly different from the era of high segregation. But it's not natural to see it that way.

In late May, on a torrid Saturday afternoon, I turned out for a coed softball tournament organized as a fund-raiser for the PTSA. My own valiant home run had been disqualified because I forgot to drop the bat (why throw away a lucky bat?). Time was almost up, and my team had been hammered by the Osceola County sheriffs' team. A male resident on the sidelines began to taunt one of the opposing team's male players up at bat. "Quit playing like a woman," he jeered. Larry Haber, the captain of our side, responded loudly from the other side of the field, "That's enough of that kind of talk. Cut it out!" The remark sliced through more than the sauna heat of the day. It was a public break with the male sporty camaraderie that had settled over the games, in spite of the presence of female players. A clumsy silence followed, before the pitcher swung her arm.

Haber's had been a mild form of gender treason, but brave enough in such a public setting. On reflection, it struck me that the sports field was a much easier place to break ranks with masculinity than with whiteness. But where could the latter occur in Celebration? As it happened, one white couple told me that the same heckler had made some apparently racist comments at a dinner party in his house. They felt uncomfortable and held their tongues rather than object to his remarks. The same scenario was probably being repeated a thousand times around the country in every setting where white folks gathered.

Celebration residents did not deserve to be singled out for these sad confirmations of white solidarity. For sure, it is a more tolerant and diverse place than many of the gated security zones that are the "natural" outcome of market behavior at the end of this century. But this town had set itself up as a model of community and housing for the future, and it was springing up in full view of a nation that had long perfected the art of segregation through its housing practices and policies. Like Levittown and Columbia, it would be very closely watched, while other communities went about their all-white business as usual. What a pity, I thought, there were not more opportunities to break bread, let alone break ranks—especially when one did not have to look far outside the White Vinyl Fence for examples of both.

In unincorporated Orange County, less than two miles from Orlando city center, I found that a different kind of experiment in restoring community and uniting races was proceeding in a forgotten

100-square-block neighborhood called Holden Heights. A formerly white middle-class area devastated by white flight after school redistricting in the early 1970s, it was now 30 percent African American, 30 percent Haitian, 30 percent Caucasian, and 10 percent Hispanic, with the highest proportion of interracial families in the city.[8] Twenty percent of its housing was abandoned, and white slumlords had a tight hold over much of the rest. The city's annexation march had swerved around Holden Heights—no tax base!—and although it was now surrounded by Orlando Metro, it had no sewage lines, too many open drainage ditches, and not a few unpaved roads. Running through its heart is the most seedy leg of South Orange Blossom Trail, ruled by liquor, guns, pornography, prostitution, and drug trafficking.

"Tourists can fly into Orlando, book into a hotel on International Drive, and within five minutes find out the name of the cross street on the South Trail where they can score drugs." Jerry Appleby was describing his new neighborhood over lunch in the soup kitchen of Restore Orlando, a nonprofit service organization he had helped organize to give Holden Heights another chance. A pastor in the Nazarene Church, which donated a church building and other facilities, Appleby and several other, mostly white, middle-class families had moved into surrounding homes as part of a rehabilitation project directed at helping build a sense of community pride and restoring neighborhood bonds. They were following the example of other Christian community development projects, like the Summerhill project in Atlanta.

Aimed at the "reinsertion of a leadership base, rather than the teaching of middle-class standards," Appleby spoke to me of building a "solid, stable, independent citizenry" among a population with many migrant, undocumented workers in addition to the large proportion of underemployed, down on their luck. He and his colleagues, like David and Bonnie Shaw who moved from a country club home in suburban Seminole County, or Darren and Julie Reed, who direct Restore's youth education program and who graduated recently from a private college, now live amid the gunshots, police sirens, and overflowing septic tanks. They are more or less missionaries, affiliated with a Christian-based organization, but their "religious drive" is played down, Appleby explained, lest their evangelism be seen as a "harassment tool."

All the same, David Shaw was quite clear about the religious nature of their mission: "We are here because we think this is what Jesus would do. This work of redeveloping is for us a way of showing the power of Christ." The Shaws had done this by sinking a good deal of money into restoring their house (with little prospect of resale value). I asked David if he had seen any changes in the neighborhood as a result. "I believe it does have a positive impact," he reported. "Our block used to be a haven for drug dealers and prostitutes, but when outsiders see this level of upkeep, they go elsewhere to do their deeds of darkness." His belief that the trim appearance of the house had a direct bearing on the moral behavior of others was clearly as robust as that of any card-carrying New Urbanist.

According to Appleby, this is a community where the whites are extremely prejudiced—both the old timers who had stayed in the neighborhood and the larger, more recent influx of Appalachian working poor—and where African Americans and Haitians are often at loggerheads. Restore Orlando, which runs a range of community programs, has emerged as a mediator of racial conflict. In the absence of any neighborhood association, it has also become the functioning lobby group for the entire area, and with the volunteer help of planners and architects, has submitted a plan for urban redesign to the county. As in Celebration, the planning concept is mixed-income, where houses will cost from $30,000 to $175,000, and they will be made available as cheaply as possible through creative financing to those seeking affordable housing. Government assistance will be avoided. The poor, Appleby insists, will not be displaced by young gentrifying professionals, they will be "restored" along with the neighborhood.

As in Celebration, the improvement plan revolves around the centrality of the porch and the gridiron street life of the traditional small town. But that is where the comparison ends. Celebration's bid to restore community life is intended to set a high-end example for the real estate industry to follow. It is a trickle-down model, and its commercial success, it is hoped, will encourage other developers to follow. The Holden Heights project starts from the opposite premise, sowing the seeds of urban rehabilitation at the lowest end. If it works, it will be an opportunity, as Appleby put it, for the "poor to teach the rich."

12

NOT AN ISLAND

"During our last visit we explored the surrounding areas including 'Old Town.' We went there around eleven o'clock at night and were not very impressed of [sic] the clientele hanging out there. We witnessed a fight between several young people. Then in the parking lot a group was hanging out drinking beer and shouting profanities at passers-by. It seems to be quite a seedy amusement park area at night, not the type of high quality attraction the Orlando area is known for worldwide."

—Celebration resident's letter to Osceola County Planning Department

In an irony of geography that no one ever mentions, Celebration's next-door neighbor on the U.S. 192 strip is a themed attraction called Old Town. Huddled around its own picture-book Main Street, Old Town's low-rent version of the bygone days is a mixed bag. Tattoo studios and psychic readers keep company with nostalgia emporiums and video arcades. Saturday evenings, I often joined the crowd on the sidewalk as the area's show car owners—Edsels, Corvettes, Studebakers, Fairlanes, Impalas—line up for a stagey drive-through. Old Town also hosts the strip's only Ferris wheel, for some years the tallest structure in Osceola County. In the summer of 1997, the Sky Coaster, a wondrous, death-defying contraption, was erected on site. The lucky customer swings in

Old Town, Celebration's "bad" neighbor. (Photo: the author)

free fall from cables slung between two sets of high poles, built with an elegant space-age monumentality that seduces the curious from miles around. The Sky Coaster terrified distant onlookers and it struck fear in the heart of Celebration Realty's sales agents. Its twenty-story poles were in full view of residents as they towered over the trees that bounded the North Village, then under construction in Phase Two of the town plan. Ever resourceful, realty agents like Greg Foxx tried to turn the Sky Coaster into a sales asset. "We tell buyers, 'It's the tallest swing in the world,' " he blithely revealed, "and we point out that it's a good landmark by which to give visitors directions." But it is no easy task to steer a sales pitch for luxury homes around the spectacle of inebriated tourists undergoing near-death experiences in midair. Overnight, the Sky Coaster became a shrieking sky fiend, casting a devilish spell on Celebration's property values. As if to add insult to injury, the owner of the attraction purchased and moved into one of the most sought-after houses in town, on Celebration Avenue. He would have a tough time currying favor among his new neighbors.

The following May, however, he had a chance to redeem himself. A rival investor in Old Town requested county approval for an even larger amusement ride—211 feet high—that would rise immediately adjacent to Celebration. Plans for the ride, called Sky Scraper, included a 116-foot tower and a 190-foot rotating arm with cars that could whirl passengers through a heady 360-degree revolution. Enough was enough. Town Hall set about mobilizing residents for collective action for the first time, roused by the latest news from Celebration Realty that estate home sales in the North Village had been on the sluggish side. Organizational meetings were announced, letters to the county's planning department were encouraged, and a mass showing at the public hearing for the proposal was planned. Behind the scenes, attorney pressure was brought into play and area businessmen began to network. Charlie Rogers, Celebration bank manager and chair of the local Chamber of Commerce branch, worked to energize outside investors with interests on the strip against what he presented as a traffic and safety hazard—a ride rotating at 70 mph alongside the most heavily congested road in the region. The goal was to reframe the Sky Scraper as a regional issue and not as "Celebration versus Old Town." Contrary to the tenor of the letters sent to the county by residents, which focused primarily on the personal plight of their property values, Rogers, ever politic and aboveboard, felt that Celebration could ill afford to go into its first local scrape from an insular position that was anti-growth, anti-entertainment, and pro–property value. "We have to pick and choose our battles carefully," he acknowledged to me.

Celebration was readying to exercise its political muscle. Luckily no heavy lifting was required. The Sky Coaster owner turned into the town's Good Fairy, interceding to offer the developer a share in another deal he was cutting. The rival developer withdrew his application at the last moment. Herrington's next newsletter nevertheless recorded his "regret that our residents' first major involvement in a public issue turned out to be our opposition to a neighboring project."

The narrowly averted showdown raised questions about the role Celebration would play in a county with a huge backlog of suspicion about its very presence. Would the new community use its rich resources and professional talent to protect its own, or would it become a publicly minded regional player? The history of Disney's own presence and behavior in the region had willed an awkward legacy, and the outcome of the company's new good neighbor policy was still unclear. But there was one thing I had learned for sure. While many of its residents were fixing to cocoon in their own ZIP code, the making of Celebration had already had a major physical impact on the regional landscape well beyond its property line.

LEGALIZING IT

The strip-malled outlands of America have thrown up some bizarre juxtapositions, but you would be hard put to find a greater mismatch anywhere than in the face-off between the sequestered pocket of genteel architectural taste in Celebration and the garish free-for-all of signage, themed retail, and honky-tonk watering holes that lies outside the White Vinyl Fence. From the riotous Water Mania across the road all the way to Gatorland, Medieval Times, and beyond, route 192 plays host to every species of franchise eatery, T-shirt shack, and factory discount outlet known to the modern consumer. Robert Stern likes to refer to this strip as "the sleaze road of all times," although, as a Disney board member, his comments in this vein often aggravate the company's PR problems with its neighbors.[1] At one point, resort and commercial property owners approached Disney for permission to name the adjacent portion of the strip as Celebration Avenue. According to Tom Lewis, vice president of Walt Disney Imagineering, the request was turned down because Celebration was supposed to set a model of good planning that would contrast with the Crazy Golf fabric of the strip. But exactly what kind of good example was Celebration to set for its county neighbors? Were they supposed to admire, copy, or simply envy it? Even if they liked what they saw, would they be able to afford it themselves? Whatever the outcome, this was the company's first try at "going intergovernmental" by dealing directly, in the sunshine, with the county's public agencies.

Of those who remained on the Celebration team after 1997, no one had labored longer and harder at this task than Lewis himself, recruited by Peter Rummell as director of residential development in 1986 and charged with negotiating Celebration's land-use entitlements and special taxing district agreements at county and state levels. An architect in Orlando in the 1970s, Lewis had followed his friend, governor-elect Bob Graham, into Florida politics, where he ran the Department of Transportation and later the Department of Community Affairs. When the time came for Disney to rationalize its transportation and building needs for the planned expansion of its theme parks, no one was better connected or more up-to-date on the state's building and zoning codes than Lewis. Cognizant of the growth management laws he had recently helped to draft and push through the state legislature, Lewis played a large role in the recommendation to develop the 11,000-acre parcel of Reedy Creek property in Osceola.

Disney had famously survived a hostile takeover bid in 1983, and a large part of its allure to corporate raiders had been the "undeveloped assets" of its film library and its unused land (at that time, only a fraction of the 28,000 acres of Florida property had been developed).[2] When the New Disney, under Eisner, set about remedying this neglect—primarily through releasing its storied backlist and its new films on home video—it soon generated unprecedented profits. Their appetites whetted for more, stockholders were promised that the 1990s would be the Disney Decade, and that Celebration would be a star turn. Lewis, Rummell, and others put together a strategic plan for expanding the company's core realty (its theme parks) and developing its other land assets. As Lewis recalls, it was evident from the outset that selling the land outright would be a bad business decision:

> If you're developing the world's premier destination resort, and you go sell land on the perimeter, you're going to put restrictions on it because you don't want it to compete with what you're doing. The more restrictions you put, the lower value the land has. . . . I was very familiar with where controls on growth were going in Florida, and holding land in Florida is not a smart decision, because it is much more difficult to develop land tomorrow than it is today. . . . We wanted to do something that was compatible with and synergistic with and noncompetitive with our primary business. Community development met that bill.

After considering retiree and second-home development, the company went for the "primary market because it would produce the best value for our shareholders and it was most compatible with the corporate values that the Walt Disney Company family held—education, and the like."

People who know real estate and who are also familiar with Disney's financial profile expressed some skepticism about the company's explanation for this decision. Celebration, like any large community development venture, would be a risky business prospect, not least because of the potential for bad media exposure, and it would be a long time before the infrastructure debt was paid off and any revenue could be recouped. For the project to make economic sense to Disney, and to outweigh the risks, there had to be another story. Celebration had to be worth much more to the company than the market value of its lots.

After hearing this skepticism from a number of quarters, I interviewed Charles Adams, formerly TCC's director of business development. At the time he was recruited in 1990, for his expertise in residential development, Adams had actually been trying to buy Disney land for Trammell Crow, one of the nation's largest property developers. By the late 1980s, Adams explained, the legal gains of the environmentalist movement had begun to take their toll on runaway growth and development. Large-scale developers were scrambling to find some way of satisfying the new legislative requirements. Adams described how Disney management used the Celebration project to obtain a permit for all the environmental impacts incurred by the expansion of its theme parks:

> Celebration was the one that carried the water on this. It was easier to have Celebration lead that effort because it was going to be adding homes and offices and economic development and more traditional real estate. It was a little harder for an agency to say, "Do we really need another water park with its impact on wetlands?" . . . At that time, the pendulum had swung over onto the side of the environmental community, and each year landowners throughout the United States were watching developable land get taken away to save one more plant species that got added to the list that year. . . . Well, by having that permit, it locked our long-term development rights in place, and that was of enormous value to the company.

The "permit" in question was obtained through an environmental mitigation agreement on a massive scale, negotiated with the South Florida Water Management District and EPA head Carol Browner, at that time Florida's top environmental official. In the customary practice of bit trading, five acres of land would have to be preserved for each acre of impact. Instead, the company did a wholesale swap. It purchased the entire 8,000-acre Walker Ranch in Osceola and turned it over to the Nature Conservancy to manage as the Disney Wilderness Preserve. In return, Disney won virtually blanket approval for twenty years of development rights on its landholdings. Given the likelihood of stiffer environmental policies down the road, this one-shot deal, negotiated by director of residential development Don Killoren, was immensely lucrative for the company, and Celebration had been the critical card to play in winning approval. However expedient, the Celebration plan would prove even more valuable to the company's effort to adapt the region's road network to its needs.

Easing the way for Disney's expanding transportation needs was Lewis's most arduous assignment. The company embarked on an aggressive campaign that, if approved, would involve building several new interstate interchanges, diverting the Central Florida Greeneway (417), and throwing in a new parkway (Osceola Parkway) for good measure. This basically meant changing the traffic map of Central Florida. What stood in the way was the 1985 Growth Management Act that Lewis had helped to draft. Among other things, the legislation requires all developers to have infrastructure—water, sewage, roads—in place before land can be developed. Under this legislation, Disney was required, for the first time, to submit a comprehensive growth plan. This presented a problem. Disney's plans for the new Animal Kingdom theme park could not have been approved because, in keeping with company policy, all details about the new park were being kept under wraps until late in the day. Estimates of the park's traffic impact that were required by the legislation could not be provided at that time. "Once again," Adams explained, "Celebration became the entity to carry the load because now we were showing a residential development that's going to generate X amount of trips, and all of a sudden we tripped the meter then that said 'Yes, now it makes sense to put in the Greeneway that comes from the airport, as well as the Osceola Parkway.' The strategic value of getting the road network in place to accommodate the Walt Disney World resort's future expansion was of tremendous value to the company."

Lewis got to work, enlisting the financial support of other large property owners whose interests were well served by paying to have the Beltway (the Southern Connector Extension of the Central Florida Greeneway) diverted south to pass through Celebration:

> It was complicated politically because you had the state, the local Department of Transportation, two different counties, and a number of large landowners, all of whom had their own agenda. The whole thing involved a 500-million-dollar public-private partnership. Tied to it was the Osceola Parkway, a new 14-mile roadway, which was the county's number one priority. But the Beltway was the priority of the landowners. Everybody was saying, 'Well, you help me with mine, I'll help you with yours,' and all of this stuff had to come together at one time when we signed six feet of documents.

The subsequent agreements were unprecedented for the federal highway system, which does not usually approve new interchanges until they are about to be built. Disney got approval for three new interstate interchanges, some of which would not be built for ten years. The entire city of Orlando had only six interchanges, and now Disney would have five of its own. Between the creation of this "huge road system" and the development permits, the deal, as Lewis put it, "created an economic development area that's probably unmatched currently anywhere in the country."

It didn't hurt that Lewis was dealing with his former colleagues in office in Tallahassee. Rummell, he said, used to cajole him: "This is a classic case of a guy who shot himself in the foot. You went up there and wrote all these laws and now you're down here trying to figure out how to get through them." Nor was anyone surprised that Disney had made the earth move under legislators' feet. In Florida, big landowners and developers dream about making this kind of sweetheart deal with local and state government. For Disney, however, it seems that nothing is impossible to fix politically, a perception that goes back to the special governmental powers obtained in the late 1960s through the Florida legislature for the multicounty Reedy Creek Improvement District (RCID). The creation of this special district gave the company sweeping fiscal and administrative powers over a virtually autonomous political unit. Through the RCID, the company won control over all planning, building, and water drainage codes, and preempted the tiresome business of asking repeatedly for permits from different agencies in two different counties. A handful of permanent residents, handpicked by the company, live in trailer parks in the two RCID municipalities of Lake Buena Vista and Bay Lake, and are required to vote on bond issues. To obtain initial approval for the RCID, however, the company had argued that the broad powers were necessary to serve "the needs of those residing there."[3] This reference was to the EPCOT population plan for 20,000 residents, never realized. In Celebration, at least, approval was secured on the basis of the guaranteed existence of a population of residents. Even so, the "needs" of these residents were still used to serve the larger needs of the company to expand its theme parks and swell its profit base.

It has long been an act of faith among critics of Disney's powerful reach that the RCID was a monstrous devolution of authority to the company's own private state within the state. Ex-legislator Marshall Harris observed, "It was a bad law. It created a feudal district in the middle of Florida."[4] Straddling two counties (Orange and Osceola), and with planning, zoning, and law enforcement authorities usually commanded by large cities and counties, the RCID was a rather unique agreement, even for a state in love with special taxing districts. Its powers included the right to build an airport and a nuclear power facility, and run the company's own criminal justice system, none of which have been fully exercised. In practice, of course, this forty-two-square-mile immunity zone, often referred to as Florida's 68th county, earned itself a lifetime of local resentment for its tax-dodging reputation. Rigorous managers of its own tourist property, RCID's regional impact took the form of a colossal tourist free-trade zone, as other attractions and theme park companies like Universal and Sea World moved in, escalating housing prices, jamming traffic routes, and delivering up the land and its lakes to blow-and-go developers. Despite its attempts at improving public relations, the company's public profile was that of an arrogant, bad neighbor that gave little prior notice of its development plans and stood aloof from community involvement.

In Osceola, the company had not developed any of its RCID land and had generated no immediate fiscal gains for the county. "Orange County got the tax base, we got the traffic" was the perception of locals. Business and political leaders had long petitioned the company to share the benefits of their development activity more equitably. Despite two decades of county appraisers' legally dubious attempts to collect assessments for commercial land use, Disney maintained an exemption for bona fide agricultural activities on its Osceola property, portions of which it leased out to cattle ranchers and timber companies. According to Mike Kloehn, director of the county's planning department, "many locals wish Disney had never arrived," and there was "a general mistrust of Disney as a large corporation that cared little for the county's welfare." When the Celebration site was surgically de-annexed from Reedy Creek and granted its own, much more limited, district authority under state law, Disney would be dealing with "the regular Joes," as Stern put it, by respecting zoning codes and paying water, sewage, and impact fees to the county.[5]

In the negotiations that followed, Kloehn describes how difficult it was for company officials to operate with the regular Joes in the public domain. They had to be educated: "The Disney decision makers were unaccustomed to following land-use regulations. Disney's departure from RCID would be difficult. They winced at adjusting to our zoning requirements." Detailed plans for Celebration had to be submitted for public review, and "if they changed their mind, an amendment and public hearing were necessary. This format ran counter to their preferred close-to-the-vest/one-stop-permitting way of doing business. They would have preferred to identify specific uses of property at the latest possible stage of plan review. However, after a few months of working with them on their [planning] documents, they finally understood that all developers are required to provide the same level of detail and that we could not make an exception."[6]

Above all, the county commissioners were hungry for *ad valorem* tax revenue from Celebration. When plans were first announced in the early 1990s, the town, had it been built out then, would have increased the Osceola property tax roll by 63 percent.[7] But the county also wanted to attract the higher-income jobs generated by the town's corporate campus, already sprouting twelve-story office buildings. As a result,

Disney bargained a good deal. Estimates of county revenue measured against its costs, for services and the like, showed a net gain, and so the company negotiated a payback from the county, in the form of either a yearly check or an agreement whereby the county would put in a road that the company wanted. This deal, along with the earlier entitlements for roads and development, all added up to an enormous benefit to the company. As a result, the strategic value of Celebration was realized even before the first lots were sold. The rate of return over ten years on the town's real estate would be about 20 percent, according to the business plan. But in the revenue stream of a $22 billion earnings-driven company, this was peanuts in comparison to high-volume videocassette sales of *The Lion King*. Celebration's cash flow potential would always be tangential to Disney's core earnings-driven business. But what Celebration made possible locally, as a convenient instrument of the company's regional development plans, and what it generated internationally, in sheer prestige and cultural capital, was of immense worth to Disney. No single Disney project has ever generated so much press attention (and, by my calculation, 90 percent of it was positive).

Few of the reporters who came to town ventured outside it, and yet one of the "reasons for Celebration" lay out there on the Beltway, currently a stunningly unclogged thruway, where you could whiz along past cow pastures and pine hammocks that will have metamorphosed into subdivisions before the next decade is out. Celebration itself may be a showpiece for traffic reduction, but it had served as a host for the road-and-development virus that now had a grip on the surrounding farmlands beyond the strip. In one of the more ironic twists of New Urbanist fate, this model town had helped secured an environmental seal of approval for a vast development zone, "unmatched," as Lewis put it, "anywhere in the country."

THE BARE NECESSITIES

Disney was not the only agent that had used the Celebration project to serve other purposes. The county's business leaders hoped the town would act as the catalyst for a different kind of economic growth. Progrowth interests in Osceola were angling for a greater share of the region's sustained development boom that had been monopolized by the richer Orange County to the north. Indeed, permits were approved, in January 1998, for two large convention center complexes on route 192, with trade show buildings, mega-malls, and hotels. One of them—the World Expo Center—was so large, at 2.4 million square feet, that its developer (who later pulled out) claimed that "like the Great Wall of China, it would be one of the few manmade objects that could be seen from the moon."[8] Servicing visitors on corporate accounts would provide marginally better, and slightly more stable, jobs than the highly seasonal tourist trade, where business was flat on twenty-eight weeks of the year. In a county where 56 percent of the jobs were in tourism, the median wage hovered at the $20,000 mark.

Osceola's economic plight was most fully reflected in its affordable housing profile. To date, Celebration's "good example" has not sparked any other mixed-housing plans, let alone anti-sprawl imitations, within the county. Its inflated price points made it an instant leader in regional housing sales and established the perception that New Urbanist homes were well beyond the range of most home buyers. The last time I visited in January 1999, the signs on route 192 still promised homes from $160,000, but no one knew of a house within Celebration that could be bought for that sum—already almost twice the price of an average home in Osceola County. Yet many locals I met in the course of the year clearly recalled that when the initial plans for Celebration were first shown around the county, low-income housing was a popular feature of the package.

Because of the scale of the Celebration plan, TCC was legally bound to include some provision for affordable housing. This was a sensitive issue, given Disney's recent record. In 1990, the company's RCID governmental arm had snapped up all of the $57.7 million in tax-exempt bonds made available to local governments for reducing costs on housing and sewage infrastructure. Reedy Creek had beaten the housing authorities in six counties to the punch in filing for the bonds, issued on a first-come, first-served basis. Local administrators were outraged that money that might have gone to low-income housing in the region would now be used to expand Disney World's sewage treatment plant. Facing a public relations nightmare, Disney elected to hand back some of the money in addition to paying out $1.5 million to Orange County to help provide home loans to families in the region. Nonetheless, the legacy in the public mind was the image of Disney as the Grinch that stole affordable housing, abusing its special powers of government to cheat revenue-strapped municipalities and their impoverished communities out of scarce public monies.

In Osceola, the affordable housing shortage would be deepened by the company's planned expansion, steadily sucking thousands of additional low-wage service workers into the county. By 1998, Disney World had become the biggest single-site employer in the United States, with over 51,500 workers on its payroll (almost 15,000 of them part-time), and its daily recruitment in Mexico and Puerto Rico supported a steady stream of migrants, swollen further by the ripple effect of additional development on the Kissimmee strip. The company's first long-range growth management plan was rejected by state officials in January 1992 because it failed to provide adequately for affordable housing for these new employees. Faced with a building moratorium, Disney renegotiated and made its first foray into the rental development business by investing in apartment buildings in both counties (including Little Lake Bryan, the pocket to the north of Celebration that Adams tried to buy for Trammell Crow). I asked Lewis how the plan for Celebration answered the requirements of the legislation. Osceola officials, he said, had made overtures to Disney: "Their initial reaction was, 'If you're going to do residential, we sure hope you're gonna do that expensive stuff. We have plenty of that affordable stuff already in our county. What we need is some of that expensive stuff.' That's exactly what they said to us."

If such an appeal were formally made, it would have been illegal. Not surprisingly, no one I talked to in the county's agencies would corroborate any request of this sort. In principle, the decision about where to locate the housing lay with the developer, and it chose to go the way of mitigation, subsidizing low-cost housing outside of Celebration. Disney agreed initially to hand over $100, 000 for each of three years for Osceola to provide assistance in down payments and closing costs to home buyers who qualified for affordable housing elsewhere in the county. Many of the recipients turned out to be Disney employees, unable to afford the dream of Celebration, not even its apartments, priced well above the local rental market value. It didn't have to be that way. Former TCC officials were generally defensive when the topic came up. The exception, Todd Mansfield, recalled that he had pushed hard for the inclusion of state-assisted public housing, and had even marked out a location on the site plan. But the prevailing point of view on the development team was that this would dissuade buyers, and so it was decided to raise the price points on the initial Phase One offerings.

While this outcome may have satisfied the county's fiscal managers, hoping for housing that would be attractive to Fortune 500 company executives, it impaired the town's public image among county residents. It did not help matters that Stern was quoted as joking to some journalists (whom he was showing around town) that low-wage workers in Celebration could "share apartments" and "have the time of their lives piling into one bedroom." Nor was the county's tax revenue from the town always in the clear. Locally, the novel nature of Celebration's governmental status sparked a taxation brawl between TCC and the county, generating further friction. Celebration was not a fully fledged town, nor the kind of exurban zone that has no center and no name, like the amorphous quadrant just to its west (called Four Corners because its only distinctive identity is that it straddles Osceola, Orange, Polk, and Lake Counties). Under a recent Florida law, the state's special tax districts, so long as their property is open to the public, are to be treated like municipalities and are thereby exempt from property taxes on their public works. Judging, to the contrary, that the Community Development District of Celebration was not a government entity, the county appraiser sent on the hefty property tax bills for 1997, and the district filed for an exemption. Local media harvested the story for all it was worth, building on the well-worn perception of Disney as a tax dodger. An *Osceola News-Gazette* editorial pointed out that the town "may hurt its image in a legal battle over taxes" and "add fodder to the argument that the Walt Disney Co. takes advantage of Osceola County. . . . As a provider of jobs, homes, attractive landscaping and upscale shops, Celebration should have a reputation as a quality development. Too bad that reputation may be tarnished by the town's efforts to circumvent its tax obligations to a county that has welcomed it with open arms."[9] Recoiling from further corrosive press, Celebration backed down within a week. "I think we are bending over backwards to be good neighbors," Tom Lewis said. "We are paying under protest."[10]

SPREADING THE GOSPEL

However they feel about the involvement of a company like Disney, many of the advocates of New Urbanism hope that the success and the visibility of Celebration will tilt the housing industry in a more responsible direction. Herrington believed that the bulk of the industry "was hoping we will fail, because we've raised the bar into very uncomfortable territory for developers. Most developers will worry about what 'values' are going to cost them," not to mention the "high concept stuff" that involves—schools, churches, nonprofit foundations, and wellness centers. Unlike Levitt and Rouse before, this project was not associated with a single figure, and so the option of spreading the gospel lay with members of the original development team who broke off to pursue their own careers elsewhere. From an early point, many of them had assumed that the research that went into Celebration would be used within the company on future projects. In the fall of 1996, a decision was made within Disney to take its name, and therefore its brand, out of the development business. The Disney Development Company (DDC), as it was then known, was folded into Walt Disney Imagineering, and TCC was created to manage Celebration alone. Adams admitted that this decision "really took some of the wind out of our sails."

Todd Mansfield, senior VP and general manager of DDC, left a few months later. When I reached him in London, he was working as head of European operations for Security Capital, a real estate venture capital group, but not involved in community development, "the riskiest business of all in the property field," as he put it. Mansfield acknowledged that, shortly before his departure, he had made a proposal for Disney to sell TCC to himself and other members of the development team. The proposal made sense for several reasons, not least as a response to Disney's squeamishness about bad press. Under the proposed arrangement, Disney would be able to avoid media exposure by having the development team take any public flak for residents' malcontent. The parent company would retain its economic interest, preserve its profits, and enjoy credit for the project. Lastly, the sale, brokered by third-party capital, would allow the team—ninety strong at that point—to stay together and extend the Celebration R&D to other development projects, providing some portion of royalties to Disney.

The proposal never got very far. At the time, Disney was smarting from the PR debacle generated by its plans for Disney's America, a three-thousand-acre history theme park in Virginia's hunt country. The America project, located six miles from Manassas National Battlefield, site of the battles of Bull Run, had run into enormous resistance from influential landowners, environmentalists, and Civil War historians, and had been shelved. To sell TCC, at that point, might have been interpreted as an open acknowledgment of the project's liability, perhaps even its failure. Given the perception, subsequently, that the company had sold out anyway, Mansfield evidently felt it was a missed opportunity.

In the months following Mansfield's departure, Peter Rummell, Charles Adams, Don Killoren (and, eventually, Chris Corr and Joe Barnes) all moved on, leaving TCC with a leadership vacuum that would injure its relations with residents. Each became engaged in the Celebration spinoff business. Rummell (who later recruited Corr) was headhunted by the St. Joe Corporation, Florida's largest private landowner, to "start managing their assets more aggressively." Having sold off its sugar and pulpwood businesses, St. Joe was gearing up to move into large-scale real estate development. In a bittersweet twist, one of Rummell's first moves as CEO was to buy up Arvida, his pre-Disney employer, to move the development plans ahead. Thirteen years earlier, Arvida had been the first company acquired by Disney, largely as a way of staving off corporate raiders in the bloody fight over control of the company. It was sold three years later, in 1987. A Florida leader in master-planned community development, Arvida's know-how was absorbed into the realty plans that would culminate in Celebration.

In May 1997, Rummell announced plans to develop 800,000 acres of St. Joe's land holdings in North Florida in the form of upscale Celebration-style communities. Among other properties, the company owns 500 acres around Seaside and will be building around the neotraditional enclave in the Panhandle. With huge tracts of land at its disposal, the company is in a position to take on the challenge of regional planning. "We have found that people welcome big thinking," reported Rummell, after six months on the job. "I've had meetings with everyone from the governor on down, and they are all thrilled that we are attacking things at a large scale and dealing with both the macro and micro. . . . The worst planning comes when everybody owns their own lot and tries to maximize their own piece. So I hope we will be able to solve some of the regional problems." Rummell, like many others, fears there "will be a lot of bad copies" of Seaside and Celebration, built on the concept of an isolated, affluent pocket. Regional planning, with the capacity to coordinate residence, workplace, traffic, and recreation, is clearly the key to altering the industry's appetite for sprawl. But for all intents and purposes, only a large corporation or landowner like Disney or St. Joe is in a position to coordinate any of these factors on such a large scale, since public planners long ago lost the power or the will to do so. The result may be the nearest thing to a regional plan, but is it the best plan for the region? Would it have been planned this way in the absence of a large corporate interest? In both cases, the private developer leads and the public planners respond, taking their cue from the market. Invariably, as the Disney example shows, it is the transportation needs of the company, rather than the public, that are served.

When they left TCC, Adams and Killoren set up shop as Celebration Associates, in the business of community development consulting and management. The Celebration name proved a valuable calling card and attracted interest from developers as far away as Abu Dhabi. Their first large projects included Morgan's Harbor, a resort property in Bermuda; Liberty, a master-planned community in California's Riverside County; and Baxter, a huge neotraditional development in Fort Mill, South Carolina. Clients can cherry-pick from a menu of elements and cornerstones similar to those that went into the making of Celebration. In each case, a pattern book is customized to fit with local architectural traditions, and local pricing. In South Carolina, for example, the "simplicity" of Upcountry styles would keep the price points down. Adams and Killoren are applying the lessons learned from Celebration. Plans for downtown retail cores are being kept to a modest or manageable minimum, and builders are being integrated at a much earlier planning stage to keep costs down and to ensure quality.[11]

Celebration's New Urbanist design had not lit any fires underneath Osceola's developers or planners, but the landscape to the north, in Orlando and Orange County, was another matter. While Disney's town was playing weekly host to curious planning teams from all across the country, Orlando had forged ahead with several ambitious New Urbanist neighborhood plans. The most high profile of these involves the decommissioned Naval Training Center, three miles east of downtown, the largest New Urbanist infill project ever undertaken. Plans for integrating the base facilities into surrounding urban fabric in the form of a large residential community, with a village center and distinct neighborhoods, involved a substantial degree of public participation. The design standards for a mixed-use, transit and pedestrian-oriented community attracted proposals from the most prominent New Urbanist firms.[12] Far from being an isolated pocket, this urban infill project is designed to emulate the civic feel of Orlando Metro's traditional city neighborhoods, like Winter Park, Thornton Park, and College Park. The Orlando planning department has also moved ahead with the Southeast Plan, a regional plan by Peter Calthorpe, along similar lines near the international airport. The site, on more than 12,000 acres, is fifteen minutes from downtown and may house more than 75,000 residents at buildout in the year 2040. Its size will allow city planners to adapt a sizable traffic and transit network to its pedestrian-friendly core. The scale also provides for a permanently protected ecological system to maintain the integrity of on-site drainage and wildlife corridors. Other New Urbanist projects in the Orlando area include the inner-city Parramore Heritage District, to be redeveloped by Dover, Kohl & Partners.

Beginning in 1985, when the city reinstated the 1926 zoning standards, private developers have been buying back into urban neighborhoods. In 1999, Orlando would become the first Florida city to institute a Traditional Neighborhood Ordinance "as a matter of right." That new code, designed by DPZ, will make a default setting out of the New Urbanist way while making it more difficult for developers to operate in conventional ways. Rick Bernhardt, Orlando's director of planning and an ardent New Urbanist, explained how the ordinance entirely changed his perception of his job. "I have moved from the realm of regulation back to the realm of community building." In the recent past, he acknowledged, something "was only good if it hadn't been done before. In the last ten years, we've understood there's a lot to learn from the way cities have been built for the last two thousand years."

The capacity of central city planners like Bernhardt to coordinate large-scale projects is envied by their counterparts in county and rural areas, where growth is elastic and where developers can jump from one jurisdiction to another until they get the best deal. Nonetheless, Orange County's planning department had recently approved Horizon West, a massive 40,000-acre development of several villages at the southwest edge of the county. Hundreds of orange growers, ruined by the hard freezes of the late 1980s, had banded together and requested county cooperation with developing the site on their land, near to Disney World. David Heath, Orange County's planning director, explained to me that the site addressed the public policy need to locate housing near to employment. But would the housing actually be within the income range of Disney workers? "It's going to be moderate," he predicted, "but not exactly affordable." Aside from a scattering of multifamily rentals, nothing would be under $120,000 ($83,000 counts as affordable in Orange County). Horizon West will be a good deal for junior executives, but the bulk of the region's tourist workers will still have to look elsewhere.

The planning department in Polk County, to the west and south of Celebration, had also been influenced by New Urbanism in drawing up a Select Area Plan with several town centers grouped in the corridor between the county line and the interstate. But Merle Bishop, the planning director, acknowledged how difficult it was to persuade multiple developers and landowners to go along with a plan that required higher density and a degree of homogeneity that would undercut competition with each other. The biggest headache, he reported, was the prospect of becoming a bedroom community for Disney service workers, as Osceola's affordable housing crisis spilled over into his county. It would not be easy to reconcile the currently high premiums of New Urbanism with the challenge of affordable housing.

After talking to these planners in three counties, I had to conclude that the biggest obstacle to sustainable development in the region remains the chronic low-wage economy. People with little access to income cannot generally afford a sustainable environment or lifestyle. This point is often made by environmentalists in developing countries.

Given the high cost of land and the equally high profit margins of builders and developers, it is just as true in Central Florida. With much fanfare and no lack of good faith, Disney had built its own ecological showpiece in Celebration. No glossy magazines, however, would be running stories about the flow of foreign minimum wage workers to the gates of the Magic Kingdom, with little prospect of decent housing, let alone the chance to live in state-of-the-art healthy communities. Charles Lee, vice president of Florida's Audubon Society, once described Disney World "as a green place . . . where the water is well managed. If you could replicate Disney a thousand times over, you'd basically have the environmental plan for Florida."[13] Locals swamped by the armies of the Mouse disgorged daily from Orlando International Airport had a different story to tell about the carrying cost upon non-Disney land of that green place. From a more responsible environmental perspective than that offered by Lee, it was easy to see that the two hands of the company were working at cross-purposes.

Neotraditional residential development is not the only domain in which the city of Orlando has come to compete directly with Disney. Like many cities looking to revitalize a languishing downtown, Orlando's business and political elites had invested in an orderly package of themed entertainment—the Church Street Station retail complex, which hosts the branches of national chain restaurants, bars, stores, and clubs. For a while, it drew some of the teenage tourist clientele in the area, eager for a nightlife alternative to Disney World's offerings. In the fall of 1997, the opening of Downtown Disney, on the Reedy Creek property, undercut some of these efforts. The massively popular complex includes a twenty-four-screen multiplex, several restaurants and speciality stores, a House of Blues, a Cirque du Soleil, DisneyQuest (a high-tech virtual reality arcade), and the sales magnets of Planet Hollywood and a Virgin Mega Store, in addition to the nightclubs of Pleasure Island. Breakdancers are paid to spin around in the streets to simulate urban spirit, and the neon and video signage is not so much decorative as in-your-face. Downtown Disney is Celebration's bad sister, a gaudy pleasure zone where the high-octane burn of consumer culture carries an intensity quite at odds with a small-town Main Street milieu. This is a different kind of new urbanism—more attractive, certainly to Celebration teens, whom I saw there almost as frequently as in Celebration itself—and it has been flourishing for some years now in cities like Baltimore, Atlanta, New Orleans, Cleveland, New York, and Denver. In these and other centers, media Goliaths like Disney, Time Warner, Viacom, Universal, and Sony are putting their footprints all over traditional downtown real estate.

To make room for its own entertainment retail zone, Orlando had acceded to a corporate makeover of the entire downtown area. In common with the New Urbanist residential developments, city managers of this zone put a high priority on maintaining good civic order and minimizing spontaneity. But the downtown development had also spawned a rich spectrum of offbeat nightlife that flourished on the margins of the compact, corporate quadrant. Alternative Orlando soon featured one of the most vibrant club cultures in the country. The Seattle of the rave scene, youth here dreamed of being hotshot DJs rather than indie rockers, and they had the good fortune to witness their idols live. For a couple of giddy years, Orlando clubs were a favored destination for the world's top DJs. In the summer of 1997, the city cracked down on the nightclubs, imposing a 3 A.M. curfew and truncating the mercurial rise of the Orlando scene. Like Times Square, the new corporate presence in urban entertainment retail would give birth to a semi-controlled mall that zoned out the maverick verve of nightlife in the name of civic order, moral security, and tidy profit. Alternative Orlando was in mourning by the time I got to sample its clubs, but they were still as lively as you could wish for in a town where the attack dogs of the American Family Association were always on the prowl.

STITCH AND GROUT

Unless you earn your living outside of town, there is no real need ever to leave Celebration. Since I did not fall into that category, I could have spent my entire year inside the White Vinyl Fence had I not found some social alternatives for myself in Orlando. Not too many residents have any appetite for life on route 192, and, for the rest, the self-contained design of the town does not equate with social isolation. But there is no escaping that Celebration, far from an island, is a nodal point on many networks. Aside from its steady stream of visitors and the omnipresence of media and professional scrutiny, the global reach of its developer's activities supplies the flavor of far and wide connections. Disney has partially de-annexed the company name, but the town remains a showy jewel in the crown of the company's assets, and its medium-term destiny is locked into Disney's doings and fortunes. Celebration may be the one place where you cannot buy Mickey Mouse T-shirts, but that does not stop anyone here from wearing them or from benefiting in some small way from their sales elsewhere. There is no visible reminder of the continuum between the stitching in the seams of the T-shirt and the packing of grout between the bricks of Celebration, but the links are there and we lose our sense of perspective by ignoring them.

When on one of his flying visits to town, I asked Bob Stern why the area of the Celebration property designated for a "Workplace" still shows up on the site plan. It is there, he explained, because Michael Eisner feels that the public has lost sight of how things that appear in stores are actually manufactured, and so the idea of showcasing these manufacturing processes in some kind of visitor attraction is still a possibility. Don Killoren had earlier described the concept to me: "The Workplace would be more or less like a Ben and Jerry's ice-cream factory where you might see the vanilla beans being mixed . . . and the making and baking of the cone through glass windows, and in the end you get your ice cream. So you would have had an educational experience through watching people work." Like most residents, I found it difficult to envisage such a building (too Disney!) in Celebration. But if it is ever built for that purpose, it is fair to assume that it will not end up featuring the wide variety of Disney merchandise that is manufactured under some of the worst labor conditions and in some of the poorest countries in the world. Ben and Jerry's socially conscious operations are a far cry from the Lion King's squalid sweatshops in Asia and Central America.

While I was in Florida, an executive from McDonald's was subletting my Manhattan apartment for the year. McDonald's was paying my rent in New York, while I was paying rent to Disney in Florida. It sounds like one of these corporate tie-ins that have become a familiar, modern business practice. More than any company, Disney has pioneered the partnership tie-in by licensing its characters, stories, and songs to other companies for a fee. Established by Walt in the 1930s, this practice has been the company's most lucrative by far. As it happens, Disney joined with McDonald's in a ten-year exclusive global marketing partnership in

1997. These two names—the world's largest retail food chain and the second largest entertainment-media conglomerate—were now linked in global media advertising and trade. The result of that partnership could be viewed in places like the Keyhinge Toys factory in Da Nang City, Vietnam, where teenage women work seventy-hour weeks for as little as six cents an hour, making giveaway promotional toys—mostly Disney characters—for Happy Meals at McDonald's. In May 1997, not long after the partnership agreement was signed, two hundred women fell ill, twenty-five collapsed, and three were hospitalized from acute exposure to acetone. Like many global sweatshops, the factory hosts appalling working conditions, and there is no health insurance coverage or compensation for these women toiling for near-starvation wages.

As a renter in Celebration, my ties to Disney/McDonald's were, of course, entirely different from these Vietnamese workers, and yet I could not disconnect myself easily from the far-flung economic circuits that make our lives touch in the global economy. Even if you have no reason or inclination to favor their products, it is difficult to elude the worldwide reach of companies like Disney and McDonald's. The Mouse and the Golden Arches are almost as ubiquitous on the earth's crust as the Christian cross or the Muslim crescent. A thoroughgoing boycott of Disney products would be a keen challenge to the everyday consumer of popular entertainment. Disney-owned TV stations reach into almost every household in the United States. Disney-owned radio stations reach 123 million people each week, and one out of every four movie tickets is for a Disney or Disney-distributed film. About 86 million people worldwide pass through its theme park turnstiles, and a good portion of these tourists use its other vacation properties. That is not to mention the company's vast empire of newspapers, magazines, and publishing companies, its educational products and sports interests, or its real estate, retail, and licensing activities, far and near.

The evening before I moved down to Celebration, I attended the Manhattan launch of a book I had edited about sweatshops in the garment industry. The Disney company comes under close scrutiny in the book, primarily for the miserable wages (less than 28 cents an hour) it paid Haitian workers to sew *Lion King* T-shirts, *Pocahontas* pajamas and *101 Dalmatians* outfits, but also for its subcontractors' abuse of factory workers in Burma, Indonesia, and China.[14] For well over a year, the company had been the target of widespread condemnation by schoolchildren and clergy, in addition to labor unions and anti-sweatshop campaigners. Responding indifferently to this public criticism, the company had then been challenged internally by some of its large, socially conscious shareholders like the Presbyterian Church and the United Methodist Church. Eventually, Disney management declared that it would take steps to clean up its act: the company would reform its contract supplier system; issue a labor code of conduct, translated into local languages and posted in factories; authorize external audits and inspections at contract facilities; and clearly define the right of workers to organize. In a more telling sign, however, Disney allowed its chief subcontractor, H. H. Cutler, to pull out of Haiti in August 1997 (as it had earlier done with Burmese subcontractors) and move operations to China, where the media spotlight is less revealing. Instead of doing the right thing—staying put and improving the conditions of these workers—Disney joined the "race to the bottom" in which companies scour the globe for the very lowest wage levels.

In May, I taught a class about sweatshops to the school's Upper 3 neighborhood. I described how the revolution in teenage fashion had changed the shape of the garment industry, encouraging the spread of sweatshops in poor countries around the world, where the counterparts of these students toiled. Of course, students wanted to know which companies were the worst offenders. One precocious boy in the front row insisted: "What about Disney?" The class froze in anticipation of my reply. Disney, I explained, was one of the many companies that did not have a great record in treating its workers well, and it was probably important for students who lived in this community to be informed about such matters. Sons and daughters of Disney executives might have more reason to care about how children of their own age suffered elsewhere to assemble the company's product. I showed a video, *Mickey Mouse Goes to Haiti,* produced by the members of the National Labor Committee who had helped uncover the terrible laboring and living conditions of Caribbean workers sewing Disney T-shirts. It was a harrowing film, and it ended with workers' pleas to Disney to preserve their jobs and pay a living wage. This slight pay increase would have virtually no impact on retail prices, since the cost of their labor added a mere 11 cents to a garment sold in the United States for about $11. The workers in the film were astonished to learn the price tags of some of these garments.

The film's closing credits noted that some of the workers may be penalized for appearing on camera. After the film ended, one boy in the front row held his hand high. "Did the workers lose their jobs, and, if so, did the film cause any of the workers to lose their jobs?" None of them lost their jobs as a result of the film, I told him, but when the subcontractor pulled out they were forced to find employment with other garment companies, no better or worse than Disney. Another boy followed the line of reasoning further. So could the film be a worthwhile educational tool even if it brought more distress to the workers? These were smart questions, and while they were partly intended to deflect attention from the poverty, they were not offered in a heartless way. They helped dissipate some of the obvious discomfort the film had generated in the room. Several students said they had heard about sweatshops, but had not imagined things could be so bad.

A few days later, I ran across Upper 3's number-one heartthrob, Nick Riccardelli, always on the move and sporting the latest buzz cut and skate pants. Of those likely to be stirred to action by our class, Nick was the last sleek teen I would have bet on. So wrong. He told me he had enlisted some friends to hand out fliers about Disney sweatshops to visitors in the theme parks. They had been thrown out by security guards. Nick shrugged as if this was all in a day's work and bustled off, lustrous and spry, in pursuit of those other things that make him tick.

13
LEARNING FROM CELEBRATION

"We're not Stepford Wives, we still have problems, it's just a nicer place to have problems."
—A Celebration resident

In a moment of sly modesty, Walt Disney once shrugged off an inquiry about the significance of one of his films. "We just try to make a good picture. And then the professors come along and tell us what it means." With my year in town drawing to an end, it was time to say what Celebration had meant to me, since most people agreed that Walt's heirs had, at least, made a "good picture." Indeed, virtually everyone who visited me in Celebration remarked that the place was like a movie set. It was a fairly obvious comment about a brand-new town, though model garden suburbs from an earlier era still exude the atmospheric quality of a theatrical set seventy years after they were built.[1] These days, however, almost every encounter with the new is rendered familiar by translating it into a media reference. The landscapes of film and TV are now our common reference points, as definitively as the Bible had once been. So much of public and political life is staged for the benefit of media coverage that the artful dodges of PR, spin, backdropping, and soundbiting are widely understood among the non-expert populace. We take it for granted that there is a facade and also a behind-the-scenes. No surprise, then, that an equally common observation among visitors was that while Celebration may be

Disney's first genuinely unscripted product, there was still an unwritten script that its residents would feel some pressure to follow, as if they were unwittingly playing the role of cast members.

CELEBRATION'S OVER

I did not need to plow my way through the mountain of press clippings about Celebration to confirm that one film, above all, encapsulated the skeptical view of the town held by many outsiders. Bryan Forbes's 1975 film adaptation of *The Stepford Wives* cropped up again and again in press accounts and in the prejudgments of visitors and locals. I suspect, rightly or wrongly, that some people who cite this film as a shorthand way of condemning high-end suburban life have not actually seen it. If so, I was among their number. It is a film whose significance has entered common currency, and so I assumed that I understood its meaning correctly, or at least the meaning it had acquired over time. At any rate, I decided early on not to view the film until near the end of my residence.

The Stepford Wives, as I discovered late in the day, is primarily a film about male opposition to early 1970s feminist ideas. In affluent Stepford, control over advanced biochemical and robotic technology allows men to reduce their wives to compliant, sexually acquiescent housewives, monstrously obsessed with cleaning their homes and gratifying their husband's desires. Any career aspirations of Stepford wives, along with their efforts to organize consciousness-raising meetings, are technologically snuffed out. The film is a science-fiction variation on the genre of antisuburban satire, but its blunt commentary on male power is arguably its strongest story line. Somewhere along the road to the cliché file of public memory, the feminist angle had been pushed to the side. The film is usually cited as a morality tale about the dramatic effect that an upscale suburban environment has on the behavior of its residents. A too-perfect community runs the risk of suppressing what it is that makes us human. The "Stepford Wife" has come to represent the socially numbing, conformist mentality that is somehow automatically triggered among new residents of highly zoned suburban housing. As for the film's particular relevance to Celebration, that was clear enough. When the nonconformist Joanna Eberhart confesses to a therapist her fears about being "changed," she predicts: "My time is coming. There will be someone with my name, and she'll cook and clean like crazy, but she won't take pictures, and she won't be me. She'll be like one of these robots in Disneyland."

It's no surprise that the Stepford Wives label is bitterly resented among the women of Celebration. Not a few described encounters with tourists who asked them directly whether they felt like a Stepford Wife. It was not always easy to separate this awareness of being typecast from normal habits of self-presentation. One remarkably independent woman, who did not seem to correspond to the stereotype in any way, confessed to me that she always "tidied herself up" to pop down to the grocery store "just in case a tourist took a picture" of her. She wanted to "represent Celebration in a good light." How did women, in general, respond to their roles in this community?

In my talks with couples, I found that women were generally less inclined to be "negative" in their opinions about Celebration, while their husbands often took pleasure in offering their own assessments of the community's problems. I also found that men alone were likely to speak in the first person of their decision to move here or to buy a house, although this habit was more chronic among older couples. As in Stepford, Celebration had its share of wealthy, nonworking wives, with a retinue of home helpers on call, but in many more cases, the economic challenge of moving in and keeping up with monthly payments obliged female homemakers to seek outside work. If anything, when I ran into resentment relating to gender roles, it was directed by women at the spectacle of "idle" men around town, especially those who were wealthy enough to buy oodles of leisure time.

Could a town like Celebration be construed, Stepford-like, as part of a male conspiracy to rein in the womenfolk? In this well-trodden domain of male behavior, no such conjecture, however far-fetched, could be entirely dismissed. But it was less easy to make the case here. New Urban design is aimed, in part, at ensuring that suburban women are no longer compelled to serve as their children's chauffeurs, nor are they required to be social prisoners in their own subdivision unit. With daycare, the school, and playgrounds all within walking distance, and with the prospect, eventually, of nearby work, this environment was intended to be much kinder on women's schedules than a typical suburban setting.

By contrast, the single-family dream homes of postwar suburbia had been built around the rigid gender role of domestic servitude. The supporting highway system was constructed to meet the assumed transportation needs of male breadwinner commuters. With the rise of the dual-income family, the undue pressure on women to cope with this ill-adapted environment was often linked to "social problems" like the latchkey child, the dysfunctional family, high divorce rates, and even the erosion of middle-class security. If this compact, postsuburban town was designed to reinforce the family bonds, it did so, in part, simply by making women's lives easier. In addition, the mixed-income and intergenerational makeup of the Celebration population yielded far from uniform expectations of male and female behavior regarding work and social roles. As for the single parents, almost all women, the gruesome label of the Stepford Wife was especially difficult to stomach.

The week I rented *The Stepford Wives*, *The Truman Show*, filmed in Seaside, started its run in the downtown theater and instantly sparked discussion among residents. Celebration was being mentioned regularly in reviews of the new film, and residents were once again on the defensive. Peter Weir's film, with its parable about the media-scripted life of an idealized small American town, promised another round of Celebration bashing. According to a *New York Times* review, Celebration was "where Truman Burbank would have fit in without changing a thing." Unlike Seaside, the reviewer pointed out, Celebration really did have lawns for Trumans to sweat over and an air of predictability that the virtuoso resort town did not exude.[2] Offended by such comments, many Celebrationites might still have envied the use that Seaside made of the money it received for serving as the film's backdrop—to help build a charter school.

In the film itself, it's the women, once again, who are causing trouble. Truman's wife, Meryl, drops her role and his sweetheart, Karen, breaks the rules of the script, inspiring the most surveilled person in TV history to outwit Christof, the controlling, patriarch producer of the show, and free himself from the artificial confines of Seahaven. For thirty years, each detail of his daily life had been available around the clock to viewers all over the world. Truman had been a model of normality in a world where norms exist only in the form of statistics, not flesh and blood. Christof informs Truman that he was more real and truthful a person on a TV set than he will be outside of Seahaven. The TV ratings confirm it. Along the way, he had to become the first child to be legally adopted by a corporation in order to smooth over any questions about his civil rights.

At the end of a century of well-earned concern about government and corporate surveillance of individuals, *The Truman Show* carries a ponderous message. Surveillance in the form of media entertainment may prove to be one of the most effective forms of social control. Forget Big Brother, the film tells us. The media corporations do a much more efficient job than government institutions of managing the emotions, aspirations, and disquiet of large populations. More often than not, it is their treatment of real life, not fiction, that commands the largest audiences, craving ever greater exposure of neighbors and nobodies alike. Hence the explosion of genres—talk shows, infotainment, tabloid news, home videos—that scorn any boundaries between public and private life, between raw reality and stage scenery. *The Truman Show* is a simple, if laborious, extension of this idea. The more chilling sequel played itself out in the impeachment proceedings on Capitol Hill. There, the media's compulsive inquiry into Bill Clinton's overpublicized private dalliances was finally outmatched in zeal by a right-wing crusade to turn personal behavior into a litmus test of public office.

Celebration's insider humor was often Trumanesque. Residents were all too aware of the outside perception of them as controlled actors in a movie set, and they had their own way of processing and putting to use this stereotype. One example was another punlike saying that I occasionally heard around town: "Celebration's Over." Depending on the speaker and the context, it had at least two different meanings. The phrase could be used, for example, as a sympathetic comment about some mishap that had changed a resident's perceptions of the town. In other words, the good life in Celebration had simply been an elaborately staged illusion, and now the show had ended, or, as Porky Pig from the Looney Tunes put it, "That's All Folks!" Alternately, "Celebration's Over" could be used to urge others to act in a mature fashion. In other words, the onset of daily problems had dispelled the hoopla surrounding the town and it was time to get real. In both cases, there was an implied comment about Disney's withdrawal from the picture. The first lamented that the pixie dust had faded, or that it would do so very soon. The second was impatient for that day to come. There were

A trick or a treat? When Mickey comes calling. Halloween in Celebration. (Photo: the author)

several other shades of meaning too, among which the notion that the days were over when the original Disney vision of the town had meant something special to its pioneers.

This broad range of sentiments was hardly surprising among pioneers who had been willing to entrust their life savings and their children's education to the real estate aspirations of a huge entertainment company, and who had put their money down on the strength of silver-tongued advertising alone. I found there were few residents whose opinion of Disney did not shift rapidly in the early period of their settlement. Many wanted to hold on to what they often referred to as the "Disney dream," but found it impossible to ignore the company's profit-seeking priorities, its mania for secrecy, or its skittishness about tart publicity. Most surprising to me, the realization that this corporation is ruled by the bottom line came as a bitter revelation to Celebrationites, even though many of the same people said they had bought in "because everything Disney does turns to gold."

A chronic ambivalence developed. One nonresident who works in a downtown store summed up her attitude toward Disney. "Hate the company, like the employees." More generally, there was the good Disney and the bad Disney, distinguishing Walt's from Michael's company. Residents also separated into two categories the many ranking employees who lived in town. There were "Disney types," intimately associated with the company's profile—aloof, tight-lipped, and close-to-the-chest—and there were "real people"—capable of switching off their corporate personalities when they were off the job. Most folks quickly learned that it was an asset to be associated with Disney in some matters and a liability in others. Despite the effective absence of Disney from the daily doings of the town, the company name was always a variable in how Celebrationites felt and talked about their home investment and the independent exercise of their rights, two quantities sometimes at odds with each other. To be sure, this was a peculiar environment for a brand name associated with fairy tales and fantasies without consequence. After all, there is nothing more consequential in America than the act of buying a home.

UNDER NEW MANAGEMENT

Home ownership is a sacred cornerstone of the American way. The percentage of Americans who own detached, single-family homes—the apex of social and economic life—far exceed those anywhere else in the world. Full membership in society can be attained only through entering into a long-term relationship with a banker, preferably through a mortgage. Americans are not fully citizens until they own a home, at which point their civic identity is anchored to their credit ratings and their property values. Non-debtors in the form of renters do not enjoy full privileges; they are regarded as immature, rootless, or untrustworthy. In addition, most homeowners are small traders because their homes are scarce assets likely to generate income through resale.[3] Zoning and the regulation of land use determine what level of citizenship homeowners will enjoy. In the geography of suburbia, the status of residents tends to increase with the distance between home and work, as well as the distance from lower priced homes. In New Urbanist geography, the reverse is true; your status increases with proximity to work and to other homes corresponding to different income levels. But mixed-income and high-density housing in places like Celebration are still enormous risks to the ironclad patterns of predictability that command the housing industry and realty market. How easy it is to backslide. It took only a year or so in Celebration for the Phase Two lot plan for the North Village to revert to some elements of the conventional suburban pattern.

Because New Urbanism marches to a different beat, the golden egg of resale value—predictability—is not guaranteed. Consequently, professional management must be as tight as a drum. What is the impact of this kind of management on the life of a place? Naturally, I wanted an answer from Andres Duany, the person who had thought longest and hardest about such questions. One spring evening, after his team completed their day's work on the Orlando Naval Training Center proposal, I dined with Duany at Café D'Antonio, around the corner from my apartment. Our dinner conversation, he warned me, would be a dry run for a presentation he would give at an architects' gathering at the Disney Institute the following day. Duany had staked his career on being provocative and being proved correct. He reeled off one success after another, as if methodically recounting a campaign of conquest for the New Urbanist cause. In his presentation the following evening, which took the form of a dialogue with Harvard professor Alex Krieger, he declared that all of the powerful bodies and institutions in the planning and housing world had been persuaded by the ideas of New Urbanism. There was one holdout—the elite academic citadels of instruction, like Harvard, Columbia, and Princeton, which remained antagonistic (one exception was Yale, where Robert Stern would be appointed to the deanship of the School of Architecture before the summer's end). The task now at hand was to capture the Ivies. There is always a studied element of swagger in Duany's showmanship, but no one had any reason to doubt the sincerity of his intentions.

Duany had just purchased a lot in Celebration, in the Lake Evalyn pocket. Styled after Key West and hosting some charming Craftsmen cottages, Lake Evalyn was considered to have potential as an artsy, neo-bohemian quarter. Duany wanted to keep track of developments here and to observe for himself the slap-up job that Celebration's creators had done. For twenty thousand dollars, he said, he was getting access to the "eight million dollars of R&D that had gone into the way the curbs are designed, the lamps they chose, the texture of the concrete." (His contract on the lot was eventually dropped, after his firm lost the Naval Training Center competition). While our dinner conversation ranged widely, there was one provocative argument he wanted to pitch.

> [This place] is clearly governed by a corporation, rather than a government, and so what happens is that an American corporation is treating you as a customer. A customer is possibly treated better than a citizen in this country. If you look at the way Land's End treats you, they're open 24 hours a day. If you pick up the phone at Land's End and see who answers, or here in Celebration, compared to who picks up in Miami at City Hall, and see what kind of illiterate hiring thing you get there—and I love minorities—but don't tell me it's the same quality of government. . . . If I show up at Coral Gables, I'm met essentially in an ugly room by an uninterested and harried bureaucrat who doesn't care, and then I have to wait two weeks for a first appointment, where my building is critiqued by four or five government hacks, architects who got their position because of friendship with the mayor. What happens here when I have my building? I make a call, Joe Barnes shows up half an hour later, apologizing for being late, and this is a guy who went to Princeton and the University of Virginia who knows what he's talking about. Objectively, that is a very superior experience. And I know they're afraid of me because I'm a customer. . . . I must say I'm very interested in being a customer

> rather than a citizen. I'm wondering whether I would like to be treated as a customer at the level of the neighborhood and then as a citizen at the level of the county and country.

I let Duany know there were many Celebrationites who felt they had been led to expect better customer treatment. In a complex community like this, you would be hard put to find a chorus of praise for the corporate offering of a "superior experience." Besides, customers are only treated well if they can pay the bills or keep up with the assessments and mortgage payments. Otherwise, they are out of luck. Even here, in affluent Celebration, there was a cash-flow problem, as the town's merchants could attest. The "maturing of the town," he responded, would take care of that problem. For the time being, a secure grip was crucial. "In order to make a real place you actually have to control it," he declared. "You have to manage it because there's a tendency for things to become false, to become literally artificial." Pushing aside his half-eaten pasta and gesturing toward the mixed range of stores around us, he praised TCC's unbending devotion to market segmentation:

> If it takes a corporation, I'll take a corporation. Because the free market will not sustain this. The free market would close this down for T-shirts. The tourist economy or cultural economy is very destructive unless it's managed. They will destroy Key West, they'll destroy Nantucket. They'll destroy the Left Bank of Paris, and eat Soho up. It takes something different, it takes a closed market, a managed market, to keep a normal place going.

I had become quite familiar with Andres's shtick, and considered myself something of a fellow traveler of New Urbanism, but there were moments like these that set me back. To my taste, the New Urbanist appetite for small-town civility often felt like a hunger for civic order at all costs. In the haste to see their designs adopted, any form of patronage would be considered: if the shoe fits, we will wear it, and whoever can supply the right size at the right price will win our loyalty. In like fashion, the modernists they scorned had gradually lost their passion for a new public order and increasingly turned to corporate patrons to bankroll their blueprints in the form of sleek office towers. New Urbanists had staked their first claims on the well-tended turf of private developers and private governments. Would they ever want to forgo the "superior experience" of dealing with expeditious, Princeton-trained peers for the public sluggishness of City Hall? In the Disney Institute debate with Krieger the next evening, the Harvard professor drew attention to the many fine "old urbanist" neighborhoods that were under stress in cities like Boston. In response, Duany suggested that a homeowner's association would offer these districts better management and a better chance of rehabilitation than current forms of city government.

Homeowner's associations have proved an efficient and popular form of common-interest management, and by now they are a semipermanent feature of the suburban landscape where planners like Duany have decided to operate. But the rage to embrace this form of governance and the willingness to salute a corporate monopoly—Duany's "managed market"—troubled folks like myself for whom efficiency, civic order, and exacting management are not overriding goals in and of themselves. When planners accept these forms of management as the price for pushing their own architectural dreams, or as pragmatic compromises in the game of competing with suburban alternatives, some features of their hallowed ideal of civility, freely endorsed by all, are sacrificed. And when citizens are viewed primarily as consumers or as property holders, with no obligations beyond the protection of their own assets, an important line gets crossed.

For one thing, some forms of civic disorder are crucial to the political life of the republic. Without civic disobedience, it has been proved, again and again, that there is little hope of changing unjust laws, discriminatory codes, and exclusive patterns of institutional behavior. The civil rights and life opportunities of a vast percentage of the population have been concessions won from the powerful only after prolonged opposition to the existing rules of civic order. Abiding suspicion of these rules is widespread, whether in the form of distrust of "white justice" or "upper middle class standards," although such distrust is often vilified and blamed for the decline of everything from public manners to the upkeep of housing stock. Moralists see this resistance to civic order as a reflection of laziness and bad character, or as part of a general weakening of respect and refinement. But most of the time it is a result of friction generated between groups who have unequal resources and advantages. In addition, the pattern of most civic disorder reveals that "civility" usually covers a very narrow spectrum of tolerable behavior and is designed as much to exclude as to invite common participation. As if to compensate for all their good civic behavior, some Celebrationites wistfully conjured up a rough-and-ready presence in the streets. One day, as we were sharing a bench, and a slow day, on Market Street, a retiree, and an ex-military man at that, observed: "What we need are a few drunks around this town."

From what I had learned, most Celebrationites were attracted to the efficiency of private government. Many spoke to me of their loss of faith in public institutions and public government, and described democratic public process as laborious, wasteful, and inept. I always found this to be a circular argument, since the capacity of public institutions—especially urban ones—to function efficiently has been decimated by the siphoning away of resources brought about by the rise of suburban privatopias. Tax starvation is one of the reasons it takes a while for someone to answer Andres Duany's phone call at City Hall in Miami. Besides, no one who has tried to be a fully functioning participant in a democratic process ever discovered it be truly efficient. Just and accountable, perhaps, but never the most economic use of time, energy, or resources. The rage for privatization that has swept the country, and much of the developed world, routinely sacrifices justice and accountability at the altar of efficiency. In practice, the efficiency of most forms of private governance is easily subverted, especially when its member-consumers take legal action. My own apartment in New York City belongs to a co-op, the most minimal form of common-interest development, and I had briefly served as vice president of the co-op board. It was an exhausting term of office, which often involved lengthy weekly meetings with lawyers when a mean-spirited set of residents repeatedly sued the co-op for weather damages to their apartment walls.

As residents found out for themselves, the early, informal attempts at democratic opinion making in Celebration were a messy business, conducted discreetly or semi-publicly among interest groups that had formed around the town's hot spots—primarily the school and home construction. Heedful of their potential labeling as "negative," Celebrationites quickly became aware of the leverage they could command if they "went to the press" to publicly embarrass the company. In this capacity, they wielded a power unavailable to almost any another residential community. Celebration may have been tarred by association with the "Truman effect," and certainly the media had generated no end of caricatures of residents who lived here. But townsfolk learned early on that the threat of media publicity could be their ally. Celebration was, and would always be, like the child of a famous public figure, basking in the warm glow of its birthright or suffering for the sins of its parent. Its private life could be ushered on to the public stage at any moment.[4]

A STRANGE BEAST

This blurring of lines between private and public eventually permeated everything that had come to interest me about this town. Celebration was a living, breathing embodiment of something called the private-public realm. This was a strange beast that had been slouching toward the millennium for much of the latter part of the century. With the end of the cold war, it picked up speed dramatically. More and more of what had been public sector was being turned over to private and corporate interests. With the spread of neoliberal economics around the globe, privatization had been urged on country after country. In comparison to other developed nations, the size of the public sector in the United States had always been modest. Now, open season was being declared on cherished holdouts like public schooling and Social Security.

Housing has always been the preserve of private developers. The record of direct government involvement in housing is scanty and limited, for the most part, to forays like the New Deal's Greenbelt towns (sold after the war in response to industry red-baiting), temporary wartime workers' towns, and the overburdened programs of public housing that have hobbled along in the postwar years. On the other hand, the private housing sector is abundantly assisted by public funding in all sorts of ways. The postwar suburban explosion would not have been possible without the VA's mortgage guarantee program, which helped tens of millions of Americans to buy a home. In addition, the annual tax benefits extended to homeowners amount to a huge portion of the public purse. Road and transportation funding is a direct subsidy to private developers and suburban homeowners. By the late 1980s, however, land was so expensive and income so polarized that the American Dream of home ownership had become a hard sell. In addition, the suburban culture of privacy and isolation, and the continuing slide in voter turnout, gave rise to widespread concerns about the erosion of public life and civic involvement among the general population. Liberals' alarm signals were set off by the flourishing of privatized exurban enclaves, while right-wing analysts like Charles Murray warned of a coming "custodial state" featuring "a high-tech and more lavish version of the Indian reservation for some substantial minority of the nation's population," who will have become "permanent wards of the state."[5]

New Urbanism's remedies promised to address some of the concerns about suburbia, at least. Who would take the gambit? Could any large private developers be persuaded to respond to the call to restore civic and community life, especially if it meant going against the grain of industry behavior? The chances seemed unlikely. Only a corporation like Disney—a company whose core business lay in culture and values—would feel it could benefit from taking on the challenge in a high-profile way. Only an entertainment company like Disney would be likely to see the fit between the values it sold and the traditional small-town virtues championed by New Urbanism.

On paper, the outcome was a win-win situation. There was little financial risk involved, since the company already owned the land, secretly bought for a song (about $180 an acre) back in 1967, and it had done its consumer market research among the target homeowners groups. The company also stood to benefit enormously from the land, road, and environmental entitlements secured through the Celebration plan. Disney would take credit for building a showcase public realm in a suburban landscape bereft of public life. Credit might even accrue to the general cause of corporate America, beset by criticisms of its greed and disregard for the common good. Privatizers would be able to contend that public interests can indeed be favorably served by private enterprise. Celebration promised visible proof that corporations could be entrusted with the charge of restoring public space. If successful, the example of this town would be a formidable weapon in the arsenal of free-marketeers who believe that putting a price on everything is the best way of preserving the common interest.

Skeptics abounded. The teeming army of Disney-bashers sharpened their bayonets. Each inkling of "trouble in paradise" that filtered out of Celebration was scooped up and magnified into a macabre tale of Mickey Mouse misadventures. The Wonderful World of Disney, it was concluded early on, was not a hospitable climate for real people; this time, it was repeatedly predicted, the company had bitten off more than it could chew.

On the ground, I had found that things were a good deal more complex. The development team had got a lot of things right in the design of the town, and had frontloaded the community plan with the best intentions. Like all real estate developers, its puffed-up advertising and sales brochures set improbable expectations, but unlike any other developer, its brand name bought instant credibility from prospective buyers. The communitarian ethos lured community builders, and the school's innovative learning design enthralled boomer parents looking for something different. Competent management professionals took up positions in Town Hall and at the Foundation.

Barely two years from the first occupancy, Celebration had prematurely aged, such was the turmoil the community had lived through. Virtually every member of the development team within TCC and the school had departed, and Disney no longer had an unambiguous brand-name attachment to the town. Any resident or merchant could tell you the town's three problem spots: schooling, home construction, and shopping. The public-private partnership behind the school was fraught from the beginning. Equity requirements of the public school system clashed with the extraordinary resources demanded by the learning design and with many of the residents' expectations of entitlement. The educational methods had produced stirring results, but not in the form that most parents wanted. The downtown retail sector, built to provide an animated public space, and administered by what Duany called a "managed market," had also proved an ordeal for many of the merchants, and had risked alienating residents' sense of proprietary rights to the town. Its streets were busy enough, attracting visitors from near and far, but the boutique retail content had been a hard sell. The quality of housing construction had suffered from the chain of subcontracting, which allowed each agent in the chain—developer, builders, and subcontractors—to disown responsibility for supervision and for delivering what had been advertised.

As these concerns had developed, spinning media headlines along the way, Disney management took a deep, dread-lined breath, and then stepped back. The golden rule of stockholder reassurance had kicked in, and residents and merchants felt the shift of mood, as if a new weather pattern had settled into the air around them. All of a sudden, the community creators had gone and the business managers, taking their cues from Burbank, were running the show from a dispassionate distance. The new policy was clear-cut. Celebration had been planned as a real community, and so it would have to stand on its own to prove its authenticity. Some residents felt abandoned, nervous about their investment in poor housing stock, and distressed about a school they felt was inadequate. Others saw a frank opportunity to take more control over the destiny of the town and organized their interests accordingly. In the meantime, the town—judged by the criterion of real estate sales—was proving a commercial success.

All of this had happened much sooner and much more boisterously than anyone bargained for. In my time there, I watched as some kind of provisional public sphere, built on blunt opinion, common sentiment, and the stoic pursuit of civic needs, pushed its snout into the moist Florida air. It was fresh, cranky, and fraught with all the noble virtues and sorry prejudices that contend in the republic at large. Kindled by self-interest, and fiercely mindful of the property values of the developer and residents alike, this public awareness was raised to a new pitch by the ever-present performance anxiety. Born and nurtured in the cool radiance of media scrutiny, the community was hooked on self-inspection. From the rumor mill to the formal caucus, residents themselves played their part. Self-surveillance of the town's progress and accomplishments was almost a built-in feature of community life. The result sometimes felt like uncharted terrain for life in a democracy. People would speak and act because they had to prove to themselves that they were free to do so, all the while knowing that any public angst could turn into a private liability.

If this was a new way of behaving, the conduct of the private and public institutions involved did not seem to have altered that much. Disney would go on doing what Disney does, as a private corporation devoted to its quarterly returns, and the community managers would hit the hard road toward civic stability, in search of a tolerable balance of residents' and developer's needs. The municipal incorporation of Celebration, if it happened, would probably result in a contract city, as close to a state of private management as was legally permissible. The practice of the corporation itself had not been modified by its experiment with town building. If anything, the lessons of Celebration may have inclined Disney to think twice about any future foray into the public domain. Other developers who took the town as an industry benchmark were likely to plan well below the expectations set by Celebration, reasoning that they could not afford the full menu of infrastructure and community software that had gone into the town's design.

On the other side, had the behavior of public institutions altered as a result of their participation in this town? Osceola County planners were sick and tired of taking calls about Celebration, and told me so. County managers were gratified with the lucrative addition to their tax rolls, and with the hope of high-end growth and development, but remained just as ineffectual in coping with the throng of minimum-wage residents and the traffic surplus that Disney would continue to attract to the region in increasing volume. The school board had inherited an educational model that none of its members seemed to regard as very practical, or desirable, to replicate. As for the state planning and environmental agencies, they had settled on living with a growth management policy, of the sort exemplified by the Celebration agreements, that ran the risk of awarding high moral credibility to Florida's runaway developers. Ravagers of the state's remaining pristine acreage could now go about their business wearing an environmental badge of honor. Increasingly starved of resources by antigovernment politics and resigned, by professional habit, to merely responding to private developer initiatives, these agencies were in no better position to act creatively and effectively in the public interest. City planners, on the other hand, could see an appreciable rise in their own prestige, and perhaps even their power, as a result of each and every New Urbanist development like Celebration.

The lessons of Celebration, drawn out in scale, suggest that any restoration of trust in these institutions, both corporate and government, requires a sea change in their character. Why rely on corporate goodwill to sustain public initiatives if executives back off whenever their company's brand name is threatened by dubious publicity? Corporations with quasi-governmental powers do not inhabit a quarantined private sector. In an age when government gives more rights to corporations than it does to people, we cannot forget that corporations were once state-chartered entities, with carefully limited powers to protect against their abuse of citizens' rights. The "due process" clause of the Fourteenth Amendment, introduced to protect the rights of freed slaves, allowed corporations to claim the same status before the law as any natural person and opened the door toward deregulation of their activities. As late as 1913, some states affirmed their right to revoke charters when corporations failed to act in the public interest, but the habit of invoking the First Amendment privilege to protect the "speech" of corporations had already taken a severe toll on public life, and would continue to do so.

The right to revoke these charters should be invoked more often to educate executives in their public obligations. One or two MBA courses in business ethics are not enough. The economic conduct of corporations is in dire need of reform. Because of its size and scope of activities, Disney is as good an example as any. With one hand, the company was accepting praise for its high-profile sponsorship of Celebration's model of urbanity. With another, it was busy recruiting foreign nationals willing to labor for a minimum wage that buys much less than it did thirty years ago. All the while, it was turning a blind eye to the uncounted Asian factory workers toiling over its T-shirts and toys for starvation wages. This is not publicly minded policy, nor is it intended to be. It is the intolerable face of capitalism with no footing in humane conduct, rewarding the affluent and punishing the poor.

On the other side, public agencies, which we need more than ever, must be funded sufficiently to pursue innovations of their own, especially in the business of housing and shelter. Their current handmaiden function is all too often limited to housekeeping regulation, ensuring legal compliance, or indirectly subsidizing private ventures. Would Celebration have been a better place if, like its British counterpart, the marble-flintstone-and-chalk Poundbury of Leon Krier and Prince

Charles, it included public housing? Many residents would applaud such a move, and it would help to soften the town's elitist profile around Central Florida.

Should the state once again become actively involved in town making? It has been almost thirty years since government dabbled in the business of community building, supporting civic-friendly alternatives to the rapacious practices of merchant subdivision builders.[6] At the high watermark of federal involvement in the early 1970s, HUD created a New Town Corporation to fund as many as 110 new towns for a population of 20 million. The initiatives were hit hard by the insolvencies of the 1974 oil crisis, and by urban mayors' protests that federal housing money should be invested instead in more pressing inner-city needs. Many communities defaulted on their federally guaranteed loans. Shortly thereafter, President Ford pulled federal government out of community building, never to return. In the face of the destructive social impact of urban disinvestment in the 1970s and 1980s, it became politically regressive to advocate state funding for building new, relatively upscale communities on undeveloped rural land. New towns of this sort, it was concluded, would not address the chronic character of America's social and environmental problems, and would benefit only the least needy. Henceforth, federal dollars would flow only to more indigent, rural, and urban communities.[7] This was sound policy, but it came at a price. With government out of the picture, the suburban secessionists had an easier time removing themselves from any responsibilities, fiscal or social, to the broader public. In the absence of any public stake in their affairs, such communities were more likely to pull their own stake from public affairs at large.

The recent acclaim for New Urbanism at several government agencies, and in state and local planning departments, is in part an expression of welcome relief at seeing civic alternatives emerge from a private suburban sector that had been written off as a source of social innovations. Yet most advocates of New Urbanism will say that planners are simply not in a position to address the major social ills of America in their designs. Their primary aim is to break the industry formula for cranking out anonymous subdivisions and prestige, golf-course communities, and to do so by working from the inside out. New Urbanist towns are "commentaries" on urban problems, they do not provide a solution to them. Before I took up residence in Celebration, Bob Stern warned me against looking for such large-scale solutions and advised me simply to compare the town to what was on offer nearby, in comparable exurban developments. To be sure, I found that most residents had migrated from such places, and regardless of the degree of their passion for the romance of Celebration, attested to the basic betterment of their lives in the new town. But this was only a small part of the story that I witnessed, and not the most telling.

Rudely dispossessed of any lingering illusions that they had moved to an instant utopia, Celebrationites encountered obstacles to happiness that compelled them to forge community bonds for which there was no planning blueprint. The strong community its creators had hoped for would come into being as much in response to adversity as to the conveniences and advantages built in the town's design. The sense of community that was most authentic and resourceful emerged in response to perceived threats, challenges, and barriers to people's well-being, and, above all, to their property values. This spirited mood, as fractious as it was cohesive, was charged by the energies released by foiled expectations of the packaged good life. Interests beyond their control, whether commercial (the developer), philosophical (the school), or cultural (media and outsider opinion), had imperiled Celebrationites' sense of security. It had taken the bitter taste of jeopardy to arouse the appetite for strong society. That was another lesson I would take away from Celebration.

What these residents would do with their strong community was another matter. Donna Sines, director of Osceola County's enormously successful Community Vision project (150 citizens' focus groups were playing a role in planning the county's future), was one of the many incredulous locals who laughed heartily when I described the conditions of adversity that Celebrationites felt they faced on a daily basis. Sines, whose office space is donated by Tupperware and sits in the back of that company's sprawling headquarters on Orange Blossom Trail, had participated in the ACT community health project in Celebration. She recalled that while some of the other communities in the project, like St. Louis, or Bethel, Illinois, had been battling teenage pregnancies, drug addictions, prostitution, and neighborhood decay, Celebration's primary social problem appeared to be weight control. An active official in the tornado relief effort earlier in the year, Sines admitted that she had not thought, at the time, of appealing to Celebrationites for money and food. She simply assumed they "would not be interested." All the same, Sines said she was "looking forward to the day when there is some overspill of Celebration's leadership potential, when all the energies of these Type A personalities starts to flow into the county."

It was a heartfelt wish, though there was more wistful hope than bright expectation in her voice. Upscale communities with strong, internal bonds have a record of looking after their own interests, rather than investing their energies outside of town limits. The suburban tax revolts of the late 1970s in southern California set a model that the Sunbelt communities have been quick to follow.[8] Persuaded that their property taxes are being squandered on public services to the "undeserving poor," affluent communities often seek to incorporate in order to capture their own tax revenue, further distancing their members from any regional responsibilities. I had already heard resentful talk among residents about the county's reliance on Celebration's tax base to look after its local "transients" and "deadbeats." Municipal rule would not alter the county's share of its tax base, but it would give townspeople control over their own fiscal identity. Outsiders who like to refer snidely to Celebration as a Disney "police state" will no doubt applaud if and when its residents vote to incorporate. But how will the municipal powers be used? To further seal the town off from the region's service worker population, or to integrate itself into the fabric of the county by serving as a resourceful public leader?

THE PURSUIT OF HAPPINESS

I had worried that my own stay in Celebration might be premature. New towns take decades to ripen, and the habit and custom that grows from residential use of a place can be a slow process of fermentation. Future authors would provide a mellowed assessment. More to the point, residents, weary of being written about, would surely publish their own biographies of the town. But it had been a formative year for Celebration, still in raw transition from a glassy Potemkin village, gussied up for media consumption, to a complex community of pioneers with their own history of residence to reflect on. What were often described around town as growing pains turned into decisive experiences that would affect the shape of the community for many years to come. The tumult within the community would not subside for some time, while media scrutiny of the town would probably never let up. But the timing of my stay had felt right. Pioneers could still recall the original vision of its creators, but its legacy was fading fast. Townspeople often remarked that they wanted to see a proper book about this phase of Celebration, before the early memories were paved over and before the official, airbrushed narratives took hold.

Near the end of my stay, one of the residents dissatisfied with the school asked me if I would consider being the headmaster of a new school in Celebration. I was often asked whether I had decided to stay there permanently. Naturally, I was pleased that people saw me as someone who had played a role in the town. By contrast, friends and colleagues in New York had predicted that life in Celebration would scare the living daylights out of me. One referred to my place of residence as Hellebration. Another assured me that I was living in a concentration camp. Elder siblings, comfortably ensconced with their families in upper-middle-class residential surroundings, hoped my stay would finally dispel the bohemian delusions of their forty-something brother and inspire him to settle down in the real world. My mother, bless her soul, kept mum.

For myself, I had worried more about being lonesome, especially since a sense of professional ethics held me back from being too cozy with residents. Scholars and journalists can all too easily exploit their informants. Neither a journalist nor a social scientist by training, I had not angled for juicy headlines—there were enough out there already—nor had I aimed at an objective or statistical survey of the town—Celebrationites had been surveyed enough already. This book, like the hybrid nature of this community, is supposed to be a cocktail of personal and public observations, laced with those ingredients of analysis that seemed most true to my experience of the town's residents and employees. So, too, I had elected not to be a mute, recording witness. After only a few months of interviewing, I knew more about the town than virtually anyone else, and respectfully volunteered information and opinion to anyone who seemed to want it. A large part of the social life of Celebration involves swapping information and tales about the town itself, and it is customary to barter stories for stories. Participation in this circuit of information absolved me from feeling and behaving like a parasite. My work at the school and various volunteer activities also helped. I left town, believing, at least, that I had contributed in small ways to the life of the community. I had made several good friends in the course of my stay. Back in Manhattan, acquaintances congratulated me on my "escape from Celebration," drawing lightly from that haughty repertoire of cosmo attitude in which the term "suburban" is automatically derogatory. In my year in Celebration I had barely encountered any reverse snobbism toward urbanites.

From time to time, the memory of a tasteless film had flirted with my doings in Osceola County. Unlike *The Stepford Wives* or *The Truman Show*, this film had no obvious relevance to the real Celebration, but it did involve a place called Celebration, the only other record of the town name that I had come across. The film is Russ Meyer's camp classic, *Faster, Pussycat, Kill! Kill!*, and it features the violent mayhem visited by a trio of tough, Amazonian disco girls on the studs and farmhands they meet while joyriding their sportsters in the Californian interior. In one scene, hunting for new kicks, they pull up for gas in a decaying farm hamlet called Celebration. The pump attendant ogles their physiques and shambles his way through his cameo role as a country yokel. With a vicious rev of their Porsche engines, they are gone, and he is left sucking dust. The name of the town is a passing reference to everything the go-go girls hold in homicidal contempt. A carefree masterpiece of exploitation film, *Faster, Pussycat* is a twisted tribute to the Californian teen fever of the 1960s—beyond good and evil, beyond gender and reason, and crazed with the high-octane gusto of a civilization burning fuel faster than the speed of its collective mind. Meyer's film is the stark antithesis, in many respects, of *The Stepford Wives'* gender parable of suburbia.

The real town of Celebration was intended to correct some of the extreme, destructive impulses featured in these two films. Among other things, its design was aimed at quelling the gas-guzzling frenzy of the

American way of life, at cracking open the stifling conformity (especially for teenagers) of its suburban sanctuaries, and at liberating women, in particular, from having to follow the path of least resistance in their careers and daily lives. The result, it was hoped, might help neutralize the amoral self-indulgence that each set of impulses has unleashed within its citizenry and on its roads. In the centurylong tradition of housing reform, improving the neighborhood was expected to produce more civic-minded conduct.

But Celebration also hosted other checks against extremes of uncivil behavior. Aesthetic controls over house and garden, political control over who would vote in the community's affairs, and social control over how many people (two, according to the rule book) slept in each bedroom. These controls were accepted by residents in return for surety of their property. In response to outsiders who saw such checks as un-American, the founding fathers could always be invoked. One Celebrationite, a retired schoolteacher from Philadelphia, cradle of liberty no less, reminded me that the ties between liberty and property were fundamental to the constitutional history of the United States. Liberty, he argued, had its root in property and was thinner without it.

There was some historical basis to this comment, but it seemed only partly accurate. Thomas Jefferson and his peers had indeed been guided by the opinions of English philosopher John Locke about the interlocking virtues of "life, liberty, and property." Indian claims notwithstanding, the most distinctive mark of early colonial life, where land appeared to be plentiful, was the right of white settlers to acquire property, denied to the majority in feudal Europe. The New World, from Locke's point of view, was a place where the natural right to property, and thus the opportunity to subsist as free men, could be realized. But Locke's idea of property had more to do with self-possession and control over one's personal liberty than with material or landed possessions. Natural property, for him, was more about free will than about the free market. When the final draft of the Declaration of Independence was drawn up, Jefferson altered Locke's "life, liberty, and estate" to "life, liberty, and the pursuit of happiness." Historian William Scott speculates that Jefferson was aware of the growing disparity between contemporary ideas about private property and Locke's increasingly antique conception of natural property. Rather than risk a reference to property being read too literally, Jefferson substituted a more symbolic term.[9] In turn, the new republic came to reflect this disparity. In this nation, all men, in principle, were "created free and equal," but only white male freeholders were so, in practice, and would hold a vote in government accordingly.

In our day, only a tiny minority of citizens are still freeholders, living off the fruits of their own labor, in the sense that Jefferson and others envisaged for their agrarian republic of small farmers. Corporations own the vast bulk of productive property, and the principal meaning of "private property" now refers to homes, automobiles, stocks, and consumer appliances. Where the chief means of upward mobility once lay in the small freeholding of productive land, now material security rests primarily on the consumer property of the home, with its appreciated resale value. As for Jefferson's pursuit of happiness, modern consumer companies like Disney, whose property is billed as "the happiest place on earth," have staked their claim to that quest on our behalf.

Celebration's version of "life, liberty, and property," with its voter restrictions, its property deeds and standards, and its devotion to communitarian ideals, is in some ways a consumer society's rendition of the concerns of the founding fathers. Walt's famous signature (which, it is alleged, he himself could not reproduce)[10] is our century's most visible, trademarked substitute for the legacy of these original signers. To weigh the principles of these eighteenth-century legislators against the current-day policies of an overextended film company, is, of course, to invite comparison between the sublime and the ridiculous. But the distant past is always overvenerated, and we tend to underestimate events that unfold on our own doorstep. The concept of a town like Celebration is no less an expression of the dominant mentality of our age than the Constitution was a reflection of the interests of the powerful landowners, lawyers, merchants, and businessmen of its day. But—to stick with this flawed analogy to the bitter end—there is one large difference. The Constitution, made by the people, would be subject to amendment by the people, by due democratic process. In Celebration, as in hundreds of communities like it, people live by consent to the developers' own rules, yet it is widely understood that everything is subject to change, at the desire of the developer. All advertising, promotional material, and company literature carries a disclaimer like the following:

> These materials are intended to provide general information about certain proposed plans of TCC. These materials, and all photos, renderings, plans, improvements and amendments depicted or described herein are subject to change or cancellation (in whole or in part) at any time without notice. Accordingly, neither these materials, nor any communications made or given in connection with these materials may be deemed to constitute any representation or warranty or may otherwise be relied upon by any person or entity. © The Walt Disney Company

On my last day in Celebration, I had been tearing around town, tying up loose ends and doing exit interviews. I ducked into Town Hall on some breathless quest. Dawn Thomas and Sarai Cowin, the grand divas of the building, accosted me as I bustled down the corridor, sweating bullets, my hair bent all out of shape. I must have been a sight. "Where have you been?" pumped one of them. "Disney legal?" quipped the other, with perfect timing. This was Celebration insider humor at its finest. Luckily, I never had any truck with the company's legal department, whose reputation in the business world rivals that of Attila the Hun in the annals of human rights, although I had been there once, in the entrails of Team Disney, to interview a company attorney who was a Celebration resident. A clerical employee casually informed me that the building's interior reminded everyone of a maximum security prison, but I knew she was just adding spice to the fearsome mystique.

In truth, however, all of us (I was now an honorary Celebrationite) had felt the shivery finger of "Disney legal" slide between our thoughts and our words, calibrating the temperature of our speech. Protector of the almighty brand name, its probing audit had once moved upon the face of the waters of the Osceola swamp, and the holy writ of its Covenants, Conditions, and Restrictions now ran with the dry land raised above. Tapping into the town's sick humor, a resident had once joked to me that "at least we don't have a Celebration tattoo stamped on our arms yet." In the age of the trademark logo, we had something much better. We had our own brand. Everyone, in time, might have his or her own brand. It had been promised.

As I motored out of town for the last time, I remembered some other things that same resident had told me. On one occasion, when a downtown parking lot was being resurfaced, TCC employees readied to tow his car to another location. Something about this intrusion unhinged him, and he complained loudly to the tow crew. The sheriff was called, and when TCC officials arrived on the scene, he lost it: "I've had enough of this," he bellowed, threatening to sue Disney, "I've got pixie dust coming out of my ass." A week later, when I ran into him again, he was agitated about the fact that a resident on the block occasionally parked her car on the back lawn, and had escaped a Town Hall reprimand for doing so. There was a perfect contradiction in his response to these two situations, and clearly this was a man in whom extremes met. But his fierce resistance to authority, on the one hand, and his equally fierce passion, on the other, for the policing of his neighbor's conduct did not seem altogether out of character in Celebration. It was what we had come to expect. After all, this was a place that many of its residents had experienced as the best and worst of towns, or so it had seemed to me.

NOTES

CHAPTER 1

1 Vincent Scully, "Disney: Theme and Reality," foreword to Beth Dunlop, *Building a Dream: The Art of Disney Architecture* (New York: Harry Abrams, 1996), p. 8.
2 Estimates provided by the Sustainable Communities Project of Florida's Department of Community Affairs.
3 Appreciation of the signage was recorded by Celebration resident Marty Treu, who was writing a book about the Main Streets of small-town America.

CHAPTER 2

1 Osceola County Comprehensive Plan, Evaluation and Appraisal Report, Executive Summary (December 1997).
2 Kevin Lynch, *What Time is This Place?* (Cambridge, MA: MIT Press, 1972).
3 According to the recollection of an architect from the firm of Skidmore, Owings, and Merrill, who worked on some of the first plans.
4 Russ Rymer, "Back to the Future: Disney Reinvents the Company Town," *Harper's*, (October 1996), p. 70.
5 Susan Hayward, "Changing Social Values and the Home," unpublished copy of a consumer report by Yankelovich Clancy Shulman (August 1988). I am indebted to Peter Katz for providing a copy of this paper.
6 "Urban or Suburban?," *Harvard Design Magazine*, 1 (Winter/Spring 1997), p. 47.

7 Compared to conventional suburban development, Traditional Neighborhood Developments (TNDs) carry extra costs—for neighborhood greens, town squares and plazas, wide sidewalks, rear lanes, facade detailing, and other attempts to build in public "character." The higher density per acre offsets these costs, since the smaller lots make roads and utilities less expensive for each unit. In addition, accessory units, or granny apartments on top of garages, provide a potential source of rental income for owners to offset mortgage payments. A study by the Ottawa-based Canada Mortgage and Housing Corporation found that TNDs should cost a developer about 24 percent less per dwelling than in a conventional design. "Density Makes New Urbanism Cheaper," *New Urban News,* July–August, 1998, p. 10. A Vancouver study by a University of British Columbia team, headed by Patrick Condon, estimates that the TNDs could be 30 percent less, while the tax base could yield 3.5 times more.

8 Mary Doyle-Kimball, "Sizing Up Disney's Celebration," *Builder Magazine,* September 1996, p. 121.

9 Mary Shanklin, "The Hottest of Spots," *Orlando Sentinel,* January 3, 1999, J-1.

10 Despite all my efforts, I could not get access to company profiles of the income and demographics of the residents. The only general statistics on income I could access were the results of AT&T's phone survey of the first 300 pioneers. According to that survey of a sample of 145 families, 54 percent had household incomes of under $75,000, 31 percent were between $75,000 and $150,000, and 10 percent were higher than $150,000. Almost 98 percent of the families had some college education, and 38 percent had graduate, medical or law school degrees.

11 The annual charges on a $400,000 house in Phase One would include about $5,106 in county and school taxes, $2,000 for the Community Development District maintenance assessment, and $360 for the Community Association, totaling about $7,500 per year. For a $155,000 townhouse, a buyer would expect to pay $1,714 in county and school taxes, $750 for the maintenance, and $360 for the Community Association dues, totaling about $2,824 per year.

12 Susan Lundine, "At Celebration, Big Tax Bills Set Off Fireworks," *Orlando Business Journal,* March 20–26, 1998, pp. 1, 48.

13 Ramond Chiaramonte, in response to Orlando architect John Henry's numerous broadsides against Celebration, "Architect on High Horse with Anti-Celebration 'Diatribe,' " *Orlando Business Journal,* October 18–24, 1996; and "Celebration Parent Defends School Innovation," *Tampa Tribune,* June 14, 1997.

14 TCC actively promoted trans2 electric vehicles, which resembled souped-up golfmobiles and were known around town as egg-cars. Almost twenty NEVs (neighborhood electric vehicles) had been purchased by residents and were in daily use. Ownership of these vehicles signified a particularly strong commitment to community life and to the ideals of Celebration.

15 Andres Duany, in "Urban or Suburban," p. 55.

16 Quoted in Mary Doyle-Kimball, "Sizing Up Disney's Celebration," p. 121.

17 Lenny Savino, "Celebration Workers Face Deportation," *Orlando Sentinel,* February 14, 1998, D-1, 6.

18 Carl Hiassen, *Team Rodent: How Disney Devours the World* (New York: Ballantine, 1998), pp. 53–57.

CHAPTER 3

1 Charles Moore, "You Have to Pay for the Public Life," originally appeared in *Perspecta: The Yale Architectural Journal,* 9/10 (1965), and was collected in Charles Moore and Gerald Allen, eds., *Dimensions: Space, Shape and Scale in Architecture* (New York: Architectural Record Books, 1976), p. 116.

2 Moore, p. 130.

3 Margaret Crawford, *Building the Workingman's Paradise: The Design of American Company Towns* (New York: Verso, 1995). The more well-known include the Kuppert Farms town of Kingsport in Tennessee, Apollo Iron and Steel's Vandergrift, the Hershey town in Pennsylvania, Tyrone, built in New Mexico by the Phelps-Dodge Copper Company, U.S. Steel's Gary in Indiana, NCR's Ohio settlement of Dayton, Colorado Fuel and Iron's Ludlow, the Kohler town in Wisconsin, Niagara Power's Echota, the Chicopee town in Georgia, and the Draper Corporation's Hopedale in Massachusetts.

4 Gwendolyn Wright, *Building the Dream: A Social History of Housing in America* (New York: Pantheon, 1981), p. 180.

5 John Reps, *The Making of Urban America: A History of City Planning in the United States* (Princeton: Princeton University Press, 1965), p. 436. Cited from a 1938 survey of planned communities by the National Resources Committee.

6 John Taylor, *Storming the Magic Kingdom: Wall Street, the Raiders, and the Battle for Disney* (New York: Knopf, 1987), pp. 33–34.

7 Quoted in Alan Bryman, *Disney and his Worlds* (London and New York: Routledge, 1955), pp. 118–120.

CHAPTER 4

1 Four samples of this kind of criticism, as applied to Celebration itself, will suffice. Longtime architecture critic for the *New York Times*, Ada Louise Huxtable's book *The Unreal America: Architecture and Illusion* (New York: New Press, 1997) is probably the most exhaustive example of the genre. Of Celebration's Pattern Book, she writes: "All of the promised 'looks' are there, but in selectively annotated and historically correct versions. Clever 'authentic' adaptation makes the ridiculous acceptable; this is a managed eclecticism of a seductive unreality that both blows and corrupts the mind" (p. 65). Renowned urbanist Jane Jacobs sees Celebration "as a theme park of a town. It'll have an artificiality, certainly, that genuine places that grew up over a course of time and weren't the brainchild of one committee don't have. You can't fake it," quoted in Craig Wilson,"Disney Gets Real, *USA Today*, October 18, 1995, A2. Rutgers professor Benjamin Barber observes: "When a government runs news stations, creates communities, defines friends and neighbors, controls architecture and rewrites history, it's called totalitarianism. When the Disney corporation does it, it's called Celebration. Except with Disney the motives are commercial, the reality is simulated, and the consequences are blandness, shallowness and the death of substance and taste alike, Disney's world is not totalitarian, it is only a simulation, a kind of totalitarian-land." "Sell-ebration: Living Inside the Book of Disney," *Forum*, Summer 1997, p. 14. Michael Sorkin, noted critic and architect, writes: "Like Disneyland—a 'city' based purely on the value of entertainment—New Urbanism asks us to believe that a shell of a city really is a city, that appearances are enough. But cities are for real; democratic culture cannot flourish in a theme park." "Acting Urban: Can New Urbanism Learn from Modernism's Mistakes?" *Metropolis* 18, 1 (August/September 1998), pp. 37–39.

2 Jane Jacobs, *The Death and Life of Great Cities* (New York: Random House, 1961).

3 Gwendolyn Wright, *Building the Dream: A Social History of Housing in America* (New York: Pantheon, 1981), p. 33.

4 Aside from the Celebration group, the list of names would include Arata Isozaki, Frank Gehry, Charles Gwathmey, Michael Rotondi, Stanley Tigerman, Thomas Beeby, Graham Gund, Peter Eisenman, Robert Siegel, Antoine Predock, Rem Koolhaas, Jean-Paul Vigier, Antoine Grumbach, Alan Lapidus, Hans Hollein, Bernard Tschumi, Arquitectonica, and Andres Duany and Elizabeth Plater-Zyberg.

5 See Beth Dunlop, *Building a Dream: The Art of Disney Architecture* (New York: Harry Abrams, 1996).

6 Deborah Dietsch, "Disney World Turns 25, Builds New Town," *Architecture,* November, 1996, p. 23.
7 Dunlop, *Building a Dream,* p. 139.
8 Darryl Owens, "Your Baby and Child—20 Years Later," *Florida Magazine,* November 1997, p. 27.
9 Hope VI, active in 53 cities, will replace existing superblocks with neotraditional public housing. According to a nationwide survey conducted by *New Urban News* in October 1997, there were over 135 New Urban developments in planning nationally, 64 of which were under active construction (most in Florida or California), while countless other "heritage developers" had adopted some of the movement's design principles in a diluted form. In January 1999, Al Gore launched the $10 billion Livability Agenda, aimed at "smart growth" to rectify "decades of ill-planned and ill-coordinated development."
10 Charles Abrams, *Forbidden Neighbors: A Study of Prejudice in Housing* (New York: Harper & Row, 1955), p. 152.
11 Dolores Hayden, *Redesigning the American Dream: The Future of Housing, Work, and Family Life* (New York: Norton, 1984), p. 56. For accounts of racial exclusion in postwar suburbanization, see Kenneth Jackson, *Crabgrass Frontier: The Suburbanization of the United States* (New York: Oxford University Press, 1985), pp. 190–230; and Abrams, *Forbidden Neighbors.*
12 James Howard Kunstler, *The Geography of Nowhere: The Rise and Decline of America's Man-Made Landscapes* (New York: Simon & Schuster, 1993), p. 124. See also *Home From Nowhere: Remaking Our Everyday World for the 21st Century* (New York: Simon & Schuster, 1996).

Other relevant books on New Urbanism include Peter Katz, *The New Urbanism: Toward an Architecture of Community* (New York: McGraw-Hill, 1994); Alex Krieger, ed., *Andres Duany and Elizabeth Plater-Zyberg: Towns and Town-Making Principles* (New York: Rizzoli, 1991); Christopher Alexander, Sara Ishikawa, and Murray Silverstein, *A Pattern Language: Towns, Buildings, Construction* (New York and Oxford: Oxford University Press, 1977); Peter Calthorpe and Sim Van der Ryn, *Sustainable Communities: A New Design Synthesis for Cities, Surburbs, and Towns* (San Francisco: Sierra Club Books, 1986); Robert Stern, *Pride of Place: Building the American Dream* (Boston: Houghton Mifflin, 1986); Doug Kelbaugh, *The Pedestrian Pocket Book: A New Suburban Design Strategy* (New York: Princeton Architectural Press, 1989); William Fulton, *New Urbanism: Hope or Hype for American Communities?* (Washington, D.C.: Lincoln Institute of Land Policy, 1996); Anton Nelessen, *Visions of a New American*

Dream (American Planning Association, 1994); David Mohney and Keller Easterling, eds., *Seaside: Making a Town in America* (New York: Princeton Architectural Press, 1991); Philip Langdon, *A Better Place to Live: Reshaping the American Suburb* (Amherst: University of Massachusetts Press, 1994).

13 Elizabeth Plater-Zyberg, in an interview with David Mohney, in Mohney and Keller Easterling, eds., *Seaside,* p. 79.

14 Andres Duany, in "The Seaside Debate," *ANY,* 1 (July–August 1993), pp. 30–31.

15 Duany in "Reasserting Spatial Difference," *ANY,* 1, p. 23.

16 Duany, "Coding America," *ANY,* 1, p. 18

17 See Peter Calthorpe, *The Next American Metropolis: Ecology, Community, and the American Dream* (New York: Princeton Architectural Press, 1993).

18 Philip Langdon, *A Better Place to Live,* p. 49.

19 Plater-Zyberg, "Five Criteria for Good Design," *ANY,* 1, p. 12.

20 Duany, in "The New Urbanism, the Newer, and the Old," *Places, 9,* 2 (Summer 1994), p. 92.

21 Plater-Zyberg, quoted in Mike Clary, "A Disney You Can Go Home To," *Los Angeles Times,* September 27, 1996, A-16.

22 The inclusion of parks and open spaces in central areas of Celebration and the large tracts of preserved wetlands make it difficult to interpret any estimate of overall density. The town's most dense single-home district, in Lake Evalyn, is about 7 units to the acre. The downtown apartments reach about 15 units to the acre. (Manhattan density is about 100, and central Paris is 380).

23 Although he had trained in the crucible of postmodernism in the late 1960s, and had cut his teeth on the opposition to the minimalist moderns, Stern's own approach to historical style quickly went beyond a witty flirtation and became a full-blown embrace. Postmodern iconoclasts like Moore and Venturi preserved an ironic distance between the old and the new. Whether in his renovations or new designs, Stern began to interpret the past literally, often identifying precisely with its ornate spirit. As a result, much of his work intersected with the ethos of the preservationist. More than any other signature architect, he would be an effective bridge between historicist postmodernism and the New Urbanism, as his commission for the Celebration master plan amply displayed.

24 Lawrence Lebowitz, "Disney Plans a Celebration of Life, Work, Play in Osceola," *Orlando Sentinel,* April 30, 1991, A-1, 4.

25 "Development Order," March 1994, *Celebration Development of Regional Impact,* Osceola County.

26 "Amended Development Order," December 1997, *Celebration Development of Regional Impact,* Osceola County.
27 "Jorge and Mimi Move to Celebration," *Front Porch,* 3 (September 1, 1997).
28 "Several American Landscapes," in *Landscapes: Selected Writings of J. B. Jackson,* edited by Ervin Zube (Amherst: University of Massachusetts Press, 1970).

CHAPTER 5

1 Greg Dawson, "Did (the) Butler Do It to Fool Everybody?" *Orlando Sentinel,* April, 23, 1997, C1.
2 Brent Herrington, Town Hall newsletter, November 1997.
3 Michael Pollan, "Town-Building Is No Mickey Mouse Operation," *New York Times Magazine,* December 14, 1997 , pp. 56ff.
4 Jeff Truesdell, "Out at the Mouse," *Orlando Weekly,* June 4–10, 1998, pp. 12–13.

CHAPTER 6

1 The title "Teaching Academy" was taken off the building in the summer of 1998. It is now known as 851 Celebration Avenue, and is used by Stetson to teach master's programs. It will eventually house Osceola school district's professional development program.
2 Promotional material for the school included a suggested reading list: *Collaborative Learning,* by Kenneth Bruffee; *The Handbook of Effective Teaching and Assessment Strategies,* by Anthony Dallmann-Jones and the Black River Group; *Multiple Intelligences,* by Howard Gardner; *The Quality School,* by William Glasser; *The Seven Habits of Highly Effective People,* by Stephen Covey; *Soar With Your Strengths,* by Donald Clifton and Paula Nelson; and *Horace's School, Horace's Compromise,* and *Horace's Hope,* all by Theodore Sizer.
3 Starting hourly wages at Universal, Disney, and Sea World are, respectively, $5.67, $5.95, and $5.80. After 5 years, Disney's wage rises to $10.07, guaranteed by union contract and based solely on seniority. Raises at the other two—$9.15, after 9 years at Universal, and $8.76, after 8 years at Sea World—are based on a "merit" system of pay for performance given at the supervisor's discretion. Disney workers also outstrip the others in paid sick leave, bereavement leave, fair disciplinary procedures, and overtime opportunities. For workers' own estimates of wage and benefit comparisons, see the May 1998 issue of *"What the *#?!" A Publication for Central*

Florida's Tourism Workers, at *http://www.what-the.org/may1998*. In the November 1998 issue, the editors also point out that "the Big 3 watch one another closely and form an unofficial cartel that keeps wages low," and that these starting wages have been stagnant for more than five years now."

4 For broad documentation of this campaign, see David Berliner and Bruce Biddle, *The Manufactured Crisis: Myths, Fraud, and the Attack on America's Public Schools* (Reading, Mass: Addison-Wesley, 1995).

5 Jonathan Kozol, *Savage Inequalities: Children in America's Schools* (New York: HarperCollins, 1992), p. 207.

6 "A Report Card on the Condition of Public Education in the 50 States," *Education Week*, XXVII (January 8, 1998).

CHAPTER 7

1 Steve Stecklow, "Disney's Model School: No Cause to Celebrate," *Wall Street Journal*, June 3, 1997, A-1.

2 "Meet the People of Celebration," MSNBC online, November 1, 1996.

3 Steve Farkas, *Different Drummers: How Teachers of Education View Public Education* (New York: Public Agenda, 1997).

4 "From THEIR Perspective: Notes from a Conversation with Concerned Students" (circulated document).

5 Holly Kurtz, "Changes for Celebration School?" *Orlando Sentinel*, January 25, 1999.

CHAPTER 8

1 Edward Erikson Jr., "The Color of Money," *Orlando Weekly*, September 18–24, 1997, pp. 8–12; and "Green Gamble," *Orlando Weekly*, November 20–26, 1997, p. 8.

2 Katherine Bouma, "A True Horror Story, Pesticides' Effects on Hormones," *Orlando Sentinel*, February 1, 1998, A-1; and "Lack of Baby Alligators Troubles Scientists," *Orlando Sentinel*, March 31, 1998, A-1, 4.

3 L. J. Guillette Jr., T. S. Gross, G. R. Masson, J. M. Matter, H. F. Percival, and A. R. Woodward, "Developmental Abnormalities of the Gonad and Abnormal Sex Hormone Concentrations in Juvenile Alligators from Contaminated and Control Lakes in Florida," *Environmental Health Perspectives*, 102 (1994), pp. 680–88; L. J. Guillette Jr., D. B. Pickford, D. A. Crain, A. A. Rooney, and H. F. Percival, "Reduction in Penis Size and Plasma Testosterone Concentrations in Juvenile Alligators Living in a Contaminated Environment," *General Comparative Endocrinology*, 101 (1996), pp. 32–42; P. M. Vonier, D. A. Crain, J. A. McLachlan, L. J. Guillette Jr., and S. F.

Arnold, "Interaction of Environmental Contaminants with the Estrogen and Progesterone Receptors from the Oviduct of the American Alligator," *Environmental Health Perspectives,* 104 (1996), pp. 1318–22.

4 *Proposal for the Celebration Learning Center: A Center for the Best Educational Practices for the 21st Century,* p. 103. I am grateful to Professor Rosen for allowing me to view this document.

5 Alfie Kohn, "Only for My Kid: How Privileged Parents Undermine School Reform," *Phi Delta Kappan,* 98, 8 (April 1998), pp. 569–77.

6 Louis Gerstner Jr., *Reinventing Education: Entrepreneurship in America's Public Schools* (New York: Penguin, 1994); RJR Nabisco Foundation, *Next Century Schools* (Washington, D.C.: RJR Nabisco Foundation, 1989).

7 Alex Molnar, *Giving Kids the Business: The Commercialization of America's Schools* (Boulder: Westview Press, 1996), p. 3.

8 An influential 1991 report issued by the U.S. Dept. of Labor outlined workplace-related skills that all students should know. SCANS, "What Work Requires of Schools: A SCANS Report for America 2000," (Washington D.C.: U.S. Department of Labor, The Secretary's Commission on Achieving Necessary Skills, June 1991).

9 Andres Duany, "Coding America," *ANY,* 1 (July–August 1993), p. 19.

10 Deborah Meier, *The Power of Their Ideas: Lessons for America from a Small School in Harlem* (Boston: Beacon Press, 1995), p. 19.

11 Molnar, *Giving Kids the Business,* chap. 2.

CHAPTER 9

1 Douglas Frantz, "Town That Disney Built is Hit by First Violent Crime," *New York Times,* August 13, 1998, A10.

2 Lenny Savino, "Father Calls Pond a Danger: Fears More Drivers Will Die at the Site," *Osceola Sentinel,* November 22, 1998, p. 1.

3 Another anomaly, pointed out to me by Brent Herrington, is that any industry analysis of Celebration's price points and housing mix would have predicted a population with predominantly high school–age kids. The high number of families with younger children presented a challenge to the school's capacity to accommodate the new residents. Celebration School would soon be full, and the district would not be in a hurry to build another school on site. As a result, there was concern that, after a certain point, TCC may not be able to guarantee enrollment to the children of incoming residents.

4 In *The Overspent American: Upscaling, Downshifting, and the New Consumer* (New York: Basic Books, 1998), Juliet Schor argues that almost a fifth of all Americans made a voluntary lifestyle change in the first half of

the 1990s. Another 12 percent were involuntarily downshifted. Both groups, she found, were happier as a result of leaving their demanding jobs and stressed-out lives.

5 Zora Neale Hurston, "How It Feels to Be Colored Me" (1928), in *I Love Myself When I Am Laughing: A Zora Neale Hurston Reader*, edited by Alice Walker (New York: Feminist Press, 1979), p. 152.

6 Lewis Mumford, *The City in History: Its Origins, Its Transformations, and Its Prospects* (New York: Harcourt, Brace, Jovanovich, 1961), p. 486. A critical mass of studies and novels in this period helped to produce what Gans called the "myth of suburbia," as a conformist and soulless wasteland. The better known include William Whyte, *The Organization Man* (New York: Simon & Schuster, 1956); John Keats, *The Crack in the Picture Window* (Boston, 1956); Eric Hodgins, *Mr. Blandings Builds his Dream House* (New York: Simon & Schuster, 1956); Jean Kerr, *Please Don't Eat the Daisies* (Garden City: Doubleday, 1957); Richard Gordon, Katherine Gordon, and Max Gunther, *The Split-Level Trap* (New York, Random House, 1962); David Riesman (with Nathan Glazer and Reuel Denney), *The Lonely Crowd: A Study of the Changing American Character* (New Haven: Yale University Press, 1950); John Seeley, *Crestwood Heights* (New York: Basic Books, 1956). Aside from *The Levittowners*, the first books to dispute this consensus view of suburbia included Bennett Berger, *Working-Class Suburb: A Study of Auto Workers in Suburbia* (Berkeley: University of California Press, 1960); and William Dobriner, ed., *Class in Suburbia* (Englewood Cliffs, N.J.: Prentice-Hall, 1963). More recent literature in this debate includes Barbara M. Kelly, ed., *Suburbia Re-Examined* (Westport, CT: Greenwood Press, 1989); John Palen, ed., *The Suburbs* (New York: McGraw-Hill, 1995); and Joel Garreau, *Edge City: Life on the New Frontier* (New York: Doubleday, 1991).

7 Herbert Gans, *The Levittowners: Ways of Life and Politics in a New Suburban Community* (New York: Pantheon, 1967).

CHAPTER 10

1 Garden Cities literature includes Ebenezer Howard, *Tomorrow: A Peaceful Path to Real Reform* (London, 1898); Raymond Unwin, *Town Planning in Practice* (London, 1911); Robert Fishman, *Urban Utopias in the Twentieth Century* (New York: Basic Books, 1977); Daniel Schaffer, *Garden Cities for America: The Radburn Experience* (Philadelphia: Temple University Press, 1982); Clarence Stein, *Towards New Towns for America* (New York: 1951); Henry Wright, *Rehousing Urban America* (New York: Columbia University Press, 1935); Lewis Mumford, *The Culture of Cities* (New York: Harcourt,

Brace, 1938); Catherine Bauer, *Modern Housing* (Boston: Houghton Mifflin, 1934). Jane Jacobs blasts away at the Garden City tradition in *The Death and Life of Great Cities.*

2 Evan MacKenzie, *Privatopia: Homeowner Associations and the Rise of the Residential Private Court* (New Haven: Yale University Press, 1994).

3 MacKenzie points out that, for large developers, the common-interest development was an efficient and profitable solution to the rising cost of land in the late 1970s, and the growing demand for common amenities like golf courses, swimming pools, and recreational areas. More residents could be squeezed onto smaller lots, common open space would be an attractive feature of the consumer package, restrictive covenants could be drawn up to favor the lender and the developer, and professional community managers would be employed to mediate any conflicts between uppity residents and the developers themselves.

4 Edward Blakeley and Mary Gail Snyder, *Fortress America: Gated Communities in the United States* (Washington, D.C.: Brookings Institution Press, 1997).

5 Quoted in Richard Schickel, *The Disney Version: The Life, Times, Art, and Commerce of Walt Disney* (New York: Simon & Schuster: 1968), p. 158.

6 Dolores Hayden, *Seven American Utopias: The Architecture of Communitarian Socialism,* 1780–1975 (Cambridge, MIT Press, 1976); Arthur Bestor Jr., *Backwoods Utopias* (Philadelphia: University of Pennsylvania Press, 1950); *Heavens on Earth: Utopian Communities in America* (New York: Dover, 1966); Y. Ovel, *Two Hundred Years of American Communes* (New Brunswick, N.J.: Transaction Books, 1988).

7 Along the way, Florida even played host to at least one version of the old-style utopia—in the settlement of Estero, a community founded near Fort Myers in 1900 in accordance with the pseudoscientific teachings of Cyrus R. Teed, a cultish patriarch who called himself Koresh long before his contemporary namesake from Waco, Texas. Teed believed that the Earth was a hollow sphere with the sun in its center, and the community was architecturally drawn up to demonstrate this belief.

8 Founded in 1973 when developers were still wary of the risk inherent in residents' representation on the boards of homeowners associations, the Community Association Institute was initially conceived as a pluralistic national forum for reconciling the potentially adversarial interests of its members. These were to include not only property managers, developers, and association professionals (lawyers and landscapers), but also association members, presidents, and public officials. Their deliberations, after all, were to have a major impact on public housing policy in the absence of

any formal government policies. McKenzie describes how the Institute evolved, over time, into a typical trade association, lobbying for the interests of its professional membership rather than serving as the quasi–public interest group it had once been. Homeowners, participating on a voluntary, unpaid basis, inevitably became "passive observers," and, after 1992, the governing board no longer included public officials. Herrington acknowledged that he and a number of other "up and comers" had been influenced by MacKenzie's book, and, in response to its "harsh" characterization, had been pushing for "a reemergence of the homeowner and resident perspective" by involving the organization more at the local level and moving it away from its focus on the legal and technical disputes generated by homeowners associations.

9 Town Hall Newsletter, January 30, 1998.

CHAPTER 11

1 Mark Pinsky, "Celebration Church to be Disney's 1st," *Orlando Sentinel*, September 20, 1996, A1–12.

2 Quoted in Deborah Kovach Caldwell, "The First Church of Disney World," *Dallas Morning News*, July 12, 1997, G-3.

3 Ibid. As it happens, the Presbyterian Church had already bared its social conscience as a major stockholder in the Disney Company. Troubled by the company's use of sweatshop subcontractors in Haiti, China, and Burma, the church had helped place resolutions for shareholder review on the annual proxy in 1997. One resolution called on management to establish supplier standards in the countries to which it outsourced low-wage work, to guarantee a living wage to these workers, and to protect their right to organize. Another resolution called for "comparison of compensation packages for company officers with the lowest and average wage of Disney contract workers in the U.S. and three low-wage countries, including Haiti." At the time, Michael Eisner was earning $97, 600 per working hour from salary and stock options, while Haitian workers were being paid 20 cents per waged hour to make Pocahontas and Lion King T-shirts. The resolutions had drawn a surprising volume of shareholder support (8 percent in favor, with 8 percent abstaining), and the company had made some limited reforms in response. Repeat resolutions in subsequent years followed on the company's unwillingness to take any further steps in improving labor conditions among its contract suppliers.

4 Leland Kaiser, "Health Care in the 21st Century," *Celebration Journal.* This "inaugural issue" is the only issue of the journal, and is undated.

5 "Celebration Gets Office OK," *Orlando Business Journal*, March 14, 1997.

6 Edward Ericson Jr., "Hospital Vote Makes Architect Sick," *Orlando Weekly,* April 3, 1997; Phil Galewitz, "Disney Isn't Used to Getting 'No' for an Answer," *Palm Beach Post,* April 20, 1997, 1F.

7 Peter Covino, "State Deal Paves Way for Hospital at Celebration," *Osceola News-Gazette,* January 8, 1998, A5.

8 *Holden Heights Community Action Plan: A Targeted Community Initiative,* Orlando, November 1998.

CHAPTER 12

1 Quoted in Beth Dunlop, "Designs on the Future," *Architectural Record,* January 1996, p. 67.

2 See John Taylor, *Storming the Magic Kingdom: Wall Street, the Raiders and the Battle for Disney* (New York: Knopf, 1987).

3 Donn Tatum, in a 1967 press release, quoted in Alan Bryman, *Disney and his Worlds* (London and New York: Routledge, 1955), p. 116.

4 "A Sweet Deal for Disney is Souring its Neighbors," *Business Week,* August 8, 1988, p. 60.

5 If Celebration had stayed within Reedy Creek, its residents would have been able to vote on the affairs of Disney World. When the idea of deannexation first came up, in the mid-1980s, Orange County officials, ever anxious about Disney's tax status, were concerned that this plan of transferring resident-voters out of Reedy Creek might be a way of eluding improvement and service fees to the county. See Stephen Fjellman, *Vinyl Leaves: Walt Disney World and America* (Boulder: Westview Press, 1992), pp. 423–24, n 91.

6 Mike Kloehn, "A Local Government's Perspective of Celebration," *Proceedings of Growth Management Short Course,* sponsored by Florida Chamber of Commerce, Kissimmee, April 10–11, 1996, p. 654.

7 Lawrence Lebowitz, "Disney Plans a Celebration of Life, Work, Play in Osceola," *Orlando Sentinel,* April 30, 1991, A-1, 4.

8 Stanley Shenkman, quoted in "Landmark Center Plan Enormous," *Osceola Sentinel,* October 1, 1997, 1.

9 "No Exemption," editorial, *Osceola News Gazette,* September 11, 1997, A4.

10 Jamie Floer, "Celebration Says It Should Get Exemption, But Pays Tax Bill," *Osceola News Gazette,* September 13, 1997, front page.

11 Joe Barnes, town architect, also left the company to be general manager of a neotraditional community called I'On, in the Charleston suburbs. Designed by DPZ and Dover Kohl, it is being developed by Vince Graham, who built the highly successful New Urbanist development of Newpoint, near Beaufort, in South California.

12 Duany Plater-Zyberg, Anton Nelessen, and Robert Kramer from Haile Plantation were on one team; St. Joe, UDA, Cooper Robertson, Arvida, and the Rouse Company on another; Peter Calthorpe on a third; with Mesirow Stein and Skidmore, Owings and Merrill heading up the winning group, as Orlando Partners.

13 David Olinger, " Disney Rules a Real Kingdom," *St. Petersburg Times,* September 30, 1996, 4b.

14 Andrew Ross, ed., *No Sweat: Fashion, Free Trade, and the Rights of Garment Workers* (New York: Verso, 1997).

CHAPTER 13

1 Forest Hills Gardens, a railroad suburb nine miles from Manhattan, developed by the Russell Sage Foundation from 1911, is perhaps the best example, as Peter Hall points out in *Cities of Tomorrow* (Oxford: Basil Blackwell, 1988), p. 124. Clarence Perry was the planner most involved in Forest Hills. His concept of the "neighborhood unit"—a compact, walkable residential area, whose population density is defined by its elementary school—had an influential impact on subsequent model plans, most famously on Radburn, New Jersey. Designed to exclude through traffic, the Radburn layout was subsequently absorbed into the auto-driven principles of postwar suburban development.

2 Michael Pollan, "Breaking Ground: 'The Truman Show' and a Seaside Lawn," *New York Times,* June 4, 1998.

3 See Constance Perin, *Everything in its Place: Social Order and Land Use in America* (Princeton: Princeton University Press, 1977).

4 In February 1999, a monthly newspaper—the *Celebration Independent*—made its debut in a community that was already information rich. Published by resident Alex Morton, the first issue carried a front-page story excoriating BFI garbage disposal company for its deficient recycling program and for its use of large trucks that ravaged the grass on back alley lawns. A cautious editorial in the second issue applauded the "changes" at Celebration School. Most of the other stories boosted events and personages around town. Neither issue alluded to the ongoing history of construction problems.

5 Charles Murray and Richard Herrnstein, *The Bell Curve: Intelligence and Class Structure in American Life* (New York: Free Press, 1994), p. 526.

6 See Edward Eichler and Marshall Kaplan, *The Community Builders* (Berkeley: University of California Press, 1970); and Marc Weiss, *The Rise of the Community Builders: The American Real Estate Industry and Urban Land Planning* (New York: Columbia University Press, 1987). Large

landowners, some of them with a clear social mission, like Robert Simon and James Rouse, had become community builders by the early 1960s, and, like Disney, none had prior experience in real estate development. Mission Viejo, Foster City, Irvine, Valencia, El Dorado Hills, Rancho Bernardo, and others were planned and built in California, Reston in Virginia, Columbia in Maryland, and several in Florida—Miami Lakes, Coral Springs, Poinciana, Weston, Palm Coast, Viera, Port LaBelle, Tampa Palms—each with thousands of acres to develop and population projections of up to 100,000. Companies like Gulf Oil, Goodyear Tire and Rubber, Mobil, Exxon, Westinghouse, and General Electric were large investors in these communities. Primarily aimed at the middle- to upper-income housing market, the towns also attracted a broad spectrum of support from local and state governments, all too happy to see property values rise and alternatives to the greed of merchant builders flourish. Most were granted special district status, or extensive zoning and planning powers under a planned community ordinance.

7 Several failed attempts were made by the Johnson administration to petition Congress to authorize loans directly to community developers. Under HUD's New Town Corporation (preceded by the New Communities Act of 1968), several hundred millions dollars of grants and loans were issued to sixteen new communities to support front-end expenditure on land and infrastructure. Contrary to popular wisdom, several of these places survived successfully—The Woodlands in Texas, Harbison in South Carolina, Jonathan in Minnesota, Riverton in New York, and Shenandoah in Georgia. See Reid Ewing, *Developing Successful New Communities* (Washington, D.C.: Urban Land Institute, 1991), and James Clapp, *New Towns and Urban Policy: Planning Metropolitan Growth* (New York: Dunellen: 1971).

8 Mike Davis, "Homegrown Revolution," in *City of Quartz: Excavating the Future in Los Angeles* (New York: Verso, 1990), pp. 151–220.

9 William Scott, *In Pursuit of Happiness: American Conceptions of Property from the Seventeenth to the Twentieth Century* (Bloomington: Indiana University Press, 1977), p. 41–42.

10 Richard Schickel, *The Disney Version* (New York: Simon & Schuster, 1968), p. 34.